PENGUIN BOOKS

THE FALL OF THE HOUSE OF HABSBURG

Edward Crankshaw has brought his narrative skill, literary power, and deep historical understanding to bear on a wide variety of topics in European history, beginning with his study *Gestapo: Instrument of Tyranny*, and including Imperial Russia and Bismarck's Germany. Among his books are *The Shadow of the Winter Palace* and *Bismarck*, also published by Penguin Books. Mr. Crankshaw lives in Kent, England.

ALSO BY EDWARD CRANKSHAW

Joseph Conrad : Aspects of the Art of the Novel
Vienna : The Image of a Culture in Decline
Britain and Russia
Russia and the Russians
Russia by Daylight
The Forsaken Idea : A Study of Viscount Milner
Gestapo : Instrument of Tyranny
Russia Without Stalin
Khrushchev's Russia
The New Cold War : Moscow v. Pekin
Khrushchev : A Biography
Maria Theresa
The Habsburgs
Tolstoy : The Making of a Novelist
The Shadow of the Winter Palace
Bismarck

NOVELS

Nina Lessing
What Glory ?
The Creedy Case

The Fall of the House of
HABSBURG

BY EDWARD CRANKSHAW

PENGUIN BOOKS

PENGUIN BOOKS
Published by the Penguin Group
Viking Penguin Inc., 40 West 23rd Street, New York, New York 10010, U.S.A.
Penguin Books Ltd, 27 Wrights Lane, London W8 5TZ, England
Penguin Books Australia Ltd, Ringwood, Victoria, Australia
Penguin Books Canada Ltd, 2801 John Street,
Markham, Ontario, Canada L3R 1B4
Penguin Books (N.Z.) Ltd, 182–190 Wairau Road,
Auckland 10, New Zealand

Penguin Books Ltd, Registered Offices:
Harmondsworth, Middlesex, England

First published in the United States of America by
Viking Penguin Inc. 1963
Published in Penguin Books 1983

5   7   9   10   8   6

LIBRARY OF CONGRESS CATALOGING IN PUBLICATION DATA
Crankshaw, Edward.
The fall of the House of Habsburg.
Reprint. Originally published : New York : Viking Press, 1963.
Includes index.
1. Austria—History—Francis Joseph, 1848–1916.   2. Habsburg, House of.
3. Franz Joseph I, Emperor of Austria, 1830–1916.   I. Title.
[DB85.C7   1983]   943.6'04   82-18071
ISBN 0 14 00.6459 1

Printed in the United States of America

For A. D. PETERS

with affection and gratitude

CONTENTS

Part Four
EMPIRE UNDER NOTICE

Part Five
AUSTRIA MUST STILL BE GREAT

Epilogue
FINIS AUSTRIAE

PREFACE

The Habsburg Monarchy is gone and largely forgotten. The problems it tried to solve have survived it: they are with us today. The Monarchy has not been treated kindly by historians. This would not matter in itself; but by dismissing the last phases of this extraordinary institution as being unworthy of serious contemplation we dismiss at the same time a considerable sector of our own past, which still bears heavily on the present. Until we understand what the Monarchy did, or tried to do, we cannot understand what went wrong. Understanding calls for the exercise of sympathy (this has nothing to do with whitewashing). There has been overflowing sympathy for the various peoples of the Empire but little, if any, for the rulers who tried to hold them together in a dangerous world. Hence this book.

ACKNOWLEDGEMENTS

It is impossible for me to thank by name all those who have helped me with this book. I should have to include everyone who has added to my understanding of the old Austria over the past thirty years. Many are now dead; many live under Communist régimes in lands which once formed part of the Monarchy; some, such are the times, would not thank me for associating them in any way with a book of this kind.

Certain debts, however, and among them the largest, I may safely acknowledge.

Above all I wish to thank the following: Prince Johannes Schwarzenberg for his invaluable assistance and encouragement, for smoothing my way with countless introductions, and for illuminating it with his own personal reminiscences; Professor Heinrich Benedikt, who with splendid generosity not only gave me the run of his mind but also, at the cost of very great trouble, went out of his way to place all the resources of a professional historian at the service of an amateur; the late Duke Maximilian of Hohenberg, the elder son of the Archduke Franz Ferdinand, for permission to work on his father's papers, now deposited in the Austrian State Archives, but so far available to only a few; Dr Fritz Meznik of the Federal Chancellery in Vienna, who put the resources of his office at my disposal; Freiherr Mayer-Gunthof for the warmth of his hospitality and the range of his practical help; Major-General Oskar Regele, who besides making me free of his latest researches into Austrian military history helped me in many ways.

There are many others. The officials of the Austrian State Archives were kindness and helpfulness itself. After Dr Gebhard Rath, the Director, I should like to thank especially Dr Blaas and Dr Anna Benna of the *Haus- Hof- und Staatsarchiv*; Dr Krauss and Dr Allmayer-Beck of the *Kriegsarchiv*; Count Nostitz-Rieneck of the *Verwaltungsarchiv*. The Austrian Foreign Office was equally helpful, and here I must thank particularly the Head of the Foreign Office, Dr Fuchs; Dr Vodak and Herr Blechner at the Ballhausplatz; Dr Verosta, lately Austrian Ambassador to Poland; the late Herr Seiffert and also Dr Cornaro of the Austrian Embassy in London.

ACKNOWLEDGEMENTS

I am also deeply grateful to Dr Steininger of the National Library in Vienna; to Frau Lolly Müller of the Federal Theatre Administration; to Dr Jedlichka of the Army Museum.

Nearer home, I must thank Mr Noel Blakiston of the Record Office in London and the Librarian of the London Library for their remarkable consideration and forbearance; and Mr John Silverlight, who read the typescript and made many valuable suggestions.

Finally, I express my gratitude to Mrs Jean Malins, who not only typed and retyped the whole book but also frequently corrected it, and to my wife, who bore the brunt and took half the load, both at home and abroad.

I am indebted to the following for permission to include copyright material: the Archduke Otto of Austria for material from the Habsburg papers and letters; Prince George Festetics for material from the papers and letters of the Countess Marie Festetics; H. Böhlaus Nachf., Graz-Köln for material from *Schicksalsjahre Österreicha—Das Politische Tagebuch Josef Redlichs*; The Macmillan Company, New York, for material from *The Emperor Franz Josef* by Josef Redlich, and Messrs John Murray, Ltd, for material from *The Life and Letters of Lord Beaconsfield*, by W. F. Monypenny and G. E. Buckle.

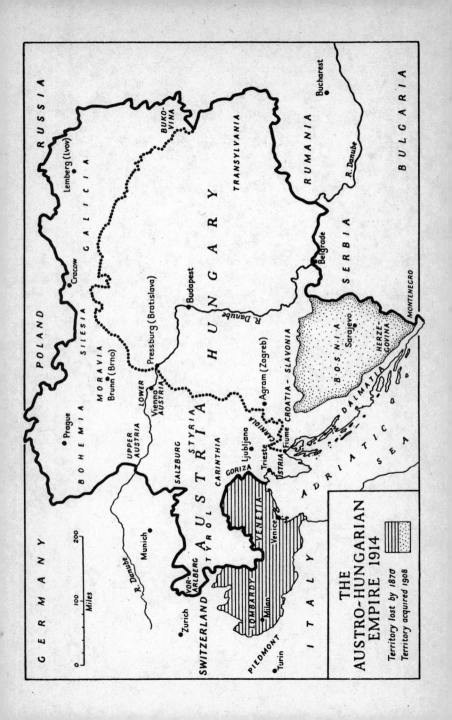

THE
AUSTRO-HUNGARIAN
EMPIRE 1914

Territory lost by 1870
Territory acquired 1908

PROLOGUE

THE HOUSE OF AUSTRIA

THE HOUSE OF AUSTRIA

I

Not many mourned the death of the Habsburg Monarchy in 1918; far more rejoiced. The national States which arose on the ruins of the supra-national Empire would surely inaugurate a new era of enlightenment, in which small nations, freed from the dead hand of Imperial oppression, would develop and unfold in prosperous amity. But the new arrangements did not last and the hope was not fulfilled. It was soon found that the new master-nations – Czechs, Poles, Serbs, Italians – had learnt all the techniques of oppression. Then came Hitler. Barely twenty years after the birth of independent Czechoslovakia, the Prime Minister of one of the Powers which had helped to create that unhappy State was calling it 'a far-away country of which we know nothing' and begging Germany to take most of it. Germany took all; and soon there was established over all the lands of the vanished Empire, and more besides, a tyranny unprecedented in the history of Europe. It was then the turn of the Russians. Now every inch of what was once the Dual Monarchy, less the rump of Austria itself and the fragments taken by Italy, lies under Communist rule. Poland, Czechoslovakia, Hungary, Yugoslavia still exist; but instead of forming the centre of Europe they are now seen as part of the East. A restoration of the Habsburgs is unthinkable; but a restoration of Europe as a complex of interdependent peoples is something to be striven for by all decent means. To understand the nature of a Europe which must include, as it once did include, not only Poland and Yugoslavia, but also a great part of Russia, it is necessary to understand the special part played for so long by the Habsburg dynasty, and, above all, the reasons for its fall.

2

Every society carries within it 'the seeds of its own decay'; and this, given the material of which all societies are made, is not surprising. What is surprising is that any society has ever managed to exist at all – unless a perfect tyranny. The Habsburg Monarchy was never that: even at the time of the Counter-Reformation there were no burnings of heretics. And yet it managed to exist for many centuries. The reason for this was that the Monarchy, or something very much like it, was felt to be necessary by most of the peoples who lived under it as well as by rival Powers. This was not due to any Austrian magic; it was due to the nature of the Empire; and the nature of the Empire was inherent in the structure of central and south-eastern Europe. In an important sense, the Habsburg system was more rational than anything seen in Europe before or since. In the eyes of its rulers, it was a supra-national organization, ordained by God, and ruled over by God's nominee. At the same time it was so modern that it anticipated problems of government as yet unresolved: its rulers could never make up their minds whether the correct way to articulate a multi-national State was through federalism or centralism. This is today a crucial question, and the Habsburgs were the first in modern history to consider it seriously: if they failed to find an answer, we also have failed.

This is not being wise after the event. The great Bohemian patriot, Palacky, said that if the Habsburg Empire had not existed it would have been necessary to invent it. The reality could not have been conceived by the most unbridled fantasist. It was a mutation, a sport, in the history of human institutions. But it was solid and real. The founder of the Czechoslovak State, Thomas Masaryk, who was largely responsible for the dismemberment of the Empire, acted only with the greatest reluctance, much more in sorrow than in anger, knowing that what he was helping to destroy was irreplaceable.

To begin with, it was homeless: it was the property not of a nation but of a single family. The recognized way of empire-building is for expanding peoples to push out beyond their frontiers, by sea or by land, and colonize, with more or less violence, the weaker peoples in their path. But there was no Austrian nation. The Habsburg lands were private possessions won by a single family by treaty and by marriage; and the colonizers, such as they were, were in every sense the personal servants of the head of that family, who had a palace in Vienna.

In Europe generally, as the consciousness of nationhood developed, the rulers of what were to become the Great Powers gradually identified themselves with their peoples, even though they themselves were often foreigners. The idea of king and country took hold as an expression of national patriotism, with the crown as its symbol; and the hereditary rulers, who belonged in fact to a great cosmopolitan family, came to be regarded as the standard-bearers of anti-cosmopolitan ideas. But not the Habsburgs. As a concept, Austrian patriotism did not exist; as a fact, Austria was not even a kingdom: it was only an Archduchy, Austria above and below the Enns, to which were added the Duchies of Carinthia, Styria, Carniola, and the County of Tirol. Except in the most local sense there was no Austrian patriotism. Habsburg archdukes ruled in Graz and Innsbruck, as well as in Vienna, until well into the seventeenth century, raising magnificent buildings to glorify their Courts. And when at the height of centralized Imperial might Vienna had become the capital of a great Empire and the dynasty ruled over nearly a dozen major races, where patriotism existed as a force it was either local or racial patriotism, usually at odds with the pretensions of the dynasty, which required nothing but loyalty to the Emperor of the day – and to a remarkable degree received it.

3

When in the year 800 Charlemagne was crowned Emperor of the Romans by Pope Leo III, the object was to unify Christendom; but Byzantium persisted in its schism and Charlemagne's authority was limited to the West. There, too, the Imperial power came into conflict with the Church. It diminished until the Holy Roman Emperor had become, in effect, the Emperor of the Germans, elective head of a loose union of Germanic princes. In 1283 Rudolf, Count of Habsburg, was chosen to be the new German king and crowned at Aix-la-Chapelle. He was not the most powerful prince and his election was bitterly contested; but his family, which possessed lands in Swabia, the Black Forest and Alsace, had for long been closely allied with the Hohenstaufens, and the Pope supported his claim, though he was never crowned in Rome. He was, moreover, a man of outstanding intelligence and a gifted soldier, and in his capacity of German king he applied himself to the task of fighting encroachments into Imperial territory. His most important action was to drive the King of Bohemia, Ottokar Premysl, out of Charlemagne's old East Mark, *Ostmark*, dominated by Vienna. In his capacity of Duke of Habsburg he made over Austria itself and the adjacent lands to members of his own family. Thenceforth, in effect, the House of Habsburg was the House of Austria.

4

The battle in which Ottokar was killed was thus one of the decisive battles of European history. It was fought on the Marchfeld, the plain on the north bank of the Danube across the river from Vienna. The Marchfeld, stretching away into the misty distance as one looks out from the tower of St Stephen's cathedral, is soaked with history. The Middle Danube basin, dominated by the great city, is the meeting-point between East and West and a continuation of the Alpine barrier between North and South. Under the cliff of the Leopoldsberg, the steep wooded hill which stands up from the city and the river, the Danube at last sweeps away from the foothills of the Alps and curves out across the great plain leading to Hungary and the East. For centuries immemorial this plain has served as a highway for successive hordes of invaders from the East – Huns, Avars, Magyars, Turks. Rome had made an eastern outpost of Vienna, and Marcus Aurelius died there.

The frontier of the old Roman Empire marched with the Danube and the Rhine, through Britain, through Africa, Arabia, Asia Minor as far as the Black Sea; but nowhere was this frontier so heavily threatened as at the point where modern Vienna now stands. Here was the old fortified camp of Vindobona and, almost in sight, the Roman headquarters, Carnuntum – Vienna's Pompeii. Nowhere else all along the frontier did two fortresses stand so close together.

Charlemagne followed Rome's example. Then came King Ottokar, who ruled from the Adriatic to the Baltic, only to be shattered by Rudolf, the first Imperial Habsburg. Thereafter the Marchfeld continued to be the arena for great events. The Habsburgs and their allies held the Turks at the very gates of Vienna and drove them painfully back in 1683. On the same ground Napoleon beat the Austrians at Wagram after he had suffered his first defeat at Aspern. In 1866, after Königgrätz, it looked as though the victorious Prussians would fight there too, but the Austrians made peace. The last great action was fought by Soviet troops in pursuit of the retreating Germans in 1945. But the most decisive battle for our civilization was Rudolf's triumph over the Bohemian king, which was to set the pattern for more than six hundred years to come.

Rudolf's successors managed to retain the Imperial Crown almost continuously until the Roman Empire, long a shadow, was done away with by Napoleon in 1806. But it was a long time before the dynasty acquired real power and weight. Indeed, in the fifteenth century, the Emperor Frederick III could barely muster an escort for his coronation journey to Rome. This was the Habsburg who devised the mystic initials A.E.I.O.U., which have been interpreted in a great variety of ways, a favourite version being *Austria Est Imperare Orbi Universo*—and proceeded to lose Vienna itself to the strong and predatory Hungarian king, Matthias Corvinus. Matthias had crusaded triumphantly against the Turks and defeated them at Jassy. He also wrested Moravia from the Bohemian king. He appeared to be succeeding where the Bohemians and the Habsburgs had failed. But the Habsburgs had not failed. Suddenly everything changed. Frederick's son, Maximilian, a ruler of genius, was dreaming in Innsbruck. He now began the process which was to carry the Habsburg name to the summit of fame and exalt the Habsburg realm so that it could take its place as an unquestioned pillar of the European edifice. From the year of Maximilian's marriage in 1477 the history of Habsburg was the history of Europe.

Maximilian was not only the first Habsburg to bring under one hand the various provinces which made up the Austrian inheritance; he was also the first to use dynastic marriage for territorial aggrandizement: his wife was Mary, daughter and heiress of Charles the Bold of Burgundy. For centuries it has been a joke that while other dynasts achieved their greatness by wars of conquest, the Habsburgs acquired their vast properties by marrying and making treaties. Indeed, they were skilled in both pursuits; but they always had to defend what they had won. And the first important conflict of this kind arose directly from Maximilian's marriage, when, in 1479, he fought and won the Battle of Guinegatte, defending his new Burgundian possessions from the French. Thus began the Habsburg opposition to the power and pretensions of France: for centuries to come Austria was to be 'the eternal counterpoise to France' – a role which, as the most brilliant of living Austrian historians has pointed out, made possible, among other things, the growth of English power and the creation of the British Empire.[1]

It was under Maximilian that the Habsburgs first made themselves felt in Italy and Spain. And it was Maximilian who brought the Renaissance to Austria.

His son, Philip the Handsome, born Archduke of Austria, married mad Joanna, daughter of Ferdinand and Isabella of Castile. This Philip had for his son the great Emperor Charles V, who, at his apogee, was master of the Netherlands, of Burgundy, of the Habsburg German lands, of Spain and all her possessions in Italy and in the New World. But this splendour of Imperial Catholic power was being undermined at the very moment of its apotheosis: two new forces arose almost simultaneously to complicate the grand simplicity – the Protestantism of the Reformation and the power of the merchant financiers, whose interests were henceforth to blur the purely strategic and political policies of the monarchs they subsidized. The sixteenth-century Fuggers were to Charles and his brother Ferdinand what the nineteenth-century Rothschilds were to later Habsburgs.

Thus when Charles abdicated in 1556 and retired to his monastery at San Gerónimo de Yuste to make clocks and contemplate his own coffin, while his son Philip took Spain, the Netherlands and the two Sicilies, his brother Ferdinand received the German lands and the Imperial Crown. And while Philip saw himself as the great Catholic potentate and wore himself out in his struggle with England, Ferdinand, by marriage, had already from the second half of the seventeenth century laid the foundations of the central European power which was to supersede and dwarf the glory of Spain. By marrying Anne of Bohemia he had put himself in a position to assume the separate Crowns of Bohemia and Hungary, when Anne's brother, Louis, was killed by the Turks at Mohacs in 1526. It was not much of an inheritance. The Bohemians only accepted him as a last resort, and Soleiman the Magnificent had turned a large part of a shattered Hungary into a Turkish province. But Ferdinand and his successors held on.

5

Somebody had to hold on. The fact that Ferdinand was possessed by no conscious mission to weld together a Christian Empire as a barrier against the Turks was neither here nor there. For centuries the fragmented races of central Europe, flotsam and jetsam of the great migrations, all intermingled, and now at the mercy of the Turks had cried out for some sort of central organization. Ferdinand of Habsburg was at last to achieve this where the Bohemian Ottokar and the Hungarian Matthias Corvinus had failed. Thenceforth the House of Austria was in fact to be, for two hundred years, a bastion against the Turks. It was also to be the main arm of the Counter-Reformation, after the Battle of the White Mountain in 1621 which finally did away with organized Protestant resistance and enabled Ferdinand II to populate Bohemia with nobles loyal to the Imperial cause. It was the raising of the Turkish siege of Vienna in 1683 which was the signal for the sudden flowering of a frontier wilderness into the glory of the Baroque, Italian inspired, which stamped all the Habsburg lands with a cultural unity no less supra-national than the military unity of a multi-racial army.

It was at this time, too, that Austria emerged finally as a great European Power. The occasion was the War of the Spanish Succession (1702–14), which brought Louis XIV of France and Leopold of Austria into conflict and resulted in the creation by William III of England of the Grand Alliance designed to curb the French drive towards the domination of Europe. This war, notable for Marlborough's tremendous feats of arms in conjunction with Prince Eugene of Savoy at the head of the Austrian forces, ended with the Habsburgs in possession of the Spanish Netherlands, Belgium, Milan and Sicily. Through it England too became a world-power.

Under Maria Theresa (1717–80) it looked as though the body was finding a soul. In the War of the Austrian Succession this remarkable woman managed to inspire among her peoples a genuine Imperial patriotism; she rallied even the Magyars to her cause, though with important reservations. The Pragmatic Sanction of 1713, which permitted the succession to follow the female line, seemed to symbolize a fresh start, so that the Empire could at last unfold and relax its cramped muscles. Already Vienna was presented with quite new problems which submitted the Habsburg lands to a new unifying pressure. The Counter-Reformation belonged to history; the Turks were no longer a menace; but the Prussia of Frederick the Great and the Russia of Catharine, expanding, made a strong central Power more of a European necessity than ever. The man who tried to hammer this Power into an administrative whole was Maria Theresa's son, Josef II, whose father, Franz Stefan of Lorraine, had brought new blood into the dynasty and caused it to change its name from Habsburg to Habsburg-Lorraine.

Josef had very clear ideas of what a modern continental empire should be. He set about organizing his possessions on rational lines. His vision was tremendous in its scope and his energy was boundless. But he lacked political sense. Maria Theresa by her administrative

9

reforms had set the stage for the gentle development of the Empire into a coherent and prosperous multi-national State. Josef perceived the opportunity and, filled with a consuming ardour for the welfare of his inheritance, tried to seize it. But he went to work like a reforming Russian Tsar. The Empire was his, and it had to be a credit to him. Life was to be made better for its millions. There were to be order and equity, education and ease; the Jesuits must be curbed. But all this had to be prescribed from above, in minute detail, by the one man who knew what was best for everybody else – by Josef, the benevolent autocrat of the Enlightenment. All this was to be achieved by a centralized bureaucracy, an Imperial civil service, staffed by the most advanced and enlightened subjects of the realm. That meant mostly by Germans, because the German subjects of the Empire were ahead of the rest. . . . It was the splendid conception of a great and fascinating man, who, with all his hectoring ways, was humble at heart. But it could not work. Josef contrived to antagonize everybody in the Empire who objected to the ordering of their lives in the name of abstract justice. The very people he so furiously desired to benefit were rushed off their feet by the speed and arbitrariness of his reforms. When they did not bite, they sulked. So this remarkable figure, Napoleonic in mood but with charity in his soul, ended his life as a disappointed and embittered man. He died in 1790, a year after the outbreak of the French Revolution, which was the last straw, convincing him of the folly of his lifework. With him died one more chance of giving his Empire an organic life of its own.

For now everything was France. Under Josef's successors, his brother Leopold, and, two years later, his nephew Franz, the dynasty returned to pre-Theresian ways in order to face the revolutionary peril and the menace of Napoleon. It ruled through the three arms which had upheld it in the past: Army, Church, Nobility. The only powers the Habsburgs enjoyed were the power of conferring privileges on those who gave them their total submission and the power of receiving privileges from a Church to which they totally submitted. The Army was the greatest estate in the realm and, at the same time, a unifying force of great value, as well as a shield. The Nobility enjoyed untold privileges, in return for which they managed the people. Once Napoleon had been defeated, Metternich bent all his energies on what is nowadays regarded as the supreme task of a statesman, the maintenance of peace.

6

With Napoleon safely on St Helena, the unifying idea of his con-
querors was to return to the *status quo*. The Powers were drained
and exhausted after twenty-three years of fighting for their existence.
The peoples, needing repose, were at first passive in the hands of
their rulers. These, stimulated into sharp activity by what they took
to be the lessons of the French Revolution, made the most of their
opportunity. With repeated hammer-blows the old pattern of Europe
had been smashed to pieces, until Bonaparte's nominees were
everywhere, sitting on new and on ancient thrones. Then the
miracle happened; and when the smoke rolled away the world for a
moment looked wonderfully as it had looked long ago. The main task
of the Congress of Vienna in 1815 was to ensure that it stayed like
that, and to put France under restraint.

Two autocracies, Austria and Russia, had survived the hurricane
apparently unscathed. A third, Prussia, had re-established itself on a
somewhat sounder basis than before. France was back behind her
pre-revolutionary frontiers, a monarchy with a Bourbon on the
throne. England, though riven by the pains of her industrial revolution, was boundlessly rich. The Emperor of Austria, Franz II, was
Europe's senior monarch, and he held out his hands with fraternal
warmth to his brother monarchs in Prussia and Russia: all were
pledged to assist each other at the first sign of revolutionary violence;
but for the time being there was no energy for violence. It was not at
once appreciated in Vienna that the old balance was already shifted
by the growing activity of Russia and the growing power of Prussia.

Another thing that was not at all appreciated was the existence of
new elements which had not been present under the ancient system.
Certainly there was a sharp fear of further revolutionary activity; but
revolution was thought of exclusively in terms of evil mobs and
regicides. It did not occur to Franz that men who were neither
guttersnipes nor potential assassins were now alight with new ideas,
above all the ideas of nationalism and democracy: these were hopelessly confused with each other, as they are still to this day, thus
forming an explosive mixture. One of the things the French Revolution had done was to show the strength of the masses; one of the
things Napoleon had done, with his conjuring up of mass armies,
was to give formal recognition to this strength when he thought he
was crushing it. But more important by far than the brute power of

the inarticulate masses was the swift development of the urban middle classes. There were other portents. For example, in the very year of Waterloo Bismarck had been born; Cavour was then five years old. Three years younger than Bismarck, Karl Marx was born at Trier on 5 May 1818.

The main architect of the new Continental system, which took no account of these things, was Metternich, the superbly accomplished Imperial Chancellor, who confused diplomacy with government. His mind was so good and his perceptions so fine that, with the help of his brilliant adviser, Friedrich von Gentz, he was more acutely aware than anyone else of the limitations of his own achievements. He was less well aware of the defects of his own character, and these were such that he allowed himself to be carried on by the momentum of his own virtuosity. He had no roots in Vienna: he was a Rhinelander making a career at a foreign Court; his obsession with France, which was natural and shared by others, involved him in a misreading of the new facts of European power. Also his intermittent perceptions of the new popular forces were nullified by the character of his master, Franz II, who had only one idea, the idea that change of any kind was a positive evil. It was not in Franz's eyes a question of resisting change; it was sufficient to forbid it.

Franz II, the grandfather of Franz Josef, was in no way a malevolent tyrant. He was the kindest of fathers, an adored uncle, and his dry, good-humoured steadiness was, for some time, what the people needed. He was clever enough to contrive things so as to divert all criticism of the evils of his régime on to his ministers. His Vienna was the Vienna of Beethoven and Schubert, of Grillparzer and the dramatists Raimund and Nestroy. On the surface all was quiet and orderly, and the Imperial Court itself was unassuming and far from ostentatious. The Court was not indifferent to the arts: opera and theatre owed much to it. But the censorship of words was, in theory, absolute, and it took a Grillparzer or a Nestroy to circumvent it at all effectively. The grossly swollen police force, the swarming spies and informers, the censors themselves – there was an internal postal censorship from which even the archdukes were not immune – not only discouraged existing talent but deterred the discovery and development of new thinking. They also barred intercourse with the world outside the Empire, so that men as different from one another as Lord Palmerston and Karl Marx could later pick up the young Disraeli's phrase and refer to Austria as Europe's China. Compared with England under the last two Georges, society in Austria was remarkable for its tidiness and decorum, indeed, for the smoothness of its running. The difference was that Castlereagh, who had represented England at the Congress of Vienna and given England's blessing to the Holy Alliance, 'the crowned conspirators' of Sydney Smith, was an openly detested figure, and, when he died by his own hand, was succeeded by a Canning. There was no Canning to supersede Metternich, and there was no Byron to execrate him and jeer over his coffin.

Franz, like other Habsburgs, was ready to trim his sails to any force other than popular feeling. It is wrong to think of the Habsburgs as for ever standing still: on the contrary, the family tendency was to move too fast, too often, too precipitately, often displaying a positive recklessness in their determination to preserve their inheritance by adapting themselves to new facts of life. Franz himself, who had had to suffer the guillotining of his father's sister, Marie Antoinette, and the presence of Napoleon as a conqueror in Schönbrunn, had all too easily accepted Napoleon's power as permanent, agreed to the abolition of his historic style of Holy Roman Emperor, and married his own daughter, Marie Louise, to the parvenu Emperor of the French. The Habsburgs, wonderful in acquisition, were scarcely less wonderful in their equanimity when it came to cutting losses—always, of course, with an eye to recovering them later. It was the most natural thing in the world for Franz II to turn on his terrible son-in-law once more when the eagle's powers were failing and to be in at the kill. But it never crossed his mind to ask who had done the fighting, or to suggest even the most limited co-partnership to his people who had carried him through. His people had a good-natured, temperate and benevolent monarch: what more could they want? Those who thought they wanted more were wicked, because their monarch was set over them by God: the Spielberg prison was the place for them. It was not merely that Franz had nothing to give to his peoples beyond the peace of a police State; he preferred them not to give to him, requiring them only to obey. When the great Tirolean patriot, Andreas Hofer, led his mountain countrymen in spontaneous insurrection against the French, against the Bavarians, to whom Napoleon had given the Tirol, then again against the French, fighting all the time for union with Austria under the Emperor's Crown, Franz was not pleased. He allowed the French to take Hofer away and shoot him. An efflorescence of Austrian national patriotism was the last thing he wanted to see. The Habsburgs were there to command, the people to obey. The Habsburgs would stand or fall by their own sovereignty: they would rather fall than be beholden to any popular hero invoking dangerous thoughts. National patriotism was a dangerous thought: it gave the people ideas above their station, and, if encouraged, would lead to demands for a share in government. Admittedly Franz carried the Habsburg idea to the point of caricature. It was he who asked the famous question which summed up the general Habsburg attitude. A distinguished servant of the Empire being recommended to him as a sterling patriot, the dry old stick asked: 'But is he a patriot for me?'

This outlook was not as absurd as it sounds. It had roots of the sturdiest kind reaching far down into the subsoil of history. But after the French Revolution it was no longer enough. It just lasted Franz's time; but when Franz, dying in 1835, was followed by a non-Emperor, the charming, feeble-minded Ferdinand, it would no longer do.

Too many people have been unkind to Ferdinand. He was an epileptic; he was rickety; he could hardly put two sentences together. But there have been many feeble-minded kings, and none perhaps so nice. 'What is the animal *implumis bipes* called Emperor?' Palmerston demanded of his Ambassador at Vienna, and answered himself: 'A perfect nullity; next thing to an idiot.'[2] And again, in another letter: 'How can an empire stand in these days without an emperor at its head? And by an emperor I mean a man endowed with intellectual faculties suited to his high station. A mere man of straw, a Guy Faux, like the present Emperor, may do very well in quiet times. . . .'[3] The Viennese knew he was a fool, but they adored him, even in the heat of the revolution which drove him to abdicate, and cheered him when he went out driving. 'I am the Emperor, and I want dumplings!' he once exclaimed, and a distinguished British historian has observed that this was his only coherent remark on record.[4] This is unfair. He left many coherent remarks, and all kind. When in 1848, after he had been thirteen years on the throne, the revolution broke, he was spirited away from Vienna by the strong men of Austria to Olmütz in Moravia and brought to abdicate in favour of his eighteen-year-old nephew. He dominated the tense and tight-lipped ceremony in the salon of the archiepiscopal palace. The new young Emperor went up to him and knelt before him: 'God bless you', the poor old man whispered. 'Be brave. God will protect you. It was done gladly.'

Then he went upstairs, the ex-Emperor, with his loyal and kind and plain ex-Empress, Marianna of Sardinia, to put their things together. Afterwards he wrote in his diary his own record of the events of that tremendous day:

> The function ended with the new Emperor kneeling to his Emperor and master, that is to say to me, and asking for a blessing, which I gave by laying my hands upon his head and making the sign of the Holy Cross. Then I embraced him and he kissed my hand. And then my dear wife embraced and kissed our new master, and then we went away to our room. Soon afterwards I and my dear wife heard Holy Mass in the chapel of the Episcopal Residence. . . . After that I and my dear wife packed our things. . . .[5]

The new Emperor was Franz Josef, a youth of eighteen. That was in December 1848, after months of insurrectionary violence, in which it seemed the Empire might be swept away. Metternich had hoped that he could use poor Ferdinand, that with a holy fool on the throne he could make himself virtual ruler of the Empire and, in his own way and time, put through reforms which he had long seen to be necessary. Under Franz his range had been restricted to foreign policy, and he had had to watch impotently while his great rival Kolowrat blocked reforms at home. But Kolowrat was still there, sitting on the Regency Council under the chairmanship of the Emperor Ferdinand's uncle, Archduke Ludwig. The stalemate remained. The new European revolutionary movement of 1848, which ended in Austria with Ferdinand's abdication, had started in France with the overthrow of Louis-Philippe. This had been the signal for a general revolt against absolutism, against master-nations. The Metternich system, absolutist and strongly Imperial in character, was the natural target for all these movements; and Metternich himself was the first considerable casualty. What happened after his fall was a vindication of his belief in the necessity for a strong central Power.

PART ONE

REVOLUTION AND REACTION

The Metternich era is
fact, it was only stagr
and undertook no rad
swift economic expar
as the time when ever
revolution got under
The newly acquired province
fertile, were included in the Austrian Cust
provided a new market for the industrial provinces or old
The Emperor himself created a Court authority for the fostering of
commerce, above all for attracting experts of all kinds from abroad.
First came looms from England, then Watt's steam-engine. Behind
the 'Chinese wall', foreign industrialists proliferated, and nearly all
the factories started up in the first half of the nineteenth century
were built by Englishmen, Frenchmen, Swiss, Belgians and Rhine-
landers. It was under Franz and Metternich that the economic unity
of the Empire was created on the lines of a regional division of labour.
Lower and Upper Austria were cotton; Bohemia and Moravia were
linen and wool; Styria and Carinthia were mining centres; while
under poor Ferdinand the first steam railway was built, the creation
of the Viennese Rothschild, who had been persuaded by Metternich
to come from Frankfurt to Austria. In this period of stagnation the
foundations were firmly laid for the immense industrial blooming of
the Franz Josef time.

Nor should it be thought that the Metternich period, too easily
dismissed as a period of oppression, brought bitterness and frustration to the lives of the Emperor's subjects.

On the contrary, Ferdinand's reign covered the *Biedermayer**
epoch, a comfortable, middle-class age with an emphasis on decency
and cosy cheerfulness and a strong philistine tinge: the philistinism

---

* Herr Biedermayer, who gave his name to the bourgeois culture of the period,
was a fictitious character invented by the writer Ludwig Pfau as a typical honest,
philistine, comfortably bourgeois fellow.

...siasm for music and the theatre. Since
...ound and since all ideas were suspect,
...hatter, eating and drinking, dressing-up,
...ided the only outlets for the surplus energy
...have to work sixteen hours a day to keep body
...It may be asked what more could anyone want in
...w-flight from the cradle to the grave? Most people
..., and it was more than most people can enjoy today,
...rity can rely on the wonders of applied science and
...sport to deaden minds and drain away surplus energy that
...tart coming out in the form of awkward questions. The only
...who in fact asked more were the radical intelligentsia, who were
...zed, as were their fellows all over Europe, by the general mood of
...evolutionary discontent. There was no revolt of the workers until
the first crisis of capitalism in the hungry forties; there was no revolt
of the peasants. Vienna, for example, was a city of craftsmen: coach-
makers, glove-makers, turners, instrument-makers, above all the
famous piano-makers; while in the enchanting suburbs were colonies
of silk-weavers, metal-workers and the rest. During the week they
earned good money, and on Sundays they spent it as though without
a care for tomorrow on music, dancing, wine and good food, always
when possible in the open air among the hills and vineyards on the
outskirts of the city. There was no unemployment until the forties,
when, as everywhere, the industrial revolution got out of hand. It
was the same among the peasants, throughout an Empire which was
still mainly agrarian. Sometimes they were hungry. That was not a
result of the social system: it was the result of a bad harvest: they
knew about bad harvests. When the harvest was good, they lived
abundantly and gave thanks to God.

But the crisis, when it came, hit hard. By the middle forties the
pull of the cities had proved too strong. The new factories were too
few to make work for the children of the poor peasants who came
swarming in from the mountains and the arid plains to seek their
fortunes, adding their number to the destitute handicraft-workers
whose ancient way of life was going to pieces under the impact of the
revolution. As in other lands, the radical and revolutionary intelligentsia now had material to work with. And what happened next
gave rise to the great question of the late nineteenth and early
twentieth century, a question which has not yet been answered, if
only because it has not yet seriously been asked. Was the rise of the

radical intelligentsia desirable, was their unchecked progress necessary in order that mankind might be led to the broad uplands of democratic freedom? Or was the very concept of democratic freedom a blind alley, developed to make the world safe for an intelligentsia which is only happy when playing at politics, at no matter what cost in suffering to the multitude?

Certainly this question did not exist for *Biedermayer* Vienna. And for the middle-class intellectuals the first slums of the industrial revolution were as remote as the slums of London and the industrial North were remote from the middle classes of nineteenth-century England. There was no visible class war. The aristocracy was also remote from the middle classes, except as an eccentric and ornamental fringe.

Today the visitor to Vienna may penetrate into innumerable palaces, great and small, used as institutes, offices, or kept as museums: he is surrounded, as in a sort of golden haze, by the masterpieces of Fischer von Erlach, Hildebrandt, and others: the stately excesses of the Baroque billow round him in luxuriant swirls of coloured marble, malachite and alabaster. The enchanting, enchanted madness of the Rococo almost suffocates him under writhing, gilded fantasy. He is in fairyland, where every tapestry is a Gobelin, every chandelier a frozen fountain of purest crystal. But this was not the Vienna of the *Biedermayer* middle classes before the 1848 revolution. The life that went on in those palaces was remote and unthought about by the generality of the Emperor's subjects. In May they would all take the traditional Prater drive, down the two-mile Hauptallee, the Emperor too; and then the citizenry would come out in their thousands to watch the carriages and the horses go by, a flashing cavalcade of brilliant paintwork, polished leather, glistening horses groomed to the minute, a whirring of wheels and a crisp drumming of hooves. Then they went back to where they belonged. In narrow streets of tall old houses and palaces great wooden gates would swing open to admit the carriages into invisible cobbled courtyards and close again to present a blank face to the world, with nothing to suggest the splendours within but the sheer weight of the frontage and perhaps a carved coat-of-arms, or a fantasy of helmets, lances, axes, sunbursts and clouds floated out of stone by one of the late-seventeenth-century masters.

The middle classes lived in their apartments or their small houses, also in narrow lanes. Almost all were employed as officials by the central government; but some were also painters, sculptors, musicians in their spare time; some, like Grillparzer, were writers, struggling with the censorship,* some were secret politicians composing manifestoes to be published under pseudonyms. They were poorly paid, and rents were very high; but they enjoyed their lives: mild official work by day, evenings of cheerful parties with endless talk and music and singing and drinking. The parties cost nothing – wine and sausages and guests to play the piano while the rest danced. It was the day of the elder Strauss and Lanner; and every time a new waltz appeared the Press (the only free and readable papers were those devoted to the theatre and the arts) gave columns to it, as nowadays to a new film or a new television feature. These two men were deified, and they made a great deal of money: the city moved and lived to their three-four beat. But when it came to more serious music it was another story. The great aristocratic families which earlier had patronized Haydn, then Beethoven, were largely out of sympathy with the new wave and the high-light of the Court Opera was the three months' season of Italian opera, with Italian conductors and singers. Even the regular director of the opera, Nicolai, who had had a great success with his *Merry Wives of Windsor*, could barely make ends meet. Lortzing, the composer of *Czar and Carpenter* and many other hits, would, in a later age, have made a fortune—but not in Vienna of the *Biedermayer* era. He directed the opera in the Theater an der Wien for a pittance; for his own operas he received a small sum down from each opera-house throughout Germany which put them on – and no more, no matter how successful. And when inspiration ran dry he was forced to return to his youthful profession as an actor in order to keep body and soul together.[1] It was a day in which quiet starvation in garrets was taken for granted as the likely end even of the most successful painters, writers and musicians as old age overtook them. It was an age in which the great eighteenth-century heritage was all but forgotten. Year after year Haydn was celebrated with performances of *The Seasons* and *The Creation*, but that was all. Mozart was neglected and misunderstood. Schubert was known only for his songs and a few piano pieces. Schumann spent a great deal of time in Vienna, but the public were not interested in his compositions, only in the piano playing of his wife, Clara Wieck,

---

* But Grillparzer himself was made Director of the Exchequer Archives and awarded the coveted title, *Hofrat*. The great and proud Prime Minister, Felix Schwarzenberg, called on him personally at his own home to honour him.

who had to support him. It was the age, also, of the great virtuosi: musicians found they could make much more by travelling about as performers than by composing; and the great man was Franz Liszt. There was a rule in those days in Vienna that nobody could give an evening concert, because no concert was allowed to clash with the officially subsidized theatres. Thus all public music-making, apart from opera, had to be done at midday: the Sunday concerts of the Vienna Philharmonic Orchestra, founded by Nicolai at this time, still start at 12.30 p.m. The only man who had the weight to beat this ban was Liszt, who gave his recitals late in the evening after the theatres had closed.

But reaction against Vienna's claims to be the natural home of music can go too far. Rossini may have driven out Beethoven in the public regard; but in 1845 Hector Berlioz came to Vienna and had an amazing success in a series of concerts which, besides *Romeo and Juliet* and *Harold in Italy*, included the *Fantastic Symphony*, that extraordinary work which was to echo down the century like a portent, or a Delphic commentary, which only began to make sense in 1914.

> The people of Vienna seem to any serious observer to be revelling in an everlasting state of intoxication. Eat, drink and be merry are the three cardinal virtues and pleasures of the Viennese. It is always Sunday, always Carnival time for them. There is music everywhere. The innumerable inns are full of roisterers day and night. Everywhere there are droves of fops and fashionable dolls. Everywhere, in daily life, in art, and in literature, there prevails that delicate and witty jesting. For the Viennese the only point of anything, of the most important event in the world, is that they can make a joke about it.[2]

The observer in question was the rebel writer, Franz Schuselka, who had to get his work published in Hamburg – one of a small but swiftly growing band of conscientious objectors to absolutism. The mood he set out to describe was the product of irresponsibility, and irresponsibility existed because people were forbidden to be responsible. Authority was all, and authority was negation. In the words of another rebel, Matthias Koch, the whole system was negation: 'It was a brazen tablet with these indestructible words engraved upon it: "No concessions, no constitution, no innovations." It stood above a prostrate living organism called the state, its limbs bound with chains. . . .'[3]

Baron Sedlitzky's police censorship was in theory all-powerful, but in fact it was Viennese. As in all would-be totalitarian systems, censorship from the outside was reinforced and made effective only by that demoralizing form of self-censorship practised by the individual who develops an exact sense of just how far he can go without offending authority. As the 1840s wore on, this self-censorship in Austria started breaking down. Austrian critics of their own system, like Schuselka, were publishing outside and having their pamphlets smuggled in. Reading clubs with innocent façades concealing self-conscious political intentions sprang up in numbers. Various journals printed in Germany and written largely by Austrians began to circulate almost openly in Vienna. The liberal middle classes found to their surprise that they were now in step with a whole cohort of aristocratic figures who were using the local Diets, above all the Lower Austrian Estates, with its building in the Herrengasse almost adjoining the Hofburg, to urge reforms: Freiherr von Doblhoff, Count Montecuccoli, Freiherr von Schmerling (later to be First Minister), Count Colloredo-Mansfeld. Von Moering, a distinguished ornament of the General Staff, tutor of the Archduke Rainer's children, produced under a pseudonym a volume called *The Sybilline Book of Austria* which attacked the system in terms which would have been a credit to Palmerston. The régime, he said, was rotten in that it placed no trust in any but the privileged nobility and treated the masses simply as beasts of burden who were also required to pay taxes and fight in the army; he attacked his own officer caste; above all he insisted that the system had alienated all the nationalities in the Empire; it had succeeded in turning Bohemians into Czechs, Hungarians into Magyars, Venetians and Lombards into Italians. It had deliberately set out to discourage the development of a common Austrian patriotism; and in the whole of the Empire there was not a solitary citizen who could be proud of being an Austrian.

This volume was inscribed to the Archduchess Sophie, the daughter-in-law of Emperor Franz and the mother of the Emperor-to-be.

There was still no call for revolution: the mood was, as indicated, one of conscientious objection to absolutism. Nothing more was required than the revitalizing of the régime, the conceding of some sort of constitution, freedom of speech, a 'liberal' Parliament, an elementary Bill of Rights. The Emperor was referred to always with a respect bordering on the fulsome. The Archduke Ludwig and the State Conference came in for all the blame. When the revolution broke out on 24 February it was carnival time in Vienna, the celebrated *Fasching*, and no *Fasching* was ever more brilliant. The public balls in endless succession were crowded night after night. Liszt was in the city, drawing packed audiences; Meyerbeer was there for the first night of his *Vielka* at the Opera; Jenny Lind, at the top of her form, was making audiences swoon and weep, and the students were planning to take the horses out of her carriage and haul her in triumph through the streets. Three weeks later the students were out in the streets in a different capacity, ordinary citizens had been shot down by the Vienna garrison, and Metternich had fled the country.

CHAPTER TWO

PEOPLES IN REVOLT

The 1848 rebellions meant different things to different people. There were profound economic causes at work; but the students who started demonstrating in Budapest, in Vienna, in Prague, were largely unconscious of these. There was an inchoate eruption of nationalistic feeling; but when the established rulers in Vienna heard echoes of savage cries – Hungary for the Magyars! Bohemia for the Slavs! Italy for the Italians! Austria for the Germans! – they had no conception of the intensity of this new passion for national self-consciousness and regarded it simply as a bizarre and ugly twist in a revolutionary impulse of destructiveness: nationalism for them was a meaningless synonym for disloyalty to the Monarchy. But it was only the Italians who wanted to rid themselves entirely of the Habsburgs, and everything that went with them; and if the men in the Hofburg had listened to what the demonstrators were saying, instead of stopping their ears so that all they could hear was the dull, ugly, generalized mutter of revolt, they would have found more than reassurance, they would have found positive encouragement. In those March days a strong Emperor could have put himself at the head of all his peoples, apart from the Italians, and led them into new ways under his own immensely strengthened authority. With a strong Empire behind him, with enhanced prestige in Germany, he could then have applied himself to the Italian provinces. But the Emperor was Ferdinand.

The radical demonstrators, to begin with, did their utmost to exalt poor Ferdinand. In Vienna, on 13 March, the day began quietly enough and the demonstrations started on a characteristic note: 'Viennese! Liberate your good Emperor Ferdinand from the bonds of his enemies! All who desire the prosperity of Austria must desire the overthrow of its rulers!'[1] That meant Metternich and his system; and it was in the spirit of this placard posted up on the cathedral wall that the students marched from their university to demonstrate, not outside the Hofburg, the Imperial residence, but outside the building of the Lower Austrian Estates in the Herrengasse close by.

The Estates had started their critical session, in the course of which their liberally minded leaders, all members of the nobility, were proposing to formulate their demands for reform: the students marched to encourage them in their deliberations. When they got there, they hardly knew what to do. Indeed, they were surprised at being there at all. Most of the Viennese, who knew all about the demonstration in advance, had assumed that it would never be permitted. Thus Grillparzer wrote in his memoirs: 'I remember laughing in the faces of several of the conspirators, all of whom I knew more or less. I asked them: "Do you really think the authorities will let your demonstration come to anything? . . ." But the unexpected actually happened. No hindrances were put in their way, and the riot of 13 March took place.'[2]

It did not start as a riot. The students just stood about on that mild, cloudy March day, wondering what to do next and how to put some passion into the deliberations of the Estates, under the chairmanship of Count Montecuccoli, behind the windows just above their heads. It might have come to nothing at all; but, exasperated into action by the indecisive mood, a young doctor from the General Hospital, Adolf Fischhof, who had brought a prepared speech with him, suddenly found courage and cried: 'Gentlemen! Listen to me!' The crowd was only too pleased to listen to anyone who thought he knew what to say. Fischhof was hoisted up on to eager shoulders, and for the first time in decades the voice of decent human aspiration was publicly heard in the heart of that beautiful city. Fischhof was not a great orator, but he was a sincere and good man, who was soon to be overtaken by events, and go back to his doctoring. He expressed, as well as anyone could, what was in the hearts of tens of thousands, beating with fearfulness and sudden hope, determined to apply some of the wild, free spirit of the French Revolution to their own land, yet not at all inclined to tear down the laborious fabric of the centuries.

His demands were modest enough. This was no destructive mob. First and foremost, a free Press, the need for it simply and movingly argued.

The desires of the individual pass unnoticed so long as they are only expressed by the individual. They are like drops of water which, when they fall singly, are drunk up by the earth, vanish in the sand, evaporate in the air. But if the individual desires can be made to flow together through the thousand channels, rivulets, brooks of the

Press, they will gradually augment themselves into mighty and irresistible streams of public opinion. Then woe to the statesman who has the impudence to steer the ship of state against the stream!

Then trial by jury; a representative assembly; freedom for teaching. Finally an appeal for strength through union and mutual tolerance in all the parts of the Empire.

Ill-advised statesmanship has kept the peoples of Austria apart. They must now meet as brothers and multiply their strength through union. . . .

Let the ambitious Germans, possessed as they are by ideas, the tenacious, hard-working, patient Slavs, the chivalrous and spirited Magyars, the clever and clear-sighted Italians – let them all concentrate on the common problems of the state. . . .

Hail to Austria and its glorious future!
Hail to the united peoples of Austria!
Hail to freedom![3]

That was all; but Fischhof was wildly applauded: he might have been a Danton. But he was nothing of the kind: he was an intelligent and level-headed Austrian radical. There were others like him; but in his writing in years to come Fischhof was to show himself not at all a simple-minded enthusiast for cloudy ideals but a liberal thinker of shrewdness and address. Neither he nor anybody like him was used by the dynasty, which he desperately wanted to serve, to broaden the base of its power and to improve its contact with the people. The dynasty did not broaden its base. It had not the least objection to using middle-class talent where it found it: it used a great deal in one way and another. But that talent for critical years to come had to be placed unreservedly at the disposal of the autocrat's will. During the years which followed the accession of the new Emperor the old nobility were to be distressed and outraged by Franz Josef's predilection for clever politicians of no family. But this, really, was a sign of his youthful contempt for the people. He made no attempt to discover who was worthy and who was not. Thus on that March day when Adolf Fischhof was making heard the voice of human decency and expressing the awakening of a social conscience in Austria, there was another young man very active in the radical interest: a brilliant lawyer called Alexander Bach. Of him Prince Adolf Schwarzenberg, in his biography of his superb ancestor, Franz Josef's first Prime Minister, wrote: 'his motto must have been "to improve is to change, to be perfect is to change often".'⁴ Quite wonderfully unprincipled, an ambitious turncoat in the grand manner, Bach was to change his position so often, so swiftly and with such *élan*, that after a series of prestigious manoeuvres he was to end up not merely as the Emperor's chief adviser but also as the most ruthless member of a reactionary régime.

That is one way of looking at it. It was the way that came naturally to nineteenth-century and early-twentieth-century liberals. But is it the correct way? Looking back over the last hundred years it is easy for us to see how Fischhof was asking too much idealistically speaking, too little materially speaking. In every country where these words are printed we have a free Press, trial by jury, a responsible Ministry, a representative assembly of some kind, and a measure of freedom when it comes to teaching. But we know how easy it is for countries which have once enjoyed these freedoms to lose them. More, we have seen how even in those countries where they flourish these freedoms are not enough to produce the sort of society of which the nineteenth-century radicals dreamed; how in all countries, whether totalitarian or free, popular education combined with industrialization goes hand in hand with a growing emphasis on material well-being and a corresponding neglect of high thinking; how the ideal of brotherhood between nations has remained the weakest of noble aspirations. It was not Metternich who kept the peoples apart, as Fischhof believed, and as the Austrian internal passport system seemed to confirm. On the contrary, it needed a Metternich – or a Maria Theresa, or a Josef II – to hold them together.

For even while Fischhof was speaking his heart to the great crowd in the Herrengasse and appealing to the rulers to allow the peoples of the Empire to combine freely in their own mutual interest, in Milan, in Venice, in Budapest, in Bratislava, in Cracow, in Prague, the various nationalities were also out on the streets demanding their own freedoms, demanding free expression for their own national spirit – which all too often really meant the freedom of the 'historic nations' of the Empire to oppress their own minorities more rigorously than they themselves had ever been oppressed by Vienna. And in Vienna too, when violence took hold, when the voice of idealism and reason was trampled down by the mob, when the shooting started, when the workmen came in from the suburbs to batter down the gates of the inner city with the lamp-posts they tore down, too many of the rebels (but not Fischhof) showed themselves to be less interested in the establishment of a sort of central European League of Nations under the patronage of a benevolent and supra-national monarch, than in joining with their German cousins in the north to form a master-nation under the black-red-yellow flag. Two days later, when the first violence had died down, when Metternich, protesting to the last, had written his letter of resignation, and slipped away into the night to find sanctuary in England, when all kinds of promises had been made by the Hofburg, the poor Emperor Ferdinand was persuaded to drive out in an open carriage in the hope that his person, trustingly exposed, would soften the mood of revolt. He was cheered everywhere he went and his progress was triumphal. Beaming at the crowds through tears, he bowed right and left, exclaiming all the time, and meaning it: 'My dear, dear people! You shall have everything, everything!' But he was cheered not as the successor of Maria Theresa, the great Empire-builder, the mistress of a community of Germans, Italians, Slavs and Magyars: he was cheered as the ruler of German Austria, under whose aegis the Germanic peoples of the north, all now in revolt against their hereditary masters, should be welded together under a Habsburg to dominate the heart of Europe. There was little supra-national feeling in that Viennese crowd. There was none at all in Milan, and there was none at all in Budapest.

2

It was the Hungarians who were making the running, as they were to go on making the running in almost every way for seventy years to come. They had their own historic constitution and, through their traditional *comitats*, had kept local government in their hands even in the teeth of Josef's centralizing drive. Bohemia and Moravia had been joined by Maria Theresa with Silesia and the Austrian lands into a so-called Unitary State; but Hungary remained outside it. The head of the Habsburg House was their king; if other nations liked to acknowledge him as king or emperor they had nothing against it; but it was no real concern of theirs. This was the mood. Sustained by that violent intensity of pride which is found in people who have nothing but their pride to lose, they looked always to the past, to the great days of St Stephen's crown, so that even their radicalism took them back from the present into the past: their refusal to recognize the very existence of the present made it impossible for them to go forward, since going forward meant accepting the present as a starting-point. Their passion for independence would have been noble in the quixotic sense had they shown the least respect for, or even interest in, the existence of similar passions in the hearts of other peoples. But they had reached the stage when they could think only of themselves. They talked incessantly about justice, but what they meant was justice for the Magyars. The Empire was to be brought to a standstill because it was unfair to the Magyars, and every high-sounding slogan left over from the French Revolution, and more besides, was turned to this end, raising echoes in the hearts of all liberals everywhere. Those minority peoples who found themselves under Magyar rule should consider themselves privileged to be accepted as Hungarians. Thus the Croats of Zagreb, the Serbs of the Voivodina, the Saxons and Wallachs of Transylvania, the Slovaks of the northern hills, were to submit to Budapest rule and use Magyar on all their official occasions, instead of Latin, which had been the common language of State until 1846. One of the main purposes behind the substitution of Magyar for Latin was to discourage the dispatch of German officials to Hungary: Magyar was a difficult language to learn.

As in Vienna and Prague a few days later, the students were the first to demonstrate. But even before they had begun their innocent pursuit of radical constitutionalism the initiative had been snatched from them by a man who knew how to appeal to the pride and arrogance, the romanticism and the obscurantism, of Magyar nationalism, kept alive for centuries under Turkish oppression by the most backward squirearchy in Europe: Lajos Kossuth. Kossuth owed his European reputation as a sort of Byronic hero to his failure. Had he succeeded in his aims the world would have seen that what it had on its hands was not a Magyar Garibaldi but an unprincipled demagogue of a new and ominous kind. Kossuth was more than a disaster for nineteenth-century Hungary: he was a portent. To an uncanny degree he was the forerunner of Hitler and Mussolini and all the tyrannous rabble of our own time who were to stir up mass hysteria to achieve their own ends, who used the appeal to militant nationalism as the way to power.

As Hitler wanted to be a German, as Mussolini wanted to be a Roman, so Kossuth wanted to be a Magyar. He was not a Magyar at all; he was a Slav, one of the peasant Slovaks accepted readily as Hungarians provided they renounced their national consciousness.

He was a petty noble, but he owned no land and his mother spoke no Magyar. But he became for a spell the greatest Magyar of them all by the simple process (simple for him with his matchless gifts as a speaker) of appealing over the heads of all the best and most progressive elements in Hungary to the vast class of petty nobility sunk in medieval squalor: 600,000 of them, whom he dignified by the name of gentry. This class consisted in the main of the small nobility multiplied throughout Hungary for lack of a law of primogeniture, so that all the children and the children's children of anyone of noble birth inherited the family honours, even though they kept geese and pigs on their middens in a village. These families in a physical sense were the backbone of Magyardom, but the real hope of Magyardom lay in the urban middle class and in certain of the great magnates, who combined liberal ideas with a passion for their country, and who for years had been treating with Metternich in the interests of their country. Kossuth decided to by-pass the magnates and break their tacit alliance with the town intelligentsia – either because he was genuinely convinced of their ineffectiveness (and Metternich had indeed clipped their wings) or because he was determined to dominate Hungary and knew that he could never hope to dominate the Szechenyis and the Deaks if he worked with them. Be that as it may, by appealing to the atavistic instincts of the squirearchy, by flattering them outrageously and exploiting their selfish passions, he managed to stir them up. The sort of spell he cast may be indicated by an extract from the speech of one of his supporters when Kossuth was standing for the Bratislava Diet:

> I can think of only four epoch-making days since the Creation of the world: the first was the day when Light was made to shine on Chaos; the second was the day when Christ was born; the third was the day of the French Revolution, bringing Freedom; and the fourth day is this very day, when it must be decided whether Kossuth will be elected Deputy or not![5]

He was elected. Thenceforth he coldly dominated the Diet. And, while the Budapest students were demonstrating on the sidelines, Kossuth put through the March Laws, which, confirmed by the Emperor on 11 April, turned Hungary into a virtually independent State, recognizing only personal union through the Crown. The new Magyar State was to include all the lands of the Crown of St Stephen, and the Diets and Governors of Croatia and Transylvania were abolished. The magnates were swamped, and with them all hope of a rational development of Hungary as an integral part of the Empire.

There was no Kossuth in Bohemia. There were magnates, but these lacked the nationalistic spirit of the great Hungarian magnates: a Szechenyi might keep his private diary in German, the common language of the Court and the higher aristocracy of the Empire, but he was an impassioned Magyar none the less. The great Bohemian magnates were wholly Imperial in their outlook and often Germanic in origin. It is not true to say, as is so often said, that they were all German Catholics settled on the estates of Protestant Czechs after the Battle of the White Mountain. Many of them came from France and Italy and other European lands, from England and Ireland, too. Some of them belonged to lines of extreme antiquity. The greatest of them all, for instance, the Schwarzenbergs, who came to Bohemia from Franconia before the Habsburgs came to Vienna, could boast that 'every square inch of the Schwarzenberg properties was inherited, purchased, exchanged or otherwise legally acquired; no parcel was derived from formerly confiscated property'.[6] But, as a whole, they saw themselves as servants of the Emperor, cosmopolitan rather than supra-national. There was no squirearchy either. There were the great landowners, virtually sovereign, their peasants, and the urban intelligentsia. Nearly everywhere the peasants also spoke German (half the peasantry of Bohemia and Moravia were in fact German). Even the first great nationalist, Palacky, the father of the Czech nation, not only wrote his history in German, but also talked German with his friends in Prague while trying to rough out the constitution of a federal Empire in which Bohemia would be another Hungary.[7] Even Masaryk had to learn to write Czech correctly when he became Professor of Philosophy at the newly founded Czech University in Prague. There was thus no cohesive national strength, and the Czech nationalists, trying to imitate the Magyars, had no force with which to oppose, or blackmail, the dynasty. It is fair to say that they also lacked the Magyar's fanatical conviction of their own innate superiority to all the world, though in fact Bohemia was far more advanced than Hungary in every way. This put them at a disadvantage when it came to a showdown with the monarchy; and Palacky was the first of a long line of gentle and idealistic Czech nationalists, ending for the time being with the younger Masaryk, who tried to reason one Great Power or another into granting the

Czechs, and helping them to maintain, a position which they could not seize for themselves.

The Prague revolution did not begin with an affair of the Bohemian Diet. Some radical intellectuals, including Germans, met at the Wenceslaus Baths, a café-concert-hall, and formulated a programme much on the lines of Fischhof's demands in Vienna; but to the usual freedoms were added at the last moment, really as an afterthought, certain more concrete political demands: above all, and with tremendous consequences for the future, a common central Chancellery and a Parliament to sit alternately at Prague, the capital of Bohemia, and Brünn, the capital of Moravia, to control the affairs of the 'lands of the Crown of St Wenceslaus' – meaning Silesia, Bohemia, and Moravia. Thus was Czechoslovak nationalism born without anybody really meaning it – and, in any case, not so much in opposition to Vienna as in fear of Budapest and the Magyar designs on the Slovaks. To Hungary's Crown of St Stephen, Bohemia riposted with its own Crown of St Wenceslaus. On this kind of shaky antiquarianism conflicting claims were based which were to shatter Europe. For centuries central and east Europe had been wholly fluid, with first one then another of the tribes coming in from the steppes and sweeping everything before them. In the tenth century St Wenceslaus, who was never a king (he was a duke), had made himself a legendary figure; a little later in the same century the Magyar St Stephen had transformed Hungary into a Christian State on the European model. But invoking those shadows from the past was a dangerous game to play: there were other races who also went back a long way, and most notable of them all the Croats, whom now, in the nineteenth century, the Magyars themselves were treating as inferiors. King Tomislav of Croatia, who died in 929, was senior to the Magyar Stephen by a hundred years, and had once commanded a fighting force of 100,000 foot soldiers, 60,000 horsemen, 80 large and 100 small warships – an impressive force for central Europe in the eleventh century. Croatia, thus, was the oldest kingdom of all the Habsburg Crown-lands – a fact no more, but no less, relevant to the realities of nineteenth-century Europe than the medieval pretensions of Bohemia and Hungary.

Neither Magyars nor Bohemians boasted very much about their culture, or even their economic life, preferring the prowess of their legendary warrior-kings. And the fact of the matter was that they had all too little native culture to boast about, the middle classes and the big towns – in Budapest and Bratislava, no less than in Prague and Brünn – being preponderantly German.

The position in Galicia, the Austrian part of Poland, was different. Here the Poles had temporarily shot their bolt two years earlier, in 1846, when the Austrian authorities had conceived the original idea of turning the oppressed peasantry – largely Ruthenians and Ukrainians, denied the status of Poles – against their proud and rebellious masters. In 1848 there were brief risings in Cracow and Lvov (Lemberg), which were put down swiftly and violently by the loyal Austrian troops. Poland, anyway, was a special case. With a history and culture of its own far grander than any other Slavonic part of the Habsburg domains, Galicia was politically entangled with the rest of old Poland, now divided between Russia and Prussia. There could be no autonomous revolution in Galicia. Russian-occupied Poland would have been drawn in as well; and Russian-occupied Poland was in no position, or mood, to rise against the Tsar. It had not yet recovered from the wounds received during the disastrous insurrections of 1830 and 1846. Most of the rebel leaders were dead or in Russian prisons. Others had found refuge in Hungary, where they were to fight for Kossuth. Another twelve years were to pass before the Poles in Russian Poland felt strong enough to start a major rising; and meanwhile Galicia was fairly quiet. Compared with the bleak, pursuing violence of the Russians, the rigid arrogance of the Prussian Junkers, the Austrian colonizers brought mildness itself to their task of holding down Galicia. Indeed, they relied largely on the great Polish magnates, corrupted by privileges emanating from the Court at Vienna, to do their work for them. It was not until later that conditions in Galicia, compared with conditions in other parts of the Empire, became a major scandal and helped to bring to white heat a broader-based Polish nationalism; and even then, much of the blame could be placed on the Polish aristocrats themselves, who, in return for helping to run the Empire, allowed their own country to continue as a sort of primitive agrarian hinterland to support the industrial growth of Bohemia and the Austrian lands.

When it came to Italy the situation was entirely different. Vienna's lordship over Bohemia, Moravia, and the lands of the Danube basin had deep roots in historical necessity. Her annexation of part of Poland, which Maria Theresa had resisted, was made inevitable by the partition policies of Russia and Prussia, and, in any case, Galicia was an integral part of an elaborate political complex forming a bastion against the East. But the only part of the Italian peninsula that had any organic or ethnographical connection with the Empire was the mountainous Trentino. This area, forming the southern approaches to the Alps, was a natural glacis for the Empire, and in its northern part was entirely German. Bozen, the capital of South Tirol, was a German city. There was never any question of Vienna becoming separated from the Trentino. The challenge came from the continued Austrian occupation of Venetia and the Lombardy plain, the position of the Austrian rulers in Tuscany and Parma-Modena, and Vienna's relations with Rome.

With the deliberate development of Trieste as the chief port of the Empire, the economic importance of Venice had dwindled. Lombardy, on the other hand, with Milan as its brilliant capital, was Austria's richest province and the one with the highest level of culture. Further, its strategic value was unbounded. Only Winston Churchill could have invented the phrase 'the soft-underbelly of Europe' as the perfect description of Italy's strategic position; but the idea expressed by that phrase was not new. The Austrians themselves used to call Italy the Achilles heel of central Europe, and already in the 1830s the magnificent old veteran, Field-Marshal Radetzky, was profoundly concerned with this Achilles heel; as Commander-in-Chief of the Austrian forces in North Italy, and Governor of Lombardy, he was obsessed with the vulnerability of his position. In fact, Lombardy as such was indefensible; but, within Lombardy, the approaches to Vienna and Trieste were controlled by the great strategic base, the famous Quadrilateral, which really was impregnable: this was an area bounded by the four fortified towns of Peschiera, on the south-east tip of Lake Garda, Mantua with its inundations, Legnano and Verona.

The Austrian position, Radetzky's position, was further complicated by the activities of the new Pope, Pius IX. This remarkable character reigned for thirty-two years, from 1846 to 1878. Towards the end of his career he had to suffer, in 1870, the annexation of the Papal States to the Kingdom of Italy, and in the same year he proclaimed the dogma of Papal Infallibility. But he had begun his reign by behaving like a liberal prince, insisting on his temporal powers and encouraging liberal and nationalist feeling for the greater glory of Italy and himself: his first act was to proclaim a general amnesty for all political prisoners. With Italy alight, with King Bomba in

Naples already forced to grant a constitution in January 1848, with the Habsburg cadets in Parma and Modena heavily beset by the forces of liberal nationalism, with Charles Albert of Savoy, King of Sardinia, sitting in Turin and waiting eagerly for a chance to go to the help of the Lombards, with an anti-Austrian Pope in Rome, Radetzky's situation was not a happy one: his army, further, was starved of men and material.

Thus, as soon as news of the revolution in Vienna reached Milan, the Italians boiled over. That was on 15 March, and on the next day, with the Piedmontese hurrying to help the Lombards, the Austrians were thrown out of Milan and back into the Quadrilateral.

CHAPTER THREE

COUNTER-ATTACK

What could Austria do to save herself? What, indeed, was Austria? The French were a nation: their February revolution had led to the establishment of a new Republic, with, as its first President, an accomplished adventurer, the nephew of the great Napoleon, soon to proclaim himself Emperor. The Russians were a nation, held in subjection by an all-powerful autocrat; and the events of 1848, although they were deeply disturbing to Nicholas I, seen as a portent and a warning, had next to no immediate impact on his realm. The German kings and princes were, in one way and another, riding out the storm; but even Frederick William IV of Prussia had been forced to concede a constitution. Even in England there were alarms and threatened rebellions; but the timid had breathed again with the collapse of Feargus O'Connor's monster Chartist demonstration and the fiasco of the great petition – so that, on 11 April 1848, Palmerston could write from the Foreign Office:

> Yesterday was a glorious day, the Waterloo of peace and order. They say there were upwards of one hundred thousand special constables – some put the number at two hundred and fifty thousand; but the streets were swarming with them, and men of all classes and ranks were blended together in defence of law and property. . . . The foreigners did not show; but the constables, regular and special, had sworn to make an example of any whiskered and bearded rioters whom they might meet with, and I am convinced they would have mashed them to jelly.[1]

That was the spirit, but not in Austria. Ten days later, Palmerston was composing for Ponsonby in Vienna his lament about the sins of Metternich and the feebleness of Ferdinand:

> There is a general fight going on all over the Continent between governors and governed, between law and disorder, between those who have and those who want to have, between honest men and rogues; and as the turbulent, the poor and the rogues in this world, though perhaps not the most numerous, are at all events the most active, the other classes require for their defence to be led and

headed by intelligence, activity and energy. But how can these qualities be found in a Government where the sovereign is an idiot?[2]

It was in that letter that Palmerston went on to recommend the abdication of the Emperor Ferdinand, the renunciation of the throne by the Emperor's brother, Karl, and the accession of Karl's son, Franz Josef, then seventeen. In fact, precisely this solution had been under active contemplation for some time: the trouble was that Franzi was not of age.

For the rest of that year, for nine months of chaos and turmoil, during the course of which the Court was twice chased out of Vienna, the dynasty, such as it was, was held together and sustained by a woman, Franz Josef's mother, the Archduchess Sophie of Bavaria, married, at nineteen, to the Emperor Franz's second son, Karl. A Wittelsbach, she was one of six sisters, all married to German kings or princes, all strong-willed, all authoritarian in temper and ardent in their Catholicism: the Prussian historian, Treitschke, called them 'the Bavarian sisters of woe'. With the Crown Prince Ferdinand an imbecile from childhood, it was clear to Sophie from the beginning that she would one day either be Empress herself or the mother of an Emperor. This was compensation for marrying a man she did not love, whose character and intellect were very much weaker than her own. From the day when Franzi was born she dedicated herself to the task of making him fit to rule. But this task was not carried out in the spirit of all-consuming ambition, regardless of human feelings, for which she came later to stand in the eyes of liberals everywhere: there was no need for ambition, for her son would be Emperor, sooner or later, without any effort on her part, unless he died young. Ambition came later, with the Empire in ruins and waiting to be rebuilt. From 1827, when she married, until 1848, when, throwing Metternich to the wolves, she became the inspiration of the counter-revolution, she could afford to take life fairly easily. When she arrived at Vienna from Munich to assume her place at one of the grandest Courts in Europe, she was tender, dutiful, gay, warm, full of the romanticism of the time, affected – and determined. She was in love with poetry and music; she adored the theatre, where she went night after night, often moved to tears. Giuditta Pasta, and, later, Jenny Lind carried her to the topless heights.[3] She spent endless pains in trying to develop Franz Josef's early talent for drawing; she delighted in the sensitive dreamer's nature of her second son, Maximilian, who was to dream himself to death before a firing squad in Mexico. She found an outlet for her romantic side in a tender and imaginative friendship with the much younger Duke of Reichstadt, Bonaparte's son and heir, l'Aiglon. When the Napoleonic Empire collapsed he had been brought to Schönbrunn by his mother, Sophie's sister-in-law, Marie Louise; and there he fretted his young life away – dreaming impossible dreams in Maria Theresa's vast formal palace, the Habsburg's retort to Versailles, which stretches its 660 feet of pale façade, its 1,400 rooms, its great park and formal gardens at the foot of the wooded hills just outside the city – a victim of high politics. He was kept there by the Emperor Franz, who loved him dearly, as a form of insurance – a pawn in the shape of a Bonapartist pretender, who could be played against France, if need be. He grew into a youth of surpassing handsomeness, to die of consumption. He was five years younger than Sophie, who helped him to bear his sequestration: they went together to the theatre; they walked in the park; Sophie read poetry to him until he was too ill even to be read to any more.[4]

In most things Sophie was enthusiastic rather than passionate. But in two things she was passionate: in her religion and in her concern for her children. She brought to the Viennese Court a new element of mystical devotion, which did not accord at all well with prevailing views; and she put up with the teasing of the archdukes and the disparagements of Princess Melanie Metternich, persisting in her devotion to the Church to the point of taking her orders from a cleric of outstanding ability, Abbot Rauscher, who was later to exercise great power as Cardinal-Archbishop of Vienna. For the rest, she was interested only in the comfort and well-being of her eldest son. Everything she did was directed to making it possible for Franzi to reign. It was not until it was on the verge of extinction that she became interested in the dynasty as such. Then she set about saving it because there was nobody else to save it. But she was saving it for Franzi. It was this which drove her to intrigue against her trusted mentor, Metternich, whose policies had brought government to a standstill and exposed the priceless heritage of her eldest son to fearful, scarcely apprehended perils. She was not in any way a liberal; but she had eyes in her head. For a long time her father, the Bavarian king, had managed his country very nicely by working through a species of constitution which seemed to keep everyone very happy and allowed useful men to play a part in government.

With the old men out of the way, why should the Austrian Court not play the same game? Somebody had to be sacrificed to keep the rioters out of the Hofburg; and that had clearly better be the man whose head they were demanding.

It is important to get Sophie into focus. Her influence in years to come was to be so great and, in some respects, so dire, that without a picture of her as she was before events turned her into a king-maker the larger picture will be false. She was for years politically illiterate. When she heard the news of the revolution in Lombardy she wrote in her diary: 'The sadness of the times we live in! Every-where the mind is inflamed by passion, above all in poor, beautiful Italy, which could be so happy if only people were reasonable!'[5] She thought the Viennese would respond with gratitude to small con-cessions; and when they did not, when passions rose still further and drove the Imperial family out of Vienna, she was suddenly dis-illusioned and furious with them for their ingratitude. She is remem-bered as the arch-type of the insufferable managing woman, the she-dragon, pushing her reluctant son into ever harsher excesses, bullying her enchanting daughter-in-law in a deliberate attempt to make life impossible for her, all in the interests of personal ambition. So one of the most perceptive writers of our time, Rebecca West, could liken her to one of those crassly domineering women, without an ounce of human feeling, who are so often chosen by all-male committees to be matrons of hospitals.[6] She was not like that at all. She was, rather, sentimental, often tiresome and silly, and stubborn to a degree. Franz Josef, who knew all about her defects, adored her. His character, too, has not been understood.

2

What Sophie did in 1848, from March to December, was to hold the Court together, in and out of exile, until the time was ripe for the striking of a counter-blow; then to assist in the abdication of Ferdi-nand and the production of her son to take his place. Meanwhile Franzi had to be kept out of the struggle so that the new young Emperor should neither be bound by the promises forced out of Ferdinand nor in any way involved in the manoeuvres of the military junta which was to break the revolution. Through a giddy sequence of ineffective Ministers, by granting concession after concession, by promising constitutions and constituent assemblies, the Court managed to survive. In May it fled to Innsbruck, leaving an in-effective liberal government to cope with chaos. Hungary had seceded, Venetia had set up a republic, Lombardy was in flames, Bohemia had its own provisional government. But action had shifted away from the centre. The Vienna liberals were by-passed by history. The Court at Innsbruck betrayed them by dealing directly with the Czechs, winning over the Bohemian moderates by promising them a Diet of their own in Prague. The soldiers did the rest. These were the 'three paladins': Field-Marshal Windischgraetz, Governor of Bohemia; Field-Marshal Radetzky, Governor of Lombardy and Venetia; and Ban Jellačić, the violent, turbulent, heavily moustachioed leader of the Croats.

Already, supported by the strong arm of Windischgraetz, the dynasty was beginning to exploit for its own ends those national contradictions and rivalries which, seventy years later, were to be its undoing. While Vienna remained in a state of turmoil, while the government was planning to abandon Italy, while there were urgent voices advocating the abandonment of Hungary and union with the German States under the black-red-yellow flag (taking Bohemia and Moravia with them into a united Germany, with a Parliament at Frankfurt), the Court and the generals were acting. The first victory was Prague. Already the Czech leader, Palacky, had refused to attend the Frankfurt pre-Parliament, a committee of fifty called into being by German nationalist radicals from all the German States to prepare for a German National Assembly. 'I am a Bohemian of Slav race', he had declared. That meant that he could take no part in the affairs of national Germany. At the same time he was equally determined in his rejection of Russia as the natural protector of the Slavs. That meant that the father of Czech nationalism was, in effect, throwing himself on the mercy of the Habsburg dynasty and asking a family which regarded nationalism as a deadly sin to father the birth of his nation. The Court at Innsbruck treated his pretensions as might have been expected. They used them and then rejected them. Rejection was made easy by the impatience of the radicals in Prague. At the beginning of June there was a grand Slav Congress, which was intended to stress the equality of the Slavs of the Empire with the Germans and the Magyars. While the Congress was sitting, rioting broke out and this gave Windischgraetz his chance. After a little street-fighting he withdrew his troops to the hills and started a brisk bombardment. The rioting stopped. The Czech moderates welcomed the action. There was now nothing in the way of moderation, and great hopes were pinned on the promised Constituent Assembly. But Prince Windischgraetz was master now, and he was not one to favour Constituent Assemblies. Moreover, during the rioting his own wife had been killed by a stray bullet.

The dynasty was recovering its strength. Windischgraetz desired the Court to stay in Innsbruck while he dealt with Vienna. But to the Imperial family the time looked ripe for a rallying of all those forces which had something to gain from the establishment of law and order. The new Ministry, moreover, led by the veteran Wessenberg, included as Minister of Justice a very strong man indeed, none other than Alexander Bach, who had abandoned the barricades because he thought the time had come to get on the side of law and order. In July the outlook for the dynasty was brighter still. Radetzky, the great Field-Marshal, who had waited so long in vain for reinforcements from Galicia and Moravia, turned on the Piedmontese and beat them soundly at Custozza: he had behind him now even the revolutionary Viennese, many of whom left the barricades they had raised against the Imperial government to fight for the greatest soldier of the Imperial government against the insolent Italians.

But there was still Hungary. And it was over Hungary that the revolution broke out again in Vienna with quite a new sort of violence. Germans, Magyars and Slavs of various branches had been united in opposition to Metternich's system; but once Metternich had fled they proceeded to tear each other to pieces. Some of the Germans wanted to unite with all other Germans, abandoning the dynasty, to form a self-consciously superior bloc; others hoped to make the best of both worlds – to annex all Germany to an Austria which also included Slav and Magyar lands. Some of the Magyars – the magnates and the city intelligentsia – wanted the maximum Hungarian independence compatible with union with Vienna; others insisted on total independence except for the bond of the Crown, which they thought they could keep while repudiating their share of the National Debt: all were united in demanding absolute jurisdiction over the Slavs in their territory (Slovaks, Serbs and Croats) as well as the Rumanians of Transylvania. Some of the Czechs and Slovaks wanted a form of independence under a Habsburg monarch; others sought equality with other peoples in a federation; some were prepared to see the Empire broken down into a series of impossibly small regions based on the ethnological pattern; others saw Prague

43

as the capital of the lands of St Wenceslaus: all resisted the pretensions of the Magyars to jurisdiction over the Slavs in the lands of St Stephen. Some of the Southern Slavs (Serbs, Croats and Slovenes) dreamed of an Illyrian kingdom within the Empire; others were prepared to serve Vienna, provided they did not come under the sway of Budapest. Only the Monarchy stood above all this and was thus able to play off one people against another. In September it was decided to tackle the Magyars by bringing into play the third of the three paladins, Jellačić, the Governor, or Ban, of Croatia, who was told to march against the insurrectory Hungarians.

This he did, at the head of a wild and savage horde, unleashing a civil war of the most desperate kind. The Magyars, now united for the time being under Kossuth (the moderates, like Deak, had long withdrawn), treated the South Slav attack as a pretext for a war of extermination against the Slav minorities in their lands. The Slavs replied in kind. The Viennese radicals, increasingly out of hand since the moderates had abandoned them, were inflamed by this show of Imperial violence against the Hungarian radicals. They rose. They tried to stop an Austrian regiment from the Vienna garrison moving to the aid of Jellačić. They stormed the Ministry of War, lynching Latour, the Minister, hanging him from a lamp-post, and nearly lynching Bach. One of the men who tried in vain to save Latour was a member of the National Guard, the idealistic young doctor, Adolf Fischhof, whose speech had fired the revolution, seven months before. The Court fled again, this time to Olmütz, where the great fortress stood which, eighteen years later, was to play so bleak a role in the defeat of Austria by Prussia. That was on 14 October. In the first days of November Windischgraetz dealt with Vienna. After bitter fighting and heavy bombardment he took over the city and established martial law.

The Empire, apart from Hungary, was now in his hands. He had no wish to be Prime Minister: he was off to take Budapest. The man he chose for the job was his much younger brother-in-law, Prince Felix Schwarzenberg. But Schwarzenberg would not take office unless under a new Emperor. Franz Josef, at eighteen, was ready in the wings, unspotted and uninvolved. He had received his baptism of fire with Radetzky in Lombardy; but he had played no part in the desperate politics of the past eight months. On 2 December 1848 his accession was proclaimed. The ceremony took place in the Archbishop's Palace, where the Court had made its headquarters. The tension was extreme. Nobody, not even Franzi's two brothers, knew why they had been told to dress in gala uniform. Sophie had put on all her jewels. Windischgraetz, Jellačić, Schwarzenberg, all the Ministers, assembled in a great half-circle round poor Emperor Ferdinand and his devoted Marianna. Ferdinand announced his abdication. Then Schwarzenberg, his voice trembling, read Karl's statement, renouncing the throne, explaining that at this juncture a younger force was needed. Then they gave their homage to Franz Josef, and after that Ferdinand and Marianna went upstairs to pack.

In this way, in turmoil and bitterness, sustained by the bayonets of the army, Franz Josef began the reign which was to last for sixty-eight years, from 1848 to 1916. He began with a throne, but he still lacked an Empire: it was Schwarzenberg's task to win it for him.

PART TWO

GOVERNMENT OF THE SWORD

CHAPTER FOUR

THE COURSE IS SET

Vienna was the *Kaiserstadt*, the Imperial city. And the Emperor who reigned for sixty-eight years came in the end to be the nearest thing to God. More than the secular father-figure, towards the end of the century he was a living sacrifice, a scapegoat, bowed down by the weight of his own personal disasters and, at the same time, bearing upon his slight shoulders the burden of the sins of all his subjects. Then he was quite alone: his brother, Maximilian, had been shot by a firing squad in Mexico and his sister-in-law driven mad; his son and heir had killed himself; his Empress, long estranged from him, had been stabbed to death on the quayside at Geneva; Franz Ferdinand, his nephew, the new heir, had married beneath him and opposed him in everything, collecting round him in Hildebrandt's dazzling palace on the hill, the Belvedere, a sort of shadow Cabinet working against the policies of the Hofburg. In the great town houses of the aristocracy the life of high society continued with all brilliance; but the ageing Emperor, ruling through professional bureaucrats and politicians, was withdrawn from that life. He toiled by day, endlessly, unrelentingly, over the paper reflections of everything that took place in his vast dominions, slept shortly by night on his narrow bed in the Hofburg or in the immense Rococo summer palace at Schönbrunn, for all the world as though should he deviate by a hair's breadth from routine the great and lovely city, the whole Empire, would fly to pieces. On 28 June 1914 Franz Ferdinand and his morganatic wife were murdered at Sarajevo in the Bosnian mountains. A few weeks later, as part of his routine, the Emperor signed the order which started the First World War. Two years later he was dead; soon after that the Empire indeed flew to pieces.

But Franz Josef had not always been Atlas: once he had been Jove. All that was required of him when they made him Emperor at eighteen, with the Empire in full revolt, was that he should look the part and come fresh to the throne, his hands not tied by the promises which the revolutionaries had forced from his gentle uncle. His advisers and his generals would do the rest – and his mother, Sophie, who had persuaded her husband to renounce his succession to the Crown in order that her son might rule. There was no need for him to be anything but a figurehead and a support for his Chief Minister. He was handsome, slender, splendid in uniform (which he always wore) and brave. This would have been enough. But in his own mind he was more than this: he was the ruler, the autocrat, divinely appointed, responsible to none but God, and charged with the sacred duty of restoring the dynasty and maintaining its European position. He saw this as a personal duty, which nobody could share. In this he differed from his chief advisers, upon whom, nevertheless, he had at first to lean. In this he differed too from others, more distant, who wished him well. Palmerston in England, who had summed up the Austrian situation long before, had seen what the Court must do eight months before it did it. With his customary insensitiveness he wrote to Lord Ponsonby, then Ambassador to Vienna, urging him to entreat Wessenberg, the then Foreign Minister, in strictest confidence that he and his colleagues should consider, 'for the salvation of their country, whether some arrangement could not be made by which the Emperor Ferdinand might abdicate, for which his bodily health might furnish a fair reason, while some more efficient successor might ascend the throne in his stead.'[1] He continued:

> I fear that his next brother is little better than he is; but could not the son of that brother be called to the succession? And though he is young, he could yet mount his horse, and show himself to his troops and his people, could excite some enthusiasm for his person as well as for his official station, and, by the aid of good Ministers and able generals, might re-establish the Austrian empire in its proper position at home and abroad.

Palmerston, who needed the Austrian Empire to maintain the uneasy continental balance, knew nothing of Franz Josef's character. Few did. All saw him as a likely kind of youth, good for mounting his horse and showing himself to the people. Even Bismarck, four years later, meeting the young Emperor at Budapest, failed to catch his real quality. Bismarck was then thirty-seven, saturnine, narrow-eyed, a bundle of nerves inside that gigantic frame, not yet at all the rugged old monument surrounded by crop-eared hounds of the familiar photographs. He met Franz Josef, twenty-two, and wrote back to Berlin:

The youthful ruler of this country makes a very agreeable impression on me: the fire of the twenties, coupled with the dignity and foresight of riper years, a fine eye, especially when animated, and a winning openness of expression, especially when he laughs. The Hungarians are enthusiastic about his national pronunciation of their language and the elegance of his riding.[2]

This was Bismarck's first trite view of the young man whom, quite soon, he was to start fighting tooth and nail, not ceasing until the Habsburg supremacy in Germany was broken and replaced by the hegemony of Prussia.

Nicholas I of Russia eulogized him and regarded him as his own particular protégé. When Franz Josef was only nineteen Nicholas wrote to the Tsaritsa: 'The more I see of him, the more I listen to him, the more I am astonished by his intellect, by the solidity and correctness of his ideas. Austria is lucky indeed to possess him.'[3] But within five years Franz Josef was to break the Tsar's heart and become an object of obsessional hatred to his successor, Alexander II.

Diplomats of every country, and German princes in their dozens, sent back their glowing impressions of this wonder-youth who had been called to such an appalling task. Only Franz Josef himself was not appalled. Young, totally inexperienced, surrounded by the toughest advisers, and perfectly well aware of the perils which beset him, he took the immediate task in his stride, as he was to take in his stride, without outwardly turning a hair, all the triumphs and disasters, mainly disasters, of the next seven decades. He was a man called by God. He was called to restore the fortunes of the divinely appointed dynasty and to rule; this was his duty and his right. Only one man in those very early days put on record a picture of the young Emperor in which may be seen the essential features of the autocrat to be, his first Prime Minister, Prince Felix Schwarzenberg, who was also the first and last Minister to dominate Franz Josef. In a letter to Metternich, living in retirement eighteen months after Franz Josef's accession, Schwarzenberg wrote:

The Emperor sees the magnitude and difficulty of his task and his will is firmly set to meet it. His intelligence is acute, his diligence in affairs astonishing, especially for one of his age. He works hard for at least ten hours a day, and nobody knows better than I how many ministerial proposals he sends back to be revised. His bearing is full of dignity, his behaviour to all exceedingly polite, though a little dry. Men of sentiment – and many people in Vienna lay claim to kindliness – say that he has not much heart. There is no trace in him of that warm, superficial goodheartedness of many Archdukes, of the wish to please, to strive for effect. On the other hand he is perfectly accessible, patient, and well disposed to be just to all. He has a rooted objection to any kind of lie and is absolutely discreet. But the quality that is most valuable to him in his present position, above all at a time like the present, is his courage. I have never seen it fail for an instant, even in the most difficult situations of whose peril he is entirely aware. Physically and morally he is fearless, and I believe the main reason why he can face the truth, however bitter, is that it does not frighten him. Time will make him more self-reliant: I do my best to assist that good work; then the country will have in him what it needs above everything – a man.[4]

He not only worked hard; he played hard too. He was a first-class dancer, a first-class horseman, and a very good shot. 'He puts an excessive strain on his physical strength by dancing, riding and doing without sleep. He gets up about four and never stops working. . . .' That was Bismarck again, already qualifying as the first hypochondriac of Europe, a little irritated by the young Emperor's animal spirits. Schwarzenberg was right about the man. What he did not see was that virility was not enough: if the Empire was to develop any sort of organic unity its ruler must have some idea of how the world at that juncture was moving.

2

Prince Felix Schwarzenberg was a statesman of genius and a man of extraordinary character. He is famous in the West for two remarks, both of which appear to be apocryphal. When asked one day whether he was not oppressed by the sense of obligation towards Tsar Nicholas for helping him put down the Hungarians in 1849, he is said to have replied: 'Austria will astonish the world by the magnitude of her ingratitude.' And when, at about the same time, somebody pleaded with him to show magnanimity and clemency towards the captured Hungarian rebels, he is said to have answered: 'Yes, yes – a very good idea. But first we will have a little hanging.' If he did not say these things he should have said them. Certainly they reflect the conscious image of the man. Tall and slender, the Hollywood dream of an Austrian aristocrat, but prematurely aged and weakened, certainly by typhus caught in Italy, perhaps by earlier excesses, he was the image of detachment, contained arrogance, and icy self-discipline. It was an image very consciously contrived and it did not reflect the reality within. He was a man of passionate ambition with a strong streak of recklessness. Behind the insolent drawl, he was touchy to a degree. His touchiness came out in violence.

At the time of his installation as Prime Minister he was forty-eight, and although he was a member of one of the most illustrious families of the Empire, very few people knew anything about him. He was to die only four years later, having in that time raised his Emperor and his country to a fresh apogee of influence and power. He was a new sort of statesman: an aristocrat of most ancient lineage, who became for a time a Jacobin dictator; but a dictator working through the medieval paraphernalia of a hereditary monarchy. Starting as a cavalry officer, he had drifted into diplomacy. In Petersburg, as a spirited and Byronic young man, he was mixed up with the spirited and Byronic young Russian officers who were involved in the Decembrist Plot against Nicholas I on his accession.[5] He had to go. Later, in London, he showed the reckless passion beneath the insolent exterior when, after innumerable affairs, he fell violently in love with Jane Ellenborough, Balzac's Lady Arabella Dudley, the wife of the Lord Privy Seal. Ellenborough was everywhere detested, but he obtained a parliamentary divorce. Once more Schwarzenberg had to go. But Metternich, who saw much promise in him, stood by him and sent him to Paris: Jane Ellenborough followed but, before long, she fled to Munich, leaving their daughter behind her.* Felix Schwarzenberg continued to cherish his child, whose descendants are still living, and took time off for self-renewal.[6] He retired to his Bohemian forests, where his family lived like kings, and bathed himself in nature and great literature. For a time it was all nature, classics, and Thomas à Kempis.[7] Then, refreshed, at thirty-one, he came out again to battle with the world.

He did so brilliantly, both in diplomacy and in war, which he seemed to find interchangeable, that Windischgraetz, his brother-in-law, chose him to be the prop and mainstay of the new young Emperor. Schwarzenberg was not grateful at all. He was filled with a profound contempt for the aristocracy which had brought the Empire to ruin, and the aristocracy included Prince Windischgraetz.

---

* She for her part went on to higher things. After a brief affair with Ludwig I of Bavaria, whose later passion for the dancer, Lola Montez, was to lose him his throne (he was Sophie's uncle) she married first a German baron, then a Greek count, and finally finished up with a flourish in the harem of a Bedouin sheik.

He had only one thought: to rehabilitate the Empire, to run it efficiently, and to restore it to its proper place in Europe, with Franz Josef firmly in the saddle. Anything that seemed likely to hinder the swift execution of this task was to be ruthlessly swept aside, regardless of personal feelings or inhibiting loyalties; anything that might help to expedite it was to be used as and how it seemed expedient. Everything had to be done through the Emperor and in his name; but since the Emperor was only eighteen and knew nothing of the world, the new Prime Minister had only to win the young man's trust and all would be well. This was easy. Felix Schwarzenberg, at forty-eight, was the most presentable man in Europe, and his character was one which would appeal strongly not only to women but also to an eighteen-year-old boy with a passion for soldiers and a profound inborn tendency towards high-handedness.

At first, of course, Schwarzenberg had things all his own way. Since Schwarzenberg's way for all practical purposes was also the young Emperor's way (Schwarzenberg did not have to persuade Franz Josef of the merits of his policies, only show him how to realize them) there was no conflict at all.

He had four main tasks. The first was to establish the authority of the Emperor in what remained of the Empire—that is to say, the Austrian lands, Bohemia, Moravia and Galicia; the second was to regain what had been lost to the Empire – that is to say, the Italian provinces (Lombardy and Venetia) and Hungary; the third was to establish Austrian hegemony in Germany, with particular reference to the rival claims of Prussia; the fourth was to look for allies to maintain the revitalized Empire as he proposed to construct it. It was a dream of the highest-vaulting kind, and, as dreams go, not absurd. For the first time the Austrian Empire was to exist as a centralized and coherent entity: Schwarzenberg went farther even than Josef II, for Hungary was, in effect, to be brought into the framework of the Unitary State; there was to be no nonsense about a special position for the Magyars, who were to be punished into the bargain. Further, the notional supremacy of Austria in Germany, enjoyed for so long, until 1806, by virtue of Charlemagne's Crown, was to be replaced by a real supremacy based on power within an all-embracing Customs Union: Prussia would submit to *force majeure* and nothing else.

There is too much hindsight in our thinking about such matters. It is easy now to look back and say that the rise of perfervid nationalism, 'devoid alike of sense and morals', made nonsense in advance of

Bruck's dream of an 'Empire of Seventy Millions'. It is even too much to say for certain that nationalism was the real inhibitor of that dream. At the close of the first half of the nineteenth century European statesmen of all kinds, not only Schwarzenberg, were thinking very much in terms of empires. The Russian Tsar ruled over an empire big enough, one would have said, even for a Russian, which he was ceaselessly trying to expand, not without success, and in the very teeth of nationalism: it had seventy years to go, then collapsed and was swiftly reassembled, rearticulated, and further aggrandized into the breath-taking Soviet imperium of today. Prussia was preparing to contest the leadership of Germany, which included Catholic States not at all amenable to Berlin's domination. Prussia, using popular nationalism as a weapon, built up the German Empire: it collapsed and was swiftly reassembled into the Third Reich which, for a few years, imposed its New Order upon the whole of Europe less Switzerland, Spain, Sweden, and a small part of European Russia. Louis Napoleon in France, the only European besides Bismarck and Cavour who really understood the spirit of nationalism, who sought deliberately and with success to ride that wave, was an empire-builder too, with his eyes on the Rhineland, Italy and Mexico. England, with no immediate claims on the Continent, was nevertheless launched on her own imperialist mission.

In the context of 1849 there was no reason at all to scoff at Bruck's dream, which became Schwarzenberg's dream, and there were good reasons for wishing that it might come true. An articulation of Europe with the main centres of power at Paris, Petersburg, Vienna and London had a great deal to be said for it, provided articulation was not confused with rigid administrative division. Louis Napoleon avoided this confusion, so did Bismarck; the Russian Tsar did not, nor did Schwarzenberg. And this led him to make his one fatal and irreparable mistake: he thought he had to hold Lombardy.

This is not hindsight. The mistake was seen by Schwarzenberg's contemporaries. It was seen by Louis Napoleon, who sought to profit by it; and it was seen by Palmerston, who deplored it:

> I cannot regret the expulsion of the Austrians from Italy. I do not believe, Sire, that it will diminish the real strength nor impair the real security of Austria as a European Power. Her rule was hateful to the Italians, and has long been maintained only by an expenditure of money and an exertion of military effort which left Austria less able to maintain her interests elsewhere. Italy was to her the heel of

Achilles, and not the shield of Ajax. The Alps are her natural barrier and her best defence.[8]

That was all there was to be said from a purely rational point of view, and Palmerston said it in a letter to Queen Victoria's beloved uncle, Leopold of Belgium, dated 15 June 1848. But hindsight comes in once more if we pretend that this diagnosis should have been self-evident to any Austrian who was not a fool.

3

It is absurd to expect a statesman to step out of his frame, but modern historians often invite their subjects to do just this. Nothing is easier than to put the Habsburg Monarchy under a microscope and show that it was the embodiment of human folly; and this has often been done. But the more brilliant and elegant the dissection the more unhelpful and irrelevant the whole operation is made to appear: mankind being given to folly, it is clear that all its institutions must to a greater or lesser degree be embodiments of that folly. Thus, to appreciate the strong points and the failings of a Schwarzenberg, we have to re-establish him firmly in his own time and to appreciate the task which, rightly or wrongly, appeared to him as the one and only, the inevitable task, not chosen by him but thrust upon him.

Europe in 1848 was for all practical purposes the civilized world. Europe consisted of a few Great Powers, who between them held some sort of balance of force, and a much larger number of small Powers, some of whom were aspiring to play a larger role. Very senior among the Great Powers was the Habsburg monarchy, which appeared to be on the verge of dissolution. If the Monarchy were allowed to disintegrate this would not be a first step towards establishing a just and equitable European society where princes would rule no more and private citizens of every degree would cultivate their gardens, living side by side in amity and concord: the pieces would be picked up by the other Powers, and not without bitter and bloody fighting among themselves. The Austrian Empire had to be restored, and it was the first duty of any new Prime Minister to see that this happened. Indeed, there was no other duty. In principle there was not a monarch or a statesman in Europe who wished it otherwise. For a variety of reasons, some purely selfish, some relatively liberal, England, France, Prussia and Russia all wished to see Austrian pretensions curtailed in one direction or another; but none wanted Austria to disappear, leaving chaos to be sorted out by war on a European scale. There were liberals in England filled with righteous indignation at the spectacle of absolute power crushing the revolutions in Italy and Hungary, who would have liked to see Austria defeated and forced to reform herself from top to bottom; but even these did not want to see the Monarchy vanish into thin air. They cheered for Kossuth and thought everything would be fine if the Habsburgs abandoned Italy and established sovereign Parliaments in Budapest and Prague and Cracow, oblivious of the contemptuous fury with which the Magyars regarded the minorities of Hungary, of the oppressive conduct of the Polish nobility towards their Ruthenian majority, of the dour antagonism between Slovak and Czech, of the bitter religious and cultural hostility between Croat and Serb. Louis Napoleon in France, whose mastery of intrigue would have carried him to the mastery of Europe had he also possessed some moral force (or even physical stamina), was busy preparing for the *coup* which would make him Emperor of the French. Although he was setting himself up as the champion of small nations and the principle of self-determination, he needed Austria as a counterpoise to Prussia. Frederick William of Prussia, who dreamed of medieval glory, nevertheless looked to the Habsburgs, heirs to the Roman crown, as his liege lords – a view which was to cause Bismarck the greatest difficulties a little later. For Nicholas I in Petersburg, Vienna was the mainstay of the European order.

We can look farther than the monarchs and the statesmen and, in England, the liberals who were beginning to influence the government in many ways. To get the mood of the times we may look to the two great revolutionaries of the day, by now deadly foes. On the one hand Bakunin, the Russian aristocrat turned anarchist, the passionate atheist who, at the time of the Dresden insurrection, hit on the idea that the revolutionaries should advance bearing before them Raphael's *Sistine Madonna*, because he was sure the troops would not fire on it; the violent opponent of the Tsarist Empire, who used the Slav Congress in Prague as a forum to persuade the Western and the Southern Slavs to look to Russia for leadership and protection from the tyrants of the West. On the other hand, the one man who was really on the way to getting something done: Karl Marx.

Three years later, in 1852, Marx, then living in London, was offered by the *New York Tribune* £1 an article, at the rate of two articles a week, to write about the European revolutions, which were regarded by all good Americans with approval.[9] In 1852, among other things, he (or Engels for him) wrote a classic analysis of the genesis and failure of the Viennese revolution; but another aspect of these articles, less generally appreciated, was the rabid pan-Germanism and anti-Slavism with which they were inspired. Marx's fury with the Serbs, the Croats (under Jellačić), above all with the Czechs of the Sudetenland, for betraying the proletarian revolution is unbounded: in article after article he speaks of the Slavs outside Russia in words which were not to be heard again until Hitler resurrected them in the 1930s.

Thus ended for the present, and most likely for ever, the attempts of the Slavonians of Germany to recover an independent national existence. Scattered remnants of numerous nations, whose nationality and political vitality had long been extinguished, and who in consequence had been obliged, for almost a thousand years, to follow in the wake of a mightier nation, their conqueror, like the Welsh in England, the Basques in Spain, the Bas-Bretons in France, and, at a more recent period, the Spanish and French Creoles in those portions of North America occupied lately by the Anglo-American race – these dying nationalities, the Bohemians, Carinthians, Dalmatians, etc., had tried to profit by the universal confusion of 1848 in order to restore their political *status quo* of A.D. 800. The history of a thousand years ought to have shown them that such a retrogression was impossible; that if all the territory east of the Elbe and Saale had at one time been occupied by kindred Slavonians, this fact merely proved the historical tendency, and at the same time the physical and intellectual power of the German nation to subdue, absorb and assimilate its ancient eastern neighbours; that this tendency of absorption on the part of the Germans had always been, and still was, one of the mightiest means by which the civilization of Western Europe had been spread in the east of that continent; that it could only cease whenever the process of Germanization had reached the frontier of large, compact, unbroken nations, capable of an independent national life, such as the Hungarians and in some degree the Poles; and that therefore the natural and inevitable fate of these dying nations was to allow this process of dissolution and absorption by their stronger neighbours to complete itself. Certainly this is no very flattering prospect for the national ambition of the Pan-Slavist dreamers who succeeded in agitating a portion of the Bohemian and South Slavonian people; but can they expect that history would retrograde a thousand years in order to please a few phthisical bodies of men, who in every part of the territory they occupy are interspersed and surrounded by Germans, who from times almost immemorial have had for all purposes of civilization no other language but the German, and who lack the very first conditions of national existence, numbers and compactness of territory?[10]

It was in this mood that Marx wrote of Palacky as 'nothing but a learned German run mad, who cannot even now speak the Czechian language correctly and without foreign accent'.[11] It was in this mood that he positively gloated over Windischgraetz's short, sharp action in Prague, which broke the Bohemian revolution while the Slav Congress was sitting.[12]

So much, for the time being, for Karl Marx. These passages are reproduced not for the light they throw on the mentality and character of this unreliable genius, of whom Windischgraetz and Schwarzenberg had never heard, but because of their relevance to the immediate problems facing the Monarchy after 1848. There were not many liberals within the Empire with the vision of a Fischhof, and Fischhof himself was one of those idealists whose plans were characterized by Marx as bearing 'the stamp of an innocuousness almost amounting to political virginity'.[13] But there were very many pan-Germans, and Marx's attitude to the Slavs within the Empire was shared by all those German Austrians who, in 1848, opposed the Imperial standard with the black-red-yellow flag of German nationalism. These were the nucleus of the German liberals, who, as the century wore on, grew stronger, until they culminated in the strident and sinister figure of Georg von Schönerer, the fanatical German nationalist demagogue, the direct precursor of the founder of the Nazi Party.

It was an attitude that was not shared by Schwarzenberg or by the young Emperor Franz Josef. Both men did everything in their power to counter it; for it was an attitude incompatible with the continued existence of the Monarchy. In all the talk about what was or what was not the Habsburg mission, one aspect of overriding importance is constantly overlooked: this family of German origin was throughout the nineteenth century and the first decade of the twentieth the sole bar to the Germanization of central and south-eastern Europe.

Schwarzenberg was playing for very high stakes, and he gathered round him a very strong team. He did not care where he found his colleagues, so long as they could do the job. His own concern was to be primarily with foreign policy and with the education of the young

Emperor. As his Minister of the Interior he appointed Count Stadion, a devoted liberal who had proved his liberalism in practice as Governor of Galicia; as Minister of Justice he took over Alexander Bach from the failing Wessenberg Ministry, not caring a rap that this extraordinarily able and assiduous administrator had started his career on the other side of the barricades; as Minister of Commerce he chose a German from Elberfeld, Baron Bruck, who had founded Austrian-Lloyd, built up Trieste as a great port, and brought as his dowry to Schwarzenberg his grandiose conception of an Empire of Seventy Millions which was to unite the Habsburg possessions economically with the rest of Germany. By his choice of a team Schwarzenberg indicated to all who did not know him that he was interested only in efficiency; that he, the greatest aristocrat in the Empire, had not the least sympathy with the pretensions or aspirations of the class to which he belonged. There was to be a clean sweep of everything except the Crown, and the Crown itself was to be freed from all the inhibitions of historic rights and customs. He brought to Austria something of the ruthless impersonality of Peter the Great of Russia, who would have nothing to do with a hereditary aristocracy and made nobility dependent, at least in theory, on service to the Crown. When Windischgraetz, distressed by the apparent liberality of the new constitution, demanded the formation of an aristocratic second chamber, Schwarzenberg replied:

> It would be a simple matter to give the new constitution an aristocratic colouring, but I consider it impossible to instil into our aristocracy true vitality and much-needed resiliency, because to this end not only respectable individuals are called for, but also a politically trained, well-organized and courageous class. This class we lack completely. I do not know of more than a dozen men of our class in the entire Monarchy who could in the present circumstances serve profitably in an upper chamber.[14]

He saw in his fellow-nobles, in Hungary, in Poland above all, but also in Bohemia and the Austrian lands, not only the negative qualities of irresponsibility and political incompetence, but also potential particularists and rebels. He distrusted them extremely; and it was because of this, almost certainly, that he devised a system which effectively excluded them as a class from government, instead of a system in which he could have put them to school to learn something of the political sense which, in spite of his dislike of England, he admired in the English aristocracy.

That was one end of the scale. At the other end he showed a similar contempt for and distrust of the people. He had seen what a few determined agitators had done to the sensible, bourgeois Viennese. He had seen the revolutionary flames engulf the whole of Europe from Paris to Dresden. Neither he nor anybody else had the least comprehension of the real forces that were stirring. When the people were not vicious they were fools. They had to be contained. He was obsessed with the threat of the international revolutionary movement (which indeed existed), exaggerated its power, and saw its hand everywhere. Revolutionaries, as well as liberals, all over Europe regarded the Hungarian rebellion as the last hope (Marx's fury with the Hungarians for their 'betrayal' of the revolution by not effectively going to the help of the Viennese was expressed in his most vituperative vein). In the minutes of the Ministerial Council which, at Olmütz on 3 April 1849, considered the desirability of calling on the Tsar for help, Schwarzenberg is reported as declaring: 'We are fighting now not merely with rebellious provinces, but also with the revolutionaries of all countries who have poured into Hungary and ruthlessly raised the banner of anarchy and communism.'[15] For him the Fischhofs of Vienna were pawns in this game, the Bathyanyis of Hungary were guilty of high treason.

He was ready for some sort of Parliament. And indeed, when he took office, the famous Constituent Assembly was still sitting, engaged in working out a constitution. So that it should be neutralized while Windischgraetz got on with the brisk and brutal task of bombarding the Viennese revolutionaries into submission, the Constituent Assembly was removed bodily to the little town of Kremsier in Moravia, not far from Olmütz, and told to get on with its job.

This was an episode of perfect comedy. The Constituent Assembly, convened in July 1848 under extreme pressure from the revolutionaries, is celebrated for one great act, which it did not in fact perform: the doing away with the *Robot*. But the abolition of the *Robot* had already been promised, and it was in fact carried out by the reactionary government of Schwarzenberg, after the Constituent Assembly had been swept into limbo.

A good deal of nonsense has been written about this feudal institution. The real gainers from its abolition were the great landowners, who had been prevented by it from developing their estates on rational lines. The peasants were in hereditary possession of their farms, but they had to put in so much work, with their own hands, or their own teams of draft animals, for the landlords. This was the *Robot*. What they were called upon to do amounted to a far less heavy burden than the taxes they have to pay today: it was so little, that although they could buy themselves out cheaply, they rarely did so. Naturally they were pleased with the prospect of being freed from all contractual obligations of any kind, and the revolutionaries exploited this feeling for purposes of propaganda. But the real driving force behind the abolition of the *Robot* was the desire of the great landowners to exchange bad and careless free labour for good and careful paid labour. It was thus that an action hailed as revolutionary came to favour the great landlords and the well-to-do peasants at the expense of the small landlords and the poor peasants.

The hereditary rights of the landlords in jurisdiction and administration (the civil service took these over) were abolished without compensation. But with the compensation for the loss of free labour service, and with the accession of efficient paid labour, the great landlords became great capitalists, able to invest in new machines, new beet factories, new saw-mills, and to work their estates scientifically and economically. More than this, they were able to branch out as industrialists and entrepreneurs as well as agriculturalists, mining coal, manufacturing paper, putting up hotels, holiday resorts and spas. The small landowners, on the other hand, went to the wall – as did many of the liberated peasants, being unable to compete, running up ruinous debts, and, in the end, losing their estates to their more powerful neighbours. The small subsistence peasants in large numbers gave up the struggle to keep afloat in a harshly competitive world and went to work in the towns. Their more prosperous brothers, on the other hand, were in time to benefit greatly from the new agricultural teaching of the magnates and their bailiffs.

The pattern was thus set which was to last until 1914: the really enduring feature of the Monarchy in its final phase was the domination of the countryside by immensely wealthy aristocrats, owning vast estates, sometimes as big as kingdoms (above all, of course, in Galicia and Hungary) and a strong, conservatively minded peasantry. A less obvious by-product of this arrangement was the flooding of the towns, hitherto dominated by educated Germans, by workers from the surrounding countryside, who brought with them to their new environment a heightened consciousness of their own nationality. This economic and cultural revolution, favouring conservatism in the countryside and nationalism in the towns, was not at all a movement of popular liberation, though represented as such by the revolutionaries of the Constituent Assembly: it was a development in the rise of central European capitalism.

The second great task of the Assembly was the drafting of a constitution. Removed from Vienna to Kremsier in Moravia, and under the eyes, now coolly sceptical, now exasperated, of Felix Schwarzenberg, it deliberated for months to produce a model democratic blueprint. Enlightened representatives of many races worked in wonderful amity to decide how those races could bind themselves together in constructive unity and freedom. Czechs and Germans, Poles and Slovenes, showed themselves for once more accommodating towards one another than they were ever to show themselves again, and reached what seemed to some of them a working answer. But there were several things they overlooked. In the first place their constitution demanded a central authority; that authority had to be the Emperor, and the Emperor endowed with very real powers; yet, in Article 1 of their new constitution, it was laid down: 'All political rights emanate from the people.' How many of them believed that a Habsburg would run the Empire for them on that understanding? In the second place they utterly ignored the existence of Hungary, which had formally broken with the Empire, and where the Magyars at that moment were engaged in an atrocious war of extermination against Serbs, Croats and Slovaks. In the third place they failed to see themselves as part of that wider picture, which Schwarzenberg had in mind. At the very time when the Austrian Assembly was deliberating at Kremsier over ways and means of bringing Slavs to lie down with Germans, the German National Assembly at Frankfurt was busy deliberating, with Austrian representatives, over ways and means of including the Empire within a larger Germany.

What Schwarzenberg was interested in was including a larger Germany within the Austrian Empire. He had to see whether anything could come out of Frankfurt; and the existence of the Kremsier Parliament was useful as an attraction to German liberals. But there was no question of a future for liberalism. Hungary and Lombardy had to be won back, and this could only be done through means that were the reverse of liberal. So he let the Assembly run on until March 1849. On 2 March the drafting committee, decked out with their new white-red-gold rosettes, solemnly entered the Assembly to announce, amid great excitement and gratification, that the drafting of the constitution was completed. The deputies resolved to consider and accept the draft on 15 March, the anniversary of Emperor Ferdinand's promise of the grant of a constitution. On 6 March, Count Stadion was sent by Schwarzenberg to call an end to the comedy, to dissolve the Assembly. Next day, on Schwarzenberg's orders, grenadiers took up posts in the Assembly hall and patrolled the little town.

It was in the Prime Minister's eyes a critical trial of strength, and for the first time, but not at all for the last, his pent-up determination came out in violence and he went too far. He ordered the arrest and imprisonment of all members of the Assembly who had played a leading part in the original Vienna revolt. They included Adolf Fischhof. Stadion, who felt his own honour at stake – after all, he had pledged himself to try to reach an accommodation – forewarned them, and they fled. Schwarzenberg was now master; but there was a gap. A constitution had been promised, and a constitution there had to be. He had his own almost ready, drafted in case by the unfortunate Stadion. It had to be promulgated before it was complete. It never worked. It set up two Chambers, both elective: Schwarzenberg refused still to have anything to do with a hereditary Second Chamber. It put strict limitations to the power of Parliament, and gave the Emperor suspensive veto. Above all it gave the Crown absolute legislative power until such time as Parliament might be convened, though any legislative acts were to be considered as provisional, pending ultimate ratification by the two chambers. Austria was to be governed for quite a time by 'provisional laws'. Still, the Empire had a constitution. It had not had one before. And the constitution itself embodied revolutionary changes. The whole Empire was comprehended in one vast Customs Union: it had become, on paper, an entity.

CHAPTER FIVE

PALMERSTON IN A WHITE UNIFORM

As far as parliamentary government was concerned, the Stadion constitution – the dictated constitution, as it was known – was a dead letter from the beginning. The Monarchy was effectively under martial law, and the Cabinet ruled in the young Emperor's name through 'provisional decrees', which, in theory, did not become law until they were ratified by Parliament – to be summoned when 'the provisional emergency' came to an end. They never were ratified. Once the Monarchy was again firmly established, Franz Josef assumed autocratic powers, and that, for the time being, was that.

With Vienna in a virtual state of siege, crushed, shocked and bitter, the first task was to settle accounts in Italy. Piedmont had to be provoked into breaking the armistice which had followed Radetzky's victory over Charles Albert at Custozza. This was easy. The King of Sardinia had been viewing with increasing unease and alarm the ineffectual and protracted negotiations between Vienna and the mediating British and the French: all that was happening, he saw, was that Austria was winning time to set her own house in order and put herself once more into an impregnable position. He decided to risk everything on striking before it was too late. But it was already too late, and the eighty-three-year-old Radetzky moved his army with wonderful skill and speed deep into Piedmont to deal an overwhelming blow at Novara, on 26 March 1849. Charles Albert's defeat was so complete and disastrous that there was nothing more for him to do; so he abdicated, to make way for his son, Victor Emmanuel, who, ten years later, Radetzky being dead, was to succeed where his father had failed.

The second task was to settle accounts in Hungary. Here Windischgraetz had forced his way quickly to Budapest, but his position was not commanding. Kossuth, aided by two doughty insurrectionary generals from Poland, Dembinsky and the cripple Bem, had made a remarkable recovery, and poor Windischgraetz found himself with a first-class war on his hands. This straight-backed, honest soldier was at one time regarded as the type of brutal tyrant, but he was no more a tyrant than the Duke of Wellington. Putting down revolutionaries with cannon he took in his stride: it was his job. But fighting a bitter civil war against a large part of the late Imperial army was not what he was made for. When on 14 April the new Magyar Parliament solemnly deposed the Habsburgs and elected Kossuth as Governor of Hungary, they based this act on Magyar constitutional law. It could be represented that the traitor to the dynasty was Windischgraetz, not Kossuth. No Habsburg could be king of Hungary until he had been crowned in Budapest: if Schwarzenberg and Windischgraetz liked to force Ferdinand to surrender the Crown of Austria, that was Austria's business. But Ferdinand was still King of Hungary, and it was to Ferdinand that the Hungarian regiments had sworn their oath of allegiance. For the officers of these regiments it was indeed an agonizing situation. Where did their true loyalty lie? Some saw more or less clearly into the confusion and tried to extricate themselves and rejoin the Imperial forces ranged against their own brothers-in-arms. Some of these succeeded, others failed – among them a young nephew of Queen Victoria. Most stayed in their ranks as Magyar officers and fought for national Hungary. All were terribly punished in the end. Meanwhile they fought like desperate men. They knew all too intimately the shortcomings of the Austrian command and they exploited their knowledge – with no holds barred – led now with extreme skill and dash by a brilliant young sapper officer, Görgey, who started winning all along the line.

Windischgraetz was broken. In the manner of his recall the new Emperor for the first time displayed that cold ruthlessness which was to mark his dealings with his generals and his Ministers for decades to come; however exalted, however noble, they were simply instruments, interchangeable, to be used for the preservation of the dynasty, which stood above all human values. Franz Josef believed that he was getting rid of a soldier who had failed. It cost him a great deal to reduce to ignominy, and so quickly, the man to whom he owed his throne. For the first and last time in his life he tried to soften the blow, which only made things worse.[1] But Schwarzenberg, who also owed his position to the grand old Field-Marshal, had other motives. It was Windischgraetz the statesman and the figurehead whom he wanted to be rid of, not Windischgraetz the soldier. The way was now clear for the Jacobin dynamism of

Schwarzenberg and Bach; the power of the Old Conservatives was shattered at a blow.

But the Hungarians still had to be beaten. The new commander, Baron von Welden, was soon crying out for help.[2] There were only two ways of helping him. One was to give up part of Italy, come to an accommodation with the Piedmontese, and switch to Hungary troops tied down in Lombardy; the other was to appeal to Russia. The first way was not even considered. The second way had in fact been discussed many times and as many times rejected. Such an exhibition of weakness, Schwarzenberg himself had argued, would destroy throughout Europe the image he was sedulously trying to create of a strong, self-sufficient, arrogant Austria, inferior to no Power and superior to most.[3] But he had to give in. Under the terms of the Holy Alliance the Tsar was asked for help, and Nicholas, who feared that the revolution would spread to Poland and had been hoping for just this, jubilantly responded. He was at one and the same time being asked to underwrite the principles of absolutist legitimacy, to put down a revolution, and to place Franz Josef under an immense personal obligation. The Russians came pouring in across Galicia, 200,000 of them under the Tsar's favourite, Count Paskiewicz, and soon it was all over. Kossuth, seeing that the game was up, handed over supreme command to Görgey and fled to Turkey. Görgey formally surrendered not to the Austrian von Welden but to the Russian Paskiewicz, who took him under his personal protection, thus underlining the Austrian humiliation. To make matters worse, the Russians began talking about mercy and chivalry towards the conquered rebels. So that Europe was treated to the remarkable spectacle of the cold, pursuing tyrant Nicholas, presiding bleakly over his own prison-house of nations, setting himself up as a model of enlightenment and clemency. This alone would have been enough to bring out the strain of arrogant savagery in Schwarzenberg, who was not going to be told how to do things by anybody, neither by Palmerston in London, nor by Nicholas in Petersburg. And so the executions followed: thirteen generals and an ex-Prime Minister, Bathyanyi. For a brief period the notorious General Haynau, a brilliant general but a psychopath, brought up from Italy, was in charge of the proceedings. It was of him that old Radetzky had said: 'He is my best general; but he is like a razor; when you have used him, put him back in his case.' It was Haynau who had outraged world opinion by his reign of terror in Brescia. After their victory in

Italy the Austrians as a whole had behaved justly and correctly: only Haynau had gone wild. But one Haynau, running berserk unpunished, was enough to make the name of Austria mud and the white tunic synonymous with butchery. Now he was at it again, hanging and shooting and sacking; and for a time Schwarzenberg let him rampage. This brilliant madman, not a born Austrian, but an illegitimate son of the Elector of Hesse, was in his element. Four hundred and seventy-five Hungarian officers had been taken prisoner, and Haynau's courts martial condemned 281 of these to death. In the event the death sentence was remitted, but nearly 400 officers were punished with up to twenty years in prison. His behaviour can be seen as an example of how the actions of one man may produce dire consequences to a whole nation. But although Haynau was the razor, and although he behaved in such a way that he soon had to be recalled, the world was right to look beyond Haynau. Schwarzenberg could have stopped him at once, but he did not: in a towering icy fury, he was determined to break Hungarian resistance by terror – and to show the world what he could do. The young Emperor could, and should, have overridden Schwarzenberg; but he did not. And here it was almost certainly pride rather than vindictiveness that guided him. The blow to pride occasioned by the appeal to Russia must have been traumatic. Listen to Paskiewicz writing to his Tsar:

> Görgey relies exclusively on the magnanimity of Your Majesty. Could I hand over to the gallows all those whose sole trust is in Your Majesty's mildness of heart, to be all the more severely punished because they surrendered to our troops? I said to Prince Schwarzenberg earlier that the Hungarian army might perhaps surrender to us, but would not surrender to the Austrians. What, in the event, was I to do? The fate of the captured army falls, in consequence, to Your Majesty to determine. You are the victor. Hungary lies at your feet and the war is at an end.[4]

Hungary was part of the Habsburg Empire. It lay at the feet of the Tsar of Russia. The Court and the Cabinet could not see beyond that. It is only if we bear this in mind that we can explain the exacerbated touchiness of Schwarzenberg on all matters relating to the Hungarian affair. He allowed Haynau to visit England, where he was set upon and badly mauled by the draymen of Barclay Perkins' brewery (Haynau had been advised at least to shave off his extravagant moustaches, but the extraordinary creature seems to have believed that he had only to show himself to the English to swing them in his favour). In his almost frenzied attempt to bully the Porte into giving up Kossuth and others he brought Austria to the verge of war with England: Palmerston actually sent the Mediterranean fleet to Constantinople to stiffen the Turkish resolve. And so on.

But already his mind was on other things. Hungary was left to Bach, who in July succeeded Stadion as Minister of the Interior; and Bach proceeded with the doctrinaire thoroughness of the lawyer turned politician to administer the conquered kingdom from Vienna, breaking it up into provinces and moving in a horde of German officials who, because they wore frogged frock-coats, came to be known as Bach's 'Hussars'. They administered, as the Austrians had already for long administered Lombardy, with thoroughness, equity and complete lack of corruption. They were hated by the proud, passionate and wildly egocentric Hungarians with a deeper and more dangerous hatred than would have been felt for a regiment of Haynaus. It is impossible to tell whether the execution of the magnate Bathyanyi, who had given way to Kossuth, was more resented than the imposition on the Hungarian countryside of the German-speaking civil service, which brought all sorts of material benefits to a backward and devastated land. As far as Bach was concerned, there was no discrimination against the Magyars. They were treated as everybody else in the Empire – as, for example, the Croats, who had helped to save it. Under the new unifying constitution the Croats lost their Diet as the Hungarians lost their constitution: 'What you get as a punishment, we get as a reward!'[5]

Almost the only man in Europe, outside Austria, who sympathized with Schwarzenberg and the young Emperor was the young Bismarck:

> You have so much sympathy for the relatives of Bathyanyi [he wrote to his mother-in-law], have you none for the thousands upon thousands of innocent persons whose wives have been widowed and whose children have been orphaned through the crazy ambition or monstrous presumption of those rebels. . . ? Can the execution of one man provide a sufficiency of even earthly justice as retribution for the burnt cities, the devastated provinces, the murdered populations whose blood cries from the ground to the Emperor of Austria, whom God has entrusted with the sword of authority?[6]

It was a bad omen for Austria to win Bismarck's early approval. On the other hand, if the Austrians had really had their heart in the business of oppression and aggression, Bismarck would have lived to regret that he had ever applauded them.

2

Bismarck did not applaud for long. Italy was recovered; Hungary was crushed; the time had now come for Schwarzenberg to try conclusions with Prussia.

Early in the eighteenth century the traditional European pattern was confused by the emergence of two new candidates for the councils of the great. The vast and unpredictable latent power of Russia, shaken out of its sleep by Peter the Great, was gathered together by Catharine to make a new force. The small kingdom of Prussia, effectively founded by the Great Elector, was transformed by a soldier of genius into a brand-new challenger to the upholders of the established order.

It was Austria, for so long the leading German Power, which first felt the impact of Prussia, losing part of Silesia to Frederick after bloody and protracted wars. After the death of Frederick two inferior monarchs found it impossible to sustain the military challenge, and, on the face of it, Brandenburg-Prussia had reverted to its old status of one small Germanic State among many. But appearances were misleading. Although the military virtues of the Prussians remained dormant, the commercial and industrial ability released by the Great Elector was still actively fermenting, turning Prussia in some ways into the most modern State in Europe. From the time of Napoleon's defeat, there was something in the atmosphere of the new University of Berlin which began to attract men of genius – men of extraordinary energy and vision who had one thing in common – a veneration for the State of a kind which had not been known since the heyday of Sparta, not even in Republican Rome. By far the most powerful influence was Hegel, not a Prussian at all, but a native of Stuttgart in Württemberg, who succeeded Fichte in the Chair of Philosophy at Berlin. When Hegel wrote of the State as 'God walking among men' he was arguing not as a patriot, nor even as a politician, but as a philosopher and a metaphysician: the State was the highest manifestation of human existence, and the fate of the individuals who composed it was neither here nor there: their only glory lay in their individual contribution to the quasi-divine organism which it was their destiny to serve. There had to be an apex to this antheap, a head of State, and this had better be a king. In return for their un-reserved service the people might be granted all kinds of liberties and rights – a Parliament, an independent Judiciary, a free Press, the whole sad, familiar catalogue. But there must be no nonsense about these rights and privileges: they were essentially conditional. The Hegelian dialectic was designed to demonstrate the inevitable development of mankind from the primitive community to the grand apotheosis when, through war and conquest (which were therefore right), all States should be merged into one global community.

This abstract thinker from Stuttgart, coming to Berlin via Jena, thus became the spiritual father of the two most rigid and concrete manifestations of the twentieth century: Prussian militarism and Russian communism. Let nobody doubt the power of ideas.

Why the tough, dour Junkers of the sandy, hungry, pine-infested plain of Brandenburg should have taken to this sort of doctrine it is outside the scope of this narrative to inquire. But take to it they did. They accepted the disciplines inherent in Hegel's glorification of the State, and the State, for them, was Prussia. The teachings of the great soldier Clausewitz about the nature of war prepared the Prussian army, much later the Prussian people, to accept and make their own the other Hegelian doctrine about the necessity of war and might being right, so sharply at odds with the ideas of nineteenth-century liberalism which the German middle classes as a whole, including many Prussians, were now in love with. It was this compact Protestant bloc in the north, homogeneous to a degree, hard-working, bursting with vitality and ideas, moving towards an acceptance of a totalitarian mystique which glorified the community as standing above all law, which now stood opposed to the sprawling, ramshackle, multi-racial Austrian Empire with no hard centre, which lacked any dynamic idea (for the very good reason that it disapproved of such things) and stood for nothing better than the preservation of the *status quo*.

Prussia's initial mistake, once the revolutionary spirit had been stifled, was, in the words of the great historian, Friedjung, to display the objects of her ambition before she had the courage to give her full strength to their achievement.[7] It was a mistake to which Berlin was to show itself peculiarly prone. But in 1850 her chief antagonist was a statesman of genius, Felix Schwarzenberg.

The Frankfurt Assembly, conceived in revolution and starting with the loftiest ideals, had long lost its impetus. As reaction began to set in, as the bourgeoisie recoiled from the ugly violence of the extremists and the proletariat, the delegates meeting in St Paul's church became increasingly preoccupied with securing some measure of German unity. German nationalism rather than libertarian ardour became the ruling spirit. But unity under whom? And what, in any case, was Germany? The senior German ruler was the head of the House of Austria; but for a variety of reasons the restoration of Austrian leadership in Germany was distasteful to a number of the smaller States. Vienna, further, was rapidly establishing itself as the very headquarters of reaction. Finally, the Habsburg realm comprehended many races which had nothing to do with Germany and whose interests were opposed to German interests. The only conceivable rivals to the Catholic Habsburgs were the Protestant Hohenzollerns; and in spite of the profound objection of the Catholic States of the south to Prussian overlordship, on 3 April 1849, while Austria was deeply and bitterly engaged with the Magyars, the Assembly solemnly offered the Imperial Crown to Frederick William of Prussia.

Frederick William drew himself up to a great height. Although he had dreams for the aggrandizement of Prussia he was himself romantic and a dynast. His ideal was a German federation under a Habsburg Emperor with the Hohenzollern King as hereditary commander-in-chief. The Imperial Crown, he said, could belong to none but a Habsburg. The Crown offered by the Frankfurt Assembly he called 'the crown of mud'. Schwarzenberg was not grateful. In refusing the Imperial Crown, which was not, anyway, in the gift of the Assembly, Frederick William had killed the last hopes of that Assembly for securing some sort of German unity by peaceful means. He had also reaffirmed the seniority of the Habsburgs, in which he passionately and romantically believed. But at the same time, almost by accident, he had removed Prussia from that voluntary entanglement with the other German States on terms which would have put limits on her action as a sovereign Power. Prussia was now on her own and in a position, when she chose, to resume her own expansionist drive at the expense of her feebler neighbours.

She chose too soon. Frederick William, erratic as always, outraged Schwarzenberg, and at the same time presented him with a golden opportunity, by going ahead with a plan for the formation of a North German Federation to consist of Prussia, Hanover and Saxony – the League of the Three Kingdoms. This was not only a threat to

Schwarzenberg's immensely ambitious plans for the creation of a central European 'Empire of Seventy Millions'; it was also, in Schwarzenberg's view, illegal – though, in fact, the law of the German Federation upon which he took his stand had been abandoned under the impact of the revolution. For eleven months the quarrel raged, with Schwarzenberg using every diplomatic artifice – threats, persuasion, promises, flattery – first to render the League abortive, then, when this failed, to destroy it. By April 1850 it looked like war; but neither side was ready for war: Austria had only 30,000 troops in Bohemia; Prussia's Silesian army was in bad shape. Both turned to Nicholas of Russia for his backing. Nicholas, immensely conscious of his worth (he had saved Austria by crushing Hungary, and the surrender at Villagos had gone to his head) at first played the impartial arbiter, then used his commanding position to force Prussia to restore Schleswig-Holstein to the Danish King in the interests of monarchic solidarity. Schwarzenberg, to get Russia wholly on his side, and seeing no immediate prospect of obtaining sole leadership of Germany, decided to compromise: he suggested that Germany should be united into a confederation of seventy million souls 'headed by a strong central executive in the hands of Austria and Prussia, exclusive of other States'. It was his way of securing the force of all Germany to help Austria hold down Italy and Hungary and, at the same time, of preventing any restricted union presided over by Prussia from growing into a rival Germanic Empire. Prussia refused; but she could do nothing but stonewall – until she made a false move to secure her position in Hesse-Kassel which enabled Austria in October 1850 to mobilize four army corps and win Bavaria and Württemberg to her side. There seemed no escape from war. The two armies stood against each other and on 24 November Schwarzenberg presented an ultimatum to expire in three days. He had made it virtually impossible for Prussia to escape without fighting or accepting his terms with ignominy. Had it come to war, Prussia would have been crushed and Bismarck might never have become Chancellor. But Schwarzenberg was reckoning without his own dynast, whose supremacy in Germany he was moving mountains to establish. Frederick William, on the edge of war, had second thoughts. He had been standing up for his honour and prestige: it was an affair between princes. He was now alarmed by the manner in which his princely quarrel was being taken up by his people, convulsed by an access of nationalistic fervour. The role of a leader of a liberal-nationalist crusade did not appeal to him in the least. He decided to appeal to family feeling. He himself wrote to Franz Josef; his Queen, Elizabeth, wrote simultaneously to her sister, Sophie. Schwarzenberg was told to extend his ultimatum, to go to Olmütz and talk peace with Manteuffel, the Prussian Foreign Minister. He did so. The effect he produced on the Prussians at the Hotel zur Krone was prodigious.[8] Manteuffel held out until the small hours and then gave way. Prussia, chastened, agreed to enter the revived Confederation, to take her troops out of Hesse, to act with Austria in evacuating Holstein, to demobilize her army. It was a dizzy personal triumph, but it was not war. 'War would perhaps have been better', Schwarzenberg said on his return to Vienna, 'and would have brought peace lasting fifty years . . . perhaps! Ah! What an embarrassment is conscience!'[9]

3

He had established Austria's ascendancy over Prussia for all the world to see, and, in so doing, he had restored the Monarchy to its former splendour. Those who had pitied Austria, now feared her. But he had sown dragon's teeth: in Italy, in Hungary, now in Prussia. And although her immediate pretensions were shattered, Prussia's latent power remained intact. It was perhaps unfortunate that the Prussian representative in the re-established Diet was Otto von Bismarck. Bismarck at first was not at all anti-Austrian. He had come out strongly against the Prussian war party. He hoped for a return to the Metternich spirit which had tacitly assumed that so long as Berlin and Vienna agreed, all matters could be arranged quietly between them. But he was not prepared to stand by and for ever watch Austria treating Prussia like an upstart and manoeuvring against her with majority decisions by inferior States.

'All the admirers of Austria consider Prince Schwarzenberg a madman', wrote Queen Victoria to her uncle Leopold in March 1852; and 'the Emperor Nicholas said that he was "Lord Palmerston in a white uniform"'.[10] But already Palmerston himself was beginning to conceive a better opinion of the man who had responded to his earlier tactlessness with such rudeness. He feared extremely a war between Austria and Prussia, which, he said, would be a calamity for Germany and a triumph for Russia and France. He admired what he took to be Schwarzenberg's moderation. Even as early as 1850 he was countering the Queen's view of the Austro-Prussian conflict, which she herself saw in ideological terms: 'the conflict between Austria and Prussia can scarcely be said to have turned upon principles of Government so much as upon a struggle for political ascendency in Germany'.[11]

Schwarzenberg was not the only man in Europe at that time to regard the rise of the spirit of nationalism with contempt and distaste, as something essentially reactionary. Disraeli characterized the aspirations towards German unity as 'dreamy and dangerous nonsense'.[12] He, too, under-estimated the force behind this 'nonsense' when he regarded the movement as something whipped up as a pretext for Prussian expansionism. As early as April 1848 he was telling the House of Commons that Prussia, in her war with the Danes, had initiated a policy which would one day make her the rival of England in the North Sea. 'That is the real reason why Denmark, supposed to be weak, is to be invaded in this age of liberty on the plea of nationality. It is to gain the harbours of the Baltic, and to secure the mouths of the Elbe, that the plea of German nationality is put forth.'[13]

As for the Monarchy: Disraeli wrote four years later in his life of Lord George Bentinck:

> It is very desirable that the people of England should arrive at some conclusions as to the conditions on which the government of Europe can be carried on. They will, perhaps, after due reflection discover that ancient communities like the European must be governed either by traditionary influences or by military force. Those who in their ardour of renovation imagine that there is a third mode, and that our societies can be reconstructed by the great Transatlantic model, will find that when they have destroyed traditionary influences there will be peculiar features in their body politic which do not obtain in the social standards which they imitate, and these may be described as elements of disturbance. A dynasty may be subverted, but it leaves as its successor a family of princely pretenders; a confiscated aristocracy takes the shape of factions; a plundered Church acts on the tender consciences of toiling millions; corporate bodies displaced from their ancient authority no longer contribute their necessary and customary quota to the means of government; outraged tradition in multiplied forms enfeebles or excruciates the reformed commonwealth. In this state of affairs, after a due course of paroxysms, for the sake of maintaining order and securing the rights of industry, the state quits the senate and takes refuge in the camp.

Let us not be deluded by forms of government. The word may be
republic in France, constitutional monarchy in Prussia, absolute
monarchy in Austria, but the thing is the same. Wherever there is a
vast standing army, the government is the government of the sword.
. . . [an] irresistible law . . . dooms Europe to the alternate sway of
disciplined armies or secret societies; the camp or the convention.[14]

The new government of Austria had indeed taken refuge in the
camp. The savagery of the reaction, the executions and the prison
sentences, above all the fate of Bathyanyi and the thirteen Hungarian
generals, shocked and embittered even those who had been horrified
and frightened by the apparitions from the lower depths who, in the
later stages of the revolution, stalked the streets and offered a standing threat to life and property. The glorious Imperial army became
an object of abhorrence. The carnival time, the *Fasching*, of February
1848, on the very eve of the revolution, had been the most brilliant
and high-spirited in memory. The *Fasching* of 1849 should have been
a thanksgiving celebration for release from the terrors of anarchy and
for the installation of the new young Emperor, untainted by the
bitterness of the past. But it was not at all like that. There were
plenty of public balls, and they were brilliant and well attended. But
the life had gone out of the city. The new mood is summed up by the
critic, Hanslick: 'I remember a ball in the *Fasching* of 1849 . . . where
about half the dancers were army officers. Not a word was exchanged
between us civilians and the officers, and we all of us tried to avoid
dancing opposite an officer in the quadrille or sitting next to one at
supper.'[15]

It was a bad beginning for a new reign, a reign that was to last
sixty-eight years and which, during all that time, was to be haunted
in one way and another by the memories of 1848 and 1849. For the
man whose reputation suffered most from the harshness and violence
of the reaction was the young Franz Josef, so uncannily cold and
collected and aloof in his nineteenth year. What was to be made of
this youth who seemed to have none of the warmth and impulsive-
ness natural to his years, who, instead of putting himself at the head
of his people and inviting their confidence and affection in the
traditional Habsburg way, stood demonstratively apart, and, far from
commanding his Chief Minister to show mercy and understanding,
at best allowed him his head, at worst encouraged him in this brief
bleak reign of terror, so that even the Tsar of Russia, even Metternich, professed outrage and dismay?

He was coldly detested. The Viennese went about their business as best they might in an Empire on the edge of financial bankruptcy. (The appalling state of the Empire's finances was another reason for Schwarzenberg's extreme intransigence. He could not afford to let the world know how close the Monarchy stood to economic ruin, how his government was completely in the hands of the bankers and repeatedly on the verge of default and public bankruptcy: he was bluffing all the time, and the harder he had to bluff, the more overbearing his attitude.) Within the limits of the economy the Bach-Stadion reforms were carried out, transforming the face of the Empire: the *Robot* was abolished; compensation was paid; the judiciary was separated from the executive; trial by jury was introduced by Schmerling, who, in July, succeeded Bach at the Ministry of Justice; every citizen of the Empire was accorded equal rights and could move about freely, without a passport, within the confines of the Empire; the tariff wall between Hungary and the rest of the Empire was abolished; taxation was rationalized; local government was strengthened. At the same time, over and above all this, the Empire was under the rule of martial law, and many and bitter were the conflicts between Bach's civil administration and the military governors. The people did not see this conflict. They saw only the military – and the new and most detested institution, General Kempen's eighteen new battalions of *gendarmerie*, who were soon spying on the Ministers themselves, their nominal superiors. Even the Russians thought this police establishment excessive. At the same time, if the people shunned the military and stared sullenly and silently as the Emperor went by, the military themselves were under orders to keep themselves aloof from the people, fraternizing as little as possible with their own fellow-citizens. And the Emperor, relying on his chief policeman, Kempen, for discipline, and his Adjutant-General, Count Grünne, for advice on the inner workings of the army, became more and more obsessed with one idea: politics was foreign politics; these served the security and the aggrandizement of the State; they were his preserve. To conduct foreign politics successfully he needed to operate from a position of strength. His strength could only come from the army, which had already succoured his throne. He must therefore cultivate the army: nothing else mattered. Bach would look after the people. He himself would look after the army. And, fortified by the boldness, the wisdom, the skill, the experience of Schwarzenberg, he would run the Empire's foreign policy.

CHAPTER SIX

I COMMAND TO BE OBEYED

One of the favourite arguments against hereditary monarchy in general and the Austrian monarchy in particular is the so-called mediocrity of so many kings and emperors. During the past hundred years or so it has been fairly conclusively established that presidents and even dictators can also be mediocre; so that today, perhaps, there is less inclination to criticize Franz Josef for not being a genius. On the face of it there is indeed some cause for wonder and even awe at the inscrutable purposes of the Almighty in delegating the temporal rule of forty million souls to a very ordinary young man. Among those forty millions there were thousands who in intellect, perception, imagination, knowledge and breadth of understanding far outshone their master, set high above them all, but who, had he been born into an ordinary bourgeois family, would probably never have distinguished himself outstandingly. But the point of the matter is that Franz Josef was not born into an ordinary bourgeois family; he was born into the ruling family of Habsburg-Lorraine. And this meant that he was by blood, tradition and training, and given health, sanity and a modicum of brains, a natural ruler. To speak of a born ruler as being ordinary is absurd. Apart from an occasional universal genius all men of specialized talent and training, whether in science, the arts, industry, politics or diplomacy are entirely ordinary in many ways. The talent for ruling is as rare as any other highly developed talent. Franz Josef possessed it as few have possessed it before or since; and it is on this talent that we should keep our eyes fixed rather than on his mediocre intellect, his non-existent imagination, his ignorance of history, his failure as a commander in the field, his deficiencies as a husband and his lack of interest in the arts. It set him apart from the ordinary run of humanity as surely as Newton was set apart by intellect. Newton, with his own hands, cut a hole in the bottom of his door so that his favourite cat could come in and go out when it felt so inclined. When the cat gave birth to kittens the great man pondered; and the outcome of his cogitation was that next to the original hole he cut a smaller one so that the kittens could also come in and go out. When the born ruler of forty millions has lapses of this kind the consequences are apt to be more serious; but the lapses are not different in kind.

Another argument against the exaltation of men like Franz Josef is that in accepting dominion over forty million souls they exhibit presumption of a megalomaniac kind. But do they? If they believe, as Franz Josef believed, that they are called upon by God to exercise a temporal vicarate there is no presumption, only piety. There is more presumption in any runner for office in a democracy, in any candidate for Parliament, in any local councillor: these are not called upon by God; they set themselves up because they think they can do things better than their neighbours or because they want power.

Franz Josef was neither presumptuous nor arrogant (Schwarzenberg was both, and justified his pretensions); he was the Lord's anointed. There was no escape from this. Equally, there was no mercy towards those who denied it. The young man burst into tears when, at that macabre ceremony in the archiepiscopal palace at Olmütz, poor old Emperor Ferdinand, his uncle, blessed him and told him to be brave. He threw himself into the arms of his mother, Sophie. 'Farewell, my youth!' he exclaimed a little later when, already Emperor, he freed himself from the last rough and tumble with his younger brothers.[1] A year later he wrote the letter of dismissal to the man who had saved his throne, Prince Windischgraetz. A little later still he could say of flatterers: 'The man who can praise me to my face I must allow to blame me likewise; which, however, may not be.'[2]

Josef Redlich, one of Franz Josef's severest and most penetrating critics, was not fanciful when he suggested that Franz Josef, even when young and raw, inherited from his forebears what can only be called the spirit of creative artistry, expressed in an irresistible compulsion 'to mould the inchoate in accordance with their will'. In Redlich's own words:

Certainly an almost aesthetic conception of politics as a means to the realization of the idea of domination for its own sake, with Catholicism as its support, was, in the old imperial race of Germany, Spain, Italy, Hungary and Austria, the key to an obstinate tenacity of purpose and to an immovable calm in the face of disaster or any crisis of human fate. This mystic inheritance of his ancestral house does not readily fit in with the dry matter-of-factness of Franz Josef. And yet in the rigid calm, the almost somnambulistic assurance, with which the young man of twenty conceived the idea of a modern, technically efficient autocracy as the only possible reply to revolution in almost every part of his inherited realm, and carried it through, simply and solely by the force of his own resolution – in this there is something analogous to the relation of the artist to the material through which he seeks to convey his thoughts and visions to the outer world.[3]

This is not far-fetched. With the passage of the years the young Emperor's instinctive impulse became conscious artistry, which, under the impact of shattering blows, achieved quite extraordinary freedom of expression, often moving into the highly experimental. It is widely supposed that what Franz Josef did was to return after 1848 to the ways of his grandfather Franz II and to persist until well into the twentieth century with a pattern of government inherited from pre-revolutionary days. This was not so. One of the remarkable things about him was the almost reckless manner in which he threw tradition overboard. How much he realized what he was doing in those first years while Schwarzenberg was still alive is very much open to question: he was not well read in history. But later on he knew exactly what he was doing, and when, after von Moltke at Königgrätz had put an end to all his hopes of German hegemony and the Empire was given, as the Dual Monarchy, its final form, this was very much a conscious creation of Franz Josef himself, owing nothing at all to traditional forms, experimental and new in every way.

At this stage of the narrative there is no question of deciding whether Franz Josef was on balance a good ruler or a bad ruler, whether another man in his position might have done better or worse. He had serious deficiencies and he made very grave mistakes. At this stage all that needs to be emphasized is that, for better or for worse, he was far from being a mediocrity. He stamped an epoch with his personality, and that epoch, as far as Austria was concerned, represented a long-drawn-out attempt, crumbling only at the end after nearly seventy years, to build and sustain a multi-national society different from anything that had gone before.

It was Schwarzenberg, aided by Bach and influenced by Bruck, who was first determined not simply to restore the Empire, but to return to old ways with the substitution of strong government for weak, to pick up the threads of the old tradition. It was Schwarzenberg who roughly and harshly did away with the traditional forms of government, central and local, and proclaimed the existence of the

Empire as a Unitary State. But it was the Emperor and the Emperor alone, then twenty-two, who carried this movement to a logical conclusion. Schwarzenberg never thought much of the famous Stadion constitution; he used to refer to it as the 'mud-constitution': when trying to win the Russian Tsar to his side in the struggle with Prussia he made it quite clear that it would be done away with at some convenient moment. But the constitution existed at least on paper, and there is nothing in Schwarzenberg's character to suggest that he would not have let it run on, that he would not, indeed, later have come to terms with some sort of Parliament if this had seemed to him opportune and expedient. It was Franz Josef and Franz Josef alone who abolished the constitution which he himself had proclaimed – without a tremor, without the least sign that he was doing anything out of the ordinary. On 20 August 1851 a programme was put out for the establishment of unconditional autocracy. The essential part of this programme was the denial of ministerial responsibility: 'Ministers are solely responsible to the Monarch.' The Tsar was overjoyed, and said so: the young Emperor of Austria was fulfilling the high hopes he had set on him from the beginning. On 31 December 1851 the programme became law, a consummation accelerated by Franz Josef's determination not to be outdone by Louis Napoleon, who had carried out his own *coup d'état* on 2 December. 'He is perfectly right', the young Emperor exclaimed when he heard the news of the Paris events. 'The man who holds the reins of government in his hands must also be able to take responsibility. Irresponsible sovereignty is, for me, a phrase without meaning'.[4]

The process which led up to the abolition of the constitution and the proclamation of the Emperor as autocrat over a Unitary State, the various limbs of which had already lost their thousand-year-old privileges, was dramatic in itself, but it has little bearing on our understanding of Franz Josef or of the future course of Austrian history. It began with an intrigue against Schwarzenberg and Bach, above all Bach, on the part of the Old Conservatives, who regarded Schwarzenberg as a reckless Jacobin and Bach as a Communist in disguise. The inspiration was Metternich, now returned to Vienna, but living in retirement, and the drive came from the venerable Baron Kübeck, a tailor's son from Iglau in Moravia. It was reinforced by the army.

Paradoxically, Austria in the nineteenth century was not a class society. In the last half of the century indeed, it was in some important ways more of a democracy than, for example, England. For too long a proper appreciation of the real nature of that society has been obscured by a simple confusion: the so-called Spanish etiquette at the Hofburg, which, in any case, has been ludicrously exaggerated; the stilted pomp of the Golden Fleece; the extravagant quarterings which were obligatory in the coat-of-arms of any family aspiring to imperial and royal intimacy; the uproar occasioned by Franz Ferdinand's marriage to a social inferior, who came from the most worthy Bohemian nobility; the Emperor's quasi-divinity. All these colourful images, and more besides, gave to the outer world the erroneous impression of a class-system of unbending rigidity because the peculiar taboos and inhibitions of the Imperial family, codified in the House Law of Habsburg-Lorraine, were taken as characteristic of the whole structure of society. It is as though one were to deduce the existence of a class-system in heaven from the existence of the Holy Family and the archangels.

It was precisely because the Emperor stood high above all parties, all interests, all aristocratic pretensions, that Austrian society became in a very real way democratic. The highest careers in the Imperial service, whether civil or military, were open to all talents. The great aristocrats and landowners could maintain as much social exclusiveness among themselves as they liked, but they could not combine to form a ruling class to put pressure on the throne in its own interests. In Britain, first the landed classes, then the new-rich bourgeoisie, working through Parliament, could form compact groupings, dominating the Church, the universities, the professions, the armed and civil services, and running the country in what they took to be their own interests. The measure of their political skill in the nineteenth century was the extent to which they were able to retreat before the rising demands of the masses without ever breaking their line. There was no young Disraeli to expose the horrors and the scandals of 'the Two Nations' in *Biedermayer* Vienna; but then there were not 'Two Nations'. There was no Shaftesbury to lead a crusade against the degradation of millions in the interests of sound commerce, or quick profits; but then, there was no Manchester School content to see in child labour in the mines the workings of an inscrutable Providence acting through iron economic laws. There were no iron economic laws in Austria: there was only the Emperor's will. The Emperor was the father of his people and his life was devoted to what he took to be the well-being of his people: the thrusting, the greedy and the predatory were not given unlimited scope to stunt and deform the minds and bodies of their fellow-men. Like all fathers, Franz Josef made wonderful blunders. But at no stage after he had reached maturity did he allow the strong and active to prey without limit on the weak and passive. Assuredly there was poverty in that remarkable Empire, assuredly the strong, as individuals, above all in Galicia, as a race above all in Hungary, were perpetually seeking to exploit the weak, often with a considerable measure of success. But classes never crystallized out, and at no stage in the nineteenth century was there anything to compare with the condition of England before – and, indeed, after – the Factory Acts, when the doctrinaire and ruthless few all but succeeded in physically destroying a great mass of the people in the interests of progress – an operation of extreme originality, which was not to be repeated until the advent of Stalin in Russia. Instead, there was the rigidly exclusive First Society clustered round the Court, the highest Aristocracy. After this, the Second Society, still largely aristocratic, but open to all the talents as well as to the rich. Then came the rest. But all were on speaking terms. Nestroy, the great satirist, a middle-class lawyer's son, went to the celebrated *Schottenschule*, kept by Benedictine monks. His fellow-pupils came from all classes, from the simplest homes, to children of the highest nobility. They included the son of Metternich.[5]

A great deal of play has been made with the feebleness and irresponsibility of the Austrian Parliament. But the existence of a strong Parliament is not, as English history shows, synonymous with the existence of democracy. Parliament in Austria was always a side-show and was so treated not only by the people but also by its members. The government of Austria was not Parliament but the Administration working for the Emperor and in the Emperor's name. The Administration drew its members from all races and all levels of society. Beneath the heel-clicking, the endless invocations of the All-highest, the uniforms, it was democratic through and through.

Thus Hans Kübeck, the man who was to talk the young Emperor into making himself supreme autocrat, was a tailor's son, while Alexander Bach, whom he hated, whose power he sought to curtail, but who was to remain for ten years nevertheless as administrator-in-chief of the Unitary Empire, was a bourgeois lawyer. Kübeck had risen by sheer merit to be a member of the State Council under the Emperor Franz and President of the Imperial Exchequer under

Ferdinand. He had fathered the first Austrian railway in 1841 and the establishment of the telegraph network in 1846. His memoirs are full of the most biting criticism of the Metternich régime, of which he was an important part; but after the revolution he allied himself with the Old Conservatives, under the banner of Windischgraetz. His efforts on their behalf, at the age of seventy-three, directed at the upstart Bach and the iconoclast Schwarzenberg, culminated in the establishment of an Imperial absolutism which was to break the power of the Old Conservatives for ever.

Schwarzenberg saw this happen and had to let it happen. He was prepared to see the abolition of the constitution and the resurrection of Metternich's old State Council, with Kübeck as its Chairman, in order to retain the confidence of the young Emperor, now determined to assert himself and, with it, his real power. There was no choice open to him. Windischgraetz and the Old Conservatives, as such, he could have dealt with. What he could not deal with was the army, which in this matter stood behind Kübeck. For three years, while Bach had been consolidating the Empire as a unit and while Schwarzenberg had been bringing that unit into play as one of the greatest powers, Franz Josef had been spending a great deal of his time establishing himself as a working commander-in-chief of the army.

This was opposed to the Austrian Imperial tradition. For a very long time the Habsburg emperors had shown no interest in soldiering. They had not aspired to lead their armies in the field, still less to submit themselves in youth to rigorous military training. There had been plenty of soldier archdukes, and Karl, the great-uncle of Franz Josef, was one of the finest generals ever produced by Austria; he distinguished himself greatly in the French wars and actually beat Napoleon at Aspern. The Archduke Albrecht, Karl's son, was also a gifted soldier, though not gifted enough to force himself by sheer merit into the supreme command under the Emperor and thus save the day at Königgrätz. But although soldiering was very well for younger sons, the heads of the House of Habsburg saw no point in barking themselves when they kept a dog. There was reason, too, in their refusal to fight: the defeat of an Emperor in the field was not to be regarded lightly. One of the more sensible characteristics of the Habsburgs was that they rarely expected to win battles – a sobriety of outlook which, less fortunately, spread to their generals. Long before Louis Napoleon made his celebrated remark after his victory at Solferino ('I don't believe in war: there is far too much luck in it for my liking') the Habsburg emperors had discovered for themselves that no prudent ruler could count on winning battles: wars sometimes had to be embarked upon when diplomacy had failed, but only reluctantly and very much as a last and regrettable resort. One did not expect to gain anything by war: the most one could hope for was not to lose too much. When it came to aggrandizement, dynastic marriages were the thing. When it came to consolidation, alliances and treaties were the proper means; but sometimes one had to fight for one's allies, and sometimes one had to fight before one could secure a treaty. The great deterrent, naturally, was the great standing army, and the standing army for a continental Power was the equivalent of the fleet-in-being for a maritime Power like England.

Franz Josef, however, had other ideas. From childhood he had been in love with soldiering, and he had received a military education of a more thorough kind than his predecessors. Where would he have been, moreover, without the army? He had been carried to power on its bayonets. It appeared to him as the only fixed and secure feature of his realm, and he put himself demonstratively at its head. He was encouraged in this by his generals, who needed his person as a figurehead. With Schwarzenberg taking care of foreign affairs, with Bach imposing his administrative system on the unified Empire, there remained one sphere which the young Emperor could make his own: the detailed control of the army. Radetzky had to be left in Italy; Windischgraetz, until his downfall, was fully engaged in Hungary. From the moment of his accession it was the most natural thing in the world for Franz Josef, appearing always in uniform, and with his capital and a great part of his realm in a state of siege, to think of himself above all as the supreme war-lord.

The man on whom he relied above all was his new Adjutant-General and personal aide, Count Karl Ludwig Grünne (who was to exercise an unfortunate influence over his young master, to say nothing of the Imperial army, for more than a decade). While Kübeck was pushing his willing pupil towards absolutist rule, Grünne was advising him to do away with the War Office, except as an administrative convenience, and make himself in fact as well as in name Supreme Commander. This consummation was achieved on 31 December 1851. Grünne became head of the Imperial Military Chancellery, and, from then on, until after the catastrophe at Solferino in 1859, this disastrous man was Franz Josef's principal adviser and right-hand.

It is easy to write off Grünne as a bully, a fool and a toady, a man of evil. But it is not the truth. He was an able man in his own right, an Imperial patriot, and, for the first eleven years of the young Emperor's reign, an important and connecting link with the pre-March tradition.

He was very much Sophie's creature. It was she who made Grünne, then forty, Master of the Household to the Archduke Franzi, then seventeen. He was thenceforward Sophie's most devoted ally, and a valuable one indeed: before long he had established himself as Franz Josef's chief lay adviser and his only confidant, and he retained this position, strengthening it all the time, for years to come. He was there when Schwarzenberg took over the government, and he was there when Schwarzenberg so prematurely died. Although he had never seen active service and had no understanding of modern military theory – or even of the elements of strategy – he was a bluff soldier through and through, at home in the world of the barracks, and also a gifted courtier. Schwarzenberg could impress Franz Josef with his brilliance as a statesman; Bach could show off as an administrator of genius; Kübeck, at eighty, could hold forth about theories of government and legitimacy; but Grünne could talk to him as a combination of elder brother and knowledgeable valet who knew everything, who could fix anything. He came to be the young Emperor's personal liaison officer with ordinary mortals, from generals to young women. And, by all accounts, he acted honourably according to his convictions, which were the convictions of the reactionary conservatives of the time. But he, more than any man, was responsible for the backwardness and inefficiency of the military machine, which was finally exposed at Solferino. Radetzky's reforms in training and organization were undone by Grünne's total failure to understand what they were about. He perpetuated the system of honorary colonels, promoted to command over the heads of the most efficient junior officers and depressing the scales of pay. He believed in parade-ground soldiering and in knocking the recruits about. But all this says no more than that he was a man of his time. Grünne's heyday lasted from 1848 to 1860. The Crimean War broke out in 1854. Nothing in the Austrian army at that time could exceed in extravagant inefficiency the British army, adorned by Lord Cardigan and managed not by an autocrat working through a favourite, but by the War Office of the Duke of Newcastle, responsible to Parliament and a constitutional monarch.

To Franz Josef, who also loved parade-ground soldiering, military discipline was certain, comprehensible to all, sensible and logical: there was no nonsense about it. It was also beautifully impersonal, and this sort of impersonalness suited down to the ground a young man called to rule over much older men of far greater experience always and far greater wisdom sometimes. Franz Josef appeared to be very sure of himself: he had to be; he owed it to himself and his exalted rank. But he was also shy and deeply sensitive. He could rule only by keeping even his most illustrious subjects at arm's length, and this was precisely what the military system was designed to do. So that when one of his most senior generals on manoeuvres permitted himself a variation on his orders the young autocrat could call him up in front of the whole Staff and send him back to do it all over again with the words: 'I command to be obeyed!'

It was a technique that worked well. To apply this technique to civil government was logical and natural, and this is what the young Emperor did, once he had proclaimed himself autocrat, and with Schwarzenberg dead. Ministers were to be used, as generals were to be used, and discarded, like failed generals, when they had served their purpose. Over the years, the decades, Franz Josef was to mature and mellow, his perceptions were to deepen, he was to learn about human beings; but to the very end of his life he was, in moments of crisis, to revert with a sense of homecoming to the cut-and-dried certitudes of those early days when, in his white tunic and scarlet pantaloons, 'Young Red-legs' to the Viennese, and under the tutelage of Grünne, the simple answer to all problems of government was order and discipline, the offhand command, the instant punishment for disobedience. 'Nothing through the people, everything for the people.' The Emperor was there to lead. He was put there by God. And before God he justified himself by working harder than anybody else, by personally making sure at the end of a gruelling day that the troops were fed and warmly bedded down before he fed himself – and then going on working through half the night in order that the troops might be brought, God willing, through yet another day.

He was still very young. When Schwarzenberg died Franz Josef was twenty-two and, as far as policy-making was concerned, entirely on his own. Four years before he had wept at his accession. He was to weep again now. Schwarzenberg's health had been shaky for some time; but nobody expected him to die. His eyes were going and his heart was not as it should be. But the doctors had lately reassured him. The only thing, they said, was that he must be on his guard against apoplexy. 'That manner of death meets with my full approval,'[6] he retorted. He worked hard on his last day, but promised himself the pleasure of a ball that evening, where he expected to meet the young Polish wife of an army officer with whom he was starting an affair. His sister-in-law had asked earlier whether she could count on him being there: 'Most certainly – unless I am dead,'[7] he replied. He was dead: he collapsed while changing for that very ball. First Bach, then Grünne, then Franz Josef came to the death-bed. Franz Josef wept, but then pulled himself together, ordered Schwarzenberg's office to be locked, and took the key with him. After that there was no office to which the Emperor did not have the key.

'Should I make Bach Prime Minister?' he asked old Kübeck, showing that he still had not grasped the full implications of his own proclamation of autocracy. Kübeck, who detested Bach, was horrified; there were to be no more Prime Ministers. He, Kübeck, as Chairman of the Imperial Council, was to be the Emperor's chief adviser. So Bach was not made Prime Minister, and soon the Emperor turned the logic of absolutism against Kübeck himself: the Imperial Council never functioned and Kübeck, himself hoist with his own petard, once more retired. There were no more Imperial Prime Ministers. Bach administered the Empire as the supreme civil servant, perpetually at loggerheads with the military; Franz Josef guided it.

It would be true to say that in these early days Franz Josef was concerned almost exclusively with dynastic prestige. The very young and totally inexperienced head of an ancient House, he was possessed above all by the determination to make the name of Austria tell with the other Great Powers: Russia under an autocrat; France under a dictatorial President, shortly to make himself Emperor; Prussia under Frederick William; England under Victoria. He was not interested in aggrandizement, only in holding on to what he had, or, rather, to what Ferdinand had once held through Metternich. For this he needed at his back a powerful army which itself could only be a product of a coherent and disciplined society. It was the job of Bach to supply that society, assisted by Ministers of finance, commerce and justice. He, the Emperor, would do the rest. In this sense only is there some justification for the view that to Franz Josef the Empire was nothing but an instrument of foreign policy. Later on his attitude was to change, but not before he had run his inheritance dangerously close to the rocks. Later on he was to find himself increasingly caught up with the business of holding the Empire together for its own sake, which, under the Bach system, he had taken too easily for granted, and for the sake of his millions of subjects. But to begin with it is fair to say that he saw it as a passive instrument to be wielded by him for the glory of his House. He was very young. When Schwarzenberg died he was only twenty-two, and when the catastrophe occurred in 1859 which brought him face to face with reality with a most fearful shock, he was no more than twenty-nine.

Just as he needed to keep his subordinates at arm's length, so, to keep his own image of himself intact, he had to be reserved to the point of coolness with his equals. Apart from the rare genius, there are three kinds of hereditary autocrat: there is the weak and feeble figurehead, who leaves everything to his Ministers, of which Ferdinand had been an extreme example. There is the comparatively rare phenomenon of the man, or woman, with a will of his own, who yet needs support and, because of a streak of genuine humility, which so often goes with an eye for character, chooses for his main support the most powerful individual in sight: William I of Prussia was an example of this. Far more common is the man who is determined to rule but cannot bear near him men of supreme ability to question his decisions. This is the norm and Franz Josef was of the norm. Such men are not interested in personality; indeed, they are more likely to be positively repelled by it. Theirs is the responsibility, theirs the direction of affairs. With more or less awareness, according to their temperament, they know very well that all their acts are open to question; but acts have to be committed. The study and the savouring of personality is a luxury that can be indulged only by the uncommitted, the onlooking, the irresponsible: it leads inevitably to the study and savouring of opposed points of view. The only point of view besides his own that a ruler wants to understand is the point of view of his active opponents, and the appreciation of this is a technical matter for specialists. Formal autocrats are not alone in this: a Prime Minister in a democracy will listen in Cabinet to what his colleagues have to say; he will pick up information from them, sometimes even ideas. If he senses a unanimous or nearly unanimous feeling in opposition to his own ideas he will give way before he has committed himself and adopt the opposition point of view as his own. But he will never submit his own ideas to be man-handled by his colleagues. Unless he is a dialectician or a debater of the first order he will not invite argument. He *knows*, and he also knows the fragility of the rational edifice upon which his knowledge is based: anybody with a lawyer's mind can knock it down. Any argument can be countered by an opposing argument. The man of sense and instinct, the two qualities above all needed in a leader, is horribly vulnerable to the first logician who turns up. If the palm is to go to the most accomplished reasoner, all countries should choose their leaders from the higher reaches of the legal profession. If speciousness and articulateness are not the highest qualities required in a leader, then the leader must protect himself from the specious and articulate. In a Cabinet a Prime Minister can do this by refusing to engage them on their own ground. In an autocracy the ruler can keep them at arm's length. It is the same with strong personalities: these are a nuisance to the man with all the threads in his hands because they introduce into the broad, vague scheme of things an element of distortion by exaggerating particular aspects. The strong personality with a wide view is a rarity: as a rule he is a man with one, or at most two or three, subjects with which he identifies himself and for which he lives: he is apt to be an obsessional character. The ruler has to consider many other objects. He is obsessional too, but his obsession is universal balance, which means universal power. He thus finds undue pressure from particular interests distasteful and embarrassing. In a Cabinet chosen from a representative assembly the Prime Minister frequently has to put up with this, just as he has to adapt himself to the fact that in the Cabinet-room with him there is at least one colleague who could step into his shoes – indeed, is only waiting for the chance to do so – and, in addition, perhaps two or three who in specialized ways are more formidable than he himself – except in the vital way of leadership. In an autocracy the temptation to exclude such awkward customers is, as a rule, irresistible. There has to be a team; the team, indeed, is everything: it had better be a team that can be easily managed.

The team which Franz Josef inherited from Schwarzenberg was not what it had been at the beginning of his reign. Stadion, the liberal aristocrat, was in a lunatic asylum; Bruck, the visionary trader and economist, had resigned, overwhelmed by incessant criticism from all sides, which came to a head when he exceeded the estimates for the building of the Semmering railway, the first mountain railway in Europe, and one of the most daring and imaginative feats of the nineteenth century. Schmerling had resigned from the Ministry of Justice, pushed out by Schwarzenberg in one of his blacker moods for resisting the arbitrary encroachments of the police and the bland prolongation of martial law. Krauss, the able Minister of Finance, had been the only one of Schwarzenberg's team to resign when the constitution was repealed.

Bach was still there. The abolition of the constitution had been for him a very bad moment indeed. He was still under forty. Only four years earlier, not a hot-headed youth, but a responsible career lawyer of thirty-five, he had been the brain and the moving spirit behind the March revolution. He had also been in the thick of the fray, calmly seated under fire on a heap of paving-stones, as he drafted new instructions for his supporters. It was he who had confronted Metternich, as he sat in his Rococo study in the Ballhausplatz, waving the citizens' demands under his nose and telling the Chancellor to his face that he must go. Now, under Schwarzenberg, he was the all-powerful Minister of the Interior, an interior which included impartially the farthest flung provinces of the Empire, their economic, judicial and social ordering prescribed minutely from Vienna and taking no account of any will but Bach's. He had justified this remarkable transition, as people like him always have done and no doubt always will do, by asking expediency to be his witness. The first purpose of the revolution, which he had led, and in which many had died, had been to free Austria from the Metternich system. That, thanks largely to him, had been fulfilled, and nothing could take that achievement away: the log-jam had been broken. There had been other hopes, the hopes expressed by Fischhof and so many others, of trial by jury, of co-operation between the nationalities – all the freedoms. These hopes, he could say, were not dead. It had been no part of his original ideas to inaugurate a reign of anarchy, or to see the Empire split asunder into its component parts. But the revolution had got out of hand, and only by force could that order be restored without which there could be none of the things of which he and Fischhof had dreamed. So he put himself on the side of force, of law and order, on the understanding that his dazzling talents should be recognized, employed, rewarded. Rome was not built in a day: not everything could be done until revolt had been everywhere put down; but a great deal was done all the same. The emancipation of the peasants stood firm; through Schmerling the judiciary had been reformed from top to bottom; through Leo Thun there had been a thorough overhaul of education; through Bruck the creation of free trade throughout the Empire. All this was something and he, Alexander Bach, at the right hand of the greatest aristocrat in the Empire, had presided not only over all this, subduing with one hand the forces of anarchy and separatism, holding off with the other the bitter attacks of the conservative nobility, but also over the streamlining of the whole administrative apparatus within which every citizen within the Empire was equal before the law, all treated with perfect fairness and impartiality, fearing nothing from their overbearing neighbours, restrained by the great central power from fratricidal bullying and strife, free as never before in their history to follow their own bent, their own opportunities, unobstructed. So that the man who sat at the apex of this system could fairly say that the foundations had been laid for the realization of Fischhof's climactic dream, the enjoyment of equality and the development of free co-operation between all the peoples of the Empire. Bach had succeeded, where Josef II had failed, in organizing a vast supranational State, a true commonwealth, undisturbed by petty national quarrels, a model for universal government. And who, pray, but Alexander Bach, could have achieved this miracle?

It was, by all standards, a stupendous feat, and it was carried out by a single individual acting as Minister of the Interior in an Empire torn by civil war and on the verge of bankruptcy.

In 1848 credit had been nil. There were 354 million paper florins in circulation; metal currency did not exist; bank notes were at a heavy discount; speculators and profiteers grew fat on inflation; and, as always under inflation, the poor and the middle classes with fixed incomes suffered heavily. In 1850, with a total revenue of 180 million florins there was a deficit of 77 million; in 1851 the deficit was 51 million; in 1852 it was 53 million.[8] Most of the money went to the upkeep of a free-spending army of 600,000 men, the Emperor's own; there could be no retrenchment there. So taxes had to be increased and new loans floated: it could be said that the proud Empire was financed mainly by the Rothschilds. There were times when Schwarzenberg had to postpone carefully considered strokes of policy on the insistence of the Minister of Finance, in case they upset his plans for raising money. But with all this, between 1848 and 1852 over 137 million florins were found for railway construction and other capital investment[9] and the abolition of the *Robot*, the emancipation of the peasants, was faithfully carried out. It cost the State 564 million florins paid out to thousands of landowning families: 1,870,000 florins went to the Schwarzenberg family alone.[10] For the great land-owners the compensation money received from the State and from their emancipated peasants was enough to enable them to modernize their estates and capitalize all sorts of enterprises; for thousands of lesser families it was not enough to compensate for the labour and services and tributes in kind which kept them going in a cosy, paternal way: they fell by the wayside; hence the bitter lament of Windischgraetz and his friends.

We have to imagine the mind of Alexander Bach, conducting this vast process and caught up by it. He, the bourgeois radical, had won the intimacy of Felix Schwarzenberg; at mixed dinner-parties the Prince's sister-in-law, Eleonore, was hostess; at all-male dinner-parties Bach took her place and was sneeringly referred to as the hostess of the Ballhausplatz. To his old associates he was a renegade, to his new ones he was a parvenu, at best a hypocrite, at worst a traitor: there were many who were convinced that he was a com-munist in disguise. Windischgraetz was sure of this. He has been laughed at since for his simplicity: Bach was a turncoat, just like that, a greedy, vain, ambitious man who sold his soul, open-eyed, for power. To believe that is to be simple in another way, and probably, if the truth could be known, Windischgraetz and the Old Conserva-tives were nearer to the truth. Bach was not a communist, of course, he was not a socialist, he was not a liberal. But he was an idealist of sorts: he cared in his way for the people, or what he took to be the people. Dizzily ambitious he clearly was, greedy too, and vain: one glance at his portrait with the fine forehead rendered dangerous by the predatory nose and the general brilliant effect of the upper part of the face brought rather frighteningly down to earth by the poor mouth, the coarse and heavy chin, is enough to show that. He wanted place quite desperately; but he also wanted to achieve great and enlightened things. It was impatience rather than greed which finally told. He was the man who knew how to do things, who had the finest organizing brain in Austria, perhaps in the world; and he was not going to be held back by the scruples of vague dreamers, who, when they had their chance, when power for one dizzy moment had been theirs, had shown themselves incompetent and foolish. Impatience and ambition, combined with practical idealism, thus carried him to the heights; and he was, indeed, on the topmost height when a slip of a boy, the Emperor, in alliance with an old, malicious and vindictive relic of the past, Kübeck, produced his ultimatum; the constitution is to be abolished, those Ministers who object to this are free to resign.

What was he to do? Start another revolution? Admit that his whole progress had been wrong and his achievement vain and go back to the barricades? Or was he simply to hand in his resignation, like Philip Krauss, and go back to his law.[11] This would have meant handing over in its entirety, to be wrecked at leisure, the splendid administrative machine he had built up from virtually nothing. If, on the other hand, he could hang on through a few years of absolutism the time would come for another great step forward: then the great Empire, with Bach at the Emperor's right hand, could be swung into the new Enlightenment. He chose this course. In no time at all, and financially on a shoestring, by colossal labour and self-glorifying devotion, he had completely reorganized the vast complex of the Habsburg lands.

Thus, for example, Bohemia, under its Governor, was divided into seven counties. Within each county were a number of administrative districts, an entirely new creation: in Bohemia there were seventy-nine of these districts. The function of the district organization was to take the place of the feudal order of the landlords. In the past all administration and justice had been supplied by the estates. Now civil servants did the job, often recruited from the old estate functionaries and legal advisers, all badly paid, most of them incorruptible and human in their approach. It was an immense upheaval. In Hungary it was worse than an upheaval; it was regarded as a cataclysm: in place of the idle, slovenly, inefficient local administration based on immemorial tradition there came a swarm of German and Czech civil servants, Bach's 'Hussars'. They ran Hungary, now treated no longer as a kingdom but simply as a province broken down into its counties, as Hungary had never been run before. They woke it from its slumber and set it to work, efficiently, briskly, but with great forbearance, for its own good. The country was transformed and the foundations of a new prosperity very quickly laid. But Bach's amazingly conscientious, able and just officials were not thanked: the Magyars resented their intrusion with a scorching hatred, preferring to go to hell in their own well-tried way. Efficiency is not all, as the great colonial Powers of the late nineteenth and early twentieth centuries have, one after another, been finding out. So much is said and written about Austrian muddle and inefficiency, easy-going slackness, frivolous *Schlamperei*, that it is important to remember that the Austrian bureaucracy, *qua* bureaucracy, was the most efficient, humane and incorruptible imaginable. It contained practically all the most able men in the Empire, selfless and devoted; chiefly, to begin with, German Austrians and German-speaking Czechs. They were hated for their efficiency, their conscientiousness, their selflessness, their devotion to duty, their equity, their foreignness.

The young Franz Josef did not really like his bourgeois Minister. He was awed by his brilliance and his talents and duly appreciative of the man who could run and organize civilian society, which held no interest for him at that stage of his life. But all might have been well for Bach had Schwarzenberg not died. Five days after his death the poor wretch found himself not only excluded from the premiership, as a result of Kübeck's machinations, but also deprived of a great slice of his own authority. On 11 April the Emperor wrote to him to say that he had decided to remove the police from the Ministry of the Interior and make its chief, Baron Kempen von Fichtenstamm, a Minister in his own right. Until then Bach had had only the military to fight; now, since Kempen loathed him, he had to fight the police as well: the new Minister of Police went so far as to set a special watch on Bach himself. The system over which he now uneasily, but with still unexampled energy, presided, was no longer the Bach system, it was, rather, the Kübeck system. And so it remained until the crash in 1859, when Franz Josef, now rising thirty, awoke from his fool's paradise on the field of Solferino and Kempen and Grünne were dismissed and, with them, Bach. Grünne had to go for ruining the army, Kempen for paralysing society, Bach for being Bach. The absolutist era had indeed come to an end. Had Bach done the right thing and resigned in 1851, or again in 1852, he might very well have been recalled, as Schmerling, who did resign, was recalled, to inaugurate a new era. As it was he lost everything: by clinging to power at all costs he fell with the system which was a contradiction of everything he believed in. He was sent to the Vatican. He lived on in obscurity, this hero of the 1848 revolution, until nearly into the twentieth century. Nobody has yet bothered to write the biography of this brilliant and fascinating man who ruined himself, and helped to ruin his Emperor, not because he was a cold and calculating turncoat, but because he told himself that if he allowed himself to be excluded it would be an admission that all he had fought for with such spirit had been in vain.

Nothing was simple and straightforward in the first decade of the new reign. It was by no means, as is sometimes presented, a case of the police and the military versus the rest. Life in Vienna had a strange ambivalence. The boisterous satirist, Nestroy, drew crowds to his theatre in the Leopoldstadt to applaud his wild extravaganzas. The dramatist Bauernfeld, who had belonged to Schubert's circle in the days of the old Emperor Franz, who had drafted with Bach the grand manifesto to be waved under Metternich's nose, who thereafter attacked Bach bitterly, was nevertheless allowed by Bach to put on his plays uncensored. And this uncompromising liberal, who turned Windischgraetz's death-bed farewell letter to his regiment into an outrageously funny one-act farce,[11] was nevertheless half attracted to the mighty and the great. One of the men who gave Bach most trouble was Baron von Welden, the man put in by Franz Josef to take over Windischgraetz's Hungarian command. Von Welden later became Military Governor of Vienna and was perpetually at loggerheads with Bach's civilian administration. He was the very type, one would have said, of the white-uniformed reactionary. Bauernfeld tells how one day in April 1849 von Welden sent for him, to discuss a matter of censorship. He presented himself at the Hofburg in a state of considerable apprehension and waited while the General, then virtual dictator of Vienna, worked quickly through a queue of petitioners. Then the great man took his cap and invited Bauernfeld to walk a little with him. What was the trouble? Bauernfeld explained. If the Governor himself had anything against his plays, it was not for him to question; what he objected to was interference by the police. Von Welden thought this reasonable. He had never read the play in question, he explained, but if Bauernfeld, as author, said it was all right, then it could be put on forthwith. Surprised, and a little shocked, Bauernfeld assured him that at most there were a few dubious lines: if the Governor cared to glance at them and delete anything he thought offensive, that would be an end of the matter. But no, the Governor would do no such thing: he left it entirely to Herr Bauernfeld. He then changed the subject and they talked about politics and the wars with Hungary and North Italy, and Bauernfeld was impressed by the soldier's moderation and 'constitutional attitude': the only people whom he had no use for at all were the Viennese. 'At this very moment', he said, 'I have a heavy task. I am on my way to tell a father that his son has been killed in Italy. I hold the accursed Viennese and their brawling directly

responsible for that!' But when Bauernfeld protested and reminded
the dictator of the evils of pre-March, against which the people had
risen, von Welden surprisingly agreed. 'Quite right!' he barked. 'We
all behaved like a lot of —s!' Bauernfeld was so taken aback that he
found himself protesting at this, and the odd interview ended with
smiles and handshakes and a heady access of mutual esteem.[12] To
Bauernfeld von Welden had seemed the type of 'gruff soldier'. Here
he now was apologizing for his class to one of the most trenchant of
the revolutionaries, only a year after the revolt. And Bauernfeld himself, the mordant independent, showed himself still under the spell
of uniformed authority. This incident illustrates to perfection the
mood of Vienna in those early days of the young Emperor's reign and
explains a very great deal: to see the situation in terms of the straight
opposition of brutal, white-uniformed martinets and noble martyred
liberals is not enough.

To Kübeck, to Bach, to Grünne, to Kempen, to Metternich in
the background, was added another adviser, Count Ferdinand Buol-
Schauenstein, who was to have the honour of formally conducting
the Empire to the verge of total disaster. Buol was a career diplomat
of Swiss descent, who had distinguished himself in Petersburg by
rubbing up the Tsar the wrong way and was Ambassador in London
when Schwarzenberg died. For some reason, which has never been
made clear, Schwarzenberg at one time had declared that if he fell
ill he would call Buol in to deputize for him: he may have mistaken
his subordinate's cold, angry and arrogant manners for strength. Be
that as it may, Franz Josef immediately sent for him, not as a stop-
gap, but to take over foreign affairs. 'Now that my name stands
alone under all decrees,' the young Emperor had said to Windischgraetz soon after the abolition of the constitution, 'criticism of those
measures is high treason.'[13] It sounded splendid, but the young man
knew very well that for a long time he would be relying largely on
his Ministers. So did Metternich, and there is no doubt at all that
Metternich spoke up for Buol – not because he had any respect for
him; Buol's personal attitude towards Russia must by itself have
seemed crass and frivolous to the old Chancellor, who set such store
by the Russian understanding – but because he thought he would
be able to work through him. Vain hope! Buol was obstinate as well
as arrogant and void. Within three years he had succeeded in
isolating Austria by quarrelling with Russia, France, and England
simultaneously. To the young Emperor, desperate in pursuit of

self-sufficiency, this looked like strength. In fact it was *folie de grandeur*: Buol had dreams of keeping Austria detached from all entanglements and becoming the arbiter of Europe, totally oblivious of the fact that Austria's security had depended for centuries, and still depended, on a complex of alliances and balances which could buttress the whole system from without and counter the centrifugal tendency which was constantly threatening to tear it asunder. Bismarck, who held Buol in perfect contempt, once recorded a saying of Pfordten's (the Bavarian Minister to Berlin): 'He is like a locomotive which does not know where it is going and, when asked, answers only with steam and whistling.'[14] Malmesbury, who as Foreign Secretary had his first interview with Buol in March 1852, found him arrogant and tricky as well as crass: 'He alternately tried to bully me and to mystify me as to diplomatic usages in a way which can only be accounted for from his supposing (and justly so) that he was dealing with an inexperienced hand.'[14] And again: 'He behaved in the most coarse and insolent manner . . . and to such a degree that I at last asked him if he was accustomed to speak to English Ministers in that style; because I must tell him at once that I would not bear it, and should inform the Court of his violence.'[15]

Schwarzenberg himself may be criticized for abandoning the traditional Viennese system of diplomacy – brilliantly developed by a succession of Foreign Ministers, above all by Kaunitz in Maria Theresa's time, and crowned by Metternich himself at the Congress of Vienna – of fixing Austria's position and influence by an intricate network of treaties. But Schwarzenberg was working under pressure in a revolutionary epoch, and although he neglected Russia, bullied Prussia, insulted England, and set himself to woo the new France of Louis Napoleon, there was reason in his madness, which (with the exception of his behaviour towards England) was always controlled and directed towards a calculated end. Buol's megalomania was purely nihilistic. Alone among Austrian statesmen he had got it into his head that the Monarchy could exist in isolation.

So the young man of twenty-two was unlucky in his advisers. He did not improve things by his marriage.

CHAPTER SEVEN

THE HEAVENLY EMPRESS

Elizabeth of Bavaria was perhaps the most beautiful woman in Europe, and the tragedy of her life has passed her down to history as a romantic and martyrized figure of perfect nobility. There are other ways of looking at it. What the young Emperor needed above all was a sensible wife who would cancel out his own shortcomings. The last thing even her most devoted admirers could claim for her was that Elizabeth was sensible, and the sum total of her effect on Franz Josef was to magnify his own failures.

Her own life was indeed a tragedy. She was only sixteen when Franz Josef swept her off her feet, and she was not cut out to be an Empress. That is usually taken to be the whole of the story; but it was by no means that. She was, when all is said, not sixteen for ever, and she enjoyed almost recklessly the perquisites of her position while refusing its obligations. To a large degree she never grew up.

She was ravishing and she was enchanting. Franz Josef was full of spirit when it came to young women, and discriminating into the bargain. He was a dashing and accomplished dancer, as Bismarck observed, and although at the formal Court balls he did not dance, confining himself to circulating in a dutiful manner among the guests as was proper to his position, Sophie arranged for his especial benefit innumerable smaller and more informal parties, highly exclusive, called balls at the Court, of which he was the life and soul: there, and elsewhere, he was naturally surrounded by enchanting countesses, all out to please, and he enjoyed every minute of it, quite throwing off the constraints of his official life and living in the moment like any other handsome young extrovert in his early twenties with all femininity quite literally at his feet. But he could not marry them all, and he very much wanted to get married. The first serious attempt, which was one of the best-kept secrets of the age, ended in a personal and political snub – from Berlin. Visiting that city at the end of 1852, he was deeply smitten by Princess Anna, a niece of the Prussian king, a girl of his own age, twenty-two, elegant, slender, pretty, intelligent and sensible, who was already unofficially engaged to one of the Hesse-Kassels. Sophie was delighted: Anna was the right sort of girl, and her marriage with Franzi would go a long way towards solving the Austro-Prussian quarrel. She was aware of the difficulties: there was the existing engagement to be got over, and Princess Anna would have to change her religion and become a Catholic. But what was an engagement among princes? And, as for religion, Anna's own Prussian aunt had changed hers to marry the Tsar. She poured out her heart to her sister, Elizabeth of Prussia, but in vain; and the very few in the know rejoiced in the whole episode as a proof that, with Schwarzenberg gone, Vienna was beginning to pay proper respect to Prussia. It is only lately, with the publication of Sophie's correspondence, that it has been understood how unreservedly she threw herself on the mercy of her sister, the Prussian Queen, in her plea for this marriage.[1]

That was in the new year of 1853. In July, Sophie tried again. If not Prussia, then the next best thing, Bavaria, her own family. Her sister, Ludovica, who had married the Bavarian Duke Maximilian, had five girls, one of them, Helena, in some ways suitable, and the same age as Franzi. So Ludovica and the two elder daughters, Helena and Elizabeth were invited to a family party at Ischl among the lakes and mountains of Salzkammergut, which had already become the favourite retreat of Franz Josef's parents and of Franz Josef too, with his growing passion for shooting.

They came in August: Ludovica, a faint and threadbare copy of Sophie herself, with all Sophie's faults and none of her strength; Helena, twenty-two, presentable and handsome, deeply religious, taking after her mother; and Elizabeth, sixteen, her father's daughter, her father's favourite, a wild, shy, lavishly poetic, scarcely awakened beauty, who had been allowed to run wild in the great park at Possenhofen on the Starnbergersee, romantic and passionate, afraid of people, dizzily brave on horseback. She had the finest forehead, with straight dark eyebrows over wonderful eyes, extravagantly long and lustrous dark hair. Her face was an oval well set on a fine neck, her nose strong and straight if a shade too long. Only her mouth turned up a little at the corners, and this, with a chin that had that slightly unfinished look that goes so often with obstinacy of the passive kind, spoilt a picture of almost perfect natural grace and beauty. Franz Josef took one look at her and fell. Poor Helena was nowhere, and within forty-eight hours he had talked his mother, at first disconcerted beyond measure, into agreeing to his choice. It was to be Elizabeth, Sisi, or nobody. And Elizabeth it was. He was like a boy with a pet bird of many colours. He could not leave her alone.

There is no reason to suppose that Elizabeth herself was not strongly attracted, although she was not ready for marriage of any kind. Apart from her incessant scribbling of verses, she had lived the life of a boy rather than of a girl. She doted on her amiable and eccentric father and cared nothing for her mother: Maximilian and Ludovica had for long occupied separate apartments at Possenhofen. There is a legend that she resisted violently, in tears, and could not stand Franzi at any price. But this is untrue. Certainly she wept, but from bewilderment and fear of the future, not from repulsion: 'How could anyone not love him?' she said through tears when her mother formally asked for her consent. 'But why, of all people, me? So young, so unimportant. Of course I shall do everything to make the Emperor happy, but will it be enough?' And to her governess, next day: 'Yes, I do love the Emperor. But if only he were not Emperor!'[2]

That was in August 1853. On 24 April 1854 they were married with all pomp and splendour in the Augustinerkirche, just outside the Hofburg. They made a splendid pair, for Franz Josef himself was handsome in those days. Clean-shaven then, the faint echo of the Habsburg chin and lower lip did not distort but, rather, gave a cavalier edge to the face, pink and white, of a boy. His hair, then thick and slightly waving, the bloom of well-nurtured youth on his cheeks, went well with the bold, rather narrow blue eyes, which later, when the Emperor was pouched and stricken and bald, his cheeks sunken and fluffed out with the famous sidewhiskers, seemed too close together.

Sisi was still a child; she behaved like one; and by all the world except Franz Josef she was treated like one. She was, moreover, a moody, brooding and stubborn child: nobody was capable of more flashing, dazzling gaiety when things were going well for her, or when she could do as she liked; but that fatal mixture of extreme sensibility and extreme self-absorption drove her back into herself at the least rebuff, at the least lack of sympathy. With this went an unforgiving heart: once Sisi had taken against anybody she detested him for life, and her schoolgirl hatreds persisted, unmitigated, into maturity. Only when the enemy was completely broken, as her mother-in-law, Sophie, was broken towards the end, or on the verge of death, as when Grünne apologized to her on his death-bed for the evil he had done, was she suddenly transformed into a radiant angel of forgiveness and consolation:[3] such moments were enough to create a legend, but they were too infrequent and specialized to make her an easy companion.

This strange creature found herself pitchforked into a world which was full of rebuffs and which showed no sympathy at all. From her dogs and her horses and the lakeside park at Possenhofen she was plunged, friendless and alone, into the stiff, glittering, extravagant ceremonial of a Habsburg wedding, surrounded by men and women old enough to be her grandparents, most of whom had never been young. Even her ladies-in-waiting were strangers, and they were presided over by a leathery-faced Countess, appointed by Sophie, who treated her from the start as a schoolgirl under instruction instead of a delicate young beauty called upon to rule.[4] Her beauty, indeed, while it aroused the enthusiasm of the populace as well as of the highly born from other lands, struck jealousy into the hearts of those who mattered at the Court of Vienna. Sophie and Grünne, above all, had had Franz Josef very much to themselves: they were not going to have his head turned away from them by a feckless slip of a girl; and since Franzi had already shown that he had a will of his own by his very choice of Sisi, and therefore had to be approached with circumspection, it was Sisi who had to be smothered. Nothing should have been easier for these two experienced and now elderly intriguers than to make her go their way; but nothing, in fact, was more difficult: the child would not be led; she showed vice and bit and kicked when they tried to bridle her. She was, when all was said, Empress, and to this irrefutable fact she clung, even when, within weeks of her marriage, she was weeping her heart out to her young husband, still very much under his mother's spell, and pouring out her soul in adolescent verses – sustained paroxysms of homesickness and revulsion.[5]

In those first days she saw little of Franz Josef. There was no honeymoon. After the shock of the wedding-night she was told that she would be expected to appear at breakfast with the family, with her new mother-in-law, that is; and although she wept bitterly and pleaded her anguish and shame, Franz Josef saw nothing wrong with this arrangement and said that of course she must appear.[6] Sophie had seen nothing wrong with it either: it was the most natural thing in the world; it was unnatural to resist. And for a day or two no doubt she did her best, not unkindly meant, to come to terms with the child, her own terms. She had advice to offer about everything, some sensible, some crass, some silly. To Sisi it was all obscene. So quite soon Sophie must have decided that if the child would not be led she must be broken.

Sisi might have found allies in the Court. If many of those who surrounded her were jealous, others had much to gain from winning her favour. But they, too, could do nothing with her. A great deal of nonsense has been talked about the black Spanish ceremonial of the Hofburg: it was not at all like that. Behind the petrified façade there was even cosiness and considerable informality; but there was no privacy at all. It was an institutional sort of life, and from the moment the young Empress emerged from her bedroom, dressed for public appearance, she was on view until the moment came to go to bed once more. Being on view in this way was normal in the European Courts of the period; but it was the last thing Elizabeth could bear. She wanted to be with her husband, and, when she could not be with him, she wanted to be alone, preferably in the open air and with horses and dogs. In those early days she spent a great deal of her time in the small but delightful palace of Laxenburg, in the country just outside Vienna, on the road to Hungary. It should have been a paradise for her with its beautiful park laid out on English lines, its splendid timber, its nightingales and golden orioles, its lake, its superb range of stables; but because Sophie was also there, while Franz Josef was off early each day to his office at the Hofburg, the paradise became a prison. And in that prison, Elizabeth sulked. She seems, poor child, to have lost for ever in her defensive self-isolation any sense of humour she may have had. Certainly she lacked all tactical sense. It never seems to have occurred to her that if she gave way on two or three small points with good grace, or a shrug, she would then be in a strong position to carry a more important point – or at least to win others, including her husband, to her side. Instead, she dug in her toes all along the line, resisting all suggestions and encroachments, however trivial or ludicrous: she would make as much fuss about some absurd convention about when and when not to wear gloves as about one of Sophie's grosser infiltrations into her strictly private life. She presented herself, in a word, as un-reasonable in all things, and this made it hard for her husband, still very much in awe of his mother, to know where to support her. Further, it discouraged those who, enchanted by her natural grace, would have liked to help her, and, worse still, it encouraged Sophie and Grünne and others who were jealous of her to develop a campaign of ridicule, which served to isolate her still further, until Sophie felt strong enough to drop all pretence of gentle guidance and simply to ride down her opposition.

The climax, the first climax, was brought on by the impending birth of her first child. When Sophie had had Franzi, the event was from beginning to end as public as a levee at the Court of Louis Soleil. The anteroom to Sophie's bedroom at Schönbrunn was crammed day and night while Sophie worked through her protracted, dangerous and agonizing labour, with uncles and aunts and cousins, ladies- and gentlemen-in-waiting, some pacing up and down, some gossiping through the uproar, some snoozing on hard sofas, some sitting upright and tense to the screams that went on hour after hour.[7] For several months before that difficult birth, Sophie, who had already had two girls, was kept indoors on the orders of her terrified doctors. She had grumbled bitterly. She believed fresh air would do her good. She was nearly sick with longing for the sun and the wind on her skin. But she obeyed without real question: it was all part of the necessary performance. And from his first days the baby who would one day almost certainly be Emperor was on view. He had a grand apartment to himself; but the rooms were *en suite*, and there was a constant procession, to and fro, of friends, relatives, servants and strangers. Franzi's own bedroom was situated directly above the lavatory used by the palace guards, and at every change of guard the drums rolled and the bugles blared beneath the infant's window. He had a wonderful chief nurse or *Aja*, the Baroness Louise Sturmfeder, who was his only protection. 'The child of the poorest day labourer', she wrote in her diary, 'is not so ill-used as this poor little Imperial Highness.'[8]

That had been in 1830. Now, in 1855, Sophie was preparing for her first grandchild, and she was outraged because Sisi tried to go her own way and retire into herself. There was bitterness when the child complained that sightseers were being allowed to penetrate into the innermost recesses of the great park at Laxenburg; Sophie replied that this was correct, that the Empress owed it to her husband and the Monarchy to show herself for all the world to see her condition.[9] After that Sisi hardly stirred out of the house. She passed the days teaching her parrots to talk, hour after hour – until Sophie again intervened: 'I also feel', she wrote in one of her notes to Franzi, 'that Sisi should not spend so much time with her parrots. It can so easily happen that when women look too much at animals in the first months the children come to take after those animals. She should spend more time looking at herself in the mirror, and at you.'[10]

But the poor child was not allowed to look much at her husband, who was away all day; and when Sisi begged to be taken into Vienna so that she could be near Franzi at his work in the Hofburg, Sophie objected very strongly: 'It is not proper for an Empress to run after her husband and dash about like an ensign.'[11] Only once did Franzi give way to her pleadings and take her with him for a whole day to the city: the subsequent scene with Sophie when they got back to Laxenburg in the evening put an end to such jaunts for ever.

Even then there were people to say that the Emperor was neglecting his duty, so wrapped up was he with his young bride. Before Sisi's pregnancy they did indeed spend many happy hours riding together. They made a triumphal journey to Bohemia and Moravia, where Elizabeth's beauty and charm did a great deal to soften hearts set glumly and resentfully against the Court. Had Elizabeth been less of a child, had she been able to project herself into her husband's problems, instead of brooding incessantly about her own, she could have found the opportunity to entwine her own life with her husband's and strengthen him in his so brittle self-sufficiency. But she could not do this. She could not stand against Sophie, she could not stand the restrictions of the Court, she was not in the least interested in politics, she hated crowds and public display. So that she remained in effect hopelessly isolated, not a wife, but an object, a precious jewel to her husband, an obstinate child to her formidable mother-in-law. So it went on.

It was all very unfortunate for Franz Josef, who, badly advised by Grünne and Buol, isolated in his own heart scarcely less than Sisi herself, was at twenty-four almost wholly preoccupied with asserting his own absolute independence as head of a great Empire and as an equal of the Tsar of Russia, beholden to none. It would have been too much to expect any young bride of seventeen to give him coherent political advice, and Franz Josef would certainly never have dreamed of asking for it. It would not have been too much to hope that a ravishingly beautiful and in some ways gifted young wife should come to realize that, since divorce was out of the question, her best course lay in developing perfect loyalty to a young husband, who at least was not physically repulsive, and in building up by subtle and private flattery and criticism his own self-assurance.

Franz Josef was an unimaginative husband; he set great store by outward show; he was, in the modern jargon, a dedicated man; he was preoccupied with things that made nonsense to Elizabeth; he was in some ways brash and hard. He was not a stick. Leopold of Belgium could write to Queen Victoria in June 1853: 'The young Emperor I confess I like much, there is much sense and courage in his warm blue eye, and it is not without a very amiable merriment when there is occasion for it. He is slight and very graceful. . . . The manners are excellent and free from pompousness or awkwardness of any kind, simple, and when he is graciously disposed, as he was to me, *sehr herzlich und natürlich*. He keeps everyone in great order without requiring for this an *outré* appearance of authority.'[12] He was also head over heels in love with Sisi, and he was as lonely and uncertain in his heart as any man has ever been. Young women of extreme sensibility and with far less opportunities than Elizabeth have done wonders in situations basically similar. Her own sister, married to the unpromising King Bomba, and just as beautiful, did wonders. But Elizabeth did nothing: she tore out her own heart and added immeasurably to her husband's burden. He was, throughout, though often misguided, immensely patient. He was, though sometimes unfaithful, always adoring. It is hard to see what she gave in return.

It is necessary to say this because for so long Elizabeth has been presented as the image of the noble, sensitive soul crushed and mangled by the hidebound pedant. But the letters discovered by Count Corti and the diaries of Elizabeth's confidante, her Hungarian lady-in-waiting, Countess Festetics, tell a different story. We find Franz Josef, long after the first spectacular breach which led to Elizabeth's flight to Madeira, pouring out his heart to her and signing himself 'Your Mannikin'. We find him, before that breach, sitting up late in his headquarters on the eve of the battle that was to lose Italy, tenderly pleading with Sisi, then no longer sixteen but in her twenties, to be patient. She had been bombarding him with letters begging him to let her come to Lombardy to be near him on the battlefield, the sort of letters that some husbands would have ignored, pretending that they had never arrived, that would have weakened others in their resolution by distracting them from the grim job in hand. But not Franz Josef. After the defeat at Magenta and when he ought to have been in bed getting a little sleep before the great battle at Solferino, he sat up, writing, writing:

My dear, dear, my only angel – I do beg you in the name of the love you have sworn to me, try to take hold of yourself, show yourself sometimes in the city, visit hospitals and institutions. You simply don't realize how much help that would be to me. It would encourage the Viennese and send up their morale, which I so desperately need. . . . And keep yourself for me, I worry so much. . . .[13]

And again:

Alas, I cannot grant your desire, though it would please me so much if I could. Women simply do not fit into the life of a military head-quarters. I can't set a bad example to my whole army – and, moreover, it is impossible to tell how long I shall be here. . . . Please, my Angel, if you love me, do not fret so much, look after yourself more, enjoy yourself as much as you can, ride and drive as you like but carefully, and keep for me your dear, precious health, so that when I come back I shall find you really well and we can be so happy together.[14]

Sophie was no better, and for her to pester Franzi in the middle of a campaign with complaints about Sisi was unforgiveable. She wrote, for example, to say that Elizabeth had taken to riding in the park alone with the chief groom, Henry Holmes. The Emperor had to take time off to cope with this: 'I have been thinking a great deal about your riding,' he wrote. 'I really can't allow you to ride alone with Holmes; it simply will not do', and he went on to explain why, and to suggest a more suitable escort.[15] He might have been forgiven for turning against Sisi in sheer exasperation at the goings on of a pack of women in the most critical and perilous hour of his reign. But he did nothing of the kind. 'My dear, my heavenly Sisi, . . . my only, most beautiful Angel', he would write, 'I can't tell you how much I love you and how much I think about you.'

But Sisi paid no attention. If she could not get to Italy with Franzi she was certainly not going to be a dutiful Empress at home. Instead, she rode and rode to excess. It became a devouring mania. She took up jumping, as though to break her neck. She developed a passion for her figure, a passion which, as the years went by, was to become a mania. She ate nothing, slept little and grew thin. When things were going badly in Lombardy she wrote panic-stricken letters. She was the sort of wife who, married to a subaltern, is the commanding officer's bane and the likely ruin of her husband. But she was not married to a subaltern; she was married to the Com-mander-in-Chief. And the Commander-in-Chief on the eve of his disastrous defeat, without mentioning the imminence of a battle, sat up late at night to write again begging her to promise him not to ride herself to death.

It was a tragic situation. It was important for two reasons. At the time when more than anything else the young Emperor needed moral support there was none forthcoming from his wife: this added to his brittleness and his rigidity. On the other hand it can hardly be doubted that what he suffered through Elizabeth in those early years helped in the end to make him the man he became. Elizabeth suffered too; we know all about that. But all her suffering did for her was to make her a bad versifier and push her to the point of recklessness which, years later, enabled her to keep up with the hounds over Irish fences.

Sophie, of course, as a mother-in-law, was intolerable. And she was, as it were, always in the house. She had passed her peak. In 1848 her strength of will and her commonsense had saved the Monarchy. Her fighting spirit had helped to prepare the way for counter-revolution and for the accession of her son. She had fulfilled her role. She was a fighter, at her best in the heat of battle, when there could be no looking to left or to right. She had gained in experience of the world, but she was still politically illiterate. She had surrendered herself heart and soul to the Church and took her ideas now from Rauscher. It is possible that given a relatively mature and sensible daughter-in-law, or a soft and biddable one, she might have been content to work through her for what she conceived to be Franzi's good. But Elizabeth, whom she had had to accept against her will, was neither mature, nor sensible, nor submissive and showed few signs of ever becoming any of these things. So she had to be schooled into being a credit to the Emperor, and it was Sophie's duty – who else could do the job? – to superintend the schooling. It was possible to get on with Sophie if one had a sense of humour and great suppleness. Sisi was too young to have a sense of humour, and when it came to suppleness, she did not know the word: she could have given lessons to her husband in rigidity.

Franz Josef owed everything to his mother, and he was well accustomed to her ways: he was to show in after life that one of his most valuable talents was his ability to get used to people's ways. He was still out of his depth and under great strain. He might impress the outside world with his extraordinary detachment and calm. But those who knew him best, Schwarzenberg as well as Sophie, knew something of the stress under which he worked: 'We now have an Emperor', wrote Schwarzenberg to Windischgraetz, 'whose character and abilities appear to be fully developed – but he is young and mistrusts his own strength.'

Schwarzenberg thought it was only a matter of time and knowledge and experience; but Sophie wondered how long he could keep it up. 'He keeps his health amazingly', she wrote to Ludwig in Munich; 'but often he is quite knocked out and exhausted.'[16] He could only carry on, she said, by gritting his teeth and slogging away at his papers with stubborn, steely application. In fact, even Sophie was over-optimistic. In those early days Franzi's health was indeed affected. The grand old Emperor, who was never to have a day's illness, who carried through for sixty-eight years the habit of industry forced upon him by the teeming demands of the chaos confronting him on his accession, began his reign by suffering from sudden seizures of faintness: the only thing that could restore him was his still boyish delight in music and dancing – light music, the music of Johan Strauss the elder above all. Later it was to be shooting: not the showy *battue*, but long, solitary and arduous days in the mountains after chamois and bear.

Elizabeth could not help him much, either in his work or in his recreation; and Franz Josef was in no position to take her education in hand. He was too busy learning himself; and, anyway, Sophie knew everything, could teach everything. So that at first, overwhelmed as he was by affairs of State, by the intense, desperately responsible and killing business of keeping his end up before all the world, he did not see the hopeless incompatibility between his mother and his young wife. Perhaps until the very end he never understood the equal hopelessness of his own incompatibility with Elizabeth, whom he constantly adored, and who was driven to ever greater spiritual excesses by her inability to escape from a love which she came to hate.

PART THREE

RETREAT FROM GLORY

CHAPTER EIGHT

DISTRUSTED AND ALONE

What the young Emperor was mainly thinking about while his child bride bickered with Sophie and talked to her parrots at Laxenburg was Austria's position in the European conflict which was to be known as the Crimean War. Until 1854 Franz Josef had been able to see himself as the supreme lord of a resurrected Great Power, presiding with military crispness and decision over a polyglot Empire which, restored to its rightful position on the map of Europe, had to be reorganized and taught a number of lessons. To assert his domestic authority he had isolated himself from his subjects, and now, to assert his international authority, he proceeded to isolate Austria from the rest of Europe. But there were two conflicting issues. In the first place the young Emperor was driven by a compulsive need to demonstrate his equality with the Russian Tsar to whom he owed so much, and whose patronizing ways he could not stomach. In the second place the very existence of Europe as understood since 1815 was being menaced by some of those pledged to maintain it. Franz Josef, with reason, felt that the established order was threatened with extinction, and the main threat came from Petersburg. Since the preservation of the established order meant very largely the preservation of the Austrian Empire he had every cause for apprehension. A strong Minister, a Schwarzenberg, could still have found a solution to the dilemma in which the Empire was now placed. But Schwarzenberg's nominee, Buol, was only one of many stridently advocating contradictory policies which led infallibly to the loss of every potential ally at a critical moment in the history of the Empire.

Because of this, Austrian policy during the Crimean War has been treated by some historians as being beneath contempt. But this attitude has to be modified by hindsight. So long as the Crimean War itself is regarded, as it was regarded by almost all those concerned in it, simply as an unfortunate episode, the common verdict on Franz Josef's policy is justifiable. But in fact it was much more than this. The mishandling of the campaign and the events leading up to it, the awe-inspiring incompetence displayed by Russians, French and

British alike, produced a traumatic effect on all the participants; and this resulted in a spontaneous averting of the gaze. The Crimean War has rarely been recollected in tranquillity or contemplated in perspective. The memory of it has survived as of a ghastly aberration to be hushed up as quickly and thoroughly as possible and, as it were, sutured off from the main stream of history: the perfect model of a frivolous and unnecessary war. But was it really like that? The war was fought in the wrong way and for the wrong reasons; but it had to be fought. It was by no means an irrelevant interlude; it was, rather, a climacteric, a critical conjuncture in the development of the modern world. What it did was to destroy the artificial balance imposed by the Congress of Vienna, upset by the revolutions of 1848, reimposed only in appearance by the Habsburg revival. From 1849 to 1854 the European balance had rested on a number of false assumptions. The action of Nicholas in 1853 removed the basis of those assumptions and revealed in their nakedness the new facts; Russia had become an expanding and dynamic Power no longer interested in holy alliances; Prussia was on the make and was not going to let anything stand in her way; France was set on the recovery of her former glory; England had at last become imperially minded; Italian nationalism was moving towards a climax; with the decline of Turkey the Balkan problem was coming into being. All these movements were in suspension. The catalyst which set them fizzing was the Russian Tsar. With so much explosive force lying about, unrecognized for what it was by anyone, though partly apprehended by Bismarck (not yet in the Prussian saddle) and Cavour in Turin, the wonder was not that the explosion took place but, rather, that it was so muffled when it came. It was muffled partly because nobody but the fighting soldiers on each side, together with a young Englishwoman called Florence Nightingale, had anything to be proud of, partly because none of the statesmen of the Great Powers wanted to recognize the real meaning of the conflict; the implications were too unsettling, frightening indeed, to be contemplated in comfort. It was easier to think of the whole affair as an unfortunate mistake to be lived down as quickly as possible. 'A war to give a few wretched monks the key of a grotto' was Thiers' characterization of that remarkable conflict; and sensible men, like Aberdeen in England, were no more conscious of what they were opposing than Palmerston was conscious of what he advocated.

Russia was on the move and had to be stopped. It looked as simple as that. Britain with her vital interest in the Mediterranean, Austria with the Balkans on her doorstep, each had a direct interest in stopping her. France, under Louis Napoleon, could not be expected to lie down for ever under the restrictions imposed upon her by the Congress of Vienna: she was bound to welcome any conflict which could weaken, or break up, the coalition which had put an end to the pretensions of the new Emperor's sainted uncle. But the trouble went deeper than that. Had it not done so, a strong, sharp warning from the other Powers would have been enough to freeze Nicholas in his tracks. The main criticism of Franz Josef has been that he refused to declare himself against the Tsar in time. Alternatively, if he were not prepared to do this, he should have sided with Russia, regardless of the consequences, and thus at least assured for his dynasty a lasting alliance with Russian power. Both courses are easily stated. Neither could be easily followed.

Paradoxically, the one man who seems, at least at the outset, to have had the most real appreciation of the issues at stake was the very man who seemed most at sea: Franz Josef himself, then twenty-four. That is not to say that he saw clearly, only that he saw deeper. And he was paralysed by what he saw. What he saw was not the simple Russian threat to his own Balkan interests, though that was bad enough. What he saw was the approaching dislocation of the delicate equilibrium on which the continuance of his dynasty depended and which had at all costs to be preserved. He had no choice of action. By siding finally with Britain and France on the one hand or Russia on the other he would let loose dynamic forces which would sooner or later sweep him and his Monarchy away. He could not articulate his profound and accurate misgivings: he was not an articulate man. But what he must have felt is plain for all to see in the light of his public manoeuvres and his secret correspondence.

The Treaty of Vienna in 1815 had taken little account of Turkey and the Balkans. But Turkey was weakening rapidly. On the edge of a Europe neatly parcelled up, there was coming into being a new power-vacuum. How could this be filled and ordered in a gentlemanly way?

The Turkish decline had been in progress for a century and a half. In 1718 Austria had swallowed Turkish Hungary. By the Treaty of Kutschuk Kainjardi in 1774 Russia had at last reached the Black Sea coast, and Catharine the Great put up an inscription at the gateway to the Crimea: 'The Road to Constantinople'. By the

Russo-Turkish Treaty of Adrianople in 1829 the Danube and the Dardanelles were open as international channels and all Moslems were banished from Wallachia and Moldavia, which became quasi-independent Principalities. Greece and Serbia at the same time became autonomous and, in 1830, elected their own princely rulers. Turkey was going back fast; but the sway of the Porte still extended into Thessaly through Macedonia; beyond the Balkan mountains through Thrace; into Bosnia, Herzegovina, Montenegro and Albania. The simultaneous extension of Russian and Austrian influence into the dwindling theatre of the Ottoman Empire had so far led to no trouble. Two great dynasties, each believing profoundly in the sacredness of the other's legitimacy, were marching in step, if not hand in hand, into a sort of no-man's-land: there was still a sizeable buffer between them. But when, in 1850, Nicholas came forward with his plan to anticipate the final demise of 'the sick man of Europe' and redistribute his possessions, the pattern changed. The idea of the Balkan States becoming autonomous under Russian protection could appeal to Vienna no more than the Russian advance to the Mediterranean could appeal to London, which would have nothing to do with the idea in spite of the Tsar's suggestion that England should take Egypt, Cyprus and Crete.

Where did Austria fit in? Every other country was expanding, or trying to expand, and appealing for its sanction to the popular will (even Tsar Nicholas himself). Only the Habsburgs wanted things to stay as they were, or as they seemed to be, and were not at any price prepared to invoke the will of peoples whom it was their appointed duty to govern. When, on 3 July 1853, Russian troops invaded Moldavia, without real warning and without any attempt on the part of the Tsar to inform Franz Josef, much less consult him, the situation as seen from Vienna began to look ugly.

Nicholas doubtless convinced himself that the Austrians had in fact been warned and had not entered an objection. At the close of 1852 the Turks had found it necessary to take punitive action against Montenegro, the fighting mountain kingdom, which had never surrendered its independence entirely and which now showed signs of breaking away from Turkish influence once for all. Austria had responded very sharply, and the Turks had withdrawn. But before he knew of this withdrawal Nicholas had seized what seemed to him a splendid opportunity for lining up Austria on his side in his impending assault on the Ottoman Empire: 'I do not know what you may decide,' he wrote to Franz Josef, 'but whatever you decide, if it should come to Turkey making war on you, you may be assured in advance that it will be precisely as though Turkey had declared war against me.'

He went on to say that he was making this clear to Constantinople and, for good measure, was mobilizing two army corps and the Black Sea fleet. 'I deeply deplore this sad necessity,' he added, 'since the end of it all might well be the collapse of the Ottoman Empire, and the consequences of that would be incalculable.'[1]

This was the inaugural letter of a long correspondence which was to embody the break-up of Austro-Russian understanding, a correspondence between Heads of State, conducted throughout in the second person, pursued against a background of the most intense diplomatic activity, and destined to achieve a peak of acrimony which has not been surpassed by the bitter and more vulgar quarrels of the twentieth century.

Here was the Tsar, so soon after the rejection of his plans for the dismemberment of Turkey, declaring that he deplored the possible collapse of the Ottoman Empire – while at the same time showing an almost indecent eagerness to find a pretext for attack. Here he was once more seeking to put Franz Josef under a debt of gratitude, and at the same time clearly inviting him to reciprocate by promising in advance to treat the Russian cause in any war with Turkey as his own.

For the moment no immediate harm was done. Franz Josef was able to reply that there was no need for Russian intervention, since Turkey had already given way; to declare his gratitude; to conclude by expressing his conviction that the happy outcome of the affair would rejoice Nicholas as much as it did him. But of course he knew that Nicholas would not be pleased; and he was left with plenty to think about.

All through 1853 the correspondence continued. In April, as the crisis between Russia and the maritime Powers developed, as the Turks – stiffened by the activities of the British Ambassador, Lord Stratford de Redcliffe, the Great Elchi, Canning's cousin – refused the Tsar's demands, the atmosphere between Petersburg and Vienna grew charged. Franz Josef postponed his promised visit to Russia, and the Tsar himself came out on the defensive. He was only doing his duty, he said. He did not want to break up the Ottoman Empire, but if the Turk remained stubborn and blind he would have to take up arms. He would keep Franz Josef, 'my dear, good friend' informed, and together they could concert their plans to foil the machinations of other Powers.

That was on 8 April. On 3 July the Tsar sent his troops across the River Pruth. Seeing that in any case the British and the French would never let him get through to Constantinople, he sought to regain Austria's confidence by a solemn declaration that his troops would not cross the Danube. Franz Josef tried to mediate between Russia and Turkey, but there could be no mediation. The Tsar was still confident that he would win Austria to his side; but Austria or no Austria he was determined to go on. It was very difficult for the young Emperor to know best how to express himself. In one breath the Tsar was talking in terms of a religious crusade to liberate the Christians under the Turkish yoke; in the next he was making it quite clear that his real objective was the Straits. Franz Josef did his best. Short of saying 'I distrust your motives, will have no part in this adventure, and may, if the worst comes to the worst, be found on the other side', he could do little but hammer away at the theme that the collapse of the Turkish Empire was likely to result in the spread of chaos and revolution, inimical to monarchies everywhere.

It had little effect. The Tsar's mind was made up. He seemed to think that if he took the young monarch more deeply into his confidence he would be bound to win his support; and this he did. He went so far as to visit Olmütz to meet Franz Josef. That was on 24 September. Almost at once there was another meeting in Warsaw and this time they were joined by the King of Prussia. But all to no purpose. Short of declaring himself in belligerent opposition to Nicholas, Franz Josef had done all he could when, on 1 October 1853, Russia declared war on Turkey. 'My hope is in God and in the justice of the cause I am defending, the cause of Christendom. The fanaticism that now dominates the unhappy Turks makes it almost a crusade, in which Russia defends Christianity while France and England are guilty of the infamy of fighting for the Crescent. Is it conceivable that Russia should have no allies in the holy cause it is defending?'

It was more than conceivable. Franz Josef evaded this very pointed question. He, too, was caught up to some extent in double-talk, basing all his objections still not on his real fear that a Russian victory might imperil his own position in the Balkans, but on the old plea that it might cause 'a new flare-up of revolutionary activity in Europe and new upheavals of incalculable outcome'. This may have seemed plain enough to Franz Josef. But to the Tsar, who had his own revolutionaries well under control, who had put Kossuth down once and could put him down again on Vienna's behalf, it could well have read like an unexpressed proposal for a bargain: 'I will help you in Turkey if you will help me overcome any consequent troubles at home.' Be that as it may, from now on Nicholas behaved towards Britain and France as though he had not only Austria but also Prussia in his pocket. From Prussia, in the event, he got only a declaration of neutrality, but from Franz Josef, the young Emperor who owed him so much and whom he regarded as his shining protégé, he received a slap in the face. For the first time Franz Josef spoke out. There should be a conference in some neutral city, to include Turkey and the maritime Powers, to work out a peace; Russia should at once evacuate the Principalities (nothing was said about the withdrawal of French and British naval forces); further, and worst of all, Austria would remain neutral only if the Tsar would give 'a most definite and solemn undertaking' that Russia would remain on the defensive on the left bank of the Danube, or 'should military developments compel you to cross it, you will not depart in the least degree from your previous declarations, according to which you seek no territorial aggrandizement, no interference between the relations of the Sultan and his subjects, no rights that do not proceed from your old treaties with the Porte'.

This was too much. Nicholas had never been spoken to like this before by anyone, anywhere. 'Can you believe that a man of honour is double-tongued, or that he could go back upon what he has once declared to be his intention?' The sombre, moody, masochistic, proud self-righteousness which was characteristic of the Russian autocrats long before the Romanovs, and which was to survive the collapse of Imperial Russia, welled with dark nobility from the man who was barely troubling to conceal the conspiratorial nature of his plotting and yet was outraged and affronted to the depths of his being if another failed for a moment to take at their face value his protestations of disinterestedness:

> ... Is there not something hatefully superfluous in permitting oneself to doubt his word, once given, or in asking him to reaffirm it? ... Are you truly to make the Turk's cause your own? Emperor Apostolical, does your conscience permit it? If it be so, well and good; then Russia alone shall raise the Holy Cross and follow its commandments. If you were to range yourself with the Crescent against me, then I say to you, that would be a parricidal war.

Franz Josef remained polite; but he stood his ground. This was his first major appearance upon the European stage since the death of Schwarzenberg. He was adamant about his refusal to let the Russians cross the Danube. He had to be. From this point on, the only question in his mind was whether to try to hold himself aloof between the conflict between East and West then impending, or whether to join Britain and France in curbing by violence the pretensions of Russia – Russia now led by a Tsar who appeared to him no longer as a fellow dynast, concerned above all with upholding the old order, but as an overweening rival from the north, to whom all things were permitted if they seemed good in his eyes. It was a difficult choice, and, in fact, Franz Josef never made it.

2

He has received nothing but blame for this, and it is easy enough to see why. There were those who wanted him to reaffirm the Habsburg-Romanov alliance, come what might; there were those who desired a declaration of unconditional neutrality – the Tsar himself in the end demanded no more than this; there were those who said that if Franz Josef was determined to stand against Nicholas his only course was to unite with Britain and France. Even Professor Redlich, whose perception of the mind of Franz Josef is deeper and more sympathetic than most, failed to see that in the nature of the Monarchy as it then was none of these three courses was in fact open to the unfortunate young man: 'Franz Josef was by no means at bottom a weak character. But he was one of those men who, lacking the resolute drive given by a passionate aspiration, an immovable conviction, a deep belief in some great idea, or even the force of imagination, are inclined to substitute for it the bare calculus of what one may call tangible immediate need.'[2]

And to illustrate his meaning Redlich quotes the famous lines of Grillparzer from his play about ancestral Habsburgs:

> Here is the curse upon our noble house,
> On half-trod ways to half-done deeds
> We strive uncertain, with but half our means.[3]

Uncertain, Franz Josef may well have been; but half-hearted he was not, and he strove with *all* his means.

Professor Redlich comes so near to the truth a moment later:

Now, in his youth, and right on up to his death, Francis Josef was dominated, spiritually and intellectually, by the notion of maintaining intact the might of the dynasty . . . and preserving the foundations of this might, namely, all the territories of his realm, as a unit. It is only with this in mind that his actions in these days of extraordinarily difficult decision in foreign policy can be rightly appraised. He hoped to attain this end by giving himself *wholly* to *neither* of the two warring parties.[4]

Nothing could be truer as far as it goes. But it must be taken a step further. The preservation of the *status quo* was for Franz Josef nothing less than 'a passionate aspiration, an immovable conviction, a deep belief in some great idea'. And it is an idea that can be better appreciated today for what it was than it could have been at any time before the Second World War. It is not necessary to attribute to Franz Josef a conscious philosophy of politics, subtle or profound. It is not necessary to believe that he was actuated by a shining vision of a multi-national State, a miniature League of Nations, centrally administered from Vienna in the interests of the peoples comprehended by it. It is certainly desirable, on the other hand, to see the Empire, as Franz Josef undoubtedly saw it, not simply as an aggregation of territory gathered together by a single family for its own aggrandizement, but rather as a divine trust, an enclave of Christian order to be preserved at all costs from the disruptive ambitions of greedy and predatory rulers on the one hand and the forces of anarchy on the other. With the Russian Tsar on the move, with Prussia abiding her hour, with the new Emperor of France threatening to harness the forces of anarchy, especially nationalism, to his own chariot, with Turkey, a pillar of the *status quo*, beginning to crumble, with England all over the place, there was nothing for him to do but strain with every nerve to recover a precarious balance which was in fact (though he could not yet perceive this) irretrievably lost. There was impending disaster no matter where he looked. If he helped France and Britain to crush Russia he would be instrumental in strengthening Louis Napoleon with his vested interest in perpetual revolution, his generalized programme of self-determination for small nations and his particular designs in Italy. At the same time he would be instrumental in removing from Prussia the shadow of the Russian threat. If he helped Russia to beat off Britain and France he would be left to cope at uncomfortably close quarters with the new Russian dynamism in face of which he could expect no help from the

Western Powers. Neither contingency could be tolerated. He had no choice but to stonewall. Indeed, as in 1849, there was only one positive step he could have taken to improve his position, perhaps decisively: the surrender of Venetia and Lombardy. Just as in 1849 this action would have enabled him to recover Hungary without Russian help, so, in 1854, it would have removed for ever the fear of France, perhaps given him a useful ally south of the Alps when passions had died down, and certainly opened up for him a wide new field for manoeuvre. It was a tragedy that he could not even consider the surrender of Italy, but it was an inevitable tragedy: it would have taken a genius to perceive the need for this surrender and to carry it through. Franz Josef was not a genius, and we have no reason to blame him for this.

He did what he could according to the light vouchsafed him. He was young and desperately conscious of his duty and responsibility towards his House. Nicholas, much older, restless and greedy behind his august and lofty attitudinizing, ruthless to the point of vindictiveness beneath his benign exterior, taking it unquestioningly for granted that he stood at the still centre of the world, above all contradiction (he would summon his victims from prison to question them sympathetically about their motives and their ideas, and then, his benevolent curiosity satisfied, send them back to solitary confinement), had first tried to patronize his young colleague, then to coax him, then to bully him. Franz Josef stood up to this and made a clean break when he had to, demanding, on 3 June 1854, the immediate evacuation of the Danubian Principalities. Bach and Buol were on his side in this; but he depended now no more on them than on Windischgraetz and Radetzky who led the pro-Russian party, a point which the Western allies failed to grasp, for they allowed themselves to be misled by Buol into believing that sooner or later Austria could be counted on to march with them.

An older and more experienced man than Franz Josef could hardly have done better with Nicholas: it is very much to be doubted whether the wisest and most venerable head in Europe could have imposed upon the 'self-conscious Caesarism' of that unholy monarch. But he could certainly have done better with England and France.

Once war was declared in March 1854 and the expedition to the Crimea under way, the false starts, the reversals, the hesitations and evasions of Austrian policy were bound to look like nothing but calculated perfidy, or at best pusillanimity, in both Paris and London, eagerly suing for the support of Austrian troops and oblivious alike of the real nature of Franz Josef and of the meaning of the conflict, as he saw it. Nothing he did was right, everything was wrong. In fact the strategy behind his actions was still right from the point of view of Austria: it was the tactics that were at fault.

Looking back calmly on Austrian policy during those years the most striking thing is the contrast between Franz Josef's firm handling of Nicholas up to the moment when war broke out, and his inept and vacillating handling of the Western Powers thereafter. It was in the spring of 1854 that he went wrong. There was every reason in the world for his stand against the Tsar; there was every reason in the world for his determination to keep out of the war and his refusal to join the Western Powers. Had he addressed London and Paris as unequivocally and reasonably as he had addressed Petersburg, making clear to Napoleon and Victoria the underlying principles which had indeed been guiding him from the beginning, he would have established for Austria a position of perfect respectability and set himself up, with some chance of success, as the staunch upholder of international law and order based on the *status quo*, to be altered only by negotiation. But he did not do this. After keeping his end up in his tremendous duel with Nicholas, much the hardest engagement he was ever called upon to fight, he seemed quite suddenly to lose both direction and will. One has to ask why.

There were two reasons. Much has been made, especially by Professor Redlich, of Franz Josef's personal handling of the whole long-drawn-out crisis. This is based chiefly on the fact that he retained in his own hands, from start to finish, the conduct of negotiations with the Tsar. The complete story is told in his own holograph letters. But appearances can deceive, and although the hand was the hand of the young Emperor, the voice was the voice of Metternich. The old man had come back to die in Vienna; in 1853 he was eighty and had six years to live. And it was he, not Franz Josef, who saw in a flash, as no other European statesman saw, the true implications of the East-West conflict. In letter after letter to his useless successor, Buol, he poured out advice and admonition. He saw – who could have seen better? – that what was at stake was the survival of his own elegant and brilliantly contrived system which alone could preserve a restless Europe not only from a general conflagration but also from the forces of revolution. His advice was passed on by Buol, who scarcely understood what it was about, to his young master, who understood it very well. 'The Russian Court is totally in the wrong,' he had written to Buol in June 1853; 'the present mood there afflicts me like a bad dream.'[5] And again: 'As regards Austria's attitude in this difficult situation, as I see it there is only one line, and that is the line taken during the Graeco-Egyptian affair [in the twenties].' This meant neutrality. And again: 'I can only compare the situation in which the Russian Cabinet has got itself to a man floundering in a bog and sinking deeper every time he moves.'[6]

These were the opinions which clarified Franz Josef's mind and fortified his resolution when he was still sparring with the Tsar and hoping to get him to see reason in the summer of 1853. And when it was conveyed to the tremendous old man that the young Emperor laid great value on his views, he wrote, characteristically, to Hübner in Paris: 'Here is the proof that his mind moves in step with mine, that is to say, towards universal peace . . . and the firmest possible base for social tranquillity and order.'[7]

But Metternich, the skilled architect of European concord, was himself out of step with the times: he never believed it would come to war. Earlier, he had regarded Schwarzenberg's warlike policy towards Prussia as unforgivable: it was not the done thing. He was the first League of Nations man, operating in this sense a hundred years too soon, but in another sense, in the belief that the future of Europe could be determined by a committee of crowned heads, fifty years too late. Combining in his scheming the aspirations of the future with the mechanics of the past, he was, when war finally came, unable to give counsel. He never spoke of enlightened self-interest, but all his policies had nevertheless been based on an innate conviction that the monarchs of his time, the tail-end of the Age of Reason, would be guided by precisely that. When this conviction was proved to be unfounded he had nothing more to offer. He could no longer be a guide. Franz Josef stood alone, and had to make what he could of the conflicting claims and counsels of lesser advisers.

The second reason for the Emperor's sudden failure was his marriage. The wedding with Sisi had taken place in April 1854; and although, as we have seen, Franz Josef put duty first, went down to the Hofburg every morning, leaving his sixteen-year-old bride in Laxenburg to be harassed and bullied by Sophie, his heart was with her. Elizabeth complained bitterly about his absences, but there were others to complain that he gave her too much time. He was twenty-four and very much in love, worried also by the disastrous way in which Elizabeth and Sophie were each bringing out the worst in each other. He had fought his great fight with Nicholas and established his position: it was too much to be expected that he should show the same sustained personal interest in the far less critical matter of his relations with France and England. Time and time again he had to tear himself away from his bride to plunge into what he himself described as 'the horrible perplexities of the moment'. And so, lacking counsel from Metternich, who was only useful in a situation which he understood, a situation involving the maintenance of peace, that is, and with his youthful nature distracted by the clamant demands of his relationship with Sisi, he left too much to his Ministers, above all to Buol.

Buol by now had got the bit between his teeth. Strengthened by Metternich, he had sustained his young master in the battle with Nicholas, helping him to withstand the heavy pressure of the Russophile conservatives, headed by Windischgraetz, and the army commanders who were appalled at the disintegration of the Austro-Russian alliance and viewed the very thought of war with Russia with total dismay. 'Do you realize', Franz Josef said to him one day, 'that here in Vienna there are only two men who are not pro-Russian? Those two are you and I.' 'Just so, Your Majesty,' replied Buol, 'but they make a very strong party – your Majesty and his Minister.' Seymour, the British Ambassador to Vienna, who reported that exchange,[8] did not go on to speculate about what the Emperor thought of his Minister's smug fatuity. Metternich had made his own position quite clear: Austria, 'the Central Power', must never allow herself to be used 'either as the advanced guard of the East against the West, or of the West against the East'.[9] She must at all costs preserve her freedom of movement. But Buol, now for the first time trying to develop a policy of his own, went further. He was determined to bring Austria into the war on the side of the West. With the news of the Crimean landing, in September 1854, he thought, not for the last time, his chance had come. In a memorandum to the Emperor he wrote:

> Our relations with Germany and with the maritime Powers must finally be clarified. . . . So long as Russia refuses to talk peace we must attach ourselves sincerely to the policies of the maritime Powers and have the courage to declare this to all the world. From the

standpoint of foreign policy, Your Majesty, I can advise no other course, for all other courses lead to isolation or to our old dependence upon Russia.[10]

Buol forgot Prussia. He still thought he could get Prussia on his side and, with Prussia, the united might of the German Confederation. This was a vain dream from the beginning. How vain is well shown in a letter from Bismarck in Frankfurt to Gerlach, dated October 1854: 'The only way of taming this *militum gloriosum* [Austria] is a heavily threatening Prussian attitude towards Austria. . . . Then we must attack, quickly and with surprise, while Bohemia is empty of troops, and overwhelm her together with Russia before France can cross the Elbe.'[11]

Bismarck was not yet the government of Prussia: he had still eight years of anonymous diplomacy before him. But he expressed a swiftly developing Prussian attitude. At its mildest and most negative this was that Prussia needed Russia at her back; she did not need Austria. At its strongest and most positive it was that with Russian friendship firmly secured Prussia could one day march against Austria and cast her down. And this, indeed, is what happened twelve years later.

If Prussia could remain neutral in the Crimean War, so could Austria. And Prussia, apart from a very exiguous and short-lived treaty with Austria, contrived to maintain her neutrality without upsetting anybody. What led to Austria's isolation was not her neutrality as such but her effective departure from it *vis-à-vis* Russia and her subsequent repeated and uncalled for raising of the hopes of the Western Powers. Both were due largely to Buol's plunging and Franz Josef's failure to keep that plunging under control. This failure, the main causes of which have already been indicated, was complicated by temptation of what looked like easy territorial gains. The whole point of the Austrian position was that no country, including Austria, should gain anything by doing violence to the existing order. By offering to share the spoils of the Ottoman Empire the Tsar had already tempted Franz Josef, and the temptation had been withstood. But now, with Buol (and Bach as well) full of the advantages that would accrue from possession of the Principalities, Franz Josef wavered. He sent a peremptory command to Nicholas to evacuate these lands, and when, in the autumn, hard-pressed by the Franco-British threat, the Tsar saw nothing for it but to agree, Austrian troops moved in and general mobilization was ordered.

Metternich complained that the general situation filled him with the uneasiest of feelings, which he could only compare with sea-sickness.[12] But Franz Josef was feeling happier than for a long time.

> In spite of all the political confusion [he wrote to his mother] I am in good spirits, since, as I see it, provided we act strongly and energetically, only good can come to us from this whole eastern saga. For it is in the East that our future lies, and we shall push back Russia's power and influence behind those borders from which, only through the weakness and disunity of earlier times, she has been able to advance in order slowly but surely – and perhaps uncon-sciously on Tsar Nicholas's part – to work for our ruin.[13]

The Tsar now had nothing to do but accept the four points as a basis of peace. But Buol was still not content. On 2 December he persuaded Franz Josef to sign a treaty of alliance with the West.

Nicholas could not be more angry than he already was. 'Do you know', he said to Esterhazy, the Austrian Ambassador to Petersburg, 'who were the two stupidest kings of Poland?' That was after the Austrian demand for the evacuation of the Principalities in June, conveyed, ironically, by the Hungarian Szechenyi. Poor Esterhazy, another Hungarian, suffering heavily under the impact of this epoch-making breach, did not understand. 'John Sobieski and myself,' said Nicholas. Sobieski, a Polish King of Poland, had saved Austria from the Turks in 1683. But now Prussia was bitter too. Austria's signing of the Treaty of Alliance with the Western Powers had been done behind her back, and Frederick William felt betrayed, and said so widely. There was still hope in Paris and London that Austria might enter the war; but Franz Josef had not the least intention of fighting except as a last resort, and Buol in Vienna and Hübner in Paris grew bitter too. On 1 January the great spire of St Stephen's in Vienna was blown down in a storm. But Vienna survived even that, and on 2 March Nicholas died, killed, it was said, by Austrian ingratitude – but actually by the strains and stresses produced by the exhibition of Russian military incompetence in the Crimea and the belated discovery that even a Russian Tsar was not almighty. Franz Josef, on the eve of becoming a father (his first daughter was born on 5 March) wrote an appropriate letter of condolence to the new Tsar, Alexander II, to which he received a stiff reply:

> You will readily understand the effect of the political events of this last year on his heart – they broke it – when instead of finding in you

a faithful friend and ally, on whom he relied and whom he loved as his own son, he saw you follow a political course which brought you ever closer to our enemies and which will still bring us inevitably, if that course does not change, to a fratricidal war, for which you will be accountable to God.[14]

This cannot have surprised Franz Josef, who already expected to find in Alexander a more determined opponent than Nicholas; but it must have been an unpleasant letter to read. Read it he did, however, and he does not seem to have been unduly affected: once a man has hardened his heart to take this sort of thing in his stride he is well on the way to success. And, indeed, it was at just this time, and when London was in a thoroughly irritable frame of mind about Austrian dilatoriness and vacillation, that Lord John Russell wrote from Vienna to Lord Clarendon, as Foreign Secretary:

The Emperor of Austria's manner is singularly agreeable; his countenance open and prepossessing. Without being one of those men who at once prove themselves qualified to hold the rudder, and guide the ship through a dangerous navigation, he seems to show an intelligence and a firmness of purpose which may enable him to rule this great Empire with ability and success.[15]

Russell also recognized Franz Josef's difficulties. A little later he reported: 'The neutrality of Prussia, the attachment of his own nobility to the Muscovite cause, the disorder of the country's finances and the desire for repose after so many and such severe internal troubles must inevitably influence the mind of the Emperor.'[16] As, indeed, they did. It was still only six years after the defeat of Hungary, only three years after the state of siege had been raised in Vienna, Graz, and Prague to celebrate Franz Josef's engagement with Elizabeth. Already the Emperor was kicking against the necessity of thinking all the time about Russia. Since the autumn of 1854 Austria had had 450,000 troops under arms, and the cost was prodigious. One of the things Franz Josef had not learnt about was money: he never used it. Without in the least understanding what he was doing, he had spent the entire army budget for the year in the first three months of 1854; and so it went on. By now even he had to understand that the country was on the verge of bankruptcy, but it certainly did not occur to him that he was laying up for his Empire financial troubles which, years later, were to cause him severe embarrassment.

In the event Austria never fought, though she lost thousands by disease; and the cholera, which was killing the French and British troops in the Crimea, spread through the Austrians standing by in the Principalities and in Galicia, reaching as far as Vienna, where it killed old Kübeck and penetrated to the Hofburg itself. Her refusal to fight aroused the bitter resentment of Napoleon and Palmerston and played directly into the hands of Bismarck and Cavour. In June the army was largely demobilized in the interests of economy, and when Sebastopol really fell, in September, Buol's desperate urging that Austria should get into the war when there was still time was brushed aside. The Emperor was letting the war take its course, and thinking of other things.

In July, under the influence of Sophie and Cardinal Rauscher, he had completed the chain of reaction by signing his remarkable Concordat with Rome, which surrendered to the Church a considerable part of his sovereignty, giving away the position so hardly won by the reforming Emperor Josef II and clung to even by Emperor Franz. 'It is indeed extraordinary', wrote Seymour, the new British Ambassador, 'that the Emperor of Austria should restore (adding of his own thereto) all that the wisdom of his ancestors has succeeded in wresting from Rome.'[17] In Paris, the Empress Eugénie at her brilliant Court begged Hübner to tell her, not as the Empress but as Eugénie, what on earth had induced his master to subscribe to this 'purely medieval' Concordat.[18] The schools were handed back to the Church; bishops once more could communicate privately with the Vatican; the Church became solely responsible for the regulation of marriage. Why? Franz Josef wanted to please Sophie; since childhood he had been swayed by Rauscher, who was made a Cardinal for pulling off the Concordat; he was glad of an authoritarian ally in his thankless task of disciplining his subjects; with an eye on Napoleon, on Victor Emmanuel, he was glad to have the Pope on his side when it came to Italy. All these things counted; but, more than these, the young man himself in the summer of 1855 was reacting from overstrain. He had been through a punishing time and pulled through. His life with Elizabeth was involving him in emotional tempests quite unforeseen. He had stood up to the Tsar without giving an inch. Pulled violently in opposing directions by his closest advisers, now in the direction of Petersburg, now in the direction of Paris and London, he had kept to what he regarded as the middle way and proved to himself that, inexperienced as he was, he could lead. He had held his own *vis-à-vis* the maritime Powers. Without admitting it to anyone, perhaps not even to himself, this by no means brilliant young man of twenty-five, who had assumed supreme command of the destinies of forty million souls, needed rest. His own need he attributed to others. And his mood is well reflected in a letter to his friend, almost his only friend, Albert of Saxony, a month after the signing of the Concordat:

> Politically now there is a dead calm, and this is for the best. Perhaps it is inhuman, but the longer the gentlemen in the Crimea keep on killing each other, the longer we can count on tranquillity – and this, I believe, is what everybody needs. We have achieved what we were striving for, and we shall hold to it. I am firmly convinced that in the end everyone will be happy to make peace on our terms.[19]

It was in this spirit that Franz Josef, who had worked himself almost to a standstill, now took off more and more time for shooting, his one luxury. In pursuit of the chamois among the mountains round Ischl he was as stubborn as he was in pursuit of the interests of his House. Buol, working up for his final demands for war, and Windischgraetz, wringing his hands over the shattered Russian alliance, both thought the Emperor, of whom much had been expected, was carrying his detachment too far.

Actually Franz Josef's mind was active. Sebastopol had fallen on 11 September and Buol's urging that Austria should join in while there was still time was brushed aside. Three weeks later the Emperor revealed that he was one move ahead of the field. He was worrying now not about the Crimean War but about Austria's position in Germany. 'I think', he wrote to Buol one day, 'that the time is soon coming when we shall have to take in hand the question of revising the Federal Constitution in a Conservative-Monarchical sense to stop the ultra-constitutional and liberal agitators in the German States from getting the upper hand.'[20]

Neutrality, consolidation in the East, alliance with the Vatican, and now bringing the German Federation to heel – all without bloodshed, all in an atmosphere of aloof tranquillity: it was a programme based on false premises. Austria and Franz Josef might feel in need of a rest, but others did not. In January 1856 Alexander agreed to discuss peace and Buol prepared to assume the role played by Metternich in Vienna forty years before. Instead, when the Powers met in Paris on 26 February, he found himself the odd man out; an odd man, moreover, being bullied by an unholy alliance between the Powers who, until a month before, had been at each others' throats. As Orlov the Russian plenipotentiary put it, vast and amiable and shrewd, to Napoleon's representative Walewski: 'We've been tearing away at each other like the honest bulldogs we are. Now we have to work together to make sure that this mongrel Austria gains nothing from our quarrel.'[21]

It was Buol himself who recounted Orlov's words to Seymour, who was greatly struck by this fact. To Clarendon he volunteered the prophecy that 'the insult thus offered to Austria is of that nature which will influence Austrian policy as long as the present Emperor occupies the throne'.

CHAPTER NINE

THE LOSS OF ITALY

The forces of popular nationalism had now broken loose all over Europe. The Crimean War had reactivated the chain reaction, started by the French Revolution, checked by Napoleon's fall, which was to continue into our own day, overwhelming the monarchies which had tried to resist it, or to use it for their own ends, sucking into their vortex countries, such as Japan, on the other side of the world, smashing utterly the lesser States which had built themselves up on the ruins of the monarchies, harnessing even the techniques of international Communism, and finally when Europe itself was beginning to have second thoughts about the validity of nationalism itself, breaching the dams and spreading to Africa, Asia and Latin America. The one man who, from the beginning, would have nothing to do with these new forces was Franz Josef of Austria, and his punishment was absolute. He was to reign for sixty years, 'and those sixty years', Mr A. J. P. Taylor has correctly observed, 'were lived out in the shadow of the Treaty of Paris'.[1] Mr Taylor finds in this matter for reproach. He is scornful because Franz Josef did not ally himself with France and Britain and fight in Galicia in 1854 the war that in the end was fought there in 1914.[2] He is contemptuous too of Schwarzenberg because he was incapable of appealing to German nationalism[3] in the interests of the Habsburgs, as Bismarck was later to do in the interest of the Hohenzollerns. It is not as though Mr Taylor could be called an enthusiast for German nationalism, or, indeed, any nationalism at all. Indeed, this brilliant historian is far closer in spirit to Schwarzenberg, also brilliant, than to any of the nationalist supermen – Louis Napoleon, Bismarck, Andrassy, Cavour, who, between them, aided by messianic Russians and imperial-minded Englishmen, were to provide the dynamic for the near destruction of this planet. Without in the least suggesting that, for example, a return to the Habsburgs would solve any problems at all, it is permissible to maintain that there is at least something to be said for a dynasty that stood out stubbornly and manfully against a thoroughly ugly trend – even though it may be argued that the trend in question was irresistible, was the inevitable outcome, indeed, of past mistakes on the part, among others, of the dynasty in question, and that things had to get very much worse before they could get better; even, again, if the equipment brought to sustain this stand was inadequate, its direction faulty and uncertain, and its management sometimes inept.

The wolves were gathering round, all of them, including the best of them (Cavour), impelled by no other purpose than the aggrandizement of nation States, none of them remotely concerned, as Franz Josef was concerned, however wrongheadedly, with the reasonable and peaceful administration of a supra-national State, none of them, alas, deeply interested in radical social reform. Franz Josef, of course, was far too deeply preoccupied with the maintenance of his dynastic inheritance as such, with his own Imperial dignity, and all the rest. But he was not concerned with grab. For more than sixty years he strove more single-mindedly than any other individual to keep the peace of Europe: obviously his motives were mixed, but at least he tried, and he got little help from anybody else. He is a tragic figure of modern times because, after all this obstinate striving, it was he, in his eighty-fifth year, who signed the paper which launched Armageddon. For Franz Josef, blinkered and unvisionary as he was, and with his pathetic belief in military discipline (not militarism) as the solvent of all evils, was nevertheless nearer in spirit to Adolf Fischhof with his cloudy dreams of international brotherhood than to any of his fellow-rulers.

He had broken with the Holy Alliance, he now had to face an unholy one. After the Peace of Paris, Napoleon was a very big noise indeed. Only three years earlier Buol had been able to write round to the crowned heads of Europe suggesting that it would be unseemly for established monarchs to address the upstart Emperor as *Mon Frère*: *Mon Ami*, he thought, would be better. In the event Buol's dabbling in protocol caused him to burn his fingers badly: Franz Josef himself called Napoleon *Mon Frère* – and so did everybody else except the Tsar, who accepted Buol's suggestion in good faith and felt badly let down by the others. Now all that was over. Napoleon was very firmly the Emperor of the French, victorious over Russia, and looking round for new worlds to conquer. On the other side of the Rhine there was much alarm. Only Bismarck among the Germans guessed correctly – he did not guess; as usual, he knew: 'France is now all velvet paws in Vienna,' he wrote to Gerlach, 'but the claws will soon be showing. His position, his character and his habits will all prevent Louis Napoleon from keeping the peace, and Italy lures him far more than the Rhine.'[4]

This fascinating adventurer was the first modern politician. He was born in 1808, too soon. Bonaparte's nephew, when the Duke of Reichstadt died at Schönbrunn in 1832, he became head of the family and set out on his path of vertiginous intrigue. Four years later he organized his first mutiny, at Strasbourg, and fled to New York when it failed. Four years after that came the landing at Boulogne, followed by arrest and imprisonment at Ham, from which he escaped very quickly. Back in London when the 1848 revolution swept Louis Philippe from the throne, he was over to France again in a flash, and by December of that year was overwhelmingly elected President of the new republic. Just three years later, smiled on by Palmerston, frowned on by everybody else, he carried out his murderous *coup d'état* and was Emperor. Now he was *Mon Frère*, and a powerful and restless one at that.

He arrived with a vaulting and elaborate set of ideas of the kind which were then revolutionary, but soon became 'modern' and contrived to remain so for something like a century, until, in 1949, the Soviet Union announced that she too had made an atom bomb. He believed that his glorious uncle had fallen only because he rode roughshod over national susceptibilities. A nationalist himself and a conspirator by nature and training, he believed in nationalism for others too and felt at home with conspirators of all nations. He believed passionately in ideas and had many good ones; but he also believed in power, which made him kin with Franz Josef. He established free trade in the teeth of his own industrialists because he thought it belonged to the future; he pushed through the Suez Canal; he adored railways and vast exhibitions; he was full of plans for pensions and profit-sharing schemes. He saw farther into the true nature of the nineteenth century than anybody except Bismarck. The difference between the two men was that Bismarck was contemptuous of that nature, as of most other things, and was content to harness it as and when required to his own special purpose, which was the aggrandizement of Prussia, while Napoleon sought to identify himself with the spirit of the age and then dominate it. But he did not see quite deep enough. 'A Government can safely break the law', he said, 'and even suppress liberty, but it will soon perish if it does not take the lead in the great causes of civilization; and, until this simple philosophical reason for its downfall is understood, it is called fate.'[5] He missed the point, which Franz Josef, infinitely less imaginative, understood: that civilization is law. He had to keep moving, and so he fell: Franz Josef who tried not to move also fell. Bismarck, who never moved at all until he knew precisely where he was going, also fell. Where is the moral?

Napoleon's obsession with nationalism and national unity had already made itself felt *vis-à-vis* Russia: he wanted to liberate the Poles and give them self-determination, come what might, and was only blocked by Austria and Prussia. He was to return to this idea at a later date; but, meanwhile, he went to very considerable lengths to reach an understanding with a Russia which believed only in Russia. His immediate interest lay, as Bismarck knew, in Italy, and his motives here, as everywhere, were very mixed indeed. He was bound to do everything in his power to assist Italian nationalism. But one of the foes of Italian nationalism was the Papacy, and the Papal States owed their very existence to the armed might not only of Austria but also of France. In his conspiratorial days, as a member of the Carbonari, he had sworn to make the cause of freedom his own. But that cause, for the new Emperor of the French, had also become a means towards domination of the peninsula and breaking the power of Austria.

At first, as Bismarck observed, he went slowly. He had to woo Russia and reassure Prussia. England, he knew, viewed with sympathy the Italian liberation movement; but popular sentiment was on the side of Mazzini, the dedicated republican, and the English would view with distrust a violent access of French influence in the Mediterranean. The running was left to Cavour.

2

This politician of genius had set himself to gamble for the highest stakes on behalf of his master, Victor Emmanuel. He played with a skill and deviousness and attack, his rear constantly uncovered, more reminiscent of the behaviour of the great oil kings half a century later than of Bismarck, the other political genius of his age. Bismarck whenever possible led from strength: he gambled only when he had to, and even then he managed to conceal what he was doing. Thus, when in 1863 he staked everything on keeping Frederick William away from the Frankfurt assembly of German princes, grandly convened by Franz Josef, he was so overcome with emotion that, his task accomplished, he tore off the door-handle as he closed the door behind him and burst into tears. Cavour was leading all the time from weakness, gambling again and again for all the world to see; but he never pulled off door-handles, he never burst into tears. At the most critical moments, until after Villafranca when he thought everything was lost and raved at his king for losing it, he looked what he was: the small landowner who discovered in himself late in life a genius first for journalism, then for practical politics, which he put at the service of an inflammatory patriotism.

He became Prime Minister in 1852, and from then on devoted himself to a single end, the breaking of Austrian rule in Italy, which seemed to have been secured for ever by Radetzky's defeat of Charles Albert at Novara in 1849. It was the Crimean War which gave him his first chance, an outside chance, and he took it in the teeth of very strong opposition. What he had hoped for was Austria's entry into the war on the side of Russia. Franz Josef dashed that hope. He then undertook the impossibly bold risk of bringing Piedmont itself into the war on the side of Britain and France. Turin was naturally aghast at this manoeuvre, which entailed the dispatch of a brigade of Piedmontese troops to the notorious Crimean front on the other side of Europe and thus wantonly embroiling a tiny, weak State, with troubles enough of its own, in a quarrel with which it had nothing at all to do. What were they fighting for? It was not even as though Austria, their only foe, was on the other side. Austria was close and disengaged and a constant threat. Only a madman would go out of his way to weaken the country in face of that threat.

Perhaps Cavour was a madman, but only in the sense that all fanatics are mad. He had embarked on a game of power politics, in which he shone as few have shone before or since, without an atom of power behind him. Only by putting the Western allies under a moral obligation could he hope to get Piedmont a seat in the council chamber where peace would one day be concluded. And only from this point of vantage could he put the condition of Italy formally and effectively on the European agenda.

He succeeded in precisely this: a tight little man in drab clothes, a little man with a brain like a razor, a little man with something of the look of an intellectualized Franz Schubert, sat in Turin, sent 15,000 of his bewildered fellow-countrymen on a dreadful journey to be shot at by Russians who had never heard of them and to die of cholera — and reaped the reward of their sacrifice.

Austria had kept two-thirds of the Russian armies tied down, thus effectively preventing Nicholas from throwing the British and French into the sea; but no Austrian troops had fought, and Austria was detested. The Piedmont contingent had made not the slightest difference to the outcome of the war, but Piedmont had become a fighting ally, and was treated as such. Buol not only had the bitterness of being cold-shouldered by both sides in the Paris Congress, he had also the humiliation of sitting at the same table with the spokesman of an insignificant State who was there for one purpose only: to make propaganda against Austria.

The skill and moderation and subtlety with which Cavour carried out his self-appointed task could still serve as a model for the leaders of small countries labouring under threats or direct oppression from their great neighbours and endeavouring to win support from a major Power without first boring, then exasperating, it by demanding too much too quickly. With a half sheet of notes, relying on his own wits, he spoke to the point always and always very briefly. He had already made his personal impact on the French and the English when he had persuaded his master, who wanted only to be fighting with his army, to make State visits to Paris and London. His aim had been to make the Sardinian monarchy respectable, to present Victor Emmanuel to the Western world as the proper champion of Italian liberation, staunch and conservative, as opposed to the inflammable revolutionary gang round Mazzini. As D'Azeglio himself pointed out, for Austria to dub Italian aspirations towards political reforms revolutionary was simply the old trick of 'making odious those whom you despoil'.[6] The Italians were no more revolutionaries than Alfred the Great or William the Silent. Victor Emmanuel was not a good advertisement. 'His Majesty seems to be frightful in person,' wrote Greville in his diary, 'but a great, strong, burly, athletic man, brusque in his manners, unrefined in his conversation, very loose in his conduct, and very eccentric in habits. When he was at Paris his talk in society amused or terrified everybody, but here he seems to have been more guarded.'[7] Cavour was extremely apprehensive about the effect of this prodigy on Queen Victoria; but he need not have worried. Malmesbury wrote in his memoirs: 'The King of Sardinia, who is here, is as vulgar and coarse as possible. He said to the Empress [Eugénie] "*On me dit que les danseuses françaises ne portent pas de caleçons. Si c'est comme cela, ce sera pour moi le paradis terrestre.*"'[8] But the tiny Queen of England had a stronger stomach than many of her Ministers and courtiers and got on splendidly with the Sardinian monster. When she conferred the Garter on him it was clear that he had arrived. On their way back to Turin, Cavour and his master stopped for one more night at Paris, and it was then that Louis Napoleon sealed their triumph: 'Write confidentially to Walewski', he said to Cavour, 'what you think I might do for Piedmont and for Italy.'

The great enemy was Austria, yet, paradoxically, life in Lombardy and Venetia, under direct Austrian rule, was materially far better and spiritually infinitely less corrupt than elsewhere. The Lombards and the Venetians may have had to pay the same taxes as any other Habsburg subjects, but they paid far less than their brothers in other parts of Italy and they enjoyed, or could have enjoyed, the benefits of an administration of very considerable efficiency and remarkable honesty. But Lombardy and Venetia were not at all grateful for the wonderful order imposed upon them by foreigners. And the Austrians themselves were frightened enough of the Italians, especially after 1848, to react fairly savagely, even for those days, to all manifestations of revolt, however trivial and absurd. They were, in effect, sent to Coventry – not so much by the common people as by the well-born, whom they sought conscientiously to woo. Radetzky, unlike his one-time lieutenant, Haynau, was not a cruel man; but he was an inflexible disciplinarian, and his ideas about the enforcement of discipline were blunt and harsh. There were floggings and crippling fines; and sometimes in the enforcement of fines there was perceptible a streak of what came in later years to be recognized as high Teutonic hysteria. This earned for Austria the hatred not only of the Italians but of the Hungarians and others too. It is not enough to say that these were the excesses of individual commanders: the same weakness of not knowing where to stop, the lack of that instinct which tells people who may be in many ways inferior where to draw a line and the importance of sticking to that line, has already been noticed in Schwarzenberg himself, and in Buol; it will reappear and reappear until it makes its last appearance in this narrative (but not in history) with the ultimatum of July 1914 to Serbia.

The lower orders, above all the peasants, but also to a lesser degree the artisans in the towns, were not easily moved to hatred of Austria: their prosperity was great; they benefited directly from the Austrian irrigation schemes and from the inclusion of their wonderfully fertile holdings in the rich Po valley within the Imperial economy. It was from the nobility and the urban intelligentsia, looking to Turin for succour, that the most stubborn opposition came, and the violent actions against them, as in Brescia, where actresses were publicly flogged for singing patriotic songs (but in fact the Brescians had massacred Austrian wounded in hospital), and in Milan where the bloody revolt of 1853 was put down with bloody severity, did not break their spirit. The sequestration of the properties of all those Venetians and Lombards who could be charged with anything remotely resembling conspiratorial activity against the régime – and this included nothing more heinous than a preference for living in Piedmont rather than in Lombardy or Venetia under Austrian rule – achieved nothing but the forging of one more weapon for Cavour. By the time it began to dawn on Franz Josef that the system would not work, it was too late to change it.

In the winter of 1856–7, with the Crimean War out of the way, he decided to make a personal appearance with his bride. Considering the mood in Venice and Milan it was a brave action, but it achieved nothing at all. First in Venice, then in Milan, the streets and squares were packed with citizenry come to stare at the Imperial progress. The handsome young Emperor in the bloom of his youth, the ravishing apparition of Elizabeth at his side, the granting of amnesties to political prisoners – all this could have marked a turning-point; but too much had happened. The army and the police were ready to cope with any trouble, but the one thing they could do nothing about was the utter silence of the vast crowds, who simply gazed. The brilliant receptions were virtually boycotted by the leading families, and those who did turn up were hissed by the crowds. In Venice, before the visit was over, the mood of the people began to soften: it was hard to go on hating Elizabeth. But the nobility still stayed away. And the performance was repeated everywhere they went. Milan was worse than Venice. There was a gala night at La Scala, and the Austrian authorities were determined at all costs that the vast auditorium should be filled. Fearing that half the boxes would be demonstratively empty, they demanded in advance to be informed by subscribers whether they proposed to be present or not: unused boxes were to be filled by Austrian officials and their wives, dressed up for the occasion. But it did not work: the great families said yes, they would be using their boxes – and when the night came they sent their servants in their place.[9] One of the by-products of this dreadful visit was its effect on poor Elizabeth, brought up in the amiable, free-and-easy atmosphere of the Bavarian Court: she had done nothing wrong, she asked only to be loved. It was a blow in the face to her. These easy-going, laughter-loving Italians hated in a way she had never before encountered. And her they hated because she was, without asking for it, the first lady at a Court she had come herself to hate.

It was shortly after this visit that Franz Josef decided to try benevolent civilian rule instead of military dictatorship. Radetzky resigned, and in his place went out Franz Josef's amiable, foolish, vain, warm-hearted younger brother, Maximilian. But that did not work either. Under Maximilian the whole system of rule was changed; but it was not enough. As one Italian patriot exclaimed: 'We don't want the Austrians to turn humanitarian; we want them to get out!'

Meanwhile, in Turin, Cavour watched these activities no less anxiously than he had three years earlier watched Austria's manoeuvres during the Crimean War. He rejoiced over the implacable bearing of his fellow-countrymen in Lombardy, schemed to sustain it and fortify it, and developed his plans for war. The first Italian patriot since Machiavelli to see his direction clearly, he showed himself a consummate master of Machiavellian intrigue, in no way inferior to his master in calculated ruthlessness. He had for some time decided to stake everything on Napoleon, even though the French Foreign Minister, Walewski, detested him, and even though the price for Napoleon's support might be high. While Napoleon, inscrutable as only a vacillating character with no principles knows how to be inscrutable, was ripening, Cavour set about the task of making Piedmont fit to fight. The burden he placed on his country's economy was immense. Everything was directed to one end, a fight to the finish between a tiny, parvenu State in the top left-hand corner of Italy and the colossal military machine of Austrian imperialism. Cavour stood to lose both ways: if war came and Piedmont was once more defeated, as she had been by Radetzky fighting with his hands tied behind his back in 1849, that was the end. It would also be the end in bankruptcy, if war did not come. Everything depended upon Napoleon, and a less dependable character than his it was impossible to imagine.

Everything, also, depended on Austria. Cavour, rightly as it turned out, was convinced that he could bring about war, with Austria as the technical aggressor, if only he could win Napoleon's pledged support. Austria knew this and still fell into the most elementary of traps with her eyes wide open. As early as December 1858, Odo Russell, then

British Minister in Rome, had a long conversation with Cavour in Turin. According to Russell, the following exchange took place:

> On my observing that Austria had only to play a waiting game to exhaust the already heavily taxed military resources of Piedmont, and that a declaration of war by Piedmont would enlist the sympathies of Europe for Austria rather than for Italy, he replied that he fully agreed with me; but that if, on the contrary, Austria declared war on Piedmont, then public opinion would side with Italy and support the cause of the weak and oppressed against the strong. On my saying that Austria was scarcely capable of committing so egregious a mistake, Cavour replied, 'But I shall *force her* to declare war against us.' I confess I felt incredulous, but asked when he expected to accomplish so great a wonder of diplomacy. 'About the first week in May', was his reply.[10]

3

In the event the extraordinary little man pulled it off by the last week in April, but it was a close-run thing. He had three obstacles to overcome: the hesitations of his own political colleagues; the vacillations of Napoleon; the almost passionate determination of the London government to prevent the outbreak of war. It was this last obstacle, at first the least considered, which all but defeated him in the end. British diplomacy during 1858 and the early part of 1859, though not brilliantly executed, formed a strange and insufficiently remembered chapter in the history of peace-making. England wanted peace of course mainly because any disturbance anywhere was liable to upset her trade, but also because she needed a period of European tranquillity in which she might recover from the strains of the war in the Crimea and the Indian Mutiny. The fact remained, she wanted peace, not war – just, for example, as Austria wanted peace for the sake of preserving the existing order. And, on top of this, there was a growing conviction in England, as well as elsewhere in Europe, that war was a bad thing. England worked very hard to prevent it. Disraeli thought she could in fact have prevented it. Writing in the 1860s he said:

> My opinion is that, even if Lord Cowley had been our Ambassador at Vienna, certainly if Lord Stratford or Sir Henry Bulwer had been there, there would have been no war. There wanted the unceasing vigilance of a commanding character to baffle the intrigues of a

miserable camarilla. Our Ambassador, Lord [*sic*] Loftus, was not fit to be resident at a third-rate German Court, and was quite despised and disregarded by that of Vienna. He was a pompous nincompoop, and of all Lord Malmesbury's appointments, the worst; and that is saying a good deal.[11]

Lord Cowley, Britain's Ambassador to the Court of Louis Napoleon, in fact bore the brunt of the whole affair. A modest, lucid, shrewd, unshowy man, a Wellesley, he had done so well at the Paris Congress that he had been rewarded with an earldom. He knew the mind of the French Emperor as well as anyone; he could speak bluntly without the least trace of offensiveness, and was respected everywhere. His only defect was a streak of that optimism which is inseparable from gentle sanity: he was not at home with megalomania, paranoia, calculated duplicity, vanity and violence. In Louis Napoleon he encountered all these qualities and, shrewd as he was, found it impossible always to disbelieve the Emperor's warm assurances. Sent to Vienna, when things were getting out of hand, to suggest a conference to settle the Italian dispute, he arrived when Franz Josef was about to dig in his hooves, eyes rolling and ears laid back, and found himself in a welter of intrigue.

By that time the real damage had been done. In March 1858 Count Orsini had been executed in Paris after his bomb attempt on Napoleon and Eugénie. This affair, and particularly Orsini's testament characterizing Napoleon, the ex-revolutionary and carbonari, as the incarnation of the spirit of reaction and therefore as the chief obstacle to the liberation of Italy, had a traumatic effect on the Emperor. The general impression was that he was afraid for his life. To quote Disraeli again:

> Ever since the Orsini business he has been, more or less, fitful and moody, and brooding over Italy. The letter of Orsini produced a great effect on him. He is alarmed for his life. Having himself belonged to the Carbonari Society, he knows that he is never safe while they continue to look upon him as a renegade. He is resolved, therefore, 'to do something for Italy'.[12]

This, the general view, was an over-simplification. Napoleon was not a physical coward. But there is no doubt that Orsini's reproaches brought out in him the romantic and reminded him of his days of reckless endeavour. From Cavour's point of view, he was beginning to ripen. A month after the attempt he had said to Della Rocca: 'Say

to M. de Cavour that we shall certainly come to an understanding.'
In May, through an intermediary, came a secret invitation to Cavour
to meet Napoleon at Plombières in the Vosges, near the frontier
between France and Savoy. In July the meeting took place. Napoleon
kept it, as so many things, from his own Foreign Minister; and a
touch of comedy was introduced when Walewski, full of his own self-
importance, sent a confidential message to his master warning him
that Cavour had arrived at Plombières and was up to no good. On
setting out for the meeting Cavour had written to La Marmora: 'Pray
Heaven so to inspire me that I shall not behave like a blockhead in
this supreme moment.[13]'

He need not have worried. Napoleon himself set the ball rolling by
announcing that he had decided to give his full support to Piedmont
in a war with Austria, provided that the war was undertaken for a
non-revolutionary cause and could be justified in the eyes of the
world.

Cavour had won the day without saying a word. But the next
step, to be taken sooner than he had foreseen, extended even his
wits to the limit: war being determined, what would do for a pretext?
It was not so easy to provoke into an act of aggression a country
which had nothing to gain from war. Cavour cast about wildly; for
once he was on the edge of being rattled. But Napoleon sustained
him. And in the end he hit on the splendid idea of arranging that the
oppressed subjects of the Duke of Modena should petition Victor
Emmanuel to take them under his protection: the King would refuse,
but he would send a warning to the Duke suggesting that it was
time he reformed his Duchy; the Duke, assured of support from
Vienna, would reply with contumely; the King would then have
no other course open to him but to send his army in; Austria would
rush to succour the miserable Francis; Napoleon would come to the
aid of Piedmont. And, because Francis was universally detested and
despised, the rest of the world, above all England, would applaud.
When it was all over, with Austria driven out of Italy, there would
be a grand rearrangement. Victor Emmanuel's House of Savoy
would unite Piedmont with Lombardy, Venetia, the Romagna and
the Legations in a Kingdom of Upper Italy. A Kingdom of Central
Italy would be set up under the Duchy of Parma, to include Tuscany
and the Papal possessions outside Rome; the Pope would still be
master of Rome and offered the Presidency of the Italian Federation;
as for the Two Sicilies – if Bomba went, they might go to Murat,

but time would tell. Napoleon's personal reward was to be Nice and Savoy.

The technical details of this conspiratorial attempt to remake the map of Europe were soon settled. The whole operation was based on the perfectly correct assumption that England, Prussia and Russia would remain neutral. Russia had already promised to allow Napoleon a free hand in Italy; Prussia would be only too pleased to see Austria hurt; England notoriously disapproved of the oppressive régimes in Italy. The prospect was fair, and Cavour went home to wait: his only real worry was Napoleon's last demand – that Princess Clotilde, Victor Emmanuel's eldest daughter, just fifteen, should be betrothed to Napoleon's notorious cousin, Plon-Plon. Even a man with Victor Emmanuel's record might be expected to draw the line at that.

Napoleon was right about England's neutrality; but he was wrong in believing that the liberation of Italy would prove a popular cause in London. In the autumn of 1858 Queen Victoria personally told Cowley to make it clear to Napoleon that England would frown on such a war of liberation. In December, to Malmesbury, she showed what was in her mind: 'If he makes war in Italy it must in all probability lead to war with Germany, and, if with Germany, will embrace Belgium, and, if so, according to our guarantees, draw us into the quarrel, and France may thus have the whole of Europe against her as in 1814 and 1815.'[14] This comprehensive misreading of the European situation was inspired by Uncle Leopold in Brussels, who was trembling for Belgium's safety: nevertheless, it made England all the more determined to keep the peace. Napoleon, too, by that time, appeared to be drifting with the tide. He was telling Hübner that it was out of the question that he should go to war, and threw in disparaging remarks about Cavour for good measure. As the year closed there was a general mood of relaxation. Austria saw her ties with England growing closer every day and felt sure that in the event of war she could count on Prussia and the rest of Germany. Napoleon temporized. Cavour began to feel abandoned and alone.

Then on 1 January 1859, Napoleon made his cataclysmic remark. At his New Year's Day reception he stopped for a moment, all affability, to chat to Hübner: 'I am sorry', he said, 'that our relations are not so good as I wish they were, but I beg you to write to Vienna that my personal sentiments for your Emperor are unchanged.'[15] It was a remark for all who stood round to hear. A few hours earlier in

Vienna, on New Year's Eve, the great Finance Minister Bruck had been looking back over his Sisyphean labours. At last, he was convinced, he had succeeded in making the Empire solvent. Relaxing, he said to his friend, Richter: 'Richter, I really believe that my mission has been accomplished, and now I can retire.'[16] But within a matter of hours after Napoleon had spoken Bruck's work was totally undone. All over Europe the Stock Exchanges slumped; in particular, there was a headlong flight from Austrian bonds. Bruck, far from retiring, was back in the arena trying in vain to raise a loan in London. Before the year was out he was dead by his own hand. In the words of Professor Benedikt, 'the war was lost before it started'.[17] Cavour was once more cock-a-hoop. On 29 January he could write: 'I believe that "the eventualities of the future" will not keep us waiting long. For we have put Austria in an impasse from which she cannot escape without firing off cannon.'[18] Before the month was out poor little Clotilde, 'true to the sense of duty which stamped the House of Savoy', had agreed to marry Prince Napoleon.

Meanwhile English diplomacy had started up in earnest. Everywhere there was feverish activity: only Austria seemed paralysed, dazed, inert like a sacrificial bull round whose vast flanks and shoulders an endless, insubstantial web of intrigue was being woven. Buol compulsively, inventively, as usual, assisted all concerned in the job of completing the net which he ought to have been tearing to ribbons. At no time did he waver in his perfectly unfounded conviction that in the last resort he could count on Germany and Prussia. At one and the same time he hamstrung the efforts of the soldiers to put the Austrian army in Italy into fighting trim by assuring the Emperor that there would be no war, while leaving undone every action which he might have taken to avert war: he did nothing effective to bind England more closely to Austria, to make up his quarrel with Russia whose benevolent neutrality Napoleon had secured, to come to a working arrangement with Prussia based on a recognition of the special position of Berlin, or to exploit Napoleon's anxieties about his projected enterprise. All the criticism wrongly directed at Vienna for its Crimean policy was fully deserved by Buol for his asinine behaviour in 1859.

Poor Cowley was sent back again to warn Napoleon a second time. Malmesbury himself tackled Buol in a most conciliatory manner, with suggestions of ways and means by which Austria could put herself in a strong moral position, then begged the Tsar to co-operate in preserving peace, then warned Cavour, whom he persistently under-estimated, regarding him as a simple adventurer in the service of a boor. Buol looked down his nose, inviting the English Prime Minister to address himself to Paris and Turin if he wished 'to preach peace'; Cavour replied that England was largely responsible for the present situation by raising Italian hopes which she had done nothing to fulfil. As for the Russian Tsar, he had no burning desire to save Austria from trouble, but if peace was to be saved he saw no reason why he, not Malmesbury, should not be the saviour. On 9 March he proposed a European Congress to thrash out the Austro-Italian and other problems, and England agreed to support this project.

Napoleon himself had not been inactive in a backstairs way. He was behind the Russian move; and on 5 March his own journal, *Le Moniteur* published the following declaration: 'The Emperor has promised the King of Sardinia to defend him against every aggressive act on the part of Austria: he has promised nothing more, and we know that he will keep his word.' The Stock Exchanges soared, and Hübner wrote in his diary: 'This is a terrible slap in the face for Napoleon and M. Cavour.'[19] Three days later Victor Emmanuel wrote to Napoleon saying that if he deserted Piedmont at this stage he, the King, would be forced to abdicate. On 29 March, in desperation, Cavour journeyed to Paris to tell Napoleon that if he went back on his pledged word he, Cavour, would publish the secret agreement signed between him and Napoleon. Napoleon, faced with war or dishonour, took to his bed, leaving Walewski to try to frighten Cavour.

Almost everything in these last days had depended on Buol. Cowley, indefatigable, and radiating commonsense, had been sent by Queen Victoria on a quasi-unofficial mission to Vienna. Everything hung, he was convinced, on Buol's acceptance of the Russian plan (but Buol refused to sit if Cavour was invited to the Congress) and on acceptance by all concerned of the principle of general disarmament (but Buol refused to disarm until Piedmont had first disarmed herself). There is a widespread belief that nineteenth-century diplomacy was heartless, frivolous and blind. As a corrective to this belief, I include in the appendices a letter from Cowley to Buol, written on 19 March after Cowley's return to Paris. It was one of several, marked by a sincerity and candour, a gentleness and a horror of war and its consequences, which speak for themselves.

But Buol was not to be moved. Although Napoleon accepted 'in principle' the general disarmament plan, Buol continued to insist that Piedmont must disarm first. There was nothing more to be done. 'England', wrote Malmesbury to Cowley, 'cannot go on running from one to another like an old aunt trying to make up family squabbles, and when I wind up it will be to put the saddle on the right horse. The papers will show that you and I have done our best to prevent a war, and to obtain a Congress which nobody but Prussia and ourselves ever intended to take place.'[20] On 12 April Buol declared in a dispatch to London that Piedmont had taken up a position of 'permanent aggression' against Austria and that Austria was about to demand her immediate disarmament. In reply Malmesbury stated that England would disapprove of any ultimatum which did not indicate that Austria herself had agreed to the principle of general disarmament. But it made no difference. On 19 April the ultimatum was sent. It arrived in Turin on the 26th and Cavour was beside himself with joy.

A little legend has grown up that this ultimatum was finally dispatched unknown to Buol himself by the Emperor's Military Council. Buol himself encouraged this belief, which had no foundation. The decision was taken at a full Ministerial Council, at which Buol was present, himself insisting on an ultimatum to Turin with a three-day limit, and at the same time opposing the wish of the Chief-of-Staff, Hess, to mobilize the whole army, 600,000 strong, part of which was to be sent to the Rhine immediately to meet all contingencies there.[21] It had been Buol's operation from beginning to end; and to the very end – according to Kempen the police chief, who attended the fatal ministerial conference – he managed to convince himself, and did his best to convince others, that Prussia and England would come in on Austria's side. That was on 19 April. Malmesbury's specific warning was dated 14 April. Buol had no excuse either for misunderstanding the English position or for allowing the Emperor to send his ultimatum without first informing Prussia, much less consulting her. Within a day or two he was gently dismissed and the war machine took over.

The stage was now set for what might have become a general conflagration and what by all reasonable calculation should have been at least a decisive conflict between Austria and France, a fight to the finish between immense continental armies of the most up-to-date kind, each led in the field by an Emperor. The war started

formally on 26 April with Cavour's rejection of the Austrian ultimatum. By 11 July it was all over. Neither side had won an overwhelming victory. At Magenta the Austrians had virtually won an
important battle, then suddenly decided that they had lost it and
ordered a swift withdrawal. At Solferino they certainly lost the day;
but they still held the Quadrilateral and could have stayed there
indefinitely. Both Emperors, however, men who for years had
dreamed of the moment when they should lead their own armies in
the field, were so shaken by the spectacle of wholesale carnage and
so apprehensive for their different reasons as to what might happen
next, that they embraced with an eagerness scarcely concealed and
called it a day. Cavour, stricken with betrayal, nearly had a fit.
The 138,000 French and Piedmontese had faced 129,000 Austrians
at Solferino. Nobody at headquarters had the least idea of how to
handle these vast numbers. But they managed to clash, and at the
end of the day there were nearly 40,000 dead and wounded on the
field. Lombardy was gained for Victor Emmanuel, but not Venetia.
Napoleon got Nice and the Savoy. But the main fruit of this massive
sacrifice was the formation of the Red Cross by a young Swiss
tourist, Henri Dunant, who found himself near Solferino when the
battle was being fought, did what he could for days to succour the
wounded, and was so shocked by the inadequacy of the medical
services on both sides that he wrote a book of his impressions which
moved the world even more radically than the revelations of *The
Times* and Florence Nightingale, five years earlier. This was not,
however, the purpose for which the war was fought.

4

It was an astonishing campaign. Armies had grown beyond the
capacity of conventionally trained general officers to handle them.

Neither the French nor the Austrian army was ready, in spite of
the fact that both sides had been talking of war for months. In the
event, however, the French moved faster than the Austrians, who
had been expected to cross the Ticino from Lombardy into Piedmont
the moment war was declared and, in overwhelming strength, to
move up from Pavia to Alessandria or Casale, a march of forty miles,
covering the approaches to Turin. Until Napoleon could get his
troops and guns across the Mont Cénis Pass, or disembarked at
Genoa, there was nothing between the Austrian host and Turin but

the Piedmontese standing alone. The exact size of Cavour's army in the field is still uncertain; but the best estimate is some 60,000 men, with 130 guns, and, in addition, Garibaldi and 3,000 of his guerrillas. It should have been a simple task for a properly led and organized Austrian army of appropriate size to have taken most of Lombardy and shattered the Piedmontese before Napoleon could come to their help. Napoleon had an army of 151,000 troops, with 300 guns, to move across the Alps, or by sea from Toulon and Marseilles to Genoa. It took some time. It was not until 12 May that Napoleon himself proudly steamed into Genoa harbour in his Imperial yacht, *La Reine Hortense*, announced that he had come to liberate Italy 'from the Alps to the Adriatic', and was accorded a reception like a Roman Triumph. It was not until 21 May that the great army was finally on the move to join forces with the Piedmontese who, after over three weeks of dreadful suspense, found themselves still unscathed. What had the Austrians been doing?

The legend puts the blame for their lack of offensive spirit squarely and exclusively on the Imperial Commander-in-Chief, Field-Marshal Gyulai. But the legend over-simplifies.

Certainly Gyulai was no ball of fire. He was a man of monumental crassness, blessed with the calm which so often goes with stupidity. He should never have been Commander-in-Chief, and he knew it himself and said so.[22] One of Grünne's peacetime nominees, he took charge of the army in Italy by virtue of seniority, and begged to be excused: he had never led an army in the field and he had scarcely more practical experience of warfare than Grünne himself. The obvious choice was old Field-Marshal Hess, at seventy-two a veteran of many campaigns, who had been the brains behind Radetzky's brilliant Italian victories: Radetzky himself freely acknowledged this, but it was not officially recognized. Hess was silent and shy and caught up entirely by the serious problems of his profession. He thought so deeply that, in military conferences, he gave an impression of hesitancy when asked for his views. He did not at all fit in with the needs of the Court in peacetime, with Grünne's parade-ground army, with, above all, the atmosphere of *pretence* which enshrouded the whole vast military machine. So Gyulai it was. Whether Gyulai, assisted by his most able Chief-of-Staff, Kuhn, would have done any better with a properly trained, equipped and mustered army it is impossible to say. Probably not. He had what came to be known just eighty years later as the Maginot mentality: his Maginot Line was the Quadrilateral, which had served Radetzky as a temporary *Lager* and a bridgehead. For Gyulai the very existence of this superb complex of fortifications was his undoing: it was there for him to fall back on, and he could think of nothing else.

But, in fairness to this simple soldier, there are other things to be said. In the first place the political and diplomatic confusion was such that there was still much loose talk about imminent support from England, Germany and Prussia; there were also daily rumours that Franz Josef himself was coming out to take command. Gyulai, in Lombardy, was looking over his shoulder, waiting for news. His hesitancies, his delayed crossing of the Ticino, his belated penetration into Piedmont, followed by retirement, were indeed entirely incomprehensible to the Piedmontese and Europe as a whole because it was assumed that he had under command an overwhelming force. Actually he had five corps and a cavalry division, all markedly under strength, many badly equipped – not more than 100,000 men.[23] And his great concern was to keep his army in being. To have destroyed the Piedmontese, with the French coming in at the rate of at least 5,000 a day, would have called not merely for competence but for the aggressive self-confidence found only as a rule in fools or the few great captains. Senior soldiers and sailors, like senior politicians, are unfortunate in their professions: they are the only professions in which the leaders of the day are expected by the public to be men of superlative quality. The odds against a soldier or a politician being a genius are quite as high as the odds against a musician or a writer being one: nobody complains when a century goes by without throwing up a Mozart or a Shakespeare; everybody, almost without exception, complains when a generation goes by without throwing up a Disraeli or a Wellington, to say nothing of a Bismarck or a Napoleon, and this in full understanding of the sort of men Napoleon and Bismarck were. Gyulai was not a Napoleon; he was not a Wellington. He was a run-of-the-mill general officer whose destiny it was to arrive at the top at a critical conjuncture in his country's history. His country needed a man who could coolly and ruthlessly open an offensive and brilliantly deploy 100,000 men for the destruction of 60,000, far from his base, while laying himself open to being caught on the wrong foot by 150,000 Frenchmen thirsting for glory. The idea never entered his head. He had been placed in command of the Italian front, as he saw it, to defend his Emperor against the French. From the beginning he felt that he had been let down by the politicians and should have been given the opportunity to strike some weeks earlier (then the French would have been held up by the snow on the passes).[24] On 25 April, two days before war was declared, he had told the Emperor that it was too late to knock out the Piedmontese before the French arrived, that he would fight a holding campaign until large reinforcements arrived, always ready meanwhile to profit by any mistakes the enemy might make, and firmly guaranteeing to keep him out of Lombardy. This was good run-of-the-mill soldierly stuff, and if it was not what was required in Vienna he should have been removed there and then. The story of Grünne's retort to Gyulai when the latter pleaded his unfitness – 'What that old ass Radetzky could get away with, you surely can!' – may or may not be true, but it expressed truly enough the mood in Vienna.

It was the Emperor's fault. He was nearly thirty now, and he had been reigning for nearly ten years, long enough to have found out the truth about men like Buol and Grünne, long enough, more importantly still, to have discovered that men counted and that there were other and better men than these. He had engaged himself personally in the long-drawn-out duel with the Russian Tsar five years earlier, partly because he stood in a special relationship with Nicholas, but still more because he could address the Tsar as a dynastic equal. But when it came to dealing with Napoleon there was no personal contact, and the pretensions of the House of Savoy were so far beneath his notice that it had been all too easy for him to leave the matter to Buol. This was understandable: where he failed, disastrously, was in not making a personal and constructive approach to Prussia: he should have known after Olmütz that he must either reckon with the perpetual enmity of Prussia or else put out all his skill to woo her. But although at the end he sent the Archduke Albrecht to Berlin to plead for dynastic solidarity, he seems to have taken it quite for granted that with Austria in dire straits the Prussians would be only too pleased to let bygones be bygones and show that they knew their place as loyal and subordinate allies. Buol, of course, kept on telling Franz Josef that this was so, but Franz Josef should have known better. In 1859 he touched his lowest point as Emperor: he was that most hopeless thing, an autocrat who was not really governing. He was frightened, too. More and more he found himself dissatisfied and apprehensive about the activities of Buol: in these critical days he was drawn back to Metternich, begging inarticulately for light.[25] But Metternich was old and palsied; he could still make phrases, but he could do nothing else. As far back as 1854 Metternich could write of Buol: 'This man is incapable of visualizing the consequences of his actions. He sees what is under his nose, but not an inch further.' But he could not, or would not, make the Emperor see this, until the Emperor, too late, saw it for himself.

More particularly the Emperor's fault was the state of the army. He was supreme Commander-in-Chief; he had effectively abolished the War Ministry; he had assumed full responsibility, and he had chosen as his right-hand Count Grünne. After ten years of this régime the army was in a deplorable state. The quartermasters were corrupt and inefficient; the conscripts were ill-trained; the field officers owed their ranks to birth or wealth; the company officers were grossly underpaid ('I can get all the subalterns I need for twenty-four gulden a month!' said Grünne, when it was pointed out to him that junior officers could hardly keep body and soul together on that pay); the armament was antiquated. The army, selected elements of it, looked splendid on parade – and the Emperor saw it only on parade. The uniforms were magnificent, and the Emperor doted on uniforms. Lord Cardigan's 'Cherrypickers' were out-glittered by the hussars with their green jackets, their scarlet shakos, yellow corded, with a black and yellow feather, their red breeches with a broken yellow stripe, their green cloaks, bordered with black fur, their red saddle-cloths with black, white and yellow piping: the officers had royal blue tunics with yellow frogs. The grenadiers with their white tunics, the officers with golden sashes; the Uhlans with their green coats and red waistcoats; Radetzky's corps of engineers with their pale blue tailcoats, cocked-hats and yellow sashes; the gunners with their cinnamon tailcoats and white breeches; the light blue Jaeger tunics; the fire on the helmets of the dragoons and the cuirassiers, both with shining breastplates . . . all this made an intoxicating display on the surface.[26]

Franz Josef was dazzled by numbers, too. In 1854, in a letter to his mother, he gloried in Austria as a land 'where in a single year 200,000 recruits can be raised without fuss'.[27] And, indeed, on paper, this was so. The mobilization strength of the army was close on 800,000 men. The standing army consisted of four armies, each of three corps, each of some 20,000 men. The reservists had all done eight years conscript or volunteer service, but their training, since

Radetzky, had not been good: they could drill, but that was all. Radezkty's great revolution, which had aimed at training the army to fight in small units, stressing the self-sufficiency of lower commands, had been forgotten. Neither the Emperor nor Grünne knew anything about war, and this applied, too, to many of the corps and divisional commanders. There were a few dedicated soldiers, like the Hungarian rough-diamond, Benedek, who did their best to follow in Radetzky's footsteps with their own commands; but the vast majority of those who were called on to face the French in Lombardy were only parade-ground soldiers, distinguished chiefly by their blood and the smart turn-out of their men.

The army was also hard up. This, again, was the Emperor's fault. He got his soldiers more cheaply than any European ruler outside Russia. General Oskar Regele, the distinguished Austrian military historian, has cited some extremely revealing figures about the nineteenth-century defence expenditure of the various European Powers.[28] Because the Austrian Emperor relied absolutely on his army and valued it above all else, because that army appeared to be so huge and presented itself with such glitter and panache, because the Emperor himself wore uniform and high Austrian society was largely composed of officers who never wore civilian clothes, except when out shooting – because of all this it was widely assumed, above all in England, that the army was immensely costly and swallowed up an altogether disproportionate amount of the revenue: Austria thus came to be regarded as a militaristic Power, and the fatal ultimatum to Serbia in July 1914 was widely regarded not as a fearful aberration but as the natural expression of a government that believed in war as an instrument of policy. But playing at soldiers is not the same as militarism. Many Austrian officers, from the Emperor downwards, liked nothing better than to play at soldiers; but the vast majority, again from the Emperor downwards, shrank from what has been called the arbitrament of arms as from an unholy abyss.

Indeed, during a critical period between the Italian war and the Prussian war, the Austrian Empire, one of the five Great Powers, (and in its own eyes the greatest) allotted a smaller proportion of its expenditure to the armed forces than eleven other European Powers. For example, in 1862 the proportion was 19·6 per cent. The figures for France, England and Russia were 25·7 per cent, 23·4 per cent and 36·4 per cent respectively.[29] Thus England, a country generally supposed to economize to excess on defence, during one of the most peaceful periods in her history spent more of her total income on the armed forces than this great continental Power. Prussia, still not a Great Power, but gathering herself for the kill, spent 27·5 per cent of her income on defence.

The numbers were there; but these were illusory. Right up to the outbreak of war Bruck, as Finance Minister, was successful in persuading the Emperor to economize on the training and equipment of the men. As a financier, he had some reason on his side: the greatest single item in Austrian State expenditure was the servicing of her National Debt. Bankruptcy was always round the corner. And it was because of this, because for all their love of playing at soldiers the Austrians thought less in terms of military conquest than any other Power except Britain, that the real sacrifices, the sacrifices imposed on the Russians by the Tsar, the sacrifices a little later accepted by the Prussians, the sacrifices the French were ready to make for glory, were not made. It was because of this that Gyulai found himself on the Ticino river with an army only 100,000 strong and with its units under strength, often ill-equipped. It was because of this that railways built for strategic reasons by the Austrian State were soon sold to French concessionaires, who ran them only for profit – so that when the need came to reinforce the army in Italy quickly it was found that these railways would not carry the necessary weight of traffic: indeed, there was a gap of seventy miles between Venice and Trieste which had to be covered on foot, and the single-track line from Vienna to Trieste itself became so jammed that at least one regiment had to march all the way from Vienna to the Po valley. It was because of this that troops had to be issued as often as not with flintlock rifles.

No wonder poor Gyulai went slowly. On top of everything else he was afflicted with dreadful weather for the time of year. It rained and it went on raining. The Po was fifteen feet above its normal level; the swamps were lakes; the tributary rivers were torrents; the dead flat countryside, cut up by innumerable irrigation channels, was a swamp. On 4 May Gyulai at last crossed the Ticino and proceeded to develop a copybook strategic deployment in the mud. Up in the High Alps the French, plodding along in their *képis* and their business-like blue uniforms, relieved only by the red trouser-stripe, were also in trouble with mud: in ceaseless rain, hungry and cold, they had to manhandle their guns and heavy wagons over the Mont Cénis and the Little St Bernard Passes. But they came through, pouring steadily down to Susa in good order, while the Austrians worked out their chessboard manoeuvres in a vacuum. It was not until 7 May that Gyulai, harassed by telegrams from Vienna, decided that he was sufficiently poised to advance. He struck not at the Piedmontese army, to destroy it, but, by-passing it, straight for Turin. He nearly got there, another day would have done it; but with Novara and Vercelli in his hands, with his forward troops under orders to take Ivrea, he suddenly wavered. Failing to bump into the opposition he expected, receiving alarming tidings of a large French force already on the way from Turin to Alessandria, knowing that his extended flank was threatened by the Piedmontese between him and the northern spurs of the Apennines, he decided that Turin, which lay virtually open, must in fact be heavily defended, and he simply turned round.

There was one incident, the sad little Battle of Montebello, before the curtain went up for the main act. Both sides retired, but 8,000 French and Piedmontese inflicted very heavy casualties on 27,000 Austrians under Stadion. Gyulai was more frightened than ever. He composed himself to meet the main attack when it came, but not in Piedmont, rather on Austrian soil, along the left bank of the Ticino. It was now Napoleon's turn. And Napoleon started his career as a fighting general with a startling and bold flank march across the whole Austrian front: instead of attacking the main body in a set battle, he decided to march swiftly north and then east from Turin, via Novara, skirting Gyulai's right, and coming round to take Milan.

Gyulai, entrenched among his swamps, was convinced that Napoleon would try to smash through his main army and take Piacenza. Even when the French and Piedmontese had exposed more than sixty miles of flank for him to strike at, he did not seize his chance. His first duty was to keep his precious army intact, not to risk an envelopment by attempting to cut through Napoleon's lines of communication. So on 2 June he gave the order to evacuate Piedmont and hurried back into Lombardy to defend Milan from the left bank of the Ticino. For all the good he had done with his stately manoeuvrings he would have done better to stay there all the time, resting his troops and making the river crossing impregnable.

5

The tourist rattling at speed along Mussolini's celebrated *autostrada* from Turin to Milan, covering nearly ninety miles in ninety minutes, or less, sweeps round in a flattened arc which follows very closely the line of Napoleon's flanking movement, but always a little to the north. Near Novara, where Napoleon stopped to concentrate his columns, while the Austrians, to the south, were streaming back to Lombardy, the motor-road approaches very closely to the old main road, and the tall, slim dome of San Gaudenzio, soaring above the high-shouldered fabric of the Romanesque cathedral, stands up imposingly across the plain. The countryside now, as much of it as can be seen between the almost unbroken lane of advertisement hoardings, is a naturalist's paradise. Away to the south-east the intensive cultivation of the Po valley proper is obscured by a belt of swamp-land with ricefields and patches of maize broken by plantations of willows and poplars and waterlogged scrub. Herons, cranes, strange water-fowl of every kind, flop about in the paddies, the swamps, the irrigation ditches and canals, which are threaded by narrow roads, or tracks, embanked, joining hamlet to hamlet and farm to farm. The old main road from Novara to Trecate and on across the Ticino to Magenta and Milan now runs very close and more or less parallel to the motor-road, and through the same country. Indeed, just across the Ticino, motor-road and old road are so close that one skirts the north end, and the other the south end, of the straggling village of Buffalora, between the river and a large canal. Between the new and the old road, overlooking the river valley, the hamlet of San Martino stands on a bluff, commanding a viaduct which carried the old road and railway across the mile-wide shallow chasm, a mass of boulders, interrupted by innumerable islands, ground out by the flood waters of the Ticino in its last stretch on its way down from the St Gotthard Pass to join the Po. This viaduct, greatly to their surprise, the French found useable: the Austrian sappers in their pale blue tail-coats and black cocked-hats had laid charges to blow it up; but they had only weakened it and had not stayed to finish the job. Another column of French found a bridge intact at Turbigo. Napoleon was into Lombardy.

But between the river and the small town of Magenta commanding the straight, short road to Milan, there is a nasty obstacle in the form of a canal – then thirty feet wide, six feet deep, and with a strong current: the canal forms a sort of ha-ha, running thirty feet or so below the level of the flat land, largely waste and scrub and paddy with patches of maize and barley, a sort of miniature jungle blotting out visibility even to a man on horseback. Across the canal the true

Lombardy plain begins. Here for the fighting man is the closest country in the world, for the farmer the richest. Flat as your hand it stretches to infinity, every inch under intensive cultivation, and marvellously irrigated. Long unbroken lines of mulberries and heavily lopped elms serve as the supports for carefully trained vines, and in between these narrow lanes the rich earth is cultivated in long strips of wheat, barley, rye, maize, gourds. Here and there the solid sea of greenery is interrupted by solidly built farm-houses, enclosing with their built-on barns and byres and stables great courtyards, blank and thickly walled: the country is virtually impassable except by the long narrow lanes serving the farms: two squadrons of cavalry could pass in broad daylight within fifty yards of each other without being any the wiser. This was the terrain through which Gyulai was bringing up his men to fight, without knowing it, the Battle of Magenta.

Neither side, the French in the scrub between river and canal, the Austrians trying to deploy among the baffling greenery, could see beyond their noses: they might have been blind.

Napoleon had expected the Austrians to attack him on the west bank of the Ticino. Gyulai, however, needed time to rest his men and redeploy them after their long march to the rear. Many had not eaten for twenty-four hours. Some were never to eat again. He expected his forward troops to put up a stiff fight at San Martino and blow the viaduct, and planned to have his main army, reinforced by a fresh army corps from Milan, in place to hem in the French and smash them in that sinister strip between the river and the canal – withdrawing over the canal and blowing the bridges there only as a last resort. It was not a bad plan, and it should have worked. Even after the failure of San Martino, which gave Napoleon an unopposed crossing of the Ticino, it could have worked. It very nearly did. When MacMahon approached Buffalora and found it full of Austrians, after a short, sharp engagement he withdrew to think again. But he omitted to tell Napoleon, who, thinking that all was going to plan, called up the Imperial Guard and sent them in to MacMahon's support. Then began a terrible battle for the bridges over the canal which went on all day. One bridge changed hands seven times. The Emperor, who had himself come up into the no-man's-land between river and canal, was totally in the dark as to what was happening and obsessed with the very natural fear that the Austrians had managed to cross the Ticino higher up and would come round at his rear to trap him between river and canal. This should have happened. But

MacMahon, having changed the battle plan without telling anybody, and leaving his Emperor in terrible danger, had been executing an act of extreme and reckless personal courage. Abandoning the fight at Buffalora he had raced up the Ticino, often within pistol shot of the enemy, to cross higher up and get behind the Austrians, as the Austrians should have been getting behind the French. After the bloodiest and most confused of fighting, with the French converging from their various canal crossings on the one landmark in that suffocating sea of green, the belfry of Magenta, the Austrians withdrew, tired out. On this day Gyulai had 113,000 men at his disposal. In a battle lasting twelve hours he had been able to bring only 58,000 men into action, none of them fresh, many of them famished and exhausted, of whom he lost over 10,000. It is true that Napoleon also managed to bring up only 54,000 men, of whom he lost 4,500, including his gifted General Espinasse. But the Austrians knew where they were: they were on home-ground in a position that could have been made virtually impregnable. Napoleon was groping and terribly exposed: he had some reason for not calling up the remainder of an army which he might all too easily need the next day. Even then the battle was neither lost nor won. There was a pause for the night, with Magenta in French hands. Napoleon planned to establish himself in his new positions and bring up 100,000 for the final attack. Gyulai set himself to deploy his own 100,000, half of them fresh to the fight. But survivors of the 58,000 had been knocked about too much. Hungry, exhausted, demoralized by bad generalship and the discovery that their arms were largely inferior, they had to be rested. Magenta was won by default. It took Napoleon two days to realize this fact. Milan, wide open, was only twelve miles away. But Napoleon let the Austrians withdraw in good order, and it was only on 7 June that he made his triumphal entry into Milan.

The shock to Vienna was unspeakable. By all standards the defeat at Magenta was a disgraceful and humiliating performance. The higher command had failed on three counts: first it had failed to mobilize its forces, which should have been overwhelming; then it had failed to equip and sustain the five army corps which were in fact available for the battle; finally it had failed to appoint a commander who knew how to fight. This is the kind of behaviour that may be grudgingly tolerated in a democracy which makes a perverse cult of always losing the initial battles of a war. But for Franz Josef there was no excuse: he had taken all upon himself. His army was on home-ground, and it was facing an invading army of inferior strength which had to fight without an effective Commander-in-Chief.

Franz Josef himself was speechless when the news came that Gyulai had given up and was retreating, unpursued, over the Mincio, which flows through Mantua, and into the heart of the Quadrilateral. He himself was in Verona, where he had arrived a few days earlier, with Hess and Grünne, to take charge of the campaign. He gave orders for the retirement to cease forthwith; but Hess, who had gone forward, told him it was too late to turn the troops round in their tracks and stand and fight: the withdrawal would have to be completed, then they could all think again. Gyulai had not thought at all. Count Crenneville, who was soon to succeed Grünne as Adjutant-General to the Emperor, visited Gyulai at his headquarters on 7 June, three days after Magenta, and found him in the best of spirits, totally oblivious of the fact that his army was on the verge of mutiny. Almost beside himself with indignation at the shocking state of the troops, declaring that it would need a miracle for 'an army so mishandled, so badly supplied, so miserably deployed' to achieve a victory, Crenneville described how he had talked to Gyulai:

> He sees nothing wrong at all; he has his own comforts, good cooking, cards after dinner – he invited me to dine, but I excused myself and went back to my splendid soldiers in their bivouacs – this Head-quarters turns the stomach and I could weep. . . . The poor 9 Corps belongs this morning to the First Army, tomorrow to the Second, and gets orders from both, which cross each other and contradict each other; so today it marches east, tomorrow west, wearing itself out to no purpose. . . .[30]

And so on, the familiar story; but this time in the camp of a proud and professional army which, having begun ignominiously, was, tomorrow, to be pushed into final defeat.

Gyulai was finally superseded on 17 June, and the Emperor himself took over, with Hess as his Chief-of-Staff. A week later he was a beaten man. Crenneville did not mention the heat, but, after all the rain, it was now getting intolerably hot. He did not mention the hunger, but the Austrians were hungry and the French and Piedmontese were on the verge of starvation. Before Magenta some of the Austrian troops had committed suicide from sheer weariness. They had been on hostile territory, and, after the battle, many Austrian wounded had been finished off by the peasants. Here in Lombardy the peasants were on the whole friendly to the Austrians: they had no use for the Piedmontese, and what with the heat and the impossibility of finding adequate food and forage, Napoleon's armies were in a bad way. But they plodded on in the general direction of Verona, with no prospect ahead of them but a major pitched battle if the Austrians would fight, or a costly assault on the formidable fortifications of the Quadrilateral if the Austrians refused to come out. Once they had crossed the Chieso their next main obstacle was the Mincio, running down from Peschiera on the south-east tip of Lake Garda to Goito, Curtatone and Mantua, and so to the Po, and forming the western bastion of the Quadrilateral itself.

After a good deal of indecision, of orders and counter-orders, Franz Josef decided to cross the Mincio to meet the enemy threat and stand behind the Chieso. It has been said often enough that the ignorant counsels of Grünne had a good deal to do with the ineffective strategy of those melancholy days; but in fairness to Grünne, all eye-witness reports insist that, although present at every council of war, he knew his place and did not interfere. Apart from the Emperor himself, it was Hess who was undecided: the weight of responsibility was too great; he had to live down the mistakes of others; he had to direct the broken armies and weld them with the reinforcements now arriving into a new machine; he had to plan a campaign to break the heart of a victorious enemy and in circumstances not of his choosing. With all this he held in his hands the reputation of his young Emperor, who, though he realized by now that his lack of experience, knowledge and sheer talent made him insufficient for the task he had undertaken, might nevertheless, with a single impulsive order, undo all that his veteran general might plan. For Hess it was too much. He was a brilliant planner and a first-class tactician; but he was also a born Chief-of-Staff: it was one thing devising plans for a Radetzky to master in a flash and then push through with dash and understanding; it was quite another to carry his Emperor on his back.

How little the quality of supreme generalship is understood! The really outstanding Commander-in-Chief will pick as his right hand, as his brain, a Chief-of-Staff with whom he can work in perfect harmony, knowing just how his mind works, knowing also that the plans laid before him to carry out will suit his own temperament and methods. He will choose and train his own army commanders, his corps commanders too, breaking them of waywardness and indiscipline, if not of vanity, so that when the day comes he can rely on them to do as they are told, and to see that their subordinates will also do as they are told. He must then be capable of sitting back, once the button has been pressed and battle is engaged, saving himself to cope with the dire emergencies that will arise – as when the plan breaks down in one vital particular; as when unforeseen enemy action calls for a radical change of plan; as when one of his subordinate commanders, in spite of training and discipline, breaks loose and starts fighting a private battle of his own, imperilling the whole. All this has to be done not in the quiet of the study, where the Chief-of-Staff works out his schemes at leisure, but in a farmhouse kitchen or a tent, with all communications broken down, with breathless orderlies galloping up from every point of the compass at once to demand immediate reinforcements, with nothing to consult but his own swift instincts, and with the knowledge that a wrong decision made in haste on insufficient information may in half an hour send thousands of unfortunates to destruction, or lose a war.

In the whole of Europe in 1859 there was only one man who possessed these qualities: the Prussian General von Moltke, whose hour had not come. Without these qualities there can be no real Commander-in-Chief. So the Battle of Solferino, as Magenta before it, was fought without direction by huge bodies of men who were effectively out of control.

The country south of Lake Garda is easier for troops than the close country round Magenta. The ground swells and undulates, dotted with farms and largely covered with vineyards. There are points of vantage, but the country is so broken up that there is little room for bold manoeuvre. The French and Piedmontese plodding on, and the Austrians rather tentatively sallying forth in a great mass to meet the enemy, were each driven, for their different reasons, to seek an engagement which neither wanted at that time, but which both felt impelled to undertake because neither could afford to spin things out much longer. Disease, as well as hunger, was now making itself felt. The French were dying of malaria; the Austrians had more than 50,000 sick within their lines. The heat was phenomenal. The whole of Europe that fine midsummer was smitten by a record heat-wave. A little later, in London, the shade temperature rose to 97 degrees, and Malmesbury recorded in his diary that in Whitehall Gardens, where he lived, the smell from the Thames was so bad that the windows had to be kept closed. Between the Chieso and the Mincio there was very little shade and there was practically no water; the children of the local peasants were dying of thirst; the drought was turning the fair green country prematurely brown.

The two great armies, 138,000 French and Piedmontese, 129,000 Austrians – numbers on a scale that even Napoleon Bonaparte, the inventor of mass armies, had never managed to control (at Leipzig he had concentrated 150,000 men against 200,000 and the result had been a shambles) – bumped into each other on the morning of 24 June: each thought it was executing a drill-book approach towards the enemy. Neither at first realized that the main bodies had made contact. The French had started early to get some of their marching done before the full heat of the day: the general idea was to move up close to the Mincio by noon. The first columns started off after a hurried bite of breakfast at half past two in the morning: the Piedmontese under Victor Emmanuel himself on the left, towards San Martino; Barageuy and MacMahon with 1 and 2 Corps in the centre, towards Solferino and Cavriana; Canrobert and Niel with 3 and 4 Corps on the right. All the glorious names. . . . The Imperial Guard stayed in reserve at Castiglione. There were 366 guns. The Austrians faced this array grouped in two armies, the first of three corps, under Wimpffen,* the second of four corps under Schlick, both army commanders being responsible directly to the Emperor. 8 Corps of the First Army, on the extreme right at San Martino, and facing Victor Emmanuel, was commanded by the man who would have been his colleagues' choice as Commander-in-Chief, Alexander Benedek, who was in the event to prove himself the only capable commander on that terrible field.

Solferino began almost as a series of independent battles. By the end of the day 270,000 men, 40,000 horses and 700 guns were engaged on a fifteen-mile front – the first great battle to range over so wide a field – and, miraculously, some sort of coherence had emerged. But not enough. At the beginning there was no coherence. By eight o'clock in the morning, the French and Piedmontese columns which had been marching first into the dawn, then into the sunrise, too far apart to support each other at all, bumped first into one Austrian corps, then into another. When the collision took place Napoleon's troops had been marching for five hours, the Austrians for the most part were just getting up from breakfast and preparing for another day of probing. Napoleon was the first of the two commanders to

---

* Not to be confused with the French general of the same name.

realize that he had stumbled into a general engagement, and when he climbed the look-out tower at Castiglione he could see from the puffs of smoke across the plain that the action was already wide-flung. Franz Josef, having spent the previous evening writing to Elizabeth ('My dear, dear angel-Sisi . . .') to cheer her up, himself enjoyed a leisurely breakfast and afterwards, at nine o'clock, moved his headquarters to Volta, behind the Austrian left. He could hear firing, but the small hills blocked the view, and communications were so bad that he had no idea at first that it was more than local skirmishing. It was not until eleven that, moving forward to Cavriana, he decided that he had the whole of Napoleon's army in front of him and took command of the battle. Schlick was to base his defence on Solferino, with its steep, commanding height; Wimpffen was to advance to Castiglione, turning Napoleon's left and taking the pressure off the Austrian centre. But as the battle developed a new pattern emerged: while the French concentrated all their force on Solferino, the Austrians massed heavily in the open ground on their left in order to smash the French right. And so it went on. By two o'clock, after the bloodiest and bravest fighting, the French drove the Austrians out of their formidably strong positions on the Solferino hill-tops. At two o'clock, after mounting two major attacks, Wimpffen on the Austrian left had to fall back in face of Niel, who would not budge. At three the French were dropping shells round Franz Josef's own headquarters. Half an hour later the Emperor decided to order a general retreat.

His heart was broken. His left and his centre had been forced back. But fifteen miles away on his right Benedek with 8 Corps had been fighting the battle of a lifetime against the Piedmontese, and he was winning. In face of incessant attack he had held the plateau at San Martino and could go on holding it. It was a position on which a regrouped army could have pivoted next day, or, better still, it was a position from which a reinforced right wing could have advanced to sweep behind the French and begin to fold them up. When Benedek, long idolized by his men, and now to be a national hero, received the general order to retreat, he burst into tears, on the edge of mutiny. But training and obedience told. He had one more attack to beat back as a matter of honour, and this he did. Then he, too, withdrew. At half past four the heat broke. One of those spectacular summer tempests against which nothing can stand suddenly broke loose, first with a tornado that swept up billowing clouds of dust, then with violent thunder, lightning, hail, flooding everything in moments. The battle broke off in disorder. Soldiers who had advanced steadily under heavy fire, dashed to find shelter, under walls, under bushes, under trees, petrified with fear of the thunder and lightning; nevertheless they could at least lap the water collected in their hands. The whole vast battlefield was blotted out, and even the spectacular lightning flashes revealed only sheeting rain, then hail. When it was all over and the fierce sun shone again, the French, to their surprise, saw the Austrians slipping away towards the Mincio, like a mirage through the misty steam which now rose from the saturated earth. They could have been caught at the passage of the Mincio and cut to pieces; but the French were too tired to move.

6

It was after this battle that Napoleon, less discreet than Franz Josef, made his celebrated remark. He had had enough of war: '*Le hazard joue un trop grand rôle.*' Franz Josef, twenty-nine, did not commit himself; but it was clear that he no longer fancied himself as a supreme commander in the field. That dream was over. Both Emperors were lacerated by the sights and sounds of the battlefield, those sights and sounds which drove Dunant to work for the foundation of the Red Cross. There were 40,000 men dead and wounded on that field; some of the wounded lay out in the terrible heat for two days for lack of services to succour them: thousands died of exposure, hunger, gangrene and sheer exhaustion. Peasants returning to their ruined farms were conscripted to bury the dead and burn the horses: that took eight days. The Emperor did not see all this; but he had seen enough. Two evenings later, back at his headquarters in Verona, he wrote to Elizabeth:

> And so I had to give the order for retreat. . . . I rode . . . through a fearful storm to Valeggio, and then drove on to Villafranca. There I spent a dreadful evening; the place was a confusion of wounded refugees, waggons and horses. . . . That is the sad history of a dreadful day, on which great things were done, but fortune did not smile on us. I have learnt and experienced much and I know what it feels like to be a beaten general. . . .[31]

Napoleon knew what it felt like to be a nearly beaten general, and he too had had enough. There was no point in going on. Honour was satisfied. He had pushed the Austrians back into the Quadrilateral. He could claim Savoy and Nice. If he went on to sweep Austria out of all Italy the cost would be immense: the main Austrian army was still intact, and strong reinforcements were being feverishly got ready by Albrecht in Vienna. And did he, in any case, want to see Victor Emmanuel and Cavour established as masters of a renascent Mediterranean Power? It was a big 'if', anyway. Prussia was now actively stirring. Berlin had refused to go to the help of Austria, when it had been a question of the invasion of Piedmont. But with the French invasion of Lombardy the matter took on a different complexion, and once the metropolitan territory of a member of the German Confederation was threatened, Prussia was bound to act. She was already mobilizing, and soon there would be a German threat to the Rhine. The time had come to strike a bargain: there was nothing in the world to stop Franz Josef from sitting down in the Quadrilateral and waiting for Prussian help.

This was not how Franz Josef saw it. Although he could write to Elizabeth: 'I do not feel myself to blame, even for faulty dispositions',[32] he knew very well that he had failed, and he was not a man to whom failure came easily. He reacted in the way inevitable in a man driven by devouring pride: the disaster had to be written off, and quickly. He would live it down in his own time, in his own way. Above all no offers of help at this stage, no demonstrative sympathy; least of all from Prussia. But for Prussia's cold-blooded desertion this would never have happened; but meanwhile he had made a fool of himself in the eyes of Berlin. Rather than concede anything to Prussia in return for belated assistance he would sacrifice Lombardy, as though without turning a hair; indeed, he would positively throw it away in his eagerness to get back to a safe place, a secure base, where, hidden from the world, he could compose himself and think again. On top of all this, Austria was on the verge of bankruptcy: it was not much use preparing for a siege in the Quadrilateral and watching French warships bombard Venice if the troops could not be paid. As a final straw, Hungary was on the verge of another explosion: far too many troops had to be kept there in garrison duty; and when some of the Hungarian units under Clam-Gallas's command found that Kossuth had arrived in Milan to raise a Hungarian legion to fight for the French they had deserted in the middle of the Solferino battle.

Thus, on both sides, all ways led to Villafranca. There was much ceremonial coming and going between the lines, beginning with

Napoleon's offer of an armistice and Franz Josef's acceptance of it, ending with the meeting of the two men. 'I look forward with dread to meeting that scoundrel',[33] Franz Josef said; but he did not show his feelings, and, after some minutes of acute mutual embarrassment, the two quickly understood each other. There was no argument about Lombardy. Austria was to keep Venetia and the Quadrilateral, and there was to be a good deal of argument about Venetia's status within the Empire. Later Franz Josef explained at great length that if Venetia were granted a special status all his other provinces would demand the same, Transylvania and Hungary too, and that would mean the end of his army, the end of his realm. About the central Italian States, Franz Josef was adamant. 'I can make personal sacrifices and renounce my own rights. What I cannot do is abandon relatives and allies who have been loyal to me.'[34] Here honour was not the sole consideration: Franz Josef was taking up Napoleon's idea of an Italian Confederation which he himself might join and come to dominate. But although Napoleon did not then care much what happened in central Italy, Cavour put a stop to that by organizing plebiscites, which ended in the annexation of the central States by Piedmont. Napoleon, indeed, cared only about one thing, to get home quickly, presenting Lombardy to Piedmont and taking Nice and Savoy for himself. After his meeting with Franz Josef he said: 'Peace is as good as concluded. I could have wished for a better one, but in the end I agreed, because I found myself dealing with a gentleman.'[35] That same evening he said to his cousin: 'I can't hang on in this position. I must get out of here, and I shall write to the Emperor in that sense.' But he could not resist a turn of the screw. In his letter he said that after hearing that the Cabinets of London and Petersburg were in full accord with his (Napoleon's) proposals, the Prussian Cabinet had told him that if Austria refused them she could count on neither material nor moral help from Berlin. 'Your Majesty perceives, therefore, that you have gained by dealing direct with me.'[36] This was not true. Whether or not Franz Josef realized its falsity is not clear. Certainly Napoleon had earlier made it clear that he was afraid of Prussian intervention; but Franz Josef was in such a state about Prussia that he could have believed anything. He gave nothing away. 'I should never have yielded to any pressure from the European areopagus', he coolly wrote in reply, 'and therefore I felicitate myself the more for having entered into direct negotiations with your Majesty.'[37]

The last thing, indeed, that Franz Josef desired was a European congress. Before the Peace of Zürich he said as much to Napoleon. He was a great respecter of treaties: a European agreement would have bound him to recognize the loss of Lombardy for ever, but, in his blindness, he was determined to keep his hands free to win it back. Thus was concluded, and in secret, to the astonishment of the world and the fury of the Prussian Court, the Peace of Zürich. But Bismarck in Petersburg was pleased: the agreement marked an important step towards the day, just seven years later, when he was to gather his strength and stake everything on his army's ability to smash Austria in the field: Bismarck himself saw this clearly enough, but his day was yet to come. As acting Ambassador to the Court of the Tsar his sole concern had been to keep Russia neutral, and Alexander had not needed much persuading.

Apart from Napoleon and Bismarck, nobody was happy. Cavour had to be kept away from the armistice negotiations at all costs; for a terrible moment, when he learnt from his King what had happened, he lost all control, accused his master of betrayal, and had to be forcibly restrained from doing violence. But he need not have worried: the central Italian States were soon manoeuvred into the Sardinian fold. Garibaldi, who had rendered great service by some dashing cutting-out operations on the shores of Lake Maggiore and, more importantly, had swung to the cause of Turin many Italians who would have preferred to fight for a republic rather than the House of Savoy, was soon to conquer Sicily and Naples. And in less than two years Victor Emmanuel was to be declared king of a united Italy, from which only Rome and Venetia were excluded. The Prussians now began to be terrified of the French, and the French themselves, flushed with victory, decided that they were invincible, a mood which persisted until 1870 and which contributed largely to that débâcle. The English, seeing Austria hard-pressed and heavily chastened, were alarmed: the idea of a Europe without an Austrian Empire to keep things in balance was unsettling and distasteful in the extreme.

But it did not turn out quite like that. By the war of 1859 Franz Josef lost Lombardy and Napoleon Italy. Since Metternich, Austrian policy had been directed towards the creation of an Italian Federation, as a counter-weight to the German Federation. Austria was shipwrecked by the resistance of France, who was pursuing the same aim. The instructions of the Directory to Bonaparte had been that Paris did not aim at the unification of Italy, but at the preservation of the separate States, and Napoleon had continued this policy as Emperor. His Kingdom of Italy was limited to Northern Italy. His nephew on the other hand, strove for an Italian federation under French protection. Cavour, with the help of the English, ruined Napoleon's policy and embroiled him in the Roman question.

English statesmen, from Palmerston onwards, realized that Austria was too weak to maintain its dominion in Italy. But an Italian federation under the protection of France would have been a menace to England. A unified Kingdom of Italy which could turn against France was, on the other hand, most welcome to England; and a unified Italy, with a long and vulnerable coastline, must set great store by England's friendship and support. Thus the real outcome of the 1859 war was defeat for Napoleon and, through the subsequent unification of Italy, victory for England.

CHAPTER TEN

AUTOCRACY IS NOT ENOUGH

Franz Josef had reigned for ten years and seven months. During all this time he had not given a thought to the principles of government. Flattered by unwise advisers, two and three times his age, who confirmed him in his deep conviction that he could do no wrong, he had gone straight ahead, relying on discipline and severe impartiality to see him through. The whole apparatus of the State had now come to pieces in his hands. To make matters worse, and as though to rub in his fallibility, his private life was also breaking down. His army had been beaten in the field, and on its own ground; he had lost Lombardy; to his burning shame, he could not even succour his relatives in Modena and Tuscany; he had quarrelled with the Tsar. He returned to Vienna to find discontent at last openly displayed: it could not be kept from him that people were discussing the desirability of his abdication in favour of Maximilian. Hungary was on the verge of another explosion, and his faithful Uncle Albrecht begged to be released from the governorship; it was out of the question, he said, to go on trying to run the country on Bach's lines. Sophie was a picture of helpless woe; her fighting spirit had gone and all she could do was wring her hands over the iniquity of the times and lament the misfortunes of her beloved son. She was still strong enough to harry Elizabeth, but that was all; and Elizabeth, far from obeying her husband's pleading to look after herself, had for months been seized by a sterile restlessness which could only be assuaged by ceaseless riding, walking, riding again, until she had worn herself to a shadow.

The Emperor, still only thirty, took all this in, swallowed it down, and proceeded to re-orientate himself according to his lights. He gave not the slightest indication that he himself was on the verge of breaking down. Instead, this time with eyes wide open, he took up the burden which he was to sustain without complaint, without the least appeal for sympathy, for half a century to come. As Jove he had failed: very well, he would be Atlas.

There was still some of the old fire. He would not forgive Prussia.

He had a new chief adviser now: Buol had gone, and his place had been taken by Count Rechberg, strongly recommended by Metternich. A career diplomat in the Austrian service, he came from antique Swabian stock and had sensible ideas of a benevolently conservative kind; unfortunately they were out of date. He was not outstandingly perspicuous and, though shrewd, was quite at sea when faced with anything outside his experience. He was happiest with the liberally minded conservatives of the old régime, above all the Magyar Old Conservatives; he appreciated the importance of the new bourgeoisie in Vienna; he did not under-estimate the mob. He knew that his task, that the whole justification of his existence, was to put an end to Austria's isolation; and first and last he addressed himself to Prussia. He was not afraid: it was he who, at Verona and after Solferino, first acquainted Franz Josef, quite fearlessly, with the hard facts about his unpopularity in Vienna. But, as Friedjung, who knew him well, has said, he lacked the power to persuade and influence people:[1] it was not enough to have a sensible policy, that policy had to be sold, and Rechberg was not a salesman. Thus he could write to Franz Josef on the eve of Villafranca: 'The vanity of Prussia is such that the appearance of standing at the head of Germany would give her extraordinary satisfaction. It seems to me advisable to gratify this vanity up to a point in order to encourage Prussia step by step along the path she is already taking towards active measures.'[2] But, having said this, he could not follow through. It would indeed have been advisable on a very short-term view, but already Franz Josef was far too deeply involved emotionally: apart from his bitterness, later to be publicly expressed, about being 'left in the lurch' by Prussia, he was still as determined as he had been ten years earlier not to concede anything at all that might be construed as recognition of the Hohenzollerns' equality of standing with the Habsburgs. On a longer term Rechberg was less sensible: blinkered by the view of the Old Conservatives, and trained by Metternich, he had not perceived that the Holy Alliance, long moribund, had been shattered for ever by the Crimean War, and he based all his policy on an attempt to restore the *status quo*. His strength and limitations as a statesman fit to cope with the world around him are shown very well in his estimate of Bismarck. It was in 1862, three years after Solferino, that Bismarck finally emerged as Prime Minister of Prussia, and by then his opposite number in Vienna had sized him up as a man of extreme ability and power without, however, at all understanding the real nature of his genius. Thus poor Rechberg could say to Grammont, the French Minister in Vienna:

> If Bismarck had had a proper diplomatic training, he would be one of the first of German statesmen, if not the *first*: he is courageous, resolute and ambitious, but incapable of sacrificing a prejudice or a party view to any higher consideration. He has no real political sense; he is a party man in the strictest sense of the word, and, as he is able and conciliatory, and moreover an enemy to Austria, we regard his appointment with distress and alarm.[3]

Rechberg, of course, had had a proper diplomatic training; he also thought he had a great deal of political sense.

It is not clear what Franz Josef thought. On a superficial view his failure in his chosen field, as a commanding general, should have shaken fatally his confidence in himself; and up to a point this may well have been so. But far more than this, the Italian fiasco had shaken his confidence in all advisers: he might not be a genius himself, but, since he had to suffer for every mistake made in his realm, there was a good deal to be said for seeing that they were his own mistakes. He had already got rid of Buol; he now, more painfully, had to get rid of Bach, Grünne and Kempen and make a clean start. Bach he sent gently to the Vatican, but Grünne he could not bear to part with altogether: he was prepared to make the honest and able soldier-diplomat, Crenneville, his Adjutant-General, but Grünne he kept close to him (Sophie had also to be listened to here) as Master of the Horse. Kempen was replaced for a very short time by the loyal and assiduous Hübner, Schwarzenberg's one-time secretary, who had served well as Ambassador to France. His new advisers he allowed to speak with remarkable openness and frankness, and it was soon clear enough that he would have to make certain concessions to the popular mood throughout the Empire and at home. But these concessions were to be made in his own time and in his own way: he was not prepared to act consistently on his Ministers' advice. Paradoxically, when at last he was beginning to think in terms of limited constitutionalism, when at last he had Ministers who would tell him the truth about the state of his Empire and indicate to him his own unpopularity, he became in practice more of an autocrat than ever: but he was to be an instructed autocrat. From now on, until the final failure in 1914, no Minister was ever any more, like Buol, to be allowed to pull the wool over his eyes; but no Minister was to be allowed in anything concrete to have his way. And so Franz Josef entered on the period when he used Ministers like generals, listening to their conflicting advice, demanding to be told everything, however unpalatable, and then using them to execute predetermined policies and dropping them with perfect ruthlessness and detachment when those policies were found not to work. Thus he allowed his new Police Minister Hübner (a man less like a police-man it would be impossible to imagine), to tell him all he knew about the evil influences exercised by his old stand-by Grünne; he argued hard and long on Grünne's behalf; but when Hübner had satisfied him that it would be catastrophic to the régime if Grünne remained, Grünne went. On the other hand, when Hübner again came to him and told him the true state of affairs in Hungary, committing himself to the belief that 'Hungary is morally lost, it must be reconquered, and this can only be done through reconciliation', and proceeding to explain why Hungary must be given back her ancient rights, Franz Josef listened attentively, encouraged Hübner to speak his mind, showed himself ready to believe everything he was told about the dangerous state of the country, but, after taking twenty-four hours to think it over, firmly rejected the policy proposed: 'I cannot accept your proposals. . . . Nothing would ever satisfy the Hungarians. If we proclaimed a constitution today, next year it would be a republic.'[4] Hübner quietly resigned, in an atmosphere of regretful amiability. The Emperor was henceforth to stand on his own feet.

He made one terrible mistake before he had quite shaken himself free.

In the search for a scapegoat for the defeat in Italy a great cry had been raised about corruption in the supply services of the army. There had to be an inquiry, the popular outcry was so great, and the inquiry led to the arrest, among others, of General Eynatten, the Quartermaster-General, who committed suicide in his cell after making a confession. In the general scandal accusations and counter-accusations flew right and left, and two men heavily involved were Richter, head of the State Bank, and Bruck, the grand old Minister of Finance, who had first dreamed up an Empire of Seventy Millions. He was a selfmade man, a bookbinder's son; he had done more to keep the Empire a going concern since 1848 than any other individual with the exception of Felix Schwarzenberg; he was modest, kind and suicidally loyal. By the worst of the aristocratic courtiers he had long been hated: he was a man of the people and a Protestant into the bargain, but above all he was a good man. Grünne had called him 'a common swindler, interested only in what he could shovel into his own pocket'![5] His hands were clean, but his enemies now had a chance to get him down, and they succeeded. He was called as a witness in the trial of Richter for embezzlement and speculation with government funds. He gave his evidence as though it was the most natural thing in the world for a Minister of Finance to be called as a witness in a criminal case. But next day he went to the Emperor and asked to be allowed to resign: a Minister of the Crown could not be publicly humiliated in this way and still retain his office. Franz Josef refused to accept his resignation, told him not to be silly, told him that everybody knew he was the most honourable man in the world. But no sooner had Bruck left, honour satisfied, than his enemies got busy. Bruck had been quite right, they told Franz Josef: it simply was not fair to him or anybody else, to the State itself, to retain in office a man involved, no matter how indirectly, in a scandal of this kind: he should be allowed to retire until the trouble had blown over. Franz Josef decided they were right. He wrote a note and sent it round by hand: 'Dear Freiherr von Bruck – As requested by you, I have decided to put you on the retired list for the time being and to replace you provisionally as head of the Ministry of Finance by my State Councillor Ignaz Edlen von Plener.'[6]

When the note was brought round Bruck was out: he had taken time off and gone to the theatre to celebrate the Emperor's show of trust. Back from the theatre, he had a cheerful supper with his family and then went off to his study to look through any messages and papers that might have arrived that evening. He read the Emperor's note, shattered and unbelieving, then took his razor and cut his throat.

Franz Josef was shattered too when he heard the news, but he did not cut his throat. He did everything he could to make life bearable for the widow, and he saw that Bruck's successor went out of his way to praise and honour the poor wretch – who was also totally and publicly exonerated when Richter was acquitted. He had learnt one more lesson the hard way, and now, besides knowing what it felt like to be a defeated general, he also knew what it felt like to be responsible for the death of a faithful servant.

He was more alone than ever before. He was, indeed, absolutely alone. Metternich had died just before Solferino. Frederick William of Prussia had had a final relapse, ending all hope that with his recovery he might put an end to the Regent's anti-Austrian policies: the Regent was soon to be William I. Count Szechyeni, the most loyal of the Hungarian magnates, had committed suicide in a lunatic asylum after writing the bitterest reproaches to Vienna for making it impossible for him to keep Hungary loyal. The old Ministers had gone. Hess followed Gyulai as an aftermath of Solferino. Franz Josef was quarrelling with Sophie about Elizabeth, and Elizabeth herself was now unmanageable. The iron was driven deep into his soul, and he embraced it. How could any professional diplomat or politician hope to influence, with easy certitudes or elaborate analyses, this young Emperor of thirty-two who saw no hope in humankind but only in his own unbreakable will? He had either to throw up the sponge, call a Grand Council, invoke the spirit of the times and let it tear his great inheritance to shreds – to abdicate, in a word – or else to go on, keeping his own counsel, as best he could. There is nothing to indicate that he ever thought of giving up. 'Never apologize; never explain. . . . ' He was committed to this discipline until it became his second nature. The Almighty, on whose behalf he volunteered this impossible ideal, took him at his word and kept him at it for fifty-five more years.

2

He had good reason, quite apart from the weight of tradition behind him, for this attitude. Bourgeois Austria in 1848 had shown itself both disloyal and inept. It had had the Court at its mercy and the government in its hands. It was in step with bourgeois Germany and with the nationalists of Bohemia, Hungary, and the rest. It had shown itself incapable of carrying out an effective revolution. The English in 1649, the French in 1793, had cut off the heads of their monarchs and contrived to run their countries by other means; but the Austrians had bungled their belated revolution and made nothing of it. Franz Josef would have been unnatural had he not distrusted his subjects, and it is hardly to be wondered at that he felt contempt for them too. It would have needed a philosopher-king to sit down and examine his conscience and the conduct of his forebears in order to discover why an Empire of forty million had been impelled to rise against the system, why the Viennese had driven his family out of the city, and why, having done so, they had proved incapable of putting anything in its place – and to go on from there to look for a reason for this in his own dynasty's conduct of affairs. Franz Josef was not a philosopher-king. He took things as he found them, as he thought he found them, and looked for expedients whereby the people could be persuaded to obey for their own good. Until 1859 he had taken the internal ordering of his Empire for granted, giving all his thought to foreign affairs. With Bach gone, and with the amiable Rechberg, clearly no man of steel, promoted to Foreign Minister, he had to take charge of the home-front too. First he had to win local popularity for himself and keep the Hungarians quiet. Since he had no intention of giving the Hungarians the special position they demanded, and which Hübner had recommended, the only thing to do was to appear to be making concessions which in fact were largely sham. Hence the manoeuvres which ended in the October Diploma of 1860 and the February Patent of 1861.

Many hard words have been levelled against him for these constitutional shifts. Of course in a sense they were fraudulent, but in the same sense every concession, or bogus concession, made by a ruler or a ruling class to popular demands has been equally fraudulent as far as motives go. The Reform Bill of 1832 was not put through for love of the masses but for fear of them. In another sense they were not fraudulent at all: Franz Josef was deeply concerned with the good of his realm, of his subjects as part of that realm, and his endeavours to appease hostility to his person by one expedient after another were directed towards maintaining the stability and prosperity of that realm, of which he could have said as truly as Louis XIV and as fervently as General de Gaulle both said of France: 'I am Austria.' He was never, however, a man for phrases. A writer who was very good at phrases, the surpassingly brilliant historian, Louis Eisenmann, contrived in a single phrase to obscure the truth of the position: 'Absolutism, bankrupt, put on a false constitutional nose to extract a few coppers from the public.'[7] It might be argued that this was the truth after all, in which case that sentence, appropriately modified, could be applied to any government compelled at any time in any place to make concessions to the governed against its better judgement.

Franz Josef had to do something and still remain Emperor. All sorts of people bombarded him with advice, but it boiled down for practical purposes to the choice between two opposed courses:

bureaucratic centralism revivified, at least in appearance, by a central Parliament, or a species of federalism based on limited provincial autonomy. The centralists were in the saddle: they included Bruck, who still had a few months to run before cutting his throat, and Schmerling, who had resigned the Ministry of Justice in 1850 because of his disapproval of Schwarzenberg's toleration of police rule. When Bruck died, his successor, Plener, took over his relatively liberal ideas. With them was the Minister of Justice, Lasser. All, by the Emperor's standards, were liberal. All believed that with a central Parliament to take the place of an individual, Bach, the Bach system could be made to work.

Opposed to them were the Old Conservatives, who had been smashed by Schwarzenberg no less effectively than the radicals. Their strength was in the countryside, where their estates and their influence lay, not in the cities. Their line with the Emperor was that since the city bureaucracy had failed he must repose his trust in his own kind and allow them to resurrect the Diets, endowed with provincial powers. The difficulty was that in certain critical cases provincial powers meant national powers; but Franz Josef decided to give the decentralizers a trial. To succeed the Jacobin lawyer, Bach, he appointed the feudal Polish aristocrat, Goluchowski. He did more than this: Bach had been Minister of the Interior, but Goluchowski was called Minister of State. As far as it went it was a perspicacious choice; but, in practice, it did not go much farther than Poland. Poland was a special case. The difficulty about the Habsburg Empire was that each and every one of its component parts was a special case. Goluchowski had everything – except that he was not a Hungarian, a Bohemian, a Croat or a German. He was an aristocrat; he wanted autonomy for Galicia, but he also wanted a Habsburg overlord to defend his country against the Russians and the Prussians. This combination of needs expressed exactly what the Habsburg Empire was for, but only the Poles knew it. The Hungarians thought they could manage very well by themselves; the Bohemians wanted to be like the Hungarians; the Croats and Serbs and Transylvanians wanted only not to be ruled by Hungarians; the remaining Italians only lived for the day when they could cut loose from Austria for ever. So the Goluchowski appointment was brilliance in a void. And the new fundamental law of the Empire, promulgated in a hurry, the October Diploma, was based on a situation which existed only between Vienna and Cracow. There were to be aristocratic Diets, of the kind that suited the Poles, in every province. It was an attempt, backed by the Hungarian magnates – one of whom, Count Szecsen, actually drafted the Diploma – to stave off the 'parliamentary' solution of the German liberals. In those days Franz Josef was afraid of the idea of Parliament: he confused it with constitutionalism and thought it might lead to almost anything. It was only much later that he understood the valuable use to which a central Parliament can be put in the hands of a skilled manager of men.

The October Diploma was engineered in secret and in a hurry, though in not so much of a hurry as has been sometimes made out. The provincial Diets which were to work out the provisions for a new fundamental law no longer effectively existed: they had to be set up and their new members consisted largely of the Emperor's nominees. Kübeck's old State Council was also resurrected. It worked away with the Diets on a report advising the adoption of an aristocratic federalism. This report, as such, was never debated, but the sense of the reinforced State Council, in which the bureaucratic liberals were heavily outnumbered by the Old Conservatives, had been filtering through to Franz Josef, who had already made up his mind. When he found suddenly that he needed a draft constitution to take to Warsaw with him where, as a result of Rechberg's persistence, he was to meet the Tsar and the new King of Prussia in a forlorn attempt to reforge, after so many years, the Holy Alliance, the final document was produced in a week.

Neither the Warsaw meeting nor the October Diploma came to anything. The new European dynamism, first expressed in the Crimean War almost by accident, was now accepted policy in Petersburg and Berlin as well as Paris. Alexander II was embarking on his new liberal policy at home and, at the same time, dreaming of foreign conquests. 'Why should we introduce a new policy towards Austria?' said Gorchakov, the Russian Foreign Minister, adding, in a phrase which sounds a bell with startling clarity across a century, 'What is the use of words? What we want is deeds. If and when Austria proves in deeds that her feelings towards us have changed, then, and only then, can we offer her our hand.'[8] Prussia, also in a liberal mood, which was to last another two years, would give no help to Austria unless she would abate her pretensions vis-à-vis Germany.

It was true enough that Franz Josef had undergone no conversion. At about this time he wrote to Napoleon himself: 'Not only for the moment, but also and more especially for the future, I should gladly welcome a close alliance between France and Austria, an alliance which I regard as the best guarantee for the order and progress of Europe.'[9] So, in his heart, Franz Josef had also recognized that the Holy Alliance could never again be revived.

Warsaw had shown that no amount of conservative emphasis could stimulate nostalgic longings for a return to the past in Petersburg and Berlin. Events in Vienna and Budapest were soon to show that federalism, or the only sort of federalism the Emperor could afford, was violently objected to by the Germans and the Hungarians alike. As far as the Hungarians were concerned, the only sort of federalism they would put up with was one based on the March Laws promulgated during the 1848 revolution, with their insistence that the only tie with Austria was personal union under a common king: the Hungarian magnates led by Szecsen, unlike their Bohemian opposite numbers, led by Clam Martinic (who saw in limited provincial autonomy their way back to influence and power, had no organic connection with the local Slav population, and only wanted to be rid of the rule of bureaucratic Germans) could not control the Magyar squires, who, grouped together again in their county associations, or *comitats*, refused to take any orders from Vienna, refused even to send their representatives to the State Council. As far as the Germans were concerned, they resisted stubbornly a system which looked like being run by conservative aristocrats and also, if the system meant anything at all, would end by swamping them under the sheer weight of non-Germans. Goluchowski, the Polish centralist, was thus assailed from two sides – and then from a third, when the Bohemian nobility weighed in because he was, they said – and correctly – manipulating the Diets in the interests of German bureaucrats. By December Goluchowski had fallen and the October Diploma had proved unworkable.

Franz Josef shed no tears. Felix Schwarzenberg had brought him up to distrust the nobility, as agents of disintegration, more than any other element in his realm. They had told him that they would work a system which could keep everybody quiet, satisfy local and national aspirations, and preserve the Empire from liberalism. He had given them their chance, reluctantly, and they had made a mess of it, interested only in so fixing things that their own privileges and power should be maintained and enhanced. Franz Josef was no more willing to pander to his nobility than to any other class; he was less willing indeed, for they were more dangerous. The collapse of the October experiment finished them off as a power for ever. As private senators, as trusted members of the Court circle, the First Society, as sensible men in their own right, individual members of the great landowning class were to exercise considerable influence, sometimes beneficent, over the Emperor's thinking right up to the end. But as a political force the First Society was never again to cut any ice at all. From now on the Second Society was to make the running. It had been the Second Society which had, in the Vienna *Landhaus*, first brought liberal ideas into the open in 1848 and given the final push to Metternich. The counter-revolution had been carried out by the First Society; but almost at once its chief ornament, Felix Schwarzenberg, had pushed it into the background and taken his brains where he could find them, partly from the Second Society, partly from below. The Emperor had continued this process until the 1859 catastrophe. Now, after once more giving the First Society its chance, he closed down. Goluchowski the Polish aristocrat was replaced by Anton von Schmerling, the perfect example of the Second Society man, well-born, autocratic by temperament, tall, gawky and inelegant, he was one of the very few strong characters in Austrian public life. A believer in Germany, he nevertheless was determined that Austria should lead in Germany. He had done well for his country as Chairman of the ill-fated Frankfurt Parliament, showing cool resolution in resisting the demands of the German radicals on the one hand, and the Prussianizers on the other. In Schwarzenberg's government he had sponsored and put through a number of reforms and introduced trial by jury. Since he had resigned in protest against Schwarzenberg's high-handed methods he was free from the odium attached to his one-time colleague, Bach. Unlike Bach, he was a manager by temperament, not a dictator, and he liked to pretend a detachment which he did not possess, presenting himself not as a career politician but as an honest man of affairs impressed into politics reluctantly, an image met with more frequently in England than on the continent of Europe. 'I have no real interest in politics,' he once declared. 'I am a soldier by nature and have got involved in politics against my will. I can't stand this perpetual turmoil. In the evenings I like to read a good book, or go to the theatre; but these political fellows exist in a state of constant excitement: something has to be happening all the time.'[10]

In fact the picture was very different. In his ideas about a centralized and unified Empire he was very close to Bach, but he thought the thing could be managed better by substituting the apparatus of parliamentary government for undisguised one-man rule. In his Germanism he far exceeded Bach. He was far from being pro-German in the sense understood by Schwarzenberg when he had expressed the view that Schmerling at Frankfurt was not to be relied on: he was, rather, pan-German. He believed in the Empire of Seventy Millions dominated by the Habsburgs; but it was to be very much a German Empire, with the other races kept in their place. Bach, and Schwarzenberg too, had run the autocracy through German civil servants, not because they were in love with Germanism, but because the most able and efficient bureaucrats were the German Austrians. Their Empire had been run on behalf of the dynasty and the Germans within the Empire had no more innate rights and privileges in their eyes than the Hungarians, the Czechs or the Croats. This system had broken down, and it was Schmerling's job, which he had very much at heart, to reintroduce centralism run by the Germans for the Germans. The best way to achieve this, he thought, was to have a central Parliament, which would appeal to the liberal inclinations of the German bourgeoisie and could at the same time be weighted in favour of the Germans as opposed to the other peoples within the Empire. Thus it was that this man who had 'no real interest' in politics showed great skill in manipulating the electoral system to give the Germans a clear majority in the new Parliament, although they were a minority within the Empire. His system, the so-called 'curial system' was of extreme complication. The curias were groups of electors determined by income, professional and geographical qualifications. The great landlords formed one curia, the chambers of commerce another, the urban districts a third, the rural districts a fourth. In the event, the wealthy landowners and the German bourgeois elements in the towns received an overwhelming advantage. For example, in Moravia the towns, with a total population of less than half a million, returned thirteen deputies to Parliament, while the surrounding countryside, with a population of over a million and a half, returned only eleven.

The new Parliament was a genuine legislative institution, complete with an Upper and a Lower Chamber. It was only a sham in the sense that it had not grown from the people but was set up by Imperial decree and could thus be abolished by Imperial decree. As recently as June 1860 Franz Josef had told his Ministerial Council that he 'would permit no curtailment of monarchical power through any constitution, he would rather face any storm than that'.[11] Now here he was, with the February Patent of 1861, decreeing a genuine constitution and handing over to Parliament very considerable powers. When granting the October Diploma, which gave considerable powers to the provincial Diets, he had written to Sophie, who was appalled by this concession: 'Now we are going to have a little parliamentarianism, but all power stays in my hands, and the general effect will suit Austrian circumstances very well indeed.'[12] Now, in February, he was retreating. He told his Ministerial Council that the February Patent marked the uttermost limits of the curtailment of the sovereign power. He went on:

> I demand from each of you the solemn pledge to defend the Throne with all your energy and the most single-minded purpose against demands for further concessions. In particular you will, as a matter of duty, keep Parliament from trespassing beyond its proper field and repulse decisively any attempt on the part of this body to concern itself with the management of foreign affairs and of army affairs and the business of the Higher Command.[13]

Some historians have gained the impression that the February Patent was never to be taken seriously. By Franz Josef, it is clear, it was taken very seriously indeed. By some of his most devoted subjects it was taken tragically. General Benedek, the hero of 1859, Gyulai's successor as Chief-of-Staff, then Archduke Albrecht's successor as Governor of Hungary, wrote to Crenneville:

> Looking back to 1848 I find myself suddenly afraid that the army, today or tomorrow, might be pressed to swear on the Constitution. I swore on the Constitution of 1848. Now I must say to you in all honesty that the Army commanded by *me* will not swear on any constitution. Indeed I am the Emperor's unconditionally loyal soldier, but I am *only* the Emperor's soldier, and I am too set in my old age to turn myself into a constitutional general. I can understand that a monarch short of cash and for many years far from short of unsound statesmen and Ministers should, with everything in a fever, reach for quinine in the form of a constitution, but the soldier's oath will not suffer this quinine.[14]

This was the reaction of the Emperor's most loyal and able general, who was later, after Königgrätz, to endure public disgrace without uttering a word in his own defence as a scapegoat for his Emperor's failure.

'Reaching for the quinine' was not a bad image. The beloved Emperor behind the cool, impassive front he turned to all the world, had for some time been near the end of his tether. He had tried to make a new start after Solferino and to put a bold face on it. But even while he had been working up to the decisions embodied in the October Diploma he had had to watch Garibaldi driving the King of Naples out of house and country without being able to raise a finger to help, an impotence that filled him with bitterness and humiliation.

> Garibaldi's banditry [he wrote to Sophie], Victor Emmanuel's thieving, the unheard-of roguery of that arch-blackguard in Paris, who is now excelling himself, the Hungarian nuisance and the inexhaustible demands and needs of all the provinces, etc., all batter my poor head so horribly that I have hardly a minute to myself. . . . There was never such baseness on the one hand, such cowardice on the other, as there is in the world today.[15]

3

The Emperor's desperation was by no means entirely due to politics, to a lost war and threatening revolution. His private life had also reached a crisis. In the summer of 1859 Elizabeth could think only of him, at first tearfully and unhappily as her letters show, then, as though suddenly brought to her senses by the fearful blow of Solferino, for an all too short time more reasonably. On the eve of Villafranca she could even write sensible advice about the need for making peace quickly with Napoleon so that her husband could get back to deal with the Hungarians. There is not the least doubt that she had come to love him in her way: 'Have you forgotten me in the middle of all these events? Do you still love me? If you did not, then nothing else that happened could matter any more.'[16] And her husband could reply: 'But my only beloved poor Sisi, you know so well how I long for you, and I don't have to repeat again the greatness of my love for you. You know this in spite of the doubtings in your letter. I rejoice to madness in the wonderful moment when I shall find myself with you, my angel, once more. . . . You are my good angel and you are helping me very much. Go on being strong and hold on, we shall soon see better times. . . . '[17]

But it did not last. They had been brought together partly because poor Sisi had nowhere else to turn. Three years earlier, in

1856, Franz Josef had proved that he was ready to quarrel with his mother on his wife's behalf, when at last he had told Sophie outright (it came as a profound shock to her and filled her with a sense of outrage) that he would no longer put up with her attempts to take the two little girls, Sophie and Gisela, entirely away from Elizabeth. After that it had been open warfare between Elizabeth and Sophie. When, in the following year, Emperor and Empress had made their visit to Hungary there were even signs that Elizabeth might be finding an interest of her own within the framework of Imperial demands. She had met few Hungarians, but simply because Sophie always spoke of them with such contempt she was already on their side, and in Budapest she was enchanted with what she saw. It was on that visit that she lost her eldest child, and in this moment she seems to have come closer than ever to her husband, who showed extreme patience with her wild outbursts against fate and incompetent and scheming doctors. A year later, in 1858, she gave birth at last to an heir, the infant Archduke Rudolf, and for the moment all was bliss. Then came the parting and, with her husband in Italy, a return of the sense, deeper than ever before, of desolated isolation in an enemy camp, expressing itself in the frenetic riding, the refusal to eat in a mania for slimming, the tearful appeals to her husband to let her join him on the battlefield. Then the short-lived attempt to take hold of herself after Solferino.

But she was worn out. She had had three children; she had been engaged for seven years in her long-drawn-out war with Sophie and the Court; she had suffered the fearful strain of the Italian campaign, which had left her on the edge of a nervous breakdown; now she had to stand by and watch her sister, married to the King of Naples, in dire peril without being able to help in any way. On top of all this there was renewed conflict with Sophie over the upbringing of Rudolf, and this time Franz Josef would not altogether take her side. In spite of her finally successful fight to gain control over the little girls, she had shown clearly enough that she was not a born mother: she would move heaven and earth to get her infant children away from Sophie, but when she had achieved this she was only intermittently active in Sophie's place. She had some eccentric ideas about the way to harden children off (later she had to be restrained from having pistols let off almost in the ear of little Rudolf to instil in him strong nerves), but she showed no desire at all to concern herself with their day-to-day upbringing, contenting herself with swooping on them when she was in the mood and leaving the routine to paid attendants. It was not as though she was overwhelmed by her duties as an Empress at this time; she refused to have anything to do with these. She would overhear with bitterness and indignation members of the Imperial Household referring to Sophie as 'our real Empress'; but she did nothing to make these words less true.

And so, while her husband was striving in his own way to pick up the pieces of his Empire, stubbornly fighting a losing battle against any form of constitutionalism, beset on all sides, the break came. Those who knew precisely what happened are all dead. If any documents survive they are under lock and key, and they will not be surrendered to the world so long as families exist who feel absolute loyalty to the Habsburgs, to Franz Josef in particular. The details do not matter: she fell ill and then she ran away. Nervous and physical exhaustion manifested itself in symptoms which threatened an affliction of the lungs. She demanded, imperatively, change and a southern climate. When Franz Josef suggested Merano in the South Tirol among the vineyards of the southern Alps, she rejected the idea with bitterness and scorn. She wanted sun, she wanted orange trees, magnolias, camellias, more sun. So they sent her to Madeira. All Europe was shocked and distressed to hear of the sudden illness of the ravishing young Empress. Advice came flowing in from princes and from quacks. The Empire had no suitable vessel for the voyage. Queen Victoria of England responded to the call and put at her disposal the royal yacht, *Victoria and Albert*, and in the *Victoria and Albert* she sailed from Antwerp into the blue, free for the first time and alone. That was on 17 November 1860, when her husband was having it brought home to him that the October Diploma would not do. She did not return, apparently cured, until May, by which time Schmerling had put through his February Patent and the Emperor had opened his first Parliament, his voice trembling slightly when he pronounced the words: 'Our fate has not ascribed to us a peaceful epoch.'[18]

A month later the old symptoms returned, and Sisi was away once more, this time to Corfu, where she remained until August of the following year. For many weeks in Madeira she had done nothing, locked up in her room for days on end, but weep and stare blindly from the window. But in Corfu she began to find herself and to develop from the shattered and helpless young girl into the mature, shy, ironic beauty with an intense inner life who, by her very mysteriousness, made such a mark in late-nineteenth-century Europe. She achieved this by escaping from reality and creating for herself a world of fantasy peopled almost exclusively by poets and ghosts and horses and their more dashing riders. Not quite entirely: in the intervals of a lifetime of flight, of innumerable journeys which took her always away from responsibility but never away from herself, this strange, peripheral creature would find herself from time to time, always in moments of deep crisis, fleetingly but sharply at the very centre of things, suddenly assuming the role of the great woman she might have been. Further, peripheral as she may have been to the Empire, she remained central to her husband, no matter where she was. And without grasping this fact it is impossible to understand the Emperor, and therefore the deeply emotional background to his attitude and his policies. So long as it was believed, as it was for long believed, that Franz Josef was incapable of feeling, the very image of his reign was out of focus. It was not until 1934, when Count Egon Corti began to uncover, among so many things, Franz Josef's correspondence with Elizabeth, and the diary of Elizabeth's confidante, Countess Festetics, that the picture came clear. The deep emotional disturbance, guilt mingled with longing to the point of desperation, which lay behind the first flight in the early winter of 1860, died down. But Elizabeth, when she had come to terms with herself and made clear how much, and how little, she could give to her husband, remained his only refuge. As the years went by he seems to have come to see her more and more as a mother-figure, even before the death of Sophie in 1873. He poured out his love for her in innumerable notes and letters. Thus, on a visit to Paris in 1867, 'This is my last letter before we see each other again. I can hardly wait for it. *Où est on mieux qu'au sein de sa famille?* I embrace you, my wonderful, most beloved wife, and the children too, and I am always – Your Mannikin.'[19]

4

Before that relationship was achieved, Franz Josef had to suffer much. The Empire was now approaching with fearful acceleration the great smash which was to be the final test of the Emperor's nerve. In the crucible of the war with Prussia and the disaster at Königgrätz in 1866 the iron in his nature was to be forged into steel, and at the same time his realm was to be transformed into the new pattern which was to endure until it finally fell apart, after surviving four years of battering in the hardest war in the then history of the world. As though his humiliation by Prussia was not enough, he also had to suffer through the years blow on blow of the severest kind; but these only served to temper the steel.

CHAPTER ELEVEN

PRUSSIA TAKES ALL

The man who engineered the great smash, Count (later Prince) Otto von Bismarck-Schönhausen, became Prime Minister of Prussia at the age of forty-seven, in 1862. He was called to power, most reluctantly, by the new King, Wilhelm I, to smash parliamentary control of the Prussian army at the very moment when the absolutist Emperor in Vienna had surrendered to the new Parliament his own unfettered control of the State. For although Franz Josef had made his solemn reservation about parliamentary interference in foreign affairs and the management of the army, he had conceded to Parliament the right to interfere in the budget; and in the years from 1861 to 1866 the army estimates were bitterly contested and heavily cut down. While Prussia was strengthening her army and equipping it with modern guns and, most importantly of all, the new breech-loading rifle, the needle-gun, with its capacity for rapid fire, Austria was steadily weakening her army and refusing to buy new weapons: the needle-gun was actually offered to her, but she turned it down, not because her armament experts did not see its value but for reasons of economy.[1] It was in these years, with Bismarck's Prussia looming as an ever more menacing threat, that the Austrian army reached its lowest point. The responsibility for this state of affairs rested squarely on the German liberals in the Austrian Parliament, who, under Schmerling, and with the Hungarians refusing to take their seats as a permanent minority, had things all their own way. The German liberals in Prussia were put in their place by Bismarck.

He was not the fire-eater of legend. He did not rejoice in war as such. He did not even say that might was right. The notorious 'blood and iron' speech, which he made so soon after his accession to power, was not intended to terrify. It threw his master into fits. It caused an outcry among his multitudinous enemies in the Prussian Parliament. It gave the Queen, his inveterate enemy, invaluable ammunition. It distressed his closest ally, Roon, the Minister of War. And he himself regretted the phrase the moment he had uttered it.

It is true [he had said] that we can hardly escape complications in Germany, though we do not seek them. Germany does not look to Prussia's liberalism, but to her power. The South German States would like to indulge in liberalism, and therefore no one will assign Prussia's role to them: Prussia must collect her forces and hold them in reserve for a favourable moment, which has already come and gone several times. Since the treaties of Vienna, our frontiers have been ill-designed for a healthy body politic. The great questions of the time will be decided, not by speeches and resolutions of majorities (that was the mistake of 1848 and 1849), but by iron and blood.[2]

He was soon explaining it away: all he had meant was that the king needed soldiers; he had not been developing a solution to the German problem. He had certainly been warning Austria and Bavaria; but he was not invoking the use of force. 'Blood and iron' was just another term for 'soldiers'. He was not to make a mistake like that again, but for ever afterwards he was the man of blood and iron. And, of course, although in 1862 he was assuredly not dreaming of an immediate war of conquest, the image was, though incomplete, for all practical purposes correct. He did not want blood and iron; but if the job to be done seemed to call for them, he used them – and ceased using them as soon as they were no longer needed.

To his great friend Motley, the American historian, he showed another side; but really it was the same side:

Here in the *Landtag* [he wrote], while I am writing to you, I have to listen . . . to amazingly foolish speeches delivered by amazingly childish and excited politicians, and this gives me a few moments of involuntary leisure. . . . When I was an Ambassador, although an official I had the feeling that I was a gentleman; but as Minister one is a slave. . . . These chatterers cannot really rule Prussia; I must resist them; they have too little wit, and too much comfort; they are stupid and arrogant . . . and yet 'stupid' (in its general sense) is not the right term. They are fairly clever in a way, have a smattering of knowledge, are typical products of German university education; they know as little about politics as we knew in our student days – no, less! As far as foreign politics are concerned they are, taken individually, children; in other matters they become children as soon as they meet together *in corpore*.[3]

It was a queer weakness in a great man, a disastrous weakness in the event, that he had to argue all this out. There is not a thought in that passage which has not been shared in essence by every leader of men since history began, and in particular by every Prime Minister of any account who in modern times has presided over a Cabinet or a Parliament. In England the great parliamentary leaders have taken the imbecilities of their flock for granted: it has not been found necessary by any of them to spell them out with the air of men making a great discovery. And with a mixture of more or less contempt and more or less tolerance they have, half-consciously at the most, adapted themselves to the human material they had to work with, seeking to draw the latent good sense out of it by example, by precept, by flattery, by cajolery, resorting, as a rule, to bamboozlement and calculated manoeuvre only as a last resort: in their general attitude there has, again as a rule, been a strong element of protectiveness: flock is the right word. Because of this general approach a climate has been fostered very favourable to the development of latent talent, to the taming of rebels once they have served their turn as irritants, to the accumulation of worldly wisdom and to the neutralization of the fools.

Bismarck, the first great German parliamentarian, had none of this approach. Too conscious of his vast superiority to the rank and file, it never occurred to him that he had a duty to lead and to educate. He saw himself not as a shepherd but as the master of a pack to be restrained with the whip, to be trained with 'rewards', to be conditioned, to be exploited when occasion arose through appeals to their base instincts. And, indeed, this element in his nature (it was far from being the only strand in one of the most complicated characters of modern times) was all too accurately expressed in a remark uttered during the course of his utterly detached and cold-blooded machinations in the Schleswig-Holstein question: needing to invoke with all his might an outburst of nationalistic feeling in the Parliament he despised, he said to Zedlitz, the Prussian Commissioner in Schleswig: 'We must let the whole pack howl!'[4] They howled.

Thus it was that this extraordinary man kept his culture and his politics in watertight compartments. He had, indeed, a more cultivated and a far more questing mind than any European statesman of his time, with the single exception of Disraeli: he delighted to argue about history and philosophy with Lassalle, the 'tragic comedian' and Karl Marx's most formidable rival, and with the author of *The Rise of the Dutch Republic*. But politics was politics, an abstract fantasy of power operations, detached from the reality of human beings and yet perversely labelled *Real*. And what politics was, when it came down to it, was neither monarchism nor republicanism, neither liberalism nor conservatism, neither revolution nor reaction, neither nationalism nor federalism: all these 'isms' were promoted and used by Bismarck at one time and another during his tenure of power as serviceable tools in the execution of his solitary purpose, the aggrandizement of Prussia, the State in which he happened to have been born, seen as an end in itself. This was the man who was to unify Germany as a means to that end, and who, in the process, corrupted German public life irreparably. This was the giant who now stood up against Austria, broke her in war as one stage towards the fulfilment of the end, and then quietly and courteously helped to put her together again in another form as part of a further stage. He would never have demeaned himself by uttering the question-begging truism about might being right: right for him did not exist, only Prussia. His supreme strength was that he never overreached himself. He had the most strict ideas about the limits of Prussian aggrandizement. Further, he was perfectly content, once he had achieved what he wanted for Prussia, to watch, even to encourage, the growth of other virile Powers, so long as these offered no direct threat to the stability of his own great edifice. In his nature there was neither megalomania nor enviousness: within the context of his own peculiar standards he had the integrity and freedom of mind of the great artist. Thus: 'His views on all subjects are original,' reported Disraeli to Queen Victoria from the Congress of Berlin, 'but there is no strain, no effort at paradox. He talks as Montaigne writes.' Britain had just secured Cyprus for herself, and Bismarck was as pleased as he would have been by any stroke of his own. Disraeli continued: 'When he heard about Cyprus, he said: "You have done a wise thing. That is progress. It will be popular; a nation likes progress." His idea of progress was evidently seizing something.'[5]

His duplicity, when called for, could be on the grand scale; but unlike many other 'forward-looking' politicians he was never intoxicated by his own cleverness and he never lied out of habit. This was not simply because he frequently found that the simplest way to put people off their guard was to tell the truth about his plans (this was simply one useful trick in a very large bagful, and one exploited to the full by later dictators who were also congenital liars) but, more often, because he had a fine sense of economy when he came to means. He lied only when he deemed it strictly necessary. In his dealings with

Austria his character was expressed with elegant lucidity. Characteristically, he felt most warmly towards Austria when about to destroy her. In his early days as Prussia's representative at the Frankfurt Diet he was bitterly resentful against the manners of the Austrians who, following Schwarzenberg, sought pettily to humiliate Prussia at every turn. It was not until 1857 that it became finally clear to him that Prussia could never achieve the position he desired for her until Austrian pretensions in Germany were broken. Then, in his great memorandum, he exhibited his flexibility by pressing the view that the natural ally for Prussia was France, arguing with all his force against the legitimist view that the Prussian monarchy could not decently ally itself with a usurper. It was by now clear to him that sooner or later it would come to war with Austria. He did not look forward to that war, and there were several occasions in the next few years when events took such a turn that it looked as though war might be avoided. He welcomed these for what they were; but war was always close to the front of his mind. One day he would be working actively with the Hungarian rebels against Austria, the next, when the unfolding of events brought Austria temporarily into step with Prussia, he would coolly break off relations with these subversive elements: he was nothing if not correct. By 1859, in Petersburg, he had crystallized his policy, which was to work for the exclusion, almost certainly by force, of Austria from Germany, and then to enter into an alliance with her. 'I regard the federal relationship as an illness of which Prussia will sooner or later have to be cured, *ferro et igne*, unless we take a treatment for it immediately, while the season is favourable.'[6] Soon he was convinced that, to use his own words, it was 'a mathematical impossibility'[7] to resolve the Austro-Prussian conflict without war. In 1865 he was saying to Benedetti, the French Ambassador to Berlin, 'If Prussia has not burned her boats yet, they are at any rate smouldering.'[8] In 1866 he said, again to Benedetti:

> I have succeeded in persuading a King of Prussia to break off the intimate relations of his House with the Imperial House of Austria; to make an alliance with revolutionary Italy; to make arrangements, for a possible emergency, with the French Emperor; and to propose at Frankfurt the revision of the Federal Act by a popular parliament. I am proud of my success. I do not know whether I shall be allowed to reap where I have sown; but, even if the King deserts me, I have prepared the way by deepening the rift between Prussia and Austria, and the liberals, if they come to power, will complete my work.[9]

On 10 June of that year he said to the Hungarian general of Kossuth's days, Turr: 'I have not yet succeeded in convincing the King that war is immediately necessary, but what does it matter? I have put the horse at the ditch and . . . he must jump.'[10]

There was no ill-feeling. If Prussia was to occupy her proper place, Austria had to be defeated decisively in war. But there was to be no rape of the body. Once Vienna had been taught its lesson and put firmly in its place, driven, that is, from Germany, the Monarchy could be approached as a friend. Bismarck undertook this operation in precisely the same spirit in which in 1863 he concluded his iniquitous treaty with Alexander II of Russia, which aroused the indignation of the world, binding him to hand over to Russia all Polish refugees who had sought asylum in the realms of the Prussian King. Indignation hurt nobody. It was unfortunate for the Poles, but in making over these unfortunates to the vengeance of the Russian Tsar he was attaching Russia to him at a critical moment in the history of Prussia. He made no attempt to justify his action. He left that to the English, to Disraeli, who told the House of Commons not to be reckless with its sympathy for the Poles. If the Partition of Poland had been a great crime, he said, it was a crime shared by the Polish people, since their national existence could not have been destroyed without some faults on their side.[11] This was the kind of exculpatory statement that Bismarck never found it necessary or desirable to make: it might have been better if he had. The two men were in many ways alike. 'A war in the centre of Europe on the pretext of restoring Poland', Disraeli continued, 'is a general war, and a long one. The map of Europe will be much changed when it is concluded, but I doubt whether the name of Poland will appear on it.' By that time Disraeli, fifty-nine to Bismarck's forty-eight, with still five years to go before he became Prime Minister, and the only statesman in Europe fit to hold a candle to Bismarck, knew all about the new Chancellor. The year before he had met Bismarck at a party in London, and Bismarck had talked to him in one of his moments of total candour:

> I shall soon be compelled to undertake the conduct of the Prussian Government. My first care will be to reorganize the army, with or without the help of the *Landtag*. . . . As soon as the army shall have been brought to such a condition as to inspire respect, I shall seize the best pretext to declare war on Austria, dissolve the German Diet, subdue the minor States, and give national unity to Germany

under Prussia's leadership. I have come here to say this to the Queen's Ministers.[12]

He made war on the Danes, on Austria, on France. Each time he won and in each case the objective was exact and limited: after Königgrätz he had his work cut out to whip the King and his generals off the hunt before they tore Austria to pieces. it was not his fault that his master later went too far in France. Nevertheless, he had firmly established the principle that a modern State was justified in undertaking calculated aggression in the interests of its own aggrandizement. He would never in any circumstances have permitted the war of 1914 to take place, but that war was the fruit of his teaching and his example. He was the ruin of a civilization.

2

Poor Austria! Easy to say – and how often said! Poor all of us. . . . The poison distilled by this superb and terrible man, having shattered our society, still infects it. Who are we to blame a young Austrian autocrat, hard-pressed, for not seeing what was coming? We can smile at Rechberg for his faulty appreciation of Bismarck's power, but Rechberg was not alone. In the eyes of most European statesmen during those four years between his accession to power and the launching of his bolt against Austria, Bismarck seemed to be more of a fantasist than a serious politician. Before he could conquer Austria he had first to conquer his own King, and he had to do this single-handed against the opposition of Parliament and all Prussia, more particularly in the teeth of the bitter hatred of the Crown Prince and the Crown Princess, who regarded him as an ogre and who were profoundly convinced that the way to establish the hegemony of Berlin was to liberalize Prussia and, through liberalization, to attract the lesser German States into her orbit. Indeed, during his first years of office, almost every action of Bismarck's – from the wresting of the Prussian army from parliamentary control to the treaty with Russia extraditing the Polish refugees – seemed to be leading straight for his downfall; even faithful adherents to the Prussian Crown found themselves increasingly repelled by Bismarck's government. Franz Josef had perfectly good reasons for believing that time was on his side and that, in any case, Bismarck would never be allowed to carry his policies to their logical conclusion. He was at this time almost quite alone: even von Moltke, the great soldier who, in the end, was to confirm Bismarck's policies in action, still viewed the notion of war against Austria with distaste and some dread: he feared that France would be the only gainer.

The first open challenge to Austria came in January 1863. While Rechberg was pursuing his mission of conciliation towards Prussia, Schmerling was seeking by every means available to him to win over the German States to the side of Vienna. These included plans for reforming the Federal Diet; but as soon as these were tabled Bismarck warned Vienna sharply that any attempt by Austria to use majority decisions of the Diet to steam-roller Prussia would be considered to be a breach of the Federal Constitution: Prussia would walk out. He further suggested to Karolyi, the Austrian Ambassador, that it would be a good thing for all if Austria forgot about Germany and turned East, towards the Balkans. It was against this background that Franz Josef fell in love with a plan designed to restore him as titular chief of all the German princes. The author of the plan was none other than Julius Fröbel, one of two extremist deputies to the revolutionary Frankfurt pre-Parliament, who had been condemned to be shot, and then pardoned. The other, Blum, had indeed been shot; but Fröbel had escaped to America, been pardoned in due course, and had then been taken by Schmerling into the Austrian service to help in lending colour to his scheme to attract the German liberals. This particular liberal flew high: he proposed nothing less than that the Emperor of Austria, the implacable enemy of liberalism everywhere, should preside over an assembly of all the German princes, resuming in essence, if not in style, his rightful place as Holy Roman Emperor. No sooner said than done. Without consulting Schmerling, who knew all about the plan, or Rechberg, who knew nothing about it at all, Franz Josef took the matter into his own hands, working through one of Rechberg's subordinates, the head of the German Department of the Austrian Foreign Office, Baron von Biegeleben, who himself cherished grand ideas about forcing Prussia to her knees, and now, in direct opposition to the policies of his chief, saw his way clear.

Seen in retrospect, the proceedings which led up to the meeting of the German princes in Frankfurt in August 1863, and the assembly itself, were pure farce. But they did not look like that at the time. In the eyes of Europe, Austria had regained her proper stature since the disaster of 1859 and, with a fresh masterstroke, was about to assert her supremacy in Germany. 'This decision of the Emperor's is the happiest thought the Austrian statesmen could have hit on',[13] wrote the Swiss ambassador to Vienna, a sober enough observer. England and France were both deeply impressed, Napoleon uneasily. The great majority of the German States, taking their cue from Saxony, fell in with the idea enthusiastically. The fact that Rechberg and Schmerling were at loggerheads was not in itself important: the plan was now the Emperor's own; it met with widespread approval; and all depended on the Emperor's capacity to put it across. With Franz Josef taking the bit between his teeth there was nothing his Ministers could do to alter the course of events. Rechberg was firmly put in his place when, furious at being consulted so late and also at seeing his cautious probings for an agreement with Prussia threatened, he submitted his resignation; he was not allowed to resign, he was to do as he was told: 'I am not going to have my Ministers dismissing me!' Then it was Schmerling's turn: to his distress and indignation he heard that the Emperor had decided to leave him behind in Vienna and take Rechberg to Frankfurt instead.

All this did not matter in the least. Franz Josef knew what he wanted to do and he put all his weight and ability into the task, in a manner that surprised and impressed all observers. But the real struggle was for the mind of the Prussian King, and this was lost before the Congress opened.

It was not a foregone conclusion. Early in August the young Emperor wrestled for the soul of the elderly and vacillating King among the fairy-lights and illuminated crags and waterfalls of Bad Gastein. Something had to be done about Germany, and quickly: the Princes had their chance to act now, as Princes, before they were caught up in the impending revolutionary tide. A little later Franz Josef was to express his line of reasoning in a letter to Sophie: 'It is the last attempt to unify Germany in order to put her in shape for fulfilling her task of maintaining the balance and peace of Europe – it is the last way open to rescue the many sovereign Germanys from going under to the growing revolution.'[14] King William had to face the young man alone. Bismarck stayed in the shadows: this thing had to be settled between the monarchs; all he could properly do was keep his master on the straight and narrow path. He had only one message, the message he had already given the Austrian Ambassador, Karolyi, in Berlin: Prussia must on no account, cost what it may, put herself in the position of being dictated to by a majority vote of the lesser Princes; any arrangements about the future of

Germany must be made between Prussia and Austria direct, as equals.

King William temporized. He was impressed by the notion of a great gathering of the Princes, but he dare not say so. Instead, he suggested a solution that has quite a modern sound: before they agreed to a 'Summit' meeting, first let the Ministers stage a preparatory conference; then, if they reached agreement, the Princes could meet in solemn State to ratify their conclusions. Meanwhile a Summit meeting that failed would do more harm than good. Franz Josef countered with the now familiar answer: Ministers had met repeatedly, with no results; it was time for the masters to take hold. King William wavered, but he went away from Bad Gastein, back to Baden-Baden, without promising anything. '*Auf wiedersehen in Frankfurt!*' Franz Josef cried. '*Auf wiedersehen!* Yes, *auf wiedersehen* when the Ministers have done their work . . .' was William's last word. It was now Bismarck's turn to wrestle. The story is familiar. 'I thought I had convinced him by the time we got to Baden. But there we found the King of Saxony, who renewed the invitation in the name of all the Princes,' he later wrote. 'My master found it hard to stand against this move. Over and over again he repeated: "Thirty reigning Princes – and a King as their courier!"' But Bismarck stuck to it, arguing on and on, 'literally in the sweat of my brow'. The King was lying on a sofa. Bismarck went on at him relentlessly, on and on, until suddenly his master burst into tears and gave way. He would boycott the Assembly. He would cut Prussia effectively out of the German Confederation. It had been a terrible scene, the first of many when Bismarck had to strain every nerve to bring his master to the sticking-point. He was, he wrote, so utterly exhausted that he could hardly keep upright. He got himself somehow to the door and closed it behind him, but his nerves were in such a state that, as he closed it behind him, he tore off the handle. He sat down at once to draft the letter of refusal, and then, flinging it at the messenger come to take it to the King for signature, swept a tray with glasses and a heavy decanter to the floor: 'I had to smash something!' he wrote immediately afterwards, 'now I can breathe again.'

The world knew nothing of this drama between the immense bag of nerves which it later came to think of as 'the Iron Chancellor' and his vacillating master. The world saw only the great and glittering assembly which gathered a few days later in the old Imperial city, and it held its breath, taking for an uneasy portent what was in fact a mocking echo of a past which was already dead. The young Emperor made the best of possible impressions. He presided over the sessions with crispness, decision, insight and tact, appearing to have the whole business at his finger-tips. But the business was vain. In the absence of Prussia, the lesser Princes, even those who leant more towards Vienna than towards Berlin, would commit themselves to nothing. And behind Franz Josef's cool exterior was fury and frustration. 'The sessions were long and exhausting,' he wrote to his mother when it was all over, 'and apart from these there were endless informal conversations; all the time we had to struggle with suspicion, cowardice and bottomless stupidity, so that our nerves were stretched to breaking-point.'[15]

Even so, it was possible for quite shrewd observers to believe that Austria was in the ascendant. On the way back from Frankfurt Franz Josef called on Queen Victoria, who was staying with the Coburgs. The Queen expressed her hopes for German unity, and when Franz Josef acquiesced in this hope, adding that Prussia made things very difficult, she expressed her apprehension that Vienna might be pushing Berlin too hard:

> I rejoined that I trusted there was no disposition to lower Prussia, for that naturally Prussia and Austria must go together, to which the Emperor answered, no one dreamt in Germany of lowering Prussia, which was an impossibility, but that, at Berlin, great pretensions were raised. . . . I said that I could not conceal from him that the King of Prussia seemed much hurt at the belief that there was an intention to show want of respect to Prussia, and thought that there was a desire to place her under Austria, which I had assured him I believed to be quite unfounded. The Emperor merely repeated the same thing, and said that he thought it was a great mistake that the King of Prussia had not come to Frankfurt, in which I agreed. . . . I went on to say that what I believed was expected, and wished, was equality between the two Powers; could there not be some arrangement of alternation on the Presidium and Directorium? He said, this was quite a new pretension of Prussia to have it also, and in Austria they would dislike extremely its being given up.[16]

This conversation took place on 3 September, the day after Franz Josef's *cri de cœur* to his mother, quoted above. It offers a vivid example of the extreme closeness and exaggerated self-containment which had now become second nature: here at least was a chance to try out his ideas on a not ill-wishing equal, or at least to float an informal appeal to William in Berlin. He said not a word, either in justification or in anger. He said nothing.

3

While Bismarck in Berlin was developing his devious strategy for the ultimate crushing of Austrian pretensions by force, Franz Josef was being threatened much more openly by more immediate dangers nearer home. The Schmerling régime, set up by the February Patent of 1861, was soon to go aground and break up on the rock of Hungarian intransigence. By all normal standards the new Parliament was a meaningless farce. It was boycotted by Magyars, Czechs and Poles. By 1863 it was to all intents and purposes a purely German assembly, and the German liberals once more proved their political incapacity and practical short-sightedness by identifying themselves with Schmerling's autocratic centralism, thus proving that they were not really liberals, that all their talk of political freedom boiled down to political freedom for Germans. The spirit behind Adolf Fischhof's moving appeal in the March days of 1848 for brotherly love between nations had left no trace; the one thing the so-called Constitutional Party unequivocally stood for was running the Empire for the benefit of Germans and establishing complete ascendancy over Magyars and Slavs.

And yet the Schmerling Parliament was not a total loss: it made Franz Josef think about politics, and supplied him with valuable insight into the minds of politicians. For a man who, until then, had thought of politics in terms exclusively of administration, with himself as unquestioned administrator-in-chief, he proved to be an astonishingly quick learner. He did not, of course, like what he learnt; indeed the very idea of a group of footloose professional politicians arguing away in a Parliament, 'Schmerling's circus', questioning his own decisions, effectively interfering with the Ministerial budgets, caused him frequent pain. But he was by no means so inflexible as to be above taking a leaf out of the politicians' book. And the deeply ironical thing was that the main use to which he put his new knowledge and understanding of political manoeuvre was to break the power of the Germans, who had taught him, and come to a fruitful accommodation, first with the Hungarians, then, much later, with some of the Slavs, over the heads of the Germans and in spite of them.

It was a very remarkable progression in the development of a born autocrat, not at all understood by the politicians of the day, and still not taken properly into account by historians and biographers. While appearing to all the world as the rigid upholder of the belief in the divine right of kings, while doing all he could to encourage this impression, Franz Josef, at thirty-two, began, almost in secret, to develop the qualities of a consummate politician. 'You see in me', he said to Theodore Roosevelt, who had journeyed across Europe to view the tremendous old phenomenon in his declining years, 'the last Monarch of the old school.' This was the image he deliberately projected. As far as manners went, it was true enough: Franz Josef knew how to be polite. As far as political activity went, it was, to say the least, an over-simplification. He was not at all the last Monarch of the old school. He was, as he knew very well, the only Monarch of the Franz Josef school; and a formidable school it was.

The one effective liberal in the whole of his vast realm in the 1860s was the great Hungarian, Ferenc Deak, and it was not without significance that Deak was the one man at that critical epoch whom the Emperor could bring himself wholly to trust and with whom he could negotiate creatively. It was an irony of the saddest kind that the liberalism of this outstanding man should, for patriotic reasons, have been placed at the service of a wholly illiberal people.

Deak had first come forward as his country's champion in 1848, only to retire to his country estate when Kossuth had been swept into power on a wave of chauvinism. Sixteen years later, in 1864, his great hour came. He rose to it with clean hands. 'He was one of those rarest statesmen', to quote Professor Redlich, 'who embody in their persons, as it were, all the best and most productive forces of spirit and mind of a race, without its adverse qualities and failings.'[17] His influence on the young Emperor has never been adequately assessed. A man of total integrity, the broadest vision (limited only, as was usual in those days even among the wisest of all lands, by ideals of national patriotism), of unsurpassed moral courage, he opened for Franz Josef windows into a country of the mind the very existence of which he had not hitherto suspected. It was a country in which the ideas of justice and human decency held sway: once glimpsed, it was never to be forgotten. The fact that Franz Josef was never to master it and make it his own is neither here nor there; he was henceforth aware of it, and his actions were to be increasingly influenced by this awareness; of very few statesmen in the history of the world can more be said. Deak himself, the great preceptor, fell short of the total realization of his own ideals: as a Magyar he was good and wise, but his goodness and his wisdom did not extend beyond the frontiers of his country.

Franz Josef did not learn all at once: there were three years of fearful trial ahead. But when the great test had been passed he was clearly a new man. The Great Compromise, the *Ausgleich*, between Austria and Hungary was reflected by a movement in the heart of the Emperor himself. 'I command to be obeyed!' and 'Those who praise me to my face may likewise blame me. That, however, may not be.' These words, and others like them, were the perfect expression of the young autocrat in the days when he imagined, vainly, that all he had to do was to command. Those days were over.

4

It was almost by accident that by 1864 the Emperor found himself on a better footing with the Magyars than with the rest of his realm. This paradox was produced by the fact that whereas German Austria, Bohemia and Moravia were effectively subject to Schmerling's parliamentary régime, the Hungarian lands were not. Totally ignoring the Vienna Parliament, and kept steady by Ferenc Deak, they ran their own local affairs through their own local government organs, which acted as though they were subordinated to the King and to nobody else. The absurdity of this situation, which seemed to escape Schmerling and the parliamentary Germans, was quite evident to Franz Josef, who proceeded to take advantage of it. On the advice of Count Esterhazy, the Hungarian Minister without Portfolio, who was a leader of the Old Conservatives, he began quite secretly to engage in a sort of shadow duologue with Deak through one of the Hungarian officials attached to the Governor-General's office. Then, when the Emperor had been acquainted with the way his thinking ran, Deak started to come out into the open. At Easter 1865 he published his famous article which in effect laid down the Hungarian's terms for co-operation with Vienna. First, he said, the Hungarian constitution of 1848 must be restored, to establish legal continuity and to excise from history the aberrations of the past sixteen years. Once that was done the Magyar Diet might well be found ready to agree to changes in that constitution. The changes Deak envisaged were as radical as his initial demand; they added up to the establishment of two distinct States under a single head, acting together towards the outer world as a single Power.

These proposals were received in Vienna with consternation and outrage. Only Franz Josef, with Esterhazy at his side, saw promise in them. Instead of drawing himself up to a great height and telling the Magyars that they were forgetting themselves and presuming too much, he took one of his sudden, reckless decisions, set off for Budapest and, once there, made it clear to all concerned that he had come to talk to them not as the head of the Empire of Austria, but as their King. His impact on Budapest was tremendous; there can be no doubt at all that he was deeply affected by the extraordinary outburst of enthusiasm with which he was received: his reign so far had not been marked by those demonstrative displays of loyalty which monarchs find so reassuring. These volatile and self-centred people were tiresome in the extreme; indeed, they were virtually unmanageable: but they clearly had to be managed, and evidently he, Franz Josef, was the only man who could do it. He would have liked more time, but he was in a hurry: at any moment now Austria might find herself at war with Prussia, and to fight Prussia with his hands tied behind his back by a disaffected Hungary was out of the question. Clearly he would have to make concessions. The first thing to do was to display a change of heart. He could do this best by getting rid of Schmerling, and he could kill two birds with one stone: with Schmerling out of the way he could disembarrass himself of the restrictions of the February Patent and make a new start. This is what he did: employing the obvious necessity of coming to an accommodation with Budapest as his lever, he used the Hungarians to defeat the German liberals, and then applied himself to the forlorn task of bridling the Hungarians.

It was a long, dour fight he had taken upon himself. He had no intention at first of transforming Hungary into an especially privileged nation, only of curtailing the pretensions of the Germans. The Hungarian vision now was of a Dual State, an Empire for the purposes of facing the outer world, with foreign policy and the army in the hands of the King-Emperor; two kingdoms, or little empires, for internal affairs, with the Magyars lording it over subject Slovaks, Croats, Rumanians, and the rest; with Vienna running Bohemia, Moravia, Galicia, and what was left of Italy. It was a clear-cut vision: once Magyar overlordship over the lands of St Stephen was acknowledged, the Hungarians would know how to look after their own. They would Magyarize their possessions and speak with one voice in Vienna. In a word they would bring to what was to be known as the Dual Monarchy, a compact, centralized State run in their own interests, while the Austrian portion would be a sprawling dissension-riven aggregation of peoples, what was left of Maria Theresa's Unitary State, speaking with half a dozen voices.

It is not clear just how far the most far-seeing of the Magyar statesmen saw ahead at this juncture: their first aim, and it was to obsess them for three years, was to achieve Hungarian autonomy. It is not clear just how far Franz Josef saw ahead when he came to the conclusion that some measure of autonomy would have to be conceded to Budapest if Hungary was to remain Habsburg. But what in fact happened as the pattern worked itself out was this: once the Dual Monarchy was set up, signifying Hungary's total victory over the centralizing Germans of Vienna, the Hungarians did everything in their power, and it was a good deal, to strengthen the rule of the German liberals over the other half of the Empire. Not content with ruling over their own minority races with a perfect disregard for nationalistic aspirations, they encouraged the German centralizers, against whom they had latterly fought with such bitterness and passion, with such an exuberance and luxuriance of invocation of the sacred rights of national independence, to sit on the Slavs of Cisleithnia. They did this because they believed, correctly, that any concessions made by Vienna to the subject-nations in her half of the Monarchy might produce demands for similar concessions from their own subjects. As in 1848, the Magyars showed in 1864, and thereafter until the final collapse of the Empire, that they were not in the least interested in the principles of self-determination for small nations, but only in winning and maintaining dominion for themselves. It was this total lack of principle behind the Magyar agitation, conducted to the accompaniment of the highest sounding invocations of the rights of man, which tarnished their romantic patriotism and introduced into their politics an element of the disreputable, preventing them from being at any time a force for goodness and enlightenment. Clearly freedom, like charity, begins at home; clearly a small nation struggling to preserve its own identity will put first things first, i.e. itself. But it is hard to discover in the history of modern Europe any nation which has exhibited such sustained and unmitigated egocentricity as the Hungarian nation, any nation which at no time in a century of rapid change ever showed the faintest, the most embryonic, flicker of interest in anything at all but its own immediately selfish interests. Many years later, the newly emergent Czechs were to affront the idealists by their treatment of the Slovaks; the newly emergent Poles were to show what subject-nations could do when they got their heads by their treatment of their Ukrainian minority and by their spectacular and short-sighted selfishness when they stabbed a prostrate Czechoslovakia in the back at the time of the Teschen incident. But the pacemakers in this competition of once-subject peoples to demonstrate how much more harsh and ruthless they could be than their one-time all-powerful masters were the Hungarians; and, in the end, it was Magyar chauvinism more than anything else which made the Empire unworkable and precipitated its final undoing.

Deak did not have this in mind, nor did the most colourful and brilliant of all Hungarian statesmen, Deak's protégé, Andrassy. But they created the conditions in which it could happen. They and their inferior successors, and they alone, steadfastly blocked all subsequent attempts on the part of Franz Josef (and these were obstinate and persevering) to achieve a working federation of south-eastern European peoples. Franz Josef could have defeated the Germanizers, and frequently did; but he could not defeat the unholy alliance of Germanizers and Magyarizers: hence Sarajevo. Ironically, the one Austro-Hungarian statesman to protest against Vienna's fatal reaction to Sarajevo was the Hungarian Prime Minister, Stepan Tisza, who saw in a war with Serbia a deadly threat to the Magyar position. But it was he and his predecessors who had brought Sarajevo about. Instead of seeing that the only hope for Hungary lay in her role as a vital part of a grand federation of peoples, they went to all possible lengths, over decades, to ensure that there would be only two peoples, the Magyars and the Germans – and the Germans only because they were too strong to be defeated. As an example, when the Monarchy went down there was still no railway between Vienna and Zagreb or Vienna and Dalmatia: the Magyars would not allow such an intimate connection between the King-Emperor and a part of his realm that came under the administration of Budapest: all rail communications had to be routed through the Hungarian capital.

Why were the Hungarians strong enough to achieve this extra-ordinary feat? Above all, of course, because they were rebels of the most self-centred kind, but also because their great nobles never ceased to be Hungarians. The Bohemians and Moravians, on the contrary, less stiff-necked and proud by nature, very much less sure of themselves, were represented in Vienna by great magnates who at the highest level put the interests of the Empire as a whole above its parts, and at the lowest put their own personal interests above the interests of their people. There is no clear answer to the question that arises from this opposition. Where does patriotism end and chauvinism begin? And, when it comes to self-interest, which is very soon, who is to say that the self-interest of the great Bohemians, who made the cause of Vienna their own, was less reputable than the self-interest of the Hungarian magnates, who wanted only to be free to run their own lands in their own way without interference from outside. It can only be said that the Hungarians who thought they could make their country viable without linking its fortunes indissolubly with Vienna were more short-sighted than the Bohemians. But the German threat was close at hand and ever present in Prague: the Russian threat seemed, until 1914, a long way from Budapest.

From the moment that Franz Josef presented himself at Budapest in the spring of 1865 it was evident that the victory of the Hungarians could not be far away. The Emperor, without knowing it, without any conscious plan, was indeed taking the first step to put into practice Bismarck's insolent advice – that Vienna should shift its centre of gravity to Budapest. It was the end of Schmerling, whose policy towards the Hungarians was to hang on and wait until they cracked. Franz Josef found it all the easier to force his resignation because of his anger with the parliamentary liberals for refusing to pass the army estimates. It was the turn once more of the nobles. Turning his back on the Germans, Franz Josef called on the Bohemian aristocrat, Count Belcredi, a gifted and accomplished Governor of Bohemia, to form a government composed almost entirely of the great magnates of the Empire. In no time at all the Schmerling constitution vanished into limbo and the national Diets came back into their own. The new Hungarian Diet, an instrument of Deak's immediately set to work under Count Julius Andrassy, Deak's own nominee, to prepare for the final struggle.

Andrassy was one of the most striking figures of the nineteenth century. Handsome and bold, intelligent and witty, he was theoretically a dead man. For throwing in his lot with Kossuth (in opposition to Deak) in 1848, he had been sentenced to death *in absentia* for high treason and hanged in effigy. All his great properties had been confiscated, and for eight years he was exiled in France. People called

him *'le beau pendu'*. This was the man who was later to become the
Imperial Minister for Foreign Affairs. He was an ardent Hungarian
patriot, but his conduct at critical moments was tempered by his
ambition: he was more interested in becoming Foreign Secretary of
the Empire than in becoming Prime Minister of Hungary. For the
moment he was simply the leader of the Hungarian Diet within the
Empire, and upon him, pushed forward by Deak, who preferred
always to remain in the background as the elder statesman, fell the
whole burden of negotiating the final settlement with Vienna. He was
still at it when war with Prussia came.

5

The events which finally precipitated that war tell us more about the
character of Bismarck, who made it, than about Franz Josef and the
Austrians. The Schleswig-Holstein imbroglio, from which Austria
sought to escape in violence, was a masterpiece of diplomatic scheming, but it possesses little significance in itself. If there had been no
Schleswig-Holstein, Bismarck would have found another issue. But
by using the quarrel over the successor to King Christian to lure
Austria into a trap of her own making, and, thereafter, by planting
his banderillas into the hide of the great, clumsy beast until the pain
and the indignity could no longer be borne, he achieved his ultimate
purpose with admirable economy of means.

In outline the story was this: after the unsuccessful Prussian
attempt to 'liberate' Schleswig-Holstein in 1848, the Treaty of
London laid it down that the two Duchies should be governed by the
Danish King but not incorporated in the Kingdom. Holstein in
fact belonged to the German Confederation; but the two had for
centuries been declared to be for ever inseparable. In 1855 the introduction of a new constitution created alarm among the German inhabitants. Together with the Duchy of Lauenburg they had been
promised local autonomy under the Danish Crown, but Denmark
was clearly bent on their ultimate incorporation. With the death of
Frederick VII, Christian IX became King and formally announced
his intention of incorporating Schleswig with Denmark. The
Germans put up a rival claimant, the Duke of Augustenburg, but
Bismarck, who had long been set on securing this bridge between the
Baltic and the North Sea for Prussia (the site of the future Kiel
Canal) was not going to tolerate this. Basing himself for once on the

sanctity of a treaty, he demanded that the two Duchies be united and restored to autonomy under the Danish King. Austria had to make a hard decision when Danish resistance gave Bismarck the pretext of going to war to restore the *status quo*. Should she take her stand with Prussia on the Treaty of London (after all, her whole being was based on the observance of treaties), and share in the spoils that might ensue? Or should she assume leadership of the rest of the German Federation and, by backing the Duke of Augustenburg, issue a direct challenge to Prussia then and there? Rechberg, still obsessed by the necessity of coming to an agreement with Prussia (he hoped to get her to guarantee Venetia), decided to act with her. It was a short, sharp little war, in which the Austrians did well and gained a misleading impression of their own military efficiency.[18] It ended in a temporary glow of mutual self-congratulation between Berlin and Vienna. But Austria had cut herself off from the German Confederation and played herself directly into Bismarck's hands: here was just what he had been constantly demanding; Austria was recognizing Prussia's special position and treating her not simply as an aberrant member of the German family of States but as an equal. And Austria soon found that anybody who thought he could treat Bismarck as an equal had made a sad miscalculation of strength.

There were deep forebodings in Vienna. Thus, in the Austrian Parliament, one of the deputies exclaimed: 'Why are we acting with Prussia? Is Prussia our friend anywhere? Is not Austria denounced as the arch-enemy of Prussia? Prussia has scarcely digested Silesia and now she is stretching out her claws into the Duchies, while we are leading her into them to the music of our own good regimental bands. What tune must we play to get her out again?'[19]

The attitude of the German liberals was quite clear-cut: Austria's future lay in the closest union with the German Confederation. Rechberg's attitude was quite clear-cut: an understanding with Prussia and reliance on the sanctity of treaties. Franz Josef, on the other hand, was badly muddled. He was not, as he saw it, treating Prussia as an equal: he was simply responding to treaty demands. And, on top of that, there was his nagging fear of the French. He was badly in need of a powerful ally: by acting in consort with Prussia, not because Prussia demanded it but because international law required it, he could win a strong ally without, as he saw it, making concessions of any kind.

To his one close friend and hitherto most loyal supporter, Albert of Saxony, he wrote on 15 February 1864:

> I only regret that you are not bringing your Saxons into the battlefield, just as I regret above all that Germany has split into two camps and that I must see you opposed to us. . . . One sees all too clearly the coming of a European war in which Austria and Prussia will have to come to your help against their will in face of the man in Paris who, in the last analysis, is the chief enemy of us all. . . . I do not want to go into what Bismarck may or may not have said. He has his great shortcomings, which we had reason to know all about in earlier times; and one of these shortcomings is that he speaks all too recklessly and exaggeratedly, trying to frighten people with words. In the proceedings in Holstein the Prussians have admittedly been wrong in form, but in essence, in my opinion, they have been correct. . . . In this alliance the position and steadily maintained objectives of Austria are enough to protect you against any further designs the Prussians may have. . . . [20]

He was far from the mark indeed. Two years later Prussia beat Austria and the whole of Germany was wide open to Berlin. Six years later, without Austrian help, Prussia beat France and Wilhelm I became Emperor of a unified Germany, excluding Austria. When Franz Josef decided to align himself with Prussia in the Schleswig-Holstein affair it never so much as crossed his mind that the Prussian King, his 'brother', would turn round on him in this way, in alliance with Italian irredentists, Hungarian revolutionaries, and Slav dissidents.

Bismarck, when he went to Schönbrunn with his master to discuss the division of the spoils, may not have foreseen it either. He did not want a war with Austria simply for its own sake; he wanted it only if it should prove essential to achieving his ultimate purpose, the expulsion of Austria from the German family with Prussia at its head. He had spoken nothing but the truth when he told Disraeli in 1862 that he saw no way of doing this except through war. He spoke nothing but the truth when, after Königgrätz, he said:

> It would have been very difficult to avoid war with Austria. But anyone with the smallest sense of responsibility for millions of human beings would shrink from making war until he had exhausted all other possibilities. . . . There were various methods of making for the goal. It was my destiny to try them one after another, until finally I had to resort to the most dangerous. [21]

But he might have said with no less truth that anyone with slightly more than a vestigial sense of responsibility would think twice about pursuing in cold blood goals the attainment of which involved the destruction of thousands of lives. This was beyond him.

6

Bismarck could almost certainly have reached an agreement with Rechberg whereby Austria would give up her Baltic interests in return for a firm guarantee of Austria's possession of Venetia. But, to cut a very long story short, he had no intention of guaranteeing the Austrian position in Italy: even though now he was at last succeeding in reducing Austrian pretensions, he still envisaged ultimate war with Austria as probable, and in that war he proposed to have the King of Italy on his side, to make it for Austria a war on two fronts. Bismarck, left to himself, could very likely have found a way first of guaranteeing Austria against Italian attack, then of making an alliance with Italy. But Bismarck was never quite left to himself: and his master, Wilhelm I, would not have tolerated such open perfidy. Indeed, in the years before Königgrätz, Bismarck had to spend rather more time and energy in softening up and conditioning his own master to see in Austria an aggressor, than in manoeuvring against Vienna and overcoming the ceaseless and sometimes violent opposition of the Crown Prince and the Crown Princess, Queen Victoria's daughter. So, after Schönbrunn, the two Powers rested on the impossible and indefensible arrangement whereby they exercised joint control over the Duchies. Bismarck took this arrangement in his stride, because no situation which held the seeds of future trouble came amiss to him. Rechberg was miserable for the reason that Bismarck was pleased. Franz Josef, though uneasy, seems to have felt that honour was satisfied.

The only man in Vienna who knew just what he wanted was the strange, anachronistic figure of the head of the German Department in the Foreign Office, Maximilian Biegeleben. He was also the only Austrian official to appreciate Bismarck for what he really was. An aristocrat and a first-class civil servant, recruited from Hesse, he made it his business, in direct opposition to the settled policies of Rechberg, his master, to oppose Prussia at every turn, even though it came to war. In the end he won the ear of Franz Josef himself, who was profoundly impressed by his industry and his lucidity. Biegeleben's great error was his failure to understand that as a civil servant with real power in one limited field he had no power at all in other related fields. Determined on a showdown with Prussia, he could see to it that Vienna adopted an intransigent attitude in her official Notes to Berlin, and he could so contrive matters that in the developing quarrel over the ultimate future of the Duchies Austria should appear to be working undeviatingly against Prussia's interest. In a word, he could make a war, but he could not prepare for one. As a departmental head in the Ballhausplatz he could recommend to his masters the desirability of an understanding with France; but he was in no position to realize this goal. Still less could he do anything effective to make the army fit to beat the enemy in the war he desired. His limited power was essentially power without responsibility. And even when it came to Germany, where the nature of his position enabled him to indulge his bent for forcing and spoiling tactics, the limitations of his highly conservative cast of mind made it impossible for him to take the necessary action to win the lesser States for Austria in the coming struggle with Prussia. He was a classic example of a strong departmental official serving a relatively weak master who can upset the balance of a government but is nevertheless powerless to swing it into a new course. It is impossible not to admire the acuteness of his reading of a highly specialized problem and the tenacity and boldness with which he championed his point of view; it is equally impossible not to wonder at the crassness of so sharp an observer in not perceiving his own inescapable limitations.

But the real interest of the Biegeleben interlude is the light it throws on Franz Josef's new determination to be independent of his Ministers and hold all the threads in his own hands. He had already shown himself capable of playing off one Minister against another, as in the Rechberg-Schmerling duel. Now, *vis-à-vis* Prussia, he was, as it were, conspiring with a permanent official against his own Foreign Secretary – and, at the same time, *vis-à-vis* Hungary, bypassing both his Ministers and entering through intermediaries into direct negotiations with the rebels. It is impossible to be sure, but it seems highly probable, that the conventional idea of the Emperor falling under the influence now of one Minister, now of his rival, is an incorrect idea. He was deeply influenced, we are told, first by Rechberg, then by Schmerling, then by Biegeleben, then by Esterhazy, then by Andrassy, dropping first one pilot, then another, in the spirit of the familiar character who is always swayed by the last man he talks to. But such a characterization does not correspond at all with the essential nature of the man, as it unfolds. It is far more likely that from 1859 onwards he was not manipulated but manipulating. Thus in the Hungarian question he was not moved by Esterhazy, but rather chose Esterhazy as the most suitable man to further a policy he had himself conceived. It was the same with Biegeleben: what he liked about the ideas of this remarkable grey eminence was that they coincided with his own view of Austro-Prussian relations; Rechberg was altogether too ready to come to an accommodation with Prussia, even if it meant admitting full equality. Biegeleben was determined to give nothing away. Franz Josef was perfectly capable of perceiving that Biegeleben was dreaming of a war; but this he would have regarded as an amiable eccentricity on the part of a man whose heart was in the right place. He, Franz Josef, could use Biegeleben: let him dream of his war; he, Franz Josef, and Wilhelm I on the other side, would see to it that this absurd consummation was never achieved. The situation was, of course, intolerable for the Ministers, over whose head the Emperor was going: they could lump it. And, as a rule, they did. When they could do so no longer, they resigned.

Over the years, there has been a great deal of sterile controversy about the responsibility, on the Austrian side, for the Austro-Prussian War. There have been many candidates for the role of the Empire's evil genius. Besides Biegeleben, the favourites have been Esterhazy and Rechberg's successor as Foreign Secretary, Count Alexander Mensdorff-Pouilly. Esterhazy, whom we have already glimpsed in his role as forerunner of the Hungarian settlement, was a high eccentric. A little, quiet, gentle, questioning man, he had immense personal charm, especially for women, and a beautiful brain. But it was the brain of a perfect sceptic. He saw with elegant lucidity deeply into every question from every point of view. Sometimes he was overcome by the bewildering complexity of life, to which there was no clear answer; then he would sulk, or go into retreat. As Austrian Ambassador to the Vatican, for example, he had sometimes sequestered himself for months at a time, leaving urgent messages from Vienna without an answer. Then he would emerge once more, fresh as a daisy, full of penetrating remarks and insights about everything under the sun: possessing no simple convictions himself, he made it impossible for lesser colleagues to act on their own by scrupulously and delicately questioning the premises of any proposed course of action just when it had been decided to do something. In the end he went melancholy mad. 'He was often peculiar in his manner,' said Rechberg to Friedjung. 'Sulky, and what the French call *maniaque*. Finally, when he took to beating his wife and set his own castle on fire, he had to be sent to a lunatic asylum.'[22]

About Mensdorff there was nothing *maniaque*. He was a cavalry officer of the gentlest, most charming and most honest kind. But through the Coburgs he was connected with the greater part of European royalty – he was, of course, a cousin of Queen Victoria – and found himself thrust into one important post after another, invariably at a most critical moment. He was a soldier, so he never refused an order. But although he, too, possessed a good brain, he was much too pleasant and unambitious to believe in himself, and he preferred the ideas of others to his own. In Friedjung's phrase, 'it never occurred to him that it might sometimes be his duty to oppose the Emperor's will'.[23]

Here were two able men, neither of them a major statesman, opposed to a statesman of genius. It seems pointless to argue about who was responsible for what. Austria lacked a Bismarck to oppose a Bismarck: it was as simple as that, and the consequences were inevitable. This can only, in honesty, be regretted by those who would like to see a Bismarck at all times conducting the affairs of every country. Bismarck, as it were, gobbled up both Mensdorff and Esterhazy before breakfast, as he had already gobbled up Rechberg. But it is to be doubted whether a Schwarzenberg, or even a Metternich in his heyday, could for long have contained that particular opponent when he put himself in league with the revolutionary forces of the day. Perhaps Kaunitz could have done it by single-mindedly devoting himself to the forging of a completely new chain of alliances and making the concessions necessary to this end. But nobody less than a Kaunitz had a chance.

We are left then with the war which Bismarck forced and the details are irrelevant to this study. Austria made what are usually regarded as two great mistakes, apart from the basic one of thinking she could manage Bismarck. She refused to sell Venetia off to the Italians for 1,000 million lire, and she refused to escape from the Holstein trap by taking cash compensation for the surrender of Holstein to Prussia. The first was the more serious, since the refusal to relinquish Venetia ensured that Italy would be on Prussia's side if it came to war. But, in the first place, the money would have all gone on building fortifications on the new frontier; and in the second place the Emperor would have seen it as highly dishonourable to sell his subjects for cash – though not at all dishonourable to lose them in war. The second would only have postponed the war until a later occasion. The drift to war was not uninterrupted. The first climax came in the summer of 1865 when Prussia showed her true intentions for the Kiel base and Austria decided after all, to join the German Confederation in support of Augustenburg's claims. Then it looked very much like war; but with the Convention of Gastein in August an appearance of amity was restored – Bismarck's 'papering over of the cracks'. In September Bismarck, not telling his King, started sounding Napoleon as to the position France would take up in the case of a war between Austria and Prussia; but Napoleon was evasive. In November came the cash offers from Prussia and Italy. All during this year the Austrian parliamentarians were doing their best to weaken Vienna's negotiating position. There were demands for freedom of the Press, which Belcredi partly met; there was sharp agitation against the Concordat with the Vatican, which was resisted; above all there was a determined and effective onslaught on the army estimates: the establishments of infantry companies were reduced to fifty-four men, and there was a 10 per cent cut on the previous year's expenditure.[24] Franz Josef's reply was to 'suspend' the constitution. Bismarck watched these developments with the liveliest pleasure. With the turn of the year Franz Josef began in earnest his negotiations with Hungary. For the whole of February and March the Court moved to Budapest, and Elizabeth, happy among the Hungarians, began to come into her own as Hungary's 'beautiful providence', in Andrassy's phrase. Then began the sinister farce of the mobilizations. For Austria mobilization was one thing, for Prussia quite another – a fact of which Bismarck and Roon made the most skilful use.

When in 1862 Bismarck had been called in to defy the Prussian Parliament on his King's behalf and railroad through the army reforms, he did his work well. He gave Prussia, in effect, a standing army of 370,000, a reserve of 126,000, and a militia of 163,000. The reserves were truly liquid. On the Prussian system the army was organized by regions. It was the quickest and simplest thing in the world for the reserves to report to their depots, which were close by their homes. Mobilization and deployment could be carried out in four and a half weeks. The Austrian system was very different. In this polygot Empire it was one of the fundamental rules that conscripts invariably served with regiments based far from their homes – e.g. Hungarian regiments were based not in Hungary, but in the Tirol, or Venetia, or Styria. This stopped the troops from becoming too friendly with the local inhabitants and effectively cut them off from the civilian life around them; but it was a drawback when it came to swift mobilization for a war, the call-up involving immense slow train journeys, sometimes across half Europe, for reservists and recruits requiring to join their regiments. Mobilization and deployment in Austria took eight weeks.[25] Bismarck knew all about this.

Once Austria had refused the cash offers, Bismarck started what would nowadays be called a war of nerves. His visit to Napoleon at Biarritz achieved nothing definite for Prussia, but a great mystery was made about it, and Vienna was deeply perturbed. On the last day of 1865 Austrian apprehensions were augmented by the signing of a commercial treaty between Prussia and Italy. At the end of January King Victor Emmanuel was solemnly awarded the Prussian Order of the Black Eagle. Gablenz in Holstein did his best to damp down the constant agitation in favour of Augustenburg, in the spirit of Gastein. But as the atmosphere grew more jumpy with Prussia's demonstrative activity in France and Italy, incidents multiplied. These were magnified by Bismarck in his reports to King William, who became gradually convinced that Austria was tolerating, if not conniving at, anti-Prussian agitation. Soon Bismarck decided he had enough ammunition to let fly; he formally accused Austria of conducting 'seditious agitation' against Prussia, which claimed complete freedom of action if Austria ignored her complaints. This was in effect a preliminary ultimatum, and Europe, aghast, took it as such. The King of Prussia was at last coming round. 'If the King is to be persuaded to demand his rights,' said Bismarck to Benedetti, 'he must first be convinced that somebody is disputing them. But when once he believes that his authority is being challenged or treated with contempt, he will concur in the most energetic measures.'[26] He said he had had a most difficult task to shake his master's faith in Austria. Now at last he was succeeding. By the end of February, with Franz Josef sitting in Budapest, William was almost brought round to the view that war was inevitable unless Austria would surrender his claim to the Duchies. But he was still insistent that war must not be provoked and that a peaceful solution must still be worked for.

This did not prevent him, after earnest prayer, from sending

Goltz, the Prussian envoy to Paris, with a formal letter asking the price of Napoleon's neutrality. At the same time Moltke was dispatched to Florence to sign an alliance with Italy. The Austrians knew nothing of these last two moves, but they were hearing enough to add to their alarm without making it finally clear that they must immediately move to action stations. It was not until March that the Austrian military were brought into the picture and told formally what they might have to reckon with. The first thought of the generals was that Bohemia lay wide open. In addition to garrison troops the establishment in Bohemia consisted on paper of a complete army corps. In fact there were only five regiments, and two of these were Italian. It was considered imperative to reinforce these immediately. Mensdorff protested that this would be to ensure the worst of both worlds. The dispatch of less than 7,000 men, which was all that was proposed, would make no difference to the issue in face of a full-scale Prussian attack, but it would give Bismarck the chance to indict Austria as a potential aggressor. And this was what happened. A great agitation was set up about the armament of Austria, which was magnified excessively in the reports fathered by Bismarck on the Prussian Press. Meanwhile, although Napoleon would not commit himself as to what he wanted from Prussia, he did everything in his power to smooth the way for the Italo-Prussian alliance by pushing the Italians into it. In fact he desired a frontier on the Rhine and the whole of Italy out of Austrian hands. He was so obsessed with the fear of an Austro-Prussian rapprochement, remote as that contingency then was, that he was ready to assist in the making of a major European conflagration to prevent it. Other Frenchmen saw more deeply, above all Thiers, whose speech in the French Chamber on 3 May was marked with high prophetic insight. Italy, he said, would soon free herself from France's tutelage and turn against her; and one day Germany, under the leadership of Prussia would become the scourge of France.

What was Franz Josef to do in the midst of so much turmoil and intrigue? Kings and Emperors were exploiting popular emotions; Prime Ministers were deceiving their masters; on every side there was movement and revolt against the *status quo*. At the heart of the confusion was one man, Bismarck, who wanted a war to gain his own ends. He was acting against the wishes of the Prussian Parliament and of the whole Prussian royal family, except the King. His cynical manoeuvres were beginning to fill Europe with dismay and disgust.

Even the Italians were apprehensive. But change was in the air, and he was the only man who was determined to harness the winds of change to a narrow and specific purpose. In spite of his unpopularity, in spite of the distrust he universally inspired, everything was in fact converging in his favour. Napoleon, who overrated Austrian strength, was happy to see him lead Europe into war, believing that he would profit from Prussia's defeat. Tsar Alexander was still in no mood to lift a finger to save Austria. Italy wanted Venetia, and, anyway, half welcomed the prospect of a victorious war as an outlet for the accumulating dissatisfaction of the Italian people. England was tied by innumerable bonds to the Protestant North and divided by religion and political institutions from Catholic Austria. Mensdorff, given greater strength of purpose, might have bought Prussia off. But to what end? Only if Austria had been prepared to identify herself unconditionally with the German Confederation could she have found the means to cut Prussia down to size; and such identification would have opened the way either to the complete domination of the Habsburg Empire by German liberals, or else to a formal revolt by Magyars and Slavs against such domination. It was out of the question: it would have meant the end of the Habsburg inheritance. It would have been the betrayal of all that Franz Josef stood for and *had* to stand for.

There was one way and one way only for Austria to avoid a war; and Bismarck knew this long before Franz Josef knew it: for Austria to surrender, without firing a shot, her pretensions as the senior German Power.

Feverish efforts were still made to appease the Prussians. To Bismarck's infinite distress an agreement was made in April whereby both sides agreed to return their armies to a peacetime footing. The Austrian generals were in despair at the hindrances put in their way – and Prussia still went on buying Bohemian horses to use against the Austrians. But then the Italians took a hand, and their threatening troop movements were the last straw: they produced the classic Austrian response. That is to say, after a display of almost infinite patience under extreme provocation, the Austrians panicked, laid back their ears and dug in their hooves, quite nullifying their past efforts and condemning their future efforts to inevitable frustration. They mobilized against Italy. Bismarck could hardly believe his luck. All he had to say, when the Austrians pointed out that the mobilization of their Southern army against the Italian threat in no way affected their agreement to disarm in face of Prussia, was that the Prussian General Staff could not possibly distinguish between regiments called up to move south and regiments called up to move north.

In June Napoleon had his great hour. In return for a promise of neutrality – a neutrality he was already determined to maintain – Austria promised to hand over Venetia, for him to give to the Italians, win or lose. Critics have found this behaviour totally inexplicable; but it is not really so inexplicable. On the face of it nothing could seem more frivolous or irresponsible than the Austrian behaviour in first refusing to consider parting with Venetia, and thus driving Italy into the arms of Prussia, and then, when war was certain, throwing Venetia away regardless of the outcome. If anything this is proof only of Franz Josef's stubborn conviction that he would be able to avoid war with Prussia (a conviction held by most of the European statesmen of the day): why should he give Venetia away to put himself in a better position to fight a war which would never take place? But when war was certain it was another story: then the overriding consideration was to keep Napoleon out of it at whatever cost, and at least no cash transaction was involved. When Napoleon told the Austrian Ambassador in Paris that unless this condition was fulfilled he would be compelled to arm and, if occasion arose, to intervene, how could Franz Josef be sure that he was bluffing? That was on 12 June. Two days earlier Bismarck had put forward a proposal for a reform of the German Confederation which, if adopted, meant the exclusion of Austria from Germany. Three days later Bismarck, heroically wrestling with his reluctant master, managed to railroad through a Prussian ultimatum to Hanover, Saxony and Hesse-Kassel and next day marched in. On 17 June Franz Josef told his people that war was unavoidable. Two weeks later it was all over.

7

The fortnight's campaign which ended at Königgrätz and brought the Prussians to the outskirts of Vienna has been brooded over and pondered by generations of military historians. What happened, in a word, was that a statesman of genius found himself working hand in glove with a soldier of genius. Von Moltke did not look like a general; he looked like an admiral. The fine-drawn features, the

distance-ranging eyes, were as far removed from the popular conception of a Prussian general as it is possible to imagine. He was
wholly without ambition in the vulgar sense; that is to say, he had
not the least desire to shine, but only to do supremely well whatever
work came to his hands. At the time of Königgrätz he was nearly
sixty-six, and virtually his whole career had been spent on the Staff.
Wherever he went on detachment he made maps, and when he was
not making maps he wrote history. His mapping operations ranged
from Rome to Constantinople; his histories from Turkey to the
Netherlands. All these things were done superbly well. At forty-five
he married an Englishwoman, Mary Burt. At forty-eight he was
contemplating retirement. He was then Chief-of-Staff of an army
corps, and retirement and the delights of country life and further
contemplation had to be postponed because of the exigencies of the
1848 revolution.

Nobody had the least idea that he was a genius. He did not then
know it himself. But events soon took a turn to bring him close to the
seats of the mighty and to give untrammelled play for gifts which
nobody had suspected. In 1855 he was picked out to be Prince
Frederick William's adjutant, and three years later the Prince Regent,
soon to be King Wilhelm I, choose him to be Chief of the General
Staff. Thus he was fifty-eight when, for the first time, he turned away
from his historical studies and unassumingly began to apply his
extraordinary mind, now enriched by his profound understanding
of the past, to the problems of the moment. In no time at all he had
worked out plans for any conceivable war in which Prussia might
find herself engaged – and he still found time to write. But his writing
now, a history of the 1859 war in Italy and of the Prussian war with
Denmark in 1848, was merging with the present and looking into the
future. His plan for the joint war between Prussia and Austria on the
one side, and Denmark on the other, aimed at the capture of the whole
Danish army in the first battle: it was upset by the incomprehension
of the Commander-in-Chief; but he did not repine and instantly
produced a new plan of great dash and boldness, which did the trick.
He now interested himself in problems of mobilization, with the
instruction and disciplining of senior officers, and with working out
new tactics to exploit the needle-gun, the breech-loading rifle. Once
it was clear to him that there would be war with Austria he set himself to devise the ideal plan, which involved striking out of the blue,
declaring war on the first day of mobilization and capturing the whole

Saxon army while it was still in barracks. In his cool, detached, almost academic way, he was the father of the *Blitzkrieg*.

European civilization at that date, however, was still dominated by dynasts. It was not yet sufficiently advanced to allow one State to strike at another without any warning at all: it was to take more than half a century and a major holocaust to liberate the peoples, so that men of the people could take over from the hereditary monarchs and make war on rational lines. Moltke knew perfectly well that his original plan would never be accepted: it was his duty to demonstrate how Austria could be most swiftly and certainly beaten, and he performed his duty. With that out of the way, he concentrated on the practicable.

He was much too sensible to be sure that Prussia would win. But he knew that his best chance lay in concentrating nearly all his force against the main Austrian armies. Hanover and Saxony had to be smashed at once, simply because they stood in the way of the Prussian deployment against the Austrians in Bohemia; but Bavaria and the rest could wait. He was, as it turned out, entirely justified in leaving his right flank exposed. The Saxon army loyally marched out of their own land to strengthen the Austrians in Bohemia, leaving their country wide open to the Prussians; the Bavarians, who, with Württemberg and Baden, should have brought an army of 100,000 to bear, did nothing: they refused to join the main battle-front in Bohemia, and they made no serious attempt to attack the exposed Prussian flank: it was betrayal on the grand scale.

Moltke's opponent, as Commander-in-Chief of the Northern army, was Field-Marshal Benedek, the hero of the right-wing at Solferino. Moltke had him weighed up, along with the other Austrian generals. He was brave, honest, chivalrous and worshipped by his men; he could fight with skill and resolution and, when occasion demanded, boldness amounting to recklessness. But he knew nothing of military history, was no strategist, and depended far too much on his Staff advisers. Because he had no book-learning himself, he exhibited an exaggerated respect for the book-learning of others, and he allowed his own natural instincts to be fettered by the copy-book planning of his Chief-of-Staff, Hennikstein, and his Chief-of-Operations, Krismanić. Further, he approached this tremendous climax to his gallant career in a spirit of morbid foreboding. In this foreboding there was certainly an element of superstition as well as a sense of personal insufficiency; but there was more than this; he knew, none better, that the Austrian armament and Austrian war-preparedness in general was far behind the Prussian.

It is necessary to get the position of Benedek clear because around his appointment, his failure, and his subsequent disgrace an enduring legend was built up over the decades which was to distort the public image of Franz Josef and, with this, of the workings of the Monarchy itself. The legend depended largely on making mysteries where no mysteries existed.[27]

There had to be two Austrian commanders, one against Prussia, one against Italy. There were two candidates for these posts – Benedek, the senior Field-Marshal and the popular hero; and the Archduke Albrecht, an able soldier but not in the same class as Benedek. Moreover, Albrecht's name was tainted by his rather inglorious role in the 1848 revolution and by his unpopular Governorship of Hungary. The Northern command was the senior command and the most critical. Albrecht wanted it; Benedek did not want it, and said so with characteristic raciness of expression. He would be a donkey in Bohemia, he said; but in Italy he knew every tree. The legend had it that Franz Josef, knowing this, insisted on putting up Benedek against the Prussians because the risk of defeat there was greatest and because it was unthinkable that a Habsburg should be allowed to expose himself to such a risk. There is no evidence of this at all. Habsburgs had led armies in the field in the past – had conquered and had been defeated. Franz Josef himself had assumed command of the Italian campaign before Solferino – and been defeated. Franz Josef, moreover, had every intention of being with his Northern army in the field, and was only with the utmost difficulty persuaded against this course long after Benedek's appointment. Benedek was appointed because there was no choice: the army and the people demanded it. He was the hero of the hour.

His own reluctance was understandable. Many generals in history have resisted critical appointments; but there was no question of Benedek's being blackmailed into accepting this one. As he wrote to his wife: 'I should have been a good-for-nothing not to have accepted the command.'[28] He could have refused, but refusal would have been the negation of all he stood for as a soldier. The next part of the legend, that he obtained from the Emperor a written assurance that in the event of defeat he would be called to account only by the Emperor himself, and by no other judge – a sort of counter-black-mail – has not a shred of evidence to support it, is out of character on both sides, and would, anyway, have been superfluous: Benedek was appointed by the Emperor and could in the nature of things be accountable only to him.

In a word, Benedek assumed the command after an initial protest, and doubting his own powers, as a matter of course; and the Emperor laid this burden on him also as a matter of course. To understand subsequent events it is necessary to bear this in mind.

The main concentration area for the Imperial forces was in the neighbourhood of Olmütz, the grim old Moravian fortress town where, nineteen years earlier, Ferdinand had abdicated and the eighteen-year-old Franz Josef had been proclaimed Emperor. It covered the approaches to Vienna and it gave Benedek a chance to tie up in the mountains any Prussian army moving in from Silesia. Once established, the Imperial quartermasters would be able to get on with the uncompleted task of equipping the great army, which was still short of many things, including boots. But events moved fast, and on 21 June the Emperor, almost certainly remembering the opportunities thrown away by Gyulai in Piedmont seven years before, ordered Benedek to move and march as fast as he could in the direction of Berlin.

The Prussians were already marching. Moltke could count initially on superior preparedness, superior discipline and training, and superior communications: he had a far better road and rail system at his command than Benedek. Directing affairs initially from Berlin, he took a long bold view which called in effect for three separate armies to be set in motion as entirely independent forces which would converge in Bohemia. Five days after the declaration of war all three Prussian armies were on Bohemian soil. On 26 June they began to win the first of a series of lightning victories, interrupted only by an initial defeat of a Prussian corps at Trautenau.

The Prussians were still fighting under remote control. Benedek had moved his main army up to the neighbourhood of Josefstadt, in front of Königgrätz, but the Saxons and an Austrian corps under Clam-Gallas were still far away on the left. The Prussian Elbe Army, under Herewarth, swept down on the right to attack the Saxons, who were moving east to link up with Benedek; the Prussian 1st Army, under Prince Friedrich Karl, came down from the north through Görlitz to link up with the Elbe Army in the neighbourhood of Münchengrätz. The Prussian 2nd Army, commanded by the Crown Prince, was engaged on the most difficult manoeuvre of all, breaking in through the mountains from Silesia in the east. It was this army which suffered an initial very sharp repulse by the Austrians at Trautenau on 27 June.

But there were no other repulses, and the Prussian 1st and Elbe Armies had already, with remarkable swiftness and decision, brought their weight to bear on the Saxon army and on Clam-Gallas: Liebenau, Turnau and Podol on the 26th; Hühnerwasser on the 27th; Münchengrätz on the 28th; Gitschin on the 29th. On the 28th, far away to the east, the Crown Prince avenged himself for Trautenau, on the 29th conquered at Königinhof, and, on the 30th, established communications with the 1st Army, now joined with the Army of the Elbe. On 1 July the King of Prussia arrived at G.H.Q. to assume command, bringing with him Roon and Moltke – and Bismarck, now playing very much second fiddle to the generals, in the uniform of a major of the reserve.

What had happened? How was it that the formidable Imperial army with 197,000 men and 770 guns had allowed the fateful junction of the two main Prussian forces, totalling 221,000 men and 776 guns, to take place under its eyes, instead of taking on first one of the great forces, destroying it, and turning to face the other?

This question has been argued for nearly a century, and it will go on being argued. Some say that Benedek should have wheeled west, advancing to meet Prince Friedrich Karl's two armies, joining with the Saxon forces to force a victory, knowing that the Crown Prince could not intervene in time. But the main line of attack has been that between the 25th and the 28th he could still have moved decisively north-east and defeated the Crown Prince, while, with the aid of the Saxons, holding off the 1st and Elbe armies. He did neither of these things, and it has been accounted to him an everlasting disgrace.

On his actual strategy nothing, one way or the other, can be said that is new. On his difficulties a good deal can be said.

In the first place, neither he nor his two Staff advisers, Krismanić and Hennikstein, had occupied the ground in front of Josefstadt with any conviction: they did not want to be there at all. They had wanted to stay based on Olmütz and fight a decisive battle there. This was what they had planned for, and their planning, good or bad in itself, had been upset by Franz Josef's imperious intervention, when he had sent his young Staff officer, Lieutenant-Colonel Beck, to tell Benedek not to dawdle round Olmütz but to advance as fast as he could.[29] Franz Josef himself had been influenced here by several considerations: first the spirit of attack, second the desirability of fighting on enemy soil, third, and above all, his determination to spare his only true allies, the Saxons, who must at all costs be supported and not left exposed to bear the brunt of a major Prussian onslaught.

In the second place, the Prussians, when they struck, did so with a swiftness and a deadliness quite unforeseen. We should be the last to criticize the Austrians for being shaken to the core by the swift and ruthless attack of Prussian troops in the opening moves of a war long and carefully planned and with superbly equipped troops trained to the minute for an operation calculated long in advance: 1870, 1914, 1940, were essentially repetitions of this kind of dedicated single-mindedness in offensive warfare. Nor was it a matter only of training and railways. Everybody was more than a little afraid of the Prussian breech-loading rifle, and all historians have since conceded its decisive impact on the campaign, in so far as the quick breech-loading action enabled the Prussian infantrymen to shoot three to five times more quickly than their Austrian opponents. Statistically, in a word, this has been generally understood and allowed for. What has been too little allowed for was the moral effect behind the statistics of mortality, first on the troops and their regimental officers, then on Benedek himself.

The series of battles listed above were no ordinary nineteenth-century battles; they were stages in a swift progress on the part of the Prussians; on the part of the Austrians they were an attempt to stem a rout, which had begun before anybody understood what was going on, and was over before the Commander-in-Chief fully realized that it had begun. In five days the Austrian right and the Austrian left had been pushed back practically to the Elbe; and nothing anyone could do could check the deadly pressure. Benedek was above all the soldiers' general: his men idolized him and he loved them. He was responsible for them. He had put them out with antique weapons to hold their own against this deadly new menace. He knew, none better, the effect on a soldier's morale, when, standing up to reload, pushing in his powder and shot and ramming the charge home, he can be shot at five times by a man, who, lying down, has only to slip a cartridge into the breech, twist home the bolt, and fire. In face of this menace there is nothing to be done except rush in and try to get home with the bayonet, all the time under rapid fire – or to give way and take cover and try to think again. The Austrians, by turns, did both. In some of these engagements they displayed extraordinary heroism; but they got shot all the same, and in the end they had to give way. This sort of thing went on for five days.

Benedek's emotions, anger, shame, a sense of total impotence, and guilt must have been past bearing when the news of these terrible blows began to come in all at once. Anger with the politicians who had prevented the proper equipment of the army; shame and impotence because he could do nothing to help; guilt, too, because although he had striven honourably and in vain to achieve the modernization of Austrian arms, he could nevertheless be blamed for failing to see that his men were trained in new tactics designed to minimize the menace of the breech-loader. It was in this state of mind that the gallant, forthright, devoted, above all *steady* father of his army quite simply lost his head. Against his better judgement he had brought his army to a place where he had much rather not have been: he had exposed it to a murderous onslaught to which there seemed to be no answer at all. Heroically as they fought, their losses were regularly anything from twice to five times the Prussian losses. The Prussians clearly had a calculated and coherent plan: they knew what they wanted to do; Benedek did not. On top of everything else, the heaviest blow had fallen on the Saxon army which the Emperor had declared himself in honour bound to succour. In five days, and without a set battle, Benedek had lost 30,000 men and also any advantage that the somewhat illusory command of interior lines might have given him. His own headquarters were now in danger of being swamped by retreating units and formations over which he had no control: the roads on all sides were a chaos of troops and their trains moving back, encountering troops and their trains moving up. It was a débâcle on a terrifying scale, the rout of perhaps the finest army ever put into the field by Austria before ever that army had been formally committed as a whole. Krismanić and Hennikstein, by no means the feeble, theoretical and spineless characters they have been made out to be, both Staff officers of the utmost distinction, but suddenly out of their depth, were over-whelmed too. So was the young Beck coming up to Benedek on one of his tireless missions from the Emperor to ensure the successful junction of the Austrians with the Saxons. He arrived to find chaos, with Benedek a broken man who had one thought and one thought only – to get out, to withdraw his main forces behind the Elbe, to put as great a distance as he could between his army and the Prussians, to fall back on the old, tested Olmütz fortifications, where he would have time to think again, to regroup, to improvise new tactics to fight a new sort of battle at least on his own ground. When Beck arrived he was past pretending. He might save the bulk of his army, but he could not even guarantee that. Nobody quite knew where Moltke's main forces were: as always on these occasions the air was thicker with rumours than with smoke; and, as usual, all the rumours said one thing: the Prussians were just down the road, were behind, were on every side. It was in this atmosphere that Beck drafted a telegram to the Emperor, which Benedek took and read in silence, and in silence signed: 'Your Majesty most urgently requested to make peace at any price. Catastrophe inevitable.'[30]

It was a remarkable scene. The thirty-six-year-old Lieutenant-Colonel seemed to be the only one capable of speech in all that stricken headquarters. He gave words to thoughts which neither Benedek nor Krismanić nor Hennikstein could utter. The army had to be taken back over the Elbe immediately. If that was not enough it would have to go back across the Danube into Hungary. Then he sent his own personal signal to Crenneville: 'Armistice or peace imperative because withdrawal scarcely possible. My heart is breaking, but I must report the truth.'[31]

The effect of these telegrams on the Emperor and his Court was unspeakable. They fell without warning from a clear sky. Anxiety, profound anxiety, there naturally had been; but the mood in Vienna had been immeasurably lightened by the news from the Italian front, where on 24 June Archduke Albrecht had inflicted on Victor Emmanuel and Lamarmora at Custozza a brilliant repetition of Radetzky's crushing blow in 1848 against Victor Emmanuel's father. There were many in Vienna who had expected the worst both in Italy and Bohemia; but the Italian attack was now broken, and there had been nothing to suggest the imminence of catastrophe in Bohemia. What could conceivably have gone wrong in so short a time? What could conceivably be done in face of this wholly inexplicable talk about an armistice and the impossibility of retreat? Only one thing: 'Impossible to conclude a peace. I order – if unavoidable – retreat in best order.' And then the pathetic, bewildered cry: 'Has there been a battle?'[32]

There had not been a battle. But by the time Beck's telegrams had arrived in Vienna it was clear that there was going to be one after all. The retreat could not begin at once: the troops needed to rest. On

2 July the heavy baggage trains still had not cleared the Elbe. The great army, covering the withdrawal of the rear echelons, was deployed in a compact semicircle in front of Königgrätz, its morale wonderfully restored after the piecemeal, planless fighting of the last few days. Benedek, though still thinking in terms of defeat, had recovered from his demoralization of the night before. The army as a whole knew nothing of those dark, void hours at G.H.Q. To them, the breech-loader notwithstanding, the Field-Marshal was still the great hero who would see them through, who could do no wrong. Hennikstein too had recovered and sent a message to Crenneville saying that things looked much better now and there was still hope. By half past three on the 2nd Benedek had firmly decided to fight and, if necessary, to go down fighting. For the ordinary soldiers, for the regimental officers, for the formation commanders in the field, the blank despair of the previous night had never been. Nothing could have been more impressive, more formidable, more comforting than the great battle array, which, with the heavy guns in their hundreds right up forward and the river at its back, presented a fighting face to the Prussians who had travelled so far and so fast.

The Prussians also were tired. That night it began to rain. The King had given his last orders: the Crown Prince was to move across to make his final junction with the 1st and Elbe Armies on the battlefield itself. When the troops began to move forward in the darkness they did not extinguish their camp fires; they left them burning, a strange and moving spectacle all over the area of their vast bivouac. Even the infantry were slipping about in the mud, while the artillery found the going heavy indeed. Bismarck, riding darkly in the rain with his master and the generals, carried with him the sense that the next day would show whether he was the supreme statesman of his age or a total failure. There were deep forebodings on the Prussian side. Their early successes had not given Moltke delusions of invincibility. He thought all would be well, he thought all would be well even if things went wrong and the Crown Prince was late. Before the royal party moved off into the night, Bismarck observed with sardonic satisfaction that when he offered Moltke his case containing his last two cigars, the great general felt them both and, considering deeply and at length, chose the better. He knew then that Moltke had put his doubts behind him, and felt content.[33]

The battle between the Prussian 1st Army and the main body of Benedek's army was formally joined at 7.30 in the morning. The Prussians had been advancing to take up their positions since 10.30 the previous night. They were hungry and shivering in the drizzle, to which now was added a cold, wet wind. At first it was an artillery duel in slow time, as each side probed the other's strength and weaknesses, and as the Prussians, cursing and now sweating, struggled to move their horse artillery forward through the slippery, summer mud. The ground was pleasant, fairly open country with, however, many little hills and undulations: these gave admirable cover for advancing troops, but they made it hard to handle the guns. Then, at about half past eight, the King gave the order to open rapid fire and the Austrians responded. Their guns were well forward and beautifully concealed, and their whole front seemed to leap into flame, until the smoke mingled with the mist and the drizzle and obscured visibility. It was a phase of plunging, screaming horses, of guns, laboriously dragged into position, being dismounted as soon as they had opened fire, of overturned and shattered caissons. But the Prussian guns kept moving forward, and on the right and on the left the Austrians were forced to give ground. It became now an infantry battle, first a battle among villages; and here the superiority of Prussian fire-power was cancelled out by the superiority of the Austrian positions. They went on fighting even though the houses which sheltered them were in flames. But, all the time, the Prussians dourly drove on. Until, suddenly, it was a battle among woods. The Austrians had massed in the woods around the village of Sadowa, and nothing but hand-to-hand fighting with bayonets could get them out. Both sides were appalled and cast down by the effects of shell-fire in woodland: branches and splinters torn from the trees caused more and worse wounds than the exploding shells themselves. But the Austrians hung on. In one of the most deadly hand-to-hand encounters of the day the 27th Prussian Regiment went into battle with 3,000 men and ninety officers; when it had worked through the wood assigned to it, having cleared out the Austrians, it had less than 400 men and only two officers.

Both wings had now been driven back; but the Prussians found themselves up against a new hard centre grouped in front of Lipa. And there, at midday, they looked like sticking. Soon after, Herewarth on the right was also held. The Prussian 1st Army, with its 150,000 men, had thrown in practically all its reserves and it began to look as though they would break. Early that afternoon Prince Friedrich Karl took all his infantry out of the battle and gathered together his cavalry so that he might have it under his hand when the great decision had to be made. If the Austrians advanced the infantry was to retire under a cavalry screen. If the Crown Prince, fighting his way forward from Miletin, arrived in time, the cavalry could go in. Nobody knew where the Crown Prince was. Until suddenly the news came that he had come through, was regrouping for an attack on Lipa, and that the artillery fire already observed on the extreme right of the Austrian position was in fact engaging him. At 3.30 he had come. The Austrians did not give up. They had to give way; but even as the retreat began the Austrian infantry, covering it, stood their ground against the Prussian cavalry with wonderful steadfastness and heroism. The artillery fought on, often with no infantry to cover them. It was a lost battle by then, but the name of the little village of Chlum, where the Austrian right took the full impact of the fresh Prussian 2nd Army, stands for one of the glories of human courage. With all hope lost, one famous battery of horse artillery fought on until not a gun or a man was left. The last Austrian reserve formation was the remnant of I Corps, which had been exhausted and shattered in the days before the great battle. It marched forward to meet the Prussians in close formation with flags flying, drums beating and to the tune of a regimental march. In just twenty minutes it lost 279 officers and 10,000 men.[34] When the break came and Prince Friedrich Karl's cavalry at last swept into action, the ground was so thickly strewn with dead and wounded that a great scream went up as the drumming hooves came nearer: the Prussian commander managed to pull up his horsemen and send them round on a wide detour to avoid trampling the wounded underfoot. It was only when the Elbe was reached that the pursuit was called off.

The Austrians were by no means finished as a military force. Benedek was finished, and Krismanić and Hennikstein. So was Clam-Gallas, for exposing the Saxons to their early defeat. Tens of thousands were lost, killed, wounded, or prisoners. The Prussians set about the methodical and very correct occupation of Bohemia. But the bulk of the Austrian forces got away, and Archduke Albrecht, now Commander-in-Chief, prepared to fight on the Danube. All that had happened was that Austria was finished as a rival to Prussia. Bismarck had achieved his first great object; but now he had another in sight, and for this he needed Austria as a strong and healthy ally. He had begun his career with a limited view: the aggrandizement of Prussia. But, imperceptibly, he had broadened his horizon, and he was now aiming at nothing less than German unity under the Prussian King, as Emperor. To achieve this aim he needed as an ally the very Power from which he had snatched the leadership of Germany and, in doing so, brought to the verge of destruction. The new enemy was France, already deeply alarmed by the great success of Prussian arms. The thing to do was to be as lenient in making peace as he had been ruthless in making war. But to do this, as a civilian Prime Minister in major's uniform, Bismarck had to fight the generals who had fought his war for him and who now, their blood up, were straining every nerve to serve the *coup-de-grâce*. How explain to soldiers who, with a supreme effort, had won a famous victory, that they must not win any more, that enough was enough, that there was to be no victory parade, not even an occupation of Vienna? It was a task which taxed to the limit all the resources of this extraordinary man; and he was not helped by the Austrians, who, suspecting that the astonishingly mild terms on which he offered peace must conceal a trap, wasted precious weeks before they would come to the point – weeks in which, supported only by the Crown Prince, and looking all the time over his shoulder at Paris, Bismarck had to hold back with one hand the whole momentum of a victorious army. In the end he got his way. At Nikolsburg, the little border town between Moravia and Lower Austria, with its castle built by the Dietrichsteins to check the Turks coming in across Hungary, Franz Josef, white-faced and exhausted, signed the peace, signed himself out of Germany, as seven years earlier he had signed himself out of Lombardy. He made only one stipulation. Just as in 1859 he had been ready to give way to Napoleon on every point save the point touching the security of his relatives in Italy, whom he felt in honour bound to protect, so, now, he stuck out, again in honour bound, for his one wholly loyal ally, his cousin Albert of Saxony, whom he had led into ruin.

8

Seen through the years it appears as a perfectly rounded story; but it did not look like that at the time. History is full of chapter-endings which, when they were reached, seemed no more than pauses in mid-argument. Austria had suffered a crushing military defeat; nobody dreamt of pretending otherwise. But the struggle, as she saw it, was very far from being over. Soon it would be resumed. And indeed, there had been victory as well as defeat. The overwhelming of the Italians at Custozza had been a splendid victory. So had been the great sea-battle at Lissa in which Admiral Tegethoff found glory by the oddest means. For history the Austro-Prussian War was Königgrätz, as it was for Bismarck too. But for Austria at the time Lissa and Custozza were more than great deeds to set against Königgrätz; they were an earnest for the future. For Lissa, indeed, history too should find a place, since on that July day in 1866 naval tactics for years to come were twisted out of shape by the boldness and impetuosity of an Austrian admiral. There were twenty-six Austrian ships with 532 guns ranged against twenty-eight Italian ships with 641 guns. Nobody quite knew what to do with this array, which included a number of the first ironclads. But Admiral Tegethoff rose to the occasion. Up went the signal: 'Armoured ships will charge the enemy and sink him!' And so they did. The confusion with the Austrian ironclads ramming the Italians and shooting and being shot at with heavy guns at point-blank range was past imagination, and when the Italian flagship was breached and sent straight to the bottom the rest of the fleet made off as best it could. Thereafter, and right up to the 1914 war, the great warships of every maritime Power were constructed with heavy steel rams, waiting for another Lissa, which never came: the development of torpedoes and gunnery as a science put an end to that.

It is against Lissa and Custozza, too, that we must see the bitter fate of Benedek. Benedek now is the general who was made a scapegoat by his Emperor for the loss of Germany. But then he was simply a failed commander who had undone the achievements of a successful general and a successful admiral. He behaved in adversity like the hero he was, and the conduct of Franz Josef fell below the occasion; but far too much has been made of the Emperor's treatment of his faithful servant. The court martial was badly managed. The picture of the fierce old man striding to meet his judgement across the courtyard of the Military Academy at Wiener Neustadt, Maria Theresa's conversion of the ancient medieval castle, with the cadets, who worshipped him, gazing down on him in silence from the windows, is a heroic one. Benedek refused to say a word in his defence that might implicate anyone else at all. He accepted the blame for defeat and never spoke. Franz Josef let it happen. He was Emperor. Benedek was his servant and the servant had failed him. Franz Josef knew that he himself was involved in this failure; but not for Emperors the luxury of confession. They must clasp their own guilt to themselves.

PART FOUR

EMPIRE UNDER NOTICE

CHAPTER TWELVE

TWO CROWNS, ONE HEAD

The Emperor was now thirty-seven. For nineteen years the history of Austria had been his personal history, its development his development, its defeats his defeats. The Empire had been his inheritance, first to restore, then to administer in undiminished glory. Once the restoration was complete, in 1849, he had been faced with four main tasks: to engender and maintain a system of alliances; to preserve and formalize his leading position in Germany; to break the will or to conquer the hearts of the Hungarians; to maintain his Italian possessions and increase his influence throughout Italy. In all these tasks, one after another, he had failed. No disgrace attached to his failure, unless it is a disgrace in a statesman not to be a visionary. He was an administrator above all, an administrator of great parts, put at the head of a mighty concern which was running down and being attacked on all sides by new forces and new men, all of whom had much to gain by aggression, some of whom had nothing to lose. A visionary might have shed Italy, leaving the upstart Napoleon to impale himself on the cutting edge of the *Risorgimento*; he might have shed Hungary; but what would Russia have said to this? And where, surrounded by Slavs, did Hungary begin and end? He might have come to an agreement with Prussia, treated as an equal Power in Germany; but would this have satisfied Bismarck? He was not a visionary. No Empire in decline has yet produced a visionary: to ask a statesman to contemplate clear-headedly the dissolution of the complex it is his first duty to uphold, and to devote himself to ensuring that in its passing the way is smoothed for its successors and that the smallest possible number will be hurt, is to ask too much.

What else could an Emperor of Austria conceivably have done but strain every nerve and sinew to continue to rule? Perhaps it takes a Marxist to appreciate Franz Josef at his true worth.

In any case, as already observed, it did not occur to him that Austria was finished. He did not even believe she was finished *vis-à-vis* Prussia. Just as, after Solferino, he looked forward to the day when he would recover Italy, so after Königgrätz he did not in the least resign himself to Prussian supremacy in Germany. And he was soon to show this in a startling gesture. But for the moment it was imperative for him to set his own house in order, and this, above all, meant reaching a final settlement with Hungary. The war with Prussia had brought to a stop the tentative negotiations with Deak and Andrassy; these now had to be resumed, more urgently, and, as far as the Emperor was concerned, from a position of comparative weakness. Hungary was once more seething with revolt; a Hungarian legion had fought with the Prussians; the prestige of Vienna was abased. But Deak was strong enough to keep his tumultuous fellow-countrymen in check, and wise and far-seeing enough to make his gesture of magnaminity. When he appeared before the stricken Emperor he said that Hungary would not ask more, after Königgrätz, than she had asked before.

This, goodness knows, was enough. Franz Josef, even now, had no intention of allowing his Empire to be split in half without a struggle. To concede to Budapest sole jurisdiction over Hungarian internal affairs meant not only the end of the Habsburg dream of a centralized realm; it meant also conceding parliamentary government to the Austrian half of the Empire, since it would clearly be impossible to leave Budapest in full enjoyment of a Parliament and a Cabinet with ministerial responsibility without granting the same privileges to Vienna. A further complication implicit in such a development was that the Austrian Germans would once more be brought forward as the only body capable of forming a government in Vienna. This, indeed, was Andrassy's plan.

Deak, who had recommended Andrassy to be the first Prime Minister of the new Hungary, took no direct part in the final negotiations, which were arduous and protracted, and time and time again suspended, with everything left hanging unresolved. The Emperor wrestled long and stubbornly, first with his own principles, then with Andrassy, the man to whose death-sentence he had put his own signature eighteen years before. At first he was upheld by his own official advisers, above all the romantic artistocrat, Belcredi, with his profound distrust of Hungary, his hatred of the German liberals, his dream of an aristocratic federalism in which Poles, Czechs, Croats, should work in harness together under feudal guidance. Belcredi tried every expedient to bring the provincial Diets to life, while keeping them under aristocratic control; but he had accepted the principle of Dualism and was concerned now only with so organizing the other peoples that they might (forlorn hope!) drown or at least muffle the voice of Hungary with their own. Thus, while encouraging the Poles and the Czechs to make their own demands for a measure of autonomy on the Austrian side of the line, he also sought to stimulate Croat nationalism on the Hungarian side in order to make difficulties in Budapest. But he was too much of a conservative to invoke the forces of popular nationalism and give them form. He held the confidence of his Emperor only because Franz Josef at first distrusted Andrassy's emphasis on the role of the German liberals: it was not the business of a Magyar spokesman to behave as though he were already the head of an independent nation and tell him, the Emperor, who were 'the peoples of State' (the Hungarians and the Germans), and that these were all that mattered. But the Hungarian was so accomplished, so able, so sure of his own mind, so incisive, so very much a man of the world, that Franz Josef soon found himself respecting him as he had respected no man since Schwarzenberg. He was a man he could do business with, and business had to be done.

On top of everything, Elizabeth, for the first time in her life, was displaying an active interest in politics. Already she had discovered, six months before Königgrätz, that the Hungarians, with their brilliance, enthusiasm and stupendous dash, were the only people in the world she really liked. Already, then, Franz Josef had written to Sophie from Budapest (in a letter contemptuously denying rumours that he might be on the verge of assenting to the establishment of an independent Hungarian Ministry), that 'Sisi is being a very great help with her politeness, her perfect tact and her mastery of Hungarian.'[1] Andrassy was enchanted with her, and she with him. He knew, as who did not, that the Emperor was still head over heels in love with her and would do everything he honourably could to please her in order to win her back. Andrassy set out to use her, and she set out to use him: it was an undertaking highly pleasurable to both. If the Empire included Hungary, she was ready, for once, to work for the Empire. She could also work for Hungary within the Empire. Already during the Prussian war she had risen to one of her peaks, tirelessly visiting hospitals and thus beginning to build up a new legend for herself. This was the sort of thing she did ineffably well and with genuine feeling; but she could not do the routine chores of royalty.

Now she was engaged on a higher level. From Budapest, where she was sent post-haste after Königgrätz, in the belief that the Vienna government would soon have to follow, she wrote letter after letter begging her husband to treat with Andrassy before it was too late. If he would not make him Imperial Foreign Minister, at least make him Hungarian Minister. He must summon him at once: the future of the Monarchy was at stake. She pleaded with him for the sake of Rudolf, their son, then eight years old. 'At least,' she concluded her most passionate appeal, 'even if you do nothing, I can tell myself that whatever may happen I shall one day be able to say to Rudolf in all honesty: "I did everything in my power. Your misfortune is not on my conscience." '[2]

It was thus that Andrassy came: 'Beloved angel', wrote Franz Josef, 'pray fervently to God, that he may guide me to do what is right and what is my duty. Today I expect G.A. I shall listen to him quietly and let him talk and then sound him out to see if I can trust him.'[3]

He liked the man, but thought him too vague and at the same time too demanding. Again and again they met and talked – while all the time the Emperor was talking peace with the Prussians – and seeking help from the French. Once Elizabeth's importunities irritated him to the point of speaking sharply. He had pleaded and pleaded that things were not to be settled as easily as she imagined. He sighed for her return and signed his letters, 'Your lonely Mannikin.' But Elizabeth was sulking. She had asked a political favour – one, moreover, designed to save the realm for her husband – for the first time in her life; for the first time in her life she was taking the interest in politics which had so often been demanded, and her husband paid no attention – or not enough. She refused to come home. And Franz Josef wrote:

My dear Sisi, my best thanks for your letter of the 5th, the whole of which has only one purpose, to demonstrate to me with a whole assortment of reasons that you want to stay in Ofen with the children, and will. Since you must know that I cannot go away from here, with the war starting up again in Italy and the peace negotiations with the Prussians, that it would go clean against my duty to adopt your exclusively Hungarian standpoint, neglecting those other lands which have borne immense suffering with steadfast loyalty and at this particular moment deserve special consideration and care, you will also understand that I cannot visit you. If you find the air here unhealthy, so be it . . . and I shall have to console myself as best I may and patiently put up with my long-accustomed loneliness. I have had plenty of practice in being alone, and in the end one gets used to it. So no more about that, or else our correspondence will become too wearisome, as you very rightly observe. I will wait here quietly until you decide what to do.[4]

This mood did not last long. Elizabeth replied shortly and coolly, and to calm herself took once more to her compulsive riding, to the distress of everyone who saw her. Her husband was once more all apprehension. He reminded her of how she had nearly ridden herself to death at the time of Solferino and pleaded with her not to do it again. He was also worrying openly, perhaps for the one and only time in his life, about Elizabeth's extravagance. She was determined to make Hungary her main headquarters, and she had her eye on a castle at Gödöllö, a dream palace, which was now a hospital for wounded soldiers.

By all means go and see the wounded at Gödöllö [Franz Josef wrote]. But don't whatever you do give the impression that we might buy it, for I have no money at all, and we have to save as hard as we can in these difficult times.* The family estates have been ruined by the Prussians and it will take years to get them back into trim. I have reduced the Court budget for next year to five million, which means that more than two million have to be saved. Almost half the horses will have to be sold, and we must cut down our living expenses all round. . . .[5]

'Your melancholy Mannikin', he signed that letter.

But Elizabeth this time responded, and said she would come to Vienna and spend a whole week there. Franz Josef was beside himself with joy: 'Now I have three days to rejoice at the thought of seeing you again, and then almost eight happy days when I shall have you entirely to myself and we shall be able to do all kinds of things together. . . . Be kind when you come, for I am so downcast and lonely and so need cheering up by you.'[6]

That was on the 10th of August 1866. All the time Franz Josef was deep in negotiations with the Prussians, and on 23 August the Peace of Prague was signed. Elizabeth had gone back to Budapest on the 19th, but she had not talked too much about the Hungarians; Andrassy himself had warned her not to bore and irritate her husband in this difficult time. 'Don't leave me alone so long, my Sisi. Don't leave me so long to pine for you, and come to me soon.'[7] That was two days after the Emperor had signed himself out of Germany.

* He bought it for her all the same, and for the rest of his life used it as his Hungarian residence, in preference to the great palace in Budapest.

He had now pretty well made up his mind about Hungary. Andrassy, he decided, could not possibly be given the Foreign Ministry because of public opinion. But he had another idea. One of the most able career diplomats in Europe was the Saxon Prime Minister, Baron Beust, now out of a job. There were two things about Beust: he was violently anti-Prussian (and the Prussians themselves had for a long time conducted a Press campaign against him of the most scurrilous kind) and he was perfectly detached from Austrian internal problems and could regard these with a fresh and unprejudiced eye. Franz Josef, with one of his swift and unexpected moves, invited him to come to Vienna to be Foreign Minister of the Empire, thus killing two birds with one stone: serving notice on Berlin that though he might be down he regarded himself as being far from out (Bismarck was furious), and providing himself with an instrument in the impending settlement with Hungary. It apparently did not occur to Belcredi that the new Foreign Minister would interest himself in Hungarian affairs, which were strictly internal to the Empire, and, as such, were the province of the Prime Minister. He continued as before, plodding away at his own unworkable arrangements, overlooking the fact that in practice his master had for some time been treating with Andrassy and Deak as one treats with the representatives of an independent Power.

Both Andrassy and Elizabeth, his pupil, were affronted. 'I cannot conceive', said Andrassy, 'that a foreigner is capable of bringing fresh life to the Monarchy. One must have been born in a country, and lived in it, before one can save it. I hope your Majesty will not think me lacking in modesty, if I express the conviction that at this juncture I alone can be of any use.' 'How often have I told the Emperor that!'[8] Elizabeth exclaimed. But Franz Josef, in his invisible way, and in the intervals of eating his heart out for Sisi, was making rings round both of them. Beust took office at the end of October and, far from confining himself to treating with the Powers, immediately announced that the government's first task must be to settle with Hungary. Within a few weeks he had personally descended on Budapest and made contact with Deak and Andrassy. At the same time he wooed the German Constitutional Party in Vienna and Prague. Then he started putting heavy pressure on Belcredi, and, with extreme skill and delicacy, manoeuvred him into resigning. Beust stepped into his shoes, summoned the central Parliament (which Belcredi had suspended), and, by March, all was ready for the Emperor to go to

Budapest himself and, amid scenes of the most heartening popular enthusiasm, concede everything that Deak and Andrassy had demanded. All that remained to be done was to get the new compromise law, the *Ausgleich* agreed by the Vienna Parliament. This Beust achieved with effortless skill by reviving Schmerling's electoral geometry, thus achieving a German liberal majority and winning German liberal support in exchange for an earnest that there would be no more attempts at absolutism. The Empire had, as it were, been dismantled and reformed overnight. The hand was the hand of Beust, but the voice was the voice of Franz Josef. The total abandonment of the centralized State of his dreams, and the establishment of a firmly constitutional Dual Monarchy, with himself as King of Hungary and Emperor of Austria, was the last act of Franz Josef as autocrat. Henceforth he was to consider himself bound by the constitution of this new Dual State of his own making no less absolutely than, hitherto, he had considered himself bound to uphold the centralized Empire of Schwarzenberg and Bach. Hitherto the history of the Monarchy had been his personal history; henceforward it was to be the history of developing peoples and conflicting social forces. The dynasty was still there. He has been criticized for putting the dynasty first. What else was there that he might have put in its place?

2

The dynasty had been Austria. It was now Austria-Hungary. One day, in the fullness of time (for the Emperor-King was not at all in love with the German liberals who had made the compromise with Hungary possible), it might be Austria-Hungary-Bohemia. One day, indeed, it might be a grand federation. . . . But that was to reckon without the Magyars. They could not rule the Empire, but they could see to it, and they did, that the partnership remained a partnership of two – and one of those two riven by internal dissensions. Hungary had its Parliament, its responsible Ministry. Hungary was now 'the lands across the Leitha', the Leitha being the little river that winds across what is now the Burgenland, almost at the gates of Vienna. It included, in effect, the lands of St Stephen's Crown – Croatia, the Voivodina with its Serbs, Transylvania, parts of the present Rumania, and the eastern part of what is now Czechoslovakia. Bohemia, Moravia, the Austrian part of Silesia, Galicia, Bukovina, together with the hereditary Austrian lands (which included Slovene-speaking districts) formed the western half.

Belcredi had resigned on 1 February 1867. On 18 February came the announcement of the appointment of an autonomous Hungarian government. The Magyars themselves, having won all along the line, quickly agreed to the changes in the 1848 constitution necessary if the Dual State was to work. For the first time Hungary agreed to contribute a fixed share of taxes; the new army law was passed to create the common army. Each half of the Empire was totally independent of the other save for the army, the common Ministry of Foreign Affairs, and certain financial arrangements connected with these. Each half had its own Ministry under a Prime Minister responsible to Franz Josef as King of Hungary and Emperor of Austria. The three common Ministers were appointed by the Emperor but were responsible to two bodies chosen from the Upper and Lower Houses of each legislature and known as the Delegations. These sat separately in Vienna and Budapest, twenty from each Upper House, forty from each Lower House. Only if disagreement on a particular point was so strong that it could not be resolved at long range did they meet for joint debate and voting. The head of the joint Ministry of Foreign Affairs acted as the common Prime Minister and formed the main link between the Emperor and the Delegations, whose members were elected annually. There was a Customs Union, but provision was made for this to be reviewed every ten years. The standing army was a completely joint affair, based on universal conscription on a two-year term, with a reserve serving as such for ten years. Auxiliary forces, however, were the concern of each separate administration, except during war, when the Emperor assumed supreme command of all forces.

This, in broad outline, was the constitutional pattern of the Habsburg Empire as we think of it today. It was to last for exactly fifty years.

3

Life in these years was not all woe. Most of the few thinking intellectuals in Vienna, Grillparzer, now a very old man, the younger poet, Anastasius Grün, prophesied immediate doom. They were appalled, above all, by the almost total lack of political understanding or even interest among the people, rich and poor alike. Even on the day after

Königgrätz there was no interruption in the mood of summer cheerfulness. There was racing in the Prater; the cafés and restaurants under the trees were full of laughing crowds listening to the bands and watching the comedians. Johann Strauss with his concerts in the Volksgarten was at the peak of his fame. Out in the wine-villages between the city and the wooded hills the usual crowds flocked to escape the oppressive heat of the narrow city lanes and sing and drink the new wine.

There was nothing else they could have done, except sit at home weeping. That was left to the mothers and sweethearts of the men who had died in battle, their homes scattered widely over the whole expanse óf the Empire, from the steep mountain valleys of the Vorarlberg to the low, sprawling Turkish villages of the great Hungarian plain. The rest got on with their jobs – and with their amusements. What were they to weep for? An Emperor and a King had clashed. For reasons scarcely apprehended by the bourgeois Viennese, let alone the peasants of Croatia, Bohemia or Tirol, the politicians and the diplomats had worked themselves into a war, the result of which could affect nobody directly, except the bereaved, except the unfortunates whose homes lay in the paths of the armies or were shattered in actual battle. Life went on, no matter who was top dog in Germany. Taxes would be more or less. Food would be abundant or scarce. But for forty million people virtually excluded from participation in the politics of the Empire, living under police rule and a heavy Press censorship, there was no part they could usefully play.

For the culturally minded, life in the cities, above all in Vienna and Prague, had a good deal to be said for it. Vienna especially, far from being finished, was fairly launched on a programme of rebuilding and expansion which, in thirty years, was to transform the face of the city and turn it into one of the most beautiful in Europe. In 1857, two years before Solferino, Franz Josef had ordered the levelling of the walls and bastions of the old fortifications and already the ground was being prepared for the laying out of the magnificent Ringstrasse, and the erection of that dazzling series of immense buildings, later to be embowered in trees, which was to turn the great circular boulevard into one of the wonders of the world.

Characteristically, the first of these to be completed was the Opera House of van der Null and von Siccardsburg, started in 1861 and opened with a performance of *Don Giovanni* on 25 May 1869. A year later the new building of the Society of Friends of Music, with its splendid concert-hall, was brought into commission. Vienna was still incontestably the musical headquarters of Europe. It was the period of Wagner and Brahms and of the bitter antagonism between their two schools. Wagner had taken some time to establish himself in Vienna. It was not until 1857, two years before Solferino, that he had an opera performed there: *Tannhäuser* in the old Thalia Theatre: the immediate reaction was for the satirist Nestroy to put on his famous Tannhäuser parody. But by the time of Königgrätz, when Ludwig of Bavaria, instead of fighting Prussia, had slipped off secretly to Zürich to try to persuade the composer to come and live with him in Munich, the Wagner cult was in full swing. For two years, from 1862 to 1863, Wagner himself had lived at Penzing while he worked on *The Mastersingers*, and from then on it was one first performance after another. In 1862 Brahms had come from Hamburg to settle in the city for life. But it was not all Brahms and Wagner, or even Johann Strauss. In 1864 Vienna made its rediscovery of Bach, with a performance of the *St John Passion*, and, in 1868, Anton Bruckner, already forty, was brought from the provinces, after seventeen years of longing, to be Court organist and to hear through the next three decades his series of immense symphonies brought to life, one after the other, by the Vienna Philharmonic. On 16 December 1866, while Beust was busily engaged in fixing Hungary and easing out Belcredi, Berlioz came to Vienna to conduct his *Damnation of Faust*. Meanwhile, in Prague, the composers Dvořák and Smetana were beginning their effective careers and, for the first time, finding artistic expression for Czech national consciousness.

It was also a time of great doctors. Josef II's original hospital buildings were being added to fast. The medical tradition which they embodied was now beginning to flower. And perhaps as characteristic of the mood of cultural Vienna as anything was the deep friendship between the highly professional composer, Brahms, with his bearded remoteness and Olympian detachment, the great surgeon Theodor Billroth, a pioneer of antisepsis and the inventor and main exponent of a bold operation for stomach cancer, and the devoted but quarrelsome critic, Hanslick, Wagner's Beckmesser. Here was a nexus of earnest and self-respecting Victorianism, carving out ground for itself in the middle of a polyglot Empire, ignoring the Court on the one hand, the politicians on the other, and consolidating the ground which was later to be irreparably undermined by men already born, or very soon to be born, also within the bounds of that Empire – by, for instance, Sigmund Freud in medicine, ten years old at the time of Königgrätz, and Gustav Mahler in music, who was six.

4

The Viennese called the new Dual State, 'The Empire under Notice'. But they did not behave as though they expected it to fall. Indeed, on the Austrian side of the Leitha, the abandonment of all interference in the internal affairs of Hungary marked the beginning of a process of rejuvenation. The German liberals had to be rewarded for their support for the new constitution, and at the same time, to bring Austria into step with Hungary, had to be given as a free gift concessions which the Magyars had won by struggle. It began to look as though some of the ideals for which Fischhof and his friends had suffered in 1848 were, twenty years later, being realized with no further effort. And the main determining event was, precisely, the divorce from Hungary: it was suddenly seen that the rigid police apparatus which had been required for eighteen years to hold the Monarchy together was no longer necessary now that the Hungarians were out – and the Italians. The other peoples of the complex might be difficult, and were; but they could be managed. In a word, once the revolution in Vienna had been broken, the whole centralized weight of the Bach system and its less harsh successor, which had borne so heavily on every citizen in the realm, had been called into being by the necessity of subduing ten million implacable Magyars. Further, if the Compromise had not been reached, it would have been the end of the milder régime of first Schmerling, then Belcredi: the Hungarians by 1866 had already got completely out of hand, and to keep them down it would have been imperative to restore throughout the whole Empire the sort of oppressive apparatus perfected by Bach.

Beust soon saw which way the wind was blowing: he was a gifted opportunist and he was also perfectly detached, looking at the Empire with the eyes of a curious foreigner. The independent Police Ministry was abolished; the censorship was greatly curtailed; the penal code was ameliorated; the Jews were largely emancipated; a school law of 1869 provided for compulsory and free elementary education (stubbornly and sometimes effectively contested by some of the provincial Diets called on to administer the law); a very determined onslaught was made on the stranglehold of the Church. Under Prince Auersperg, the first Prime Minister of the new Austrian Parliament (Beust was now the Imperial Foreign Secretary), war was joined with Rome. The 1855 Concordat, Sophie's supreme creation, was not destroyed at once, but the privileges of the Church were gradually whittled away to the accompaniment of incessant popular agitation. First civil marriage was legalized; then the schools were taken away from Church control. Then came a law putting all Christian creeds on an equal footing. The driving force came from the German liberals; but the man who did the work, fighting tooth and nail against all the weight and majesty of Cardinal Rauscher, who tried to bully and terrorize the aristocrats in the Upper House, was Auersperg himself, from one of the grandest and most ancient families in the Empire. Finally the Pope moved into action, denouncing the new laws as 'truly unholy', as 'absolutely null and void', as 'destructive, abominable and damnable'.[9] Some bishops took heart from this and instructed their flocks to disobey the laws. One was actually sent to prison, though subsequently pardoned.[10] Beust threw his weight into the scales and started talking about 'the spirit of the age'. The Pope had gone too far. He was to go farther still. In 1870, by proclaiming the doctrine of Papal Infallibility, he gave Franz Josef his chance. The adoption of the doctrine of infallibility, he said in an Imperial Rescript, had changed the nature of the party with which the Concordat had been signed: the treaty was therefore cancelled. It was the end of an epoch.

5

Where was Sophie when all these revolutionary events were proceeding? How could Franz Josef himself be so easily persuaded to concur in the revision of a whole string of measures which he had made so very much his own?

She was still alive, eighty-two, with two more years to live; but she was broken. What had broken her was the execution in Mexico in 1867 of her second son, Maximilian. It had been she above all who had nourished the dreams of glory which found fatal expression in Maximilian's acceptance from Louis Napoleon of the Imperial Crown of Mexico in 1864. She had desired for him glory and fame to rival his brother's; and although she opposed the Mexican adventure, her earlier encouragement had helped to send him to his death. Franz Josef's part in this sombrely lunatic episode has been heavily criticized: it is hard to see why this should be, unless on the general assumption that everything Franz Josef did was wrong.

As children, Franz Josef and his younger brother Ferdinand Max had always got on well together. Franzi had been practical and brisk, full of feeling and not without a sense of the enchantment of living. He had never been a serious reader, but he had a gift for drawing, worked hard at it, encouraged by Sophie, and, in his teens, left amusing and sometimes witty and sensitive records of the sights he saw on his travels. He might well have developed this side of his nature, which came out also in the choice of Sisi for a bride. But at eighteen he was Emperor and coolly, without dreams of glory, put away childish things. If, however, he would henceforward have no time in his own life for the graces of living, he nevertheless continued to feel protective to his younger brother – tall, dreamily handsome with silky blond hair, and a dreamer through and through. There was a place in the family for a poetic dreamer and a patron of the arts, and Max should have that place.

But when the dreamer began to have dreams of power, that was quite another matter: it was eating one's cake and having it. Franz Josef had paid for power and responsibility by dedicating his life and everything in it to the service of his dynasty: Maximilian was already showing the signs of wanting power without responsibility; he had the makings of a megalomaniac dilettante. He was also jealous of his brother, whose nature he did not in the least understand, and whom he came to despise for his narrowness and brusqueness. He knew that he was more popular with the Viennese than the aloof, cold figurehead of the counter-revolution. His ambitions were aroused, and they were encouraged by Sophie, who would have liked all her sons to be Emperors. Franz Josef saw this happening. He distrusted his brother profoundly, and he also suddenly found himself jealous. When, in 1857, in his convulsive effort to recover lost ground in Lombardy and Venetia, he sent Maximilian to be Governor-General in Milan, he hoped to exploit his charm and humanitarian instincts, and at the same time cut him down to size. But Maximilian was now being urged on by two women: in that same year he had married Charlotte, the daughter of Leopold of Belgium, beautiful, highly strung, intelligent, witty but a self-dramatizer and devoured by ambition. Any basic commonsense

Maximilian may have had was soon driven out of him by the promptings of his wife and his mother: Sophie was already beginning to realize that Franz Josef had moved away from her and was no longer to be deeply influenced; she transferred her remaining drive to her younger son.

Napoleon had long had dreams of restoring French influence in the New World. His opportunity came when the Mexican radical dictator, the Indian Juarez, defaulted on a French loan. The American President, Abraham Lincoln, was at that time in no position to interfere, being engaged in his own Civil War. French troops under Bazaine were sent to punish Juarez, and Napoleon, looking round for a satellite prince, hit on the idea of causing the Imperial Crown of Mexico to be offered to Ferdinand Maximilian, second in the line of succession to the Habsburg throne. Maximilian, dreaming of founding an Empire in the New World which should eclipse the glory of Vienna, wanted immediately to accept and, urged on by his wife (but not, this time, by Sophie), was quite incapable of questioning the credentials of the nondescript group of Parisian bankers and *émigré* Mexican politicians who came to lay at his feet the dubious Crown. Lincoln, engaged in his cataclysmic war with the South, drew attention to the Monroe Doctrine, but was incapable of enforcing it. Franz Josef conscientiously pointed out the absurdity of the idea, but this was put down to jealousy. He could, as head of the House, have forbidden it flatly. He did everything short of this. He said that he would agree that Max should accept the crown only if France, Great Britain and Spain all pledged their support and only if it could be shown that the Mexican people really wanted him to accept. The guarantees did not come; the support of the people was expressed only in a series of rigged plebiscites. But Maximilian, far from Vienna in his castle at Miramar, spectacularly perched on the grey rocks above the Adriatic just outside Trieste, had taken the bit between his teeth. He accepted without guarantees. Franz Josef made one more effort. He insisted absolutely that if his brother went to Mexico he must renounce his right of succession to the Habsburg throne. Maximilian was so far out of touch with reality that when this demand arrived at Miramar he was genuinely shocked. Franz Josef was still young, but there could be accidents, and he, Maximilian, was still younger. The heir presumptive, the infant Rudolf, was a delicate child, and relations between Franz Josef and Elizabeth being what they notoriously were in 1863, it seemed improbable that there would be another child. He might still succeed Franz Josef and be Mexican Emperor too. He fought back with bitterness and indignation; Franz Josef, not knowing whether to laugh or cry at the thought of a possible joint Empire of Austria and Mexico, went at it dourly, dryly, legalistically. In the end he had to go to Trieste himself and stand over his brother until the deed of renunciation was signed. Both men wept, embraced, tears pouring down their faces at the railway station; they never saw each other again.[11]

Maximilian's four-year reign was the ghastliest tragi-comedy. His territories extended to the ground that could be cleared by French bayonets, and nowhere beyond. As Emperor he affronted the Mexicans by being there at all, and he affronted his supporters by his initial refusal to sanction punitive measures and his attempt to win unwilling subjects to his side by humane and liberal measures. The French grew tired of an operation that was bringing no glory to France and no cash to the bankers; Rome was outraged by Maximilian's liberalism and put out feelers to Juarez; on 5 April 1865 the American Civil War was brought to an end by General Lee's surrender, and Lincoln could now turn his attention to this last anachronistic attempt by a European Power to carve an Empire out of the American continent. A year later Maximilian was ready to give up the game in disgust. He got as far as writing out his own instrument of abdication; but Charlotte turned on him, accused him of cowardice, announced that she would go herself to Paris to make Napoleon renew his support, to Rome to see the Pope. She did both, while Maximilian hung on. Her mind was going: she poured out mad, apocalyptic letters. Napoleon did not help; Eugénie did not help; the Pope could only give his blessing, although she threw herself at his feet and wept and raved and pleaded for three hours on end. Next morning she was back again at the Vatican: dishevelled and bareheaded she forced herself into the Pope's presence and implored him to save her from Napoleon's assassins. Her mind had quite given way. It never came back, but the body of this fated and fateful woman, so beautiful, proud, intense and taunting, lived on for more than fifty years.

Maximilian was luckier: captured, escaping, recaptured, tended only by two or three utterly devoted friends, on 19 June 1867, he was shot by a firing squad. Garibaldi tried to save him; so did the Americans. As so often with the weak but idealistic he died with perfect bravery. Bareheaded, his long fair hair and silky beard slightly stirred by the light airs of dawn, this child of the Old World and the counter-revolution who had come to the New World to inaugurate a new kind of society, fell to the bullets of that radical nationalism which, in its own way and at its own tempo, was transforming the face of the globe: 'May my blood be the last to be shed,' he said, 'and may it bring peace and happiness to my unhappy adopted fatherland.'[12]

This, for Sophie, his mother, was the end. With her final eclipse, although she lingered on for some years, the way was clear for Franz Josef to act as he saw fit to save his own Crown.

CHAPTER THIRTEEN

THE IRON RING OF FATE

Although nobody realized it at the time, the defeat at Königgrätz and the Compromise with Hungary had given the Empire its final shape. It took the failure, in 1869, of Beust's attempts to form a triple alliance with France and Italy against Prussia to set the seal on the new pattern. And with the Prussian victory over Napoleon in 1870 there could clearly be no going back. The following decade, strained and desperately confused for all who had to live and act through it, appears in retrospect as a period of steady and orderly progression: smoothly, with sleep-walking certainty, the Dual Monarchy, with diminishing space for manoeuvre, advanced to take up the position which led almost infallibly to the explosion of 1914. By 1879, when Count Taaffe came forward with his no-party government designed to conciliate the Slavs and force the German Austrians to live in amity with the 'lesser breeds', his famous 'Iron Ring', the iron ring of fate was already sealed round the Empire as a whole. The main elements in this ring were the clash of interest in the Balkans between Russia and the Dual Monarchy; the Austro-Prussian alliance of 1879; the Compromise with Hungary which, while saving the dynasty for another fifty years, was in effect a sort of Enabling Act, permitting the Magyars to bully the Transleithnian Slavs and to blackmail Vienna; and the irreconcilability of Germans and Slavs in Austria proper (or, to give it its technical title, 'The Kingdoms and Lands Represented in the Reichsrat').

Beust, while presiding at home over the liberalization of Austria, was devoting himself more especially to foreign affairs; and foreign affairs for him meant the construction of an anti-Prussian coalition. Already in August 1867 Napoleon and Eugénie had come to Salzburg, nominally to offer their condolences to Franz Josef on the death of Maximilian, which lay heavily on Napoleon's conscience, more actually to establish contact with a view to a future alliance. Nothing was settled, but contact was made. A few months later, in October, Franz Josef made the visit to Paris which had been postponed because of Maximilian's death. There were still no formal negotiations, but each Emperor now knew what was in the other's mind. Napoleon, quite desperately needed Austria's support in face of Prussia. Beust, less urgently but no less determinedly, wanted a coalition, including the South German States and Italy, for a later showdown with Prussia and also to cover future contingencies in the Balkans. Bismarck looked on with the liveliest interest, but his mood was sardonic rather than apprehensive. He knew that he had Andrassy in Budapest on his side, that he had a fifth column, which he despised, among Austria's German Ministers, who still hankered after some sort of union with Bismarck's Germany. Further, Napoleon was *in extremis*, ill and almost paralysed by indecision and swaying giddily in the saddle from which he was sooner or later bound to fall. There was never much hope for the Franco-Austrian alliance. Napoleon, who needed it most, allowed it to be wrecked on the question of Rome. The Austrian higher command, very rightly, refused flatly to be embroiled in any new war with Prussia unless Italy were at least neutralized. Italy would enter no alliance with France unless Napoleon withdrew his troops from Rome. Napoleon, under intolerable pressure from Eugénie, felt, almost certainly quite rightly, that to withdraw his protection from the Pope would be an admission of final defeat and the signal for his fall.

It was a fall postponed by one year. In July 1870, forced to activity again by his fear of losing all prestige, he protested against the selection of Prince Leopold of Hohenzollern-Sigmaringen to occupy the empty Spanish throne. This was Bismarck's opportunity and he seized it with both hands. He knew that the Prussian army was ready and that the French army was not. When, to his dismay, it looked as though his master, William, was providing an opportunity for both sides to climb down, he took decisive action by publishing to the world a doctored version of William's private account to him of his meeting with the French Ambassador, Benedetti, at Ems: the famous Ems telegram, Bismarck's version of which made it appear that the Prussian King had broken off relations. Napoleon, over-confident in his army and, in any case, swept along by the public outcry, declared war on 19 July. On 3 September he had surrendered in person at Sedan. Three weeks later Paris was invested. On 18 January 1871, after a terrible winter of siege, William was proclaimed German Emperor at Versailles. On the 28th was signed the peace which cost France an indemnity of £200,000,000 and the loss of Alsace and Lorraine.

Austria was outside all this. Beust, the Saxon, wanted to fight: it was his only chance of revenging himself on Prussia. But the generals thought of Italy; and Bismarck's allies in Budapest and Vienna did their work; Andrassy above all, who had everything to lose by victory or defeat in war against Prussia. The consequences of defeat were obvious, the consequences of victory scarcely less so: the dynasty as part of a victorious coalition would no longer be dependent for its very existence on Magyar support. The discussions in the Crown Council on 18 July were not clear-cut in this sense. Beust was deeply concerned about the possibility of Russian intervention in Galicia. The Chief-of-Staff, Kuhn (Gyulai's old Chief-of-Staff in the Italian campaign, better known as a strategist than a policy-maker) was convinced that Russia would intervene and must be fought now, 'even at the risk of setting the whole of Europe alight'... 'Now or later this war will have to be fought out, the sooner, then, the better. . . .' For with every year Russia would become stronger in arms and in communications:

> We must harness the revolutionary Poles in the fight against Russia, we must promise the separation of this land from Russia, even if it means sacrificing Galicia, so that this giant may be weakened and driven back on Asia, unless the whole earth is not to be sooner or later divided between two powers: the North Americans and the Russians.[1]

While Kuhn, like Conrad von Hötzendorf his ill-fated successor, must take his share of the criticism to which all proponents of preventive wars lay themselves open, it can no longer be held against him (as, for decades, it was) that he was wholly lacking in foresight. It needed imagination – and courage – to introduce into a Court Council in the Vienna of 1870 a vision of a planet dominated by Washington and Moscow. The Beust-Andrassy debate was conducted strictly within the Metternichean framework, and the ultimate decision to stay neutral was arrived at in the spirit of Metternich. But Kuhn's apocalyptic vision serves to bring vividly to mind the magnitude of the movements which lay behind the more or less cut-and-dried, more or less elegant manoeuvres through which the European Powers sought to maintain their uneasy balance, the newer ones to expand, the older ones to survive. Kuhn was not mad. Nor was he talking in a vacuum. He was simply better read than anybody else in that cool, Rococo council-chamber with its creaking parquet floor.

And he was putting two and two together, as the first European soldier to see the globe as a whole – though even he did not think of China – or Japan.

It was 1870. In 1867 while Hungary and Austria were negotiating their portentous Compromise, the United States had bought Alaska from Russia. 'They have taken California, Oregon, and sooner or later they will get Alaska. It is inevitable. It cannot be prevented; and it would be better to yield with good grace and cede territory', ran a Petersburg memorandum in 1860 – the year after Solferino.[2] 'Russia too has a manifest destiny on the Amur, and further south, even in Korea.' Celebrating the Alaska deal, the New York *Herald* wrote that 'the young giants' were engaged on the same work, 'that of expansion and progress' . . . 'The interests of both demand that they should go hand in hand in their march to Empire.'[3] It was a beautiful dream. In central Europe only Field-Marshal Kuhn seems to have been aware of its existence.

Beust hung on until late in 1871. The unification of Germany under the Hohenzollerns had made nonsense of his foreign policy; but he was to fall in the end because of his failure to conciliate the Slavs within the Empire. Then Andrassy at last came into his own and for eight years conducted the affairs of the Monarchy as though it were an appendage of the Magyar nation.

The Deak-Andrassy plan, in 1867, as we have seen, called for Magyar rule in the East and German rule in the West. 'You look after your barbarians, and I'll look after mine!' Beust is supposed to have said cheerfully to Andrassy. He spoke as a German; but it was not as simple as that, and he knew it. Although he had made use of Schmerling's electoral geometry to pack the new Parliament in order to put the Compromise through, he was not by any means a German nationalist; and one of the tasks he set himself was to come to an accommodation with the Czechs, who were at least on his side *vis-à-vis* Prussia. Prince Carlos Auersperg's Ministry of German liberals was easy to make fun of. It suffered from all the faults ever committed by the parliamentary Germans. It included prominently three men, Giskra, Herbst and Berger, who had done more than anybody else to ensure Austria's defeat at Königgrätz when in Schmerling's Ministry they had heavily cut the army estimates, displaying in their arguments a perfect lack of any understanding of the realities of power or the character of Bismarck (the Parliamentary Committee concerned with army expenditure was known as

Dr Giskra's String Quartet: in German *Streichquartet*, '*Streich*' also meaning to strike out, or cut).[4] They tried to woo Bismarck, who despised them; they in turn despised the Slavs, and drove the Czechs to contract out of the Vienna Parliament. But, with all these manifestations of cloud-cuckoo-land crassness, it has to be set to their credit that it was they, working under Auersperg, who brought Vienna into the nineteenth century with the 1868 reforms. Their most glorious hour was the climax of the *Kulturkampf*, when Austria threw off the shackles of the Concordat.

The Germans had the education and the power. No less than the Magyars, they regarded the Slavs as inferior beings. Nothing had changed since Karl Marx, writing in exile, had characterized the 'Slavonian hordes' as inferior beings who had lost the race and whose only hope lay in submissive loyalty to the culture-bringers, the Germans. There was nothing in the world, it seemed, to prevent them taking charge and 'organizing' the Slavs of the western half of the Empire as the Magyars were 'organizing' the Slavs of the eastern half. All, at least, except the Galician Poles: the existence of these spirited and self-centred magnates offered a problem before which even the most self-confident Germans quailed, and there were many who would have been only too pleased to have seen Galicia given up. But, in fact, there was one stumbling-block: no less than the Emperor himself.

The German liberals not unnaturally made no appeal to Franz Josef, who was antipathetic to liberals of any kind. But his refusal to let them have everything their own way went deeper than simple dislike: it would have been the same had they been German conservatives. He, in feeling, was not a German: he was supra-national; he was Habsburg. As such he detested nationalism of any kind. He was the father of all his peoples, and his peoples included Slavs as well as Germans, as well as Magyars. It was his privilege to be served by all; and it was his duty to protect all and enable them to live in concord. It was a genuine vision. The fact that he was not prepared to die for it did not alter the reality of the vision. In face of Magyar intransigence he had yielded to *force majeure* in order to hold his inheritance together. This aim came first, indeed had to come first. He had divided his authority with Budapest, and, in so doing, he knew that he had sold into slavery Croats, Serbs, Slovaks and Transylvanian Germans. The less said about that the better: one day things might change. But that was no argument for selling the Czechs of Bohemia and Moravia and the Slovenes of Carinthia and Carniola into slavery to the Germans.

Here he still had jurisdiction. As a constitutional monarch he could no longer give orders to his Ministers – until, in 1879, he found one so close to him that orders as such were not necessary – but he could see that they were curbed. The twelve years between the Compromise and the advent of Count Taaffe as Prime Minister were devoid of positive progress towards the goal of reconciling Slav and German (in this context and at this time 'Slav' above all meant Czech); but at least Franz Josef managed to prevent the Germans from running head-on into the Czechs. The Auersperg Ministry fell on this issue, and so did the Potocki Cabinet (which included Taaffe). Early in 1870 Giskra was back again, but before the year was out the Emperor had one more try. There was already a new spirit in Bohemia. In 1868 the romantic pan-Slavism represented by the veteran Bohemian politician, Rieger, Palacky's son-in-law, who spoke of Moscow as his mother-city, was giving way to a more sensible and formidable rapprochement between the great Bohemian magnates and the Prague intelligentsia. These now began to demand a place within the Empire analogous to Hungary's. Towards the end of 1870 Franz Josef, already in a state of considerable irritation with Hungarian pretensions (he was keeping his side of the Compromise bargain; Andrassy was not), decided that he could afford to do some irritating in his turn. Prompted by representatives of the great Bohemian nobility, who were never far from his person and helped, indeed, to form a sort of personal bodyguard within the Delegation of the Austrian Upper House, he turned his back on German liberals and German centralists alike and brought into being a brand-new Ministry of unknown men with a federalistic turn of mind whose main purpose was to reach a working agreement with the Czechs. The new Prime Minister was Count Hohenwart, an admirable and idealistic conservative, who had as his right-hand a Professor Schäffle, an economist by training, who had some revolutionary ideas. Schäffle was doomed from the start. Not only did he recommend that the Czechs should be given a measure of autonomy, but he also attacked the very foundations of the dogma of German liberalism in its first flush of embryo capitalism. He had, indeed, been lecturing in Vienna on this very subject. 'I glossed over nothing. I made no secret of my conviction that a purely Liberal and individualistic form of society, or, as I first christened it, a purely capitalist order, could not survive.

My thoughts and feelings were greatly influenced by the spectacle of misery in the industrial suburbs which I had seen with my own eyes.'[5] He was an honest German, a Swabian, a Protestant. He had thought he was a liberal, but he found that liberalism had nothing to do with social reform as such, but only with freedom for the bourgeoise and a free-for-all for the moneyed entrepreneur. He found, too, that not all Slavs were inferior to Germans:

> Among those Conservatives who were most savagely maligned I discovered distinguished men, while many of the liberal idols of the Parliamentarians were tainted with corruption. I discovered, moreover, that the so-called inferior races whom it was the fashion to deride could produce a far higher culture, and far more talented and interesting personalities, than I had supposed possible.

He was a humourless man, but deadly earnest, and as honest as the day. To recognize these things was to proclaim them. He was a lustreless Cobbett denouncing Manchester, a dim shadow of Disraeli in his 'Two Nations' mood. He was more. He was the innocent precursor of a movement for social justice and human equity which was to develop powerfully towards the end of the century under Catholic idealists inspired by Baron Carl Vogelsang and led by Prince Alois Liechtenstein, which paradoxically was much later to get itself inextricably intertwined with an anti-semitic dynamic. This was the man who was now summoned by Franz Josef. He talked to his Emperor for two hours, as though addressing a university seminar.

> Without any disguise I pointed out the deplorable and unnatural consequences of a concentration of power in the hands of a Parliamentary minority from which whole races and classes were excluded. I explained to him that the domination of this minority signified, in truth, domination of the big capitalists, with the support of the Professors of Liberalism. It was the rule of money dressed up in intellectual garb by Liberal servants, lawyers, writers and professors.

He went further: he had concrete proposals for breaking the power of the bourgeoisie by introducing universal suffrage and for writing the principle of racial equality into the constitution. It was a new sort of experience for Franz Josef; but he listened to what this remarkable little man with his back-room mentality had to say, digested it, and, with Hohenwart as a figurehead, put him in charge of affairs.

The Ministry lasted just five months. Neither Hohenwart nor Schäffle was a politician, and they would have needed political skill of a consummate kind to ride the hysteria of opposition that now broke out. The German-controlled Press thundered against the appointment of the new Ministry as a crime against Germanism and liberty. When the Czechs, encouraged by the new mood, published their so-called 'Fundamental Articles' setting out their demands for Czech autonomy on Hungarian lines, the students of Vienna University rioted. Beust, seeing which way the wind was blowing, himself started sniping and obliquely demonstrating against the Hohenwart government. Things indeed had got so far that in his message for the opening of the Bohemian Diet Franz Josef had said: 'We gladly recognize the right of this Kingdom and are prepared to renew this recognition with our kingly oath.'[6] But it was not Beust who struck the deadly blow against this first serious attempt to turn the Empire into a close-knit federation; it was Andrassy. This gifted and mobile statesman had been going very quietly and biding his time. He saw his chance when, in tune with the new ideas, three weeks after the message to the Bohemian Diet, on 8 October, the Southern Slavs came into action. There was a revolt in the Voivodina, the old military frontier area. It was suppressed in three days, but not before the aims behind it had been widely published: to establish a new State of Illyria, consisting of Croatia, Slavonia, Dalmatia, Bosnia and Herzegovina. This shook even Franz Josef. And Andrassy struck. He appeared before the Emperor, blamed Beust for all the trouble, took the line that the whole agitation had been conceived as a move against Prussia, described the fearful effect produced in Hungary by concessions to the Czechs and asked Schäffle point-blank how he proposed to establish by force Bohemian ascendancy over Moravia and Silesia, which did not want to be ruled by Prague.

He was in a strong position. Backed by the strange alliance of Bismarck and Elizabeth he knew he could take liberties. He was, moreover, the embodied spirit of the Compromise, which since his coronation at Budapest Franz Josef had accepted and clung to: he had solemnly sworn to uphold it, and to Franz Josef his kingly oath was everything. The fact that Andrassy had been breaking the Hungarian side of the bargain by interfering in Austrian internal affairs was neither here nor there: it was exasperating; it was vulgar; but it did not release the King-Emperor from his own most solemn obligations. Andrassy was also able to speak with unshakable conviction. He was at last about to exchange the premiership of Hungary for the Foreign Ministry of the Empire; but he was interested above all in Hungary, and in the Empire only as Hungary's shield. Concessions to the Czechs would have been bad enough: they would not only have wrecked the special position of Hungary *vis-à-vis* the Hofburg, but they would also have made it very hard indeed for the Magyars to continue in peace the absorbtion of their own minorities, above all the Slovaks in the north. The 'Illyrian' revolt was worse, since Croatia and the Voivodina came directly under the jurisdiction of Budapest. Andrassy knew exactly what he wanted. Beust was uncertain, divided against himself and already in the Emperor's bad books. The inevitable happened. Franz Josef was frightened into getting rid of Hohenwart and Schäffle and, for the moment, out of his attempts to reconcile Vienna with Prague. Andrassy took over from Beust. Andrassy, for his part, had killed for the time being the dream, Fischhof's dream, of a harmonious multi-racial Empire at the very moment when, after more than two decades, the Emperor had come round to it himself: the Magyars, to establish their own position invincibly, had saddled the western half of the Empire with a German liberal government for another eight years.

2

The new Austrian Ministry was headed by Carlos Auersperg's brother. Andrassy let it run. His Magyar friends in Budapest, with Kolomon Tisza at their head, could continue quietly with their task of Magyarization. The Vienna Ministry, less the Czechs, who once more refused to take their seats in the Vienna Parliament, counted for very little. The interests of Andrassy were now almost exclusively devoted to foreign affairs: foreign affairs for him meant exploiting Franz Josef's great name, power and resources to make the world safe for ten million Magyars. Let it not be thought that the Hungarians were the only egocentrics: they were more single-mindedly selfish than any other people, and more persistent and ruthless in pursuit of what they took to be their own interests (unlike Field-Marshal Kuhn, they did not see very far). But they were helped beyond measure by the Poles. If the Germans despised the Slavs and sought to deny them their rights, if the Magyars despised Slavs and Germans, and sought to oppress the one and exploit the others, the Poles were also self-absorbed, though less obsessively and flamboyantly than the Magyars and less naggingly and arrogantly than the Germans. There was not much evidence of solidarity among the Slavs.

The Poles, had they cared to, could have come to the rescue of their co-racials and made life very difficult for the Hungarians by making common cause with the Czechs, the Slovaks and the Southern Slavs. They were careful not to do anything of the kind. By quiet political manoeuvring they had already achieved a considerable degree of effective autonomy for themselves: effective autonomy in this context meant freedom for their Polish magnates to express their own personalities, augment their own wealth and power, and exploit and oppress their own fellow-Slavs, the Ruthenians, or Little Russians, nearly all peasants on the great estates, who were denied the name of Pole. The last thing the Galician magnates wanted was for any other Slavs, anywhere, to interfere with their game. In a word, it can be said without exaggeration that in 1871, when Andrassy took over, there was only one man in the whole Empire who was exploiting and oppressing nobody: that was the Emperor himself. Franz Josef was well aware of this; and it is not to be doubted that his constant close-up view of the behaviour of freedom-loving Germans, Magyars, Poles and Czechs towards their minorities and each other helped to confirm an inborn scepticism towards freedom and politicians. What he thought about Andrassy has never been made clear. Always slightly larger than lifesize, this brilliant, charming, hectoring, moody, stubbornly cunning, gypsy figure from another world certainly fascinated him profoundly. He had all the attack and self-confidence and flexibility that his other Ministers so markedly lacked. Clever as a bagful of monkeys, he was yet steadfast in a crisis, and always lucid and clear-cut. Time and time again Franz Josef was irritated almost beyond endurance by his presumption and his crowding tactics; also, perhaps, by his influence over Elizabeth (when she was staying by herself at Gödöllö he would carry her off for long *tête-à-têtes* to his own hunting-lodge in the deep countryside). Time and time again he would recover lost ground with an inspired exercise of charm or sudden deference. Always he knew what he wanted, and Franz Josef knew what he wanted: these rare qualities the Emperor greatly prized, even though what Andrassy wanted was by no means always what he himself wanted.

He was, as Franz Josef knew from his own experience, a diplomat of extreme accomplishment. Almost at once he started making friends with Prussia. Demonstratively turning his back on Beust's pro-French policy, he addressed himself to England, who had not the least objection to his avowed intention of preventing a too close understanding between Prussia and Russia. But, at the same time, he himself was determined to get on terms with Russia. The role he had assumed was that of the great peacemaker. He sent round a circular to the Foreign Offices of Europe to that effect. At home he announced: 'The aims of Austro-Hungarian policy are first to be able to say to the peasant: Sow your seeds without anxiety; they are not going to be ravaged. Secondly to be able to say to the town: Build your houses; they are not going to be destroyed. Thirdly, to be able to say to the whole population: Your sacrifices will serve the cause of peace.' With all this, and as a buckler for peace, he increased the armed forces and added a year to the two-year conscript term in face of bitter opposition from his German liberal protégés.

This sort of approach, a mixture of grandiloquence and down-to-earth demagogy which was to become more familiar a century later in the speeches of a great Soviet statesman, was sincere enough. Hungary wanted peace: it was the only thing that could preserve her special position. But to his proclaimed intention of inducing prosperity all round there was a little setback. The Empire had enjoyed a miraculous seven years. After the horrors of 1866, 1867 had been a year of natural calamities. There had been every kind of bad weather, and the harvest had failed all over the Empire. Then, suddenly, everything smiled. There was a long succession of bountiful harvests; in the new-found freedom which resulted from the abandonment of the attempt to subdue Prussia with one hand while running a centralized Empire with the other, trade and industry, building and railways, had flourished exceedingly. Into Hungary in particular, money had been poured. Then came the slump. It came on Black Friday, 9 May 1873, and at the very worst moment. Only nine days before, the Emperor had opened the World Exhibition in the Prater at Vienna, the biggest of its kind ever held until then, some of the monuments of which – notably the Rotunda, 200 yards across – remain to this day. It was a triumphant and imposing display of the wealth and resources of the Empire. It was designed to show that poor old 'Chinese' Austria had shaken herself free from her obscurantist past and was riding the glorious wave of nineteenth-century capitalist enterprise. Ironically, the Power which had looked most sceptically at *laissez-faire* and material progress was the first major casualty of the new system which, all over the world, on and on and up and up, was to lead mankind to the commanding heights. The great slump came when Vienna was full of foreign royalty. Tsar

Alexander himself arrived for the opening. The new German Emperor, William I, should have come, but he was ill and sent Augusta and the Crown Prince. Franz Josef was deeply upset and personally wounded by the crash. True, there was a world depression in the making (the word had not yet been invented; capitalism was so new), and the collapse of the Vienna Stock Exchange touched off a financial disaster as the collapse of the Credit-Anstalt was to do nearly sixty years later. This did not interest the Emperor: what did interest him was the discovery that more than twenty-five per cent of the active deputies to the Vienna Parliament held directorships, or were otherwise actively engaged in business enterprises (most of whom used their positions to push their own wares), that this scandal also heavily affected the Upper House, and that speculation and corruption extended to members of the First Society, those who were free of the Court. Giskra himself was involved, ultimately confessing that he had himself accepted 100,000 florins in bribes.[7] If Franz Josef had not understood the full import of Schäffle's anti-capitalist theories when they were first presented to him, he understood them now.

But the programme had to go on. It involved profitable conversations with the Tsar. Later in the year it was the turn of Wilhelm I. He brought with him Bismarck, who felt shy, as well he might. But all went well. Then Franz Josef had to go to Petersburg. The first thing he did was to lay a wreath on the tomb of Nicholas I, a gesture which affected Alexander deeply, after all that had gone before. So that went well too, though Bismarck was more than a little apprehensive, largely because of a remark made by Andrassy to Gorchakov, which got back to Berlin, that Austria needed Russia's friendship against the possible day when the new united Germany might start trying to attract the Austrian Germans into their orbit.

Austria, in a word, after more than two decades of almost perfect isolation, was beginning to make friends again. England regarded her with favour, partly because of her internal reforms and her new attitude to Hungary, more especially as a bulwark against Russian Middle East ambitions; Bismarck would need her help one day in the matter of Constantinople. Before the year was out Victor Emmanuel had also come to Vienna, an action which deeply offended the Pope, and was received with proper decorum as the King of a united Italy. In March 1874 Pius IX shot his last bolt in the form of an Encyclical condemning the liberal laws and, in effect, threatening Franz Josef with excommunication.[8] The Emperor took it calmly. He regarded himself, as indeed he was, as a devout servant of the Church; but he was Caesar, and he had had quite enough of clerical intrigues. The Pope, however, was still the Pope, and when in 1875 it was the turn of Franz Josef to visit Victor Emmanuel, the last strand he had to pick up in the business of disentangling old, inhibiting quarrels, he refused to meet the King of Italy in Rome, on the Pope's own ground, and insisted on Venice as a meeting-place.

Then just as the past seemed to be safely buried and all was set for a peaceful course new trouble blew up out of the Balkans – or old trouble in new form. It was to continue, intermittently, until 1914.

In 1875 there was a bloody revolt against Turkish misrule in Herzegovina. Russians, as well as Austrians, had helped to stimulate the revolt, and the whole Eastern Question was once more reopened. Out of this rising grew the Serbo-Turkish War. Andrassy made frantic efforts to force Turkey to mend her ways. But the Turks refused to budge. Britain was taking her old line of the Crimean days, and although France was still out of action after her defeat by Prussia, the Turks were convinced that this time, if it came to war with Russia, they would have Austria-Hungary unequivocally on their side, as well as England. They were wrong. Andrassy's one aim now, as Franz Josef's aim had been in 1854, was to avoid war with Russia. But for different reasons. Then the young Emperor's ruling instinct had told him that any war between the Powers would unleash forces inimical to Austria, and, when war broke out, that Austria must keep out of it at almost any cost, in the hope that the old balance, or something like it, might be restored. The reasons for Andrassy's need for peace were more particular. In the first place the motives which had made him oppose participation in the Franco-Prussian War still held good; in the second place almost any change in the Balkans would be perilous for Hungary. Russia's grand ideas of wholesale partition were also unattractive. Russia thought Austria might be tempted by an agreement which would give her a free hand in Serbia and in the whole of the Western Balkans, leaving Bulgaria and the Principalities in the Russian sphere. There were two things against this, one political, one economic. Politically, the Monarchy would find itself saddled with a lot of tough and unmanageable Slavs, all too susceptible to Russian influence; economically, such a partition would have cut the Monarchy's greatest and most valuable trade-route, the Danube, and prevented the free development of the proposed railway from Belgrade to Constantinople. So all that happened when Andrassy met Gorchakov at Reichstadt in Bohemia was the conclusion of a secret agreement whereby in the event of a Russo-Turkish war, Russia would regain Bessarabia, between the Dniester, the Pruth and the Black Sea, which she had lost after the Crimean War while, in return for her neutrality, Austria should have the right to occupy Bosnia and Herzegovina.

This agreement was reached under the impact of the Serbo-Turkish War. When, three months later, the Serbs were prostrate, Russia decided to act. In September a mission arrived in Vienna from Petersburg to revise the Reichstadt Agreement. This time Russia wanted Austria to join her. Austria was to move into Bosnia, Russia into Bulgaria, to force the Porte to grant autonomy to these two lands. An Austrian occupation of Bosnia and Herzegovina was one thing; the liberation of these Turkish provinces was another: other provinces, this time in Austria, would ask for autonomy too. The quarrel was on. Austria wanted no disturbance of the Balkans, and might have to fight to keep the Russians away and the Turkish power intact. Russia, while talking largely about the miseries of Christians under the Moslem yoke, had her eyes very firmly fixed on Constantinople and the Straits, her sally-port into the Mediterranean.

And so there ensued yet another personal correspondence between Franz Josef and a Russian Tsar, this time Alexander the liberator of the serfs; but Alexander's letters had the same strange, hieratic, boding quality, like an Aztec sculpture, of the doomed Nicholas: Alexander was also doomed![9]

If we synchronize our actions the prospect of avoiding greater complications will be much better. . . . Thus your troops must be ready to move into Bosnia, while mine do the same in Bulgaria. . . . Should my proposals not suit you and should you have others to put forward, I am prepared to examine them in the sincere desire to reach agreement with you. I only request you to take my situation into consideration, in that it forces me to adopt a clear-cut, tidy and definite position and to follow it through energetically. . . . Under these conditions I consider that it should be possible for an understanding to be reached between us, and this I desire not only for the present but also for the future, for this is one of those moments which can determine the fate of our two lands for many generations to come.

At the time of the Crimean War the young Emperor had been very much alone. Now he had Andrassy behind him, and it was Andrassy who drafted the reply to Alexander's first appeal: 'A joint intervention seems to me not a little dangerous. The armed invasion of the two most interested States would arouse the distrust of all Europe.' And he went on to say that before promising anything he, the Emperor, must secure the constitutional approval of the representative chambers 'to which I myself have given this power'. It was a half-hearted letter. But it contained a half promise, and encouraged Alexander to announce the imminent mobilization of his army and to offer Austria-Hungary 'an *unconditionally* secret treaty' to regulate the details of Austro-Russian co-operation. Franz Josef was ready for an agreement, but had doubts about Alexander's motives:

> You seem to take it for granted that I desire to hasten the dissolution of the Ottoman Empire through military action. . . . But, in fact, an action which would lead to the dismemberment of Turkey does not at all correspond with my thought. . . . Everything I have said was conditional on a general European conviction that the maintenance of Ottoman sovereignty was no longer possible.

This called forth the old, authentic Muscovite tones:

> Impossible to see an end to an ever more intolerable situation. I for my part am resolved to set a term to it and alone to bring about the solution which the world has already declared in principle to be proper, humane and necessary. I confess I regret that you do not wish to act openly and jointly with me. Nevertheless I count on your indirect help in achieving the aim which we have together agreed upon. And this particularly so that the disadvantages of divided action may be excluded, which could allow events to take a course wholly opposed to my intentions.

With this scarcely veiled threat Franz Josef was almost back where he had been in 1853. Once more the Austrian generals were demanding an immediate accord with Russia; once more there was a war party, this time headed by the Hungarian gentry. Once more England, this time through Disraeli, sought to engage Vienna in an anti-Russian alliance. But Franz Josef and Andrassy still kept their lines open to Petersburg, and in January 1877 arrived at a completely secret agreement, pledging Austrian neutrality, assuring Austria of Bosnia and Herzegovina, and excluding Russian activity from Rumania, Serbia, Bulgaria and Montenegro. The driving force behind this treaty was Franz Josef himself who, in opposition to most of his advisers, had set his heart on the bloodless gain of Bosnia and

Herzegovina to compensate for what he had lost in the first twenty years of his reign.

On 19 April Alexander wrote jubilantly to Franz Josef: 'The moment for action has come. My armies will now receive the order to march into Turkey. I have done everything humanly possible to avoid these extreme measures. It is in the interest of all the world that the coming war should be short.'

On 24 April the Russian armies marched, and the war was indeed short. Few people understood how close they had been to war between Russia and Austria-Hungary before the Treaty of Neutrality was signed. Both sides had applied to Bismarck, who, with the smallest cost to himself, managed to reassure them equally. But it was a problem only very temporarily shelved. The two Empires, now brought so close together in the Balkans, were from now on to bump into each other every time one of them stirred. Until the Russo-Turkish War it could have been fairly said that Russia and Russia alone was responsible for the perilous reduction of the buffer area between the two Powers, just as she was simultaneously responsible for diminishing the area of neutrality between herself and British India. There was plenty to worry about. One of the great Russian soldiers of the time, H. D. Skobelev, had helped with the capture of Khiva, was then sent to fight the Turks where he made his name at Plevna and the Shipka Pass, and then went back to Turkestan to conquer at Geok Tepe. He did not in the least dream of laying India at the feet of his Tsar, but he did express one very revealing truth: 'The stronger Russia is in Central Asia, the weaker England is in India and the more conciliatory she will be in Europe.'

This was the kind of wide-ranging and dynamic thinking which Austria-Hungary now found herself quite literally up against. And by responding so eagerly to the fateful lure of Bosnia and Herzegovina Franz Josef, for the first time, but for ever, put himself into direct competition with the spirit of Skobelev, and, as it were, on the Russians' own ground.

The English, meanwhile, were very far from conciliatory; in spite of the approaching threat to India (or, rather, because of it), they were in a sharply hostile frame of mind. After initial setbacks, the Russians quickly made a clean sweep of the Turks. While Austria watched her swift advance with apprehension for the Balkans, England, with increasing fury, saw the way being cleared to Constantinople. Unaware of the secret treaty of neutrality, she still tried hard to woo Vienna into a new alliance. Andrassy kept cool. At first he was convinced that Russia was running herself into a bog, and must be allowed to flounder there. While with one hand he restrained his fellow-Magyars, calling for a war of revenge, he was utterly sceptical of any lasting agreement with Russia. 'I want no enmity with Russia so long as there is no direct threat to our interests. But should such a threat arise, then not only a Crimean War, but war to the knife. The first aim of our policy must be to discourage pan-Slavism in the Balkans.'[10] There were still twenty-seven years to go before it was war to the knife. War in 1877 was avoided by Andrassy's diplomacy, in 1878 by the action of Disraeli and Bismarck.

The Treaty of San Stefano was signed on 3 March 1878. Single-handed the Russians had broken the Turkish Empire, and single-handed they now proposed to enjoy the fruits of their costly and by no means easy action. This involved, above all, ignoring the Russo-Austrian agreements. Far from limiting herself to the acquisition of Bessarabia, Russia forced on Turkey an agreement whereby a large Bulgarian State was created, nominally under Turkish sovereignty, actually wide open to Russian influence. Rumania, Serbia and Montenegro were all declared independent. The Balkans were thrown open to Russian intrigue and also to a free interplay between those Slavs outside Austria-Hungary and those inside. On top of every-thing else the Russian armies were at the very gates of Constantinople. Andrassy was wounded in his vanity, which was profound (he con-sidered himself, correctly, to have been outmanoeuvred), and deeply disturbed at the injury to Austrian interests. He faced about. The time had come, he insisted, to strike quickly, attacking the Russians in the back while the going was good. Franz Josef would not agree to this: instead he resumed his correspondence with the Tsar, this time in tones of high acrimony. Andrassy stormed. Once or twice before there had been a slight displacement of the façade of the elegant, flexible man of affairs. This time it simply disappeared as he clamoured for an ultimatum. Franz Josef did not like people who shouted, any more than he valued men who allowed him to be manoeuvred into false positions. From this moment Andrassy lost his magic, and it was only a matter of time before he went. Disraeli and Bismarck saved him for the moment by taking up the running. It was the moment in England when 'jingoism' was born. While Franz Josef and Andrassy racked themselves and wrestled in Vienna, a wild mood of Russophobia swept through London and beyond. The music-hall singer Macdermott became a national hero with the song which was to symbolize England's contribution to the reckless, violent scramble for extra-territorial dominion which was the European mood (American too) of the last quarter of the nineteenth century and the first decade of the twentieth:

> We don't want to fight, but, by jingo, if we do,
> We've got the ships, we've got the men, and got the money too!

It was against this pre-view of the vulgarity which was to drown the age not only of Edward VII in England, but of Wilhelm II in Germany and the France of the Dreyfus affair, that on Disraeli's initiative the Congress of Berlin was called, with Bismarck as the 'honest broker' in the chair. San Stefano was undone, Russia humiliated, Austria received the right to occupy and provisionally administer Bosnia and Herzegovina. 'I know very well', Franz Josef said to Hübner, still after all these years and so many disappointments, very much in his confidence, 'that this step is highly unpopular with us, not only in Hungary, but also here; but public opinion is in error: the gain of this territory is a necessity, for otherwise Dalmatia will be lost.'[11]

It was no triumph for Andrassy, who was now the most unpopular man in the Empire. The army generals (all but Archduke Albrecht), the German liberals, above all the Slav populations of the Empire, had been united in rejecting his war policy, which had not even got the Emperor behind it; and the fact that the Emperor *was* behind the occupation of two new difficult provinces could not save him. Particularly when the occupation itself turned out to be a major military operation. Andrassy, in order not to exasperate his Hungarians, had tried to carry it out quietly as a parade operation with only two divisions. It was not a parade operation at all: the army had to fight hard to enter into what should have been a peaceful occupation and, before it could move on Sarajevo, it had to be heavily reinforced – as the generals had said all along. It was an unhappy episode, and everything went wrong. The idea was that the occupation of Sarajevo should be announced as a birthday-present for Franz Josef: it arrived a day late, and it turned out to be in fact a death-sentence for Franz Josef's successor, for the Empire, and for the Renaissance tradition which, for so long, and with so many setbacks, had inspired all that was best in Europe.

Andrassy had one more action to perform before the ring of fate was sealed. This was the consummation of the Dual Alliance with Germany.

It was, of course, Bismarck's *tour de force*. He had obtained all he needed by war. He was not interested in aggrandizement for his new Germany; indeed he feared it. The man who had used war, when it came to his hand, with perfect ruthlessness to secure particular and limited ends had become since 1870 the supreme champion of peace. Thus he was now, in a sense, on the defensive. Further, being for once without a clearly defined limited objective, he became the victim of his own moods and his own surpassing cleverness. After the Congress of Berlin, to secure the peace of Germany and his own celebrity, he started playing chess with the whole of Europe as his board. In 1875 there had been an ominous little flare-up which could have embroiled Germany, ruled by any other man than Bismarck, in another war with France. Gorchakov, the aged and excessively vain Russian Foreign Minister, sought to obtain the credit for preventing a war which Bismarck had never envisaged. Bismarck, perhaps because for once he had perfectly clean hands, flew into a towering temper; and it was from this point that he began to turn from his settled policy of solidarity with Russia, first towards holding the ring between Austria and Russia in the Balkans, later towards an alliance with Austria directed against Russia. 'I am holding two powerful heraldic beasts by their collars, and I am keeping them apart for two reasons: first of all, lest they tear one another to pieces; secondly, lest they should come to an understanding at our expense.'[12] That was in the summer of 1875, when Russia and Austria were eyeing each other with inflamed suspicion on the occasion of the rising in Herzegovina. It was then that Bismarck made his famous remark about the Balkans not being worth the bones of a single Pomeranian grenadier. His immediate answer was to bring the two Balkan Powers together with Prussia into the Three Emperors' League. That, of course, did not survive the Congress of Berlin, which in Gorchakov's eyes was rigged by Bismarck for the express purpose of humiliating Russia. Soon after came a personal letter from the Tsar to the Emperor William, now eighty-two, heavily reproaching him for allowing German agents to intrigue against Russian interests and for seeming to support Austria against Russia at every turn.

William was horrified. For him the Russian connection was the rock upon which the new Germany was built. It was unthinkable that anything should be allowed to come between him and his nephew. Bismarck thought otherwise. Alexander's letter was all that was needed to put him into a towering rage. He had already invited Andrassy to meet him at Bad Gastein; now he brought the meeting forward. He had made up his mind that Germany, strong, had more to lose from being tied to a strong Russia than to a weak Austria. He rationalized this primitive need to dominate with the utmost ingenuity all through the fierce and protracted struggle with his master which went on for the next few weeks. The last time he had quarrelled with William about Austria was when he had wrestled, not in vain, to keep Prussia out of the Frankfurt assembly of German princes. Now in this even more violent struggle, in which Bismarck's threats to resign were countered by William's threats to abdicate, he was arguing from a perfect volte-face – to tie Germany to Austria. 'Let us never tie our trim Prussian frigate to the worm-eaten Austrian galleon!' he had once exclaimed. Now, of an Austria beaten and humiliated by Prussia, he was saying:[13]

> Perhaps, of all the Powers, Austria is the one whose internal condition is the healthiest, and the rule of the Imperial house is firmly established among the component nationalities. But in the case of Russia no one knows what eruption of revolutionary elements may not suddenly occur in the interior of that great Empire.

William fought back: 'I would rather retire from the scene, and hand the government over to my son, than act in defiance of my best convictions and commit an act of treachery against Russia. . . . There shall be no alliance. I will not have it.'

But an alliance there was. Not the one that Bismarck wanted. Austria would not have that. There was to be no Austrian guarantee of Germany against France, only a mutual defensive alliance against Russia. 'Why should we support Austria against Russia with all our strength, while being content that Austria should remain neutral if France attacks us?' the old King cried out in despair and indignation.

> What we propose to do for Austria against Russia, Austria ought to do for us against France. . . . This is *partie inégale*! The proposed treaty will inevitably drive Russia into the arms of France, and that will foster the French longing for vengeance! What better situation could France hope for than to place Germany and Austria between two fires? . . . As soon as the proposed treaty becomes known, or when its existence is suspected, France and Russia cannot fail to unite!

The King was not blind. But Bismarck? This is how Bismarck appeared to a contemporary, Karl Marx, in a letter to Engels:

> The most characteristic thing in Bismarck is the way in which his
> antagonism to Russia originated. He wanted to depose Gorchakov
> and instal Shuvalov. Since he failed to get his way, the rest follows
> as a matter of course. *Voilà l'ennemi* . . . *En attendant*, the black
> cloud in the East is serviceable to him: once more he is the indispens-
> able man.[14]

This is not the sort of political analysis we have come to expect from
Marxism; but then Karl Marx lived and worked without the advantage of sitting at the feet of Lenin. It was part of the truth, but the
main truth seems to have been Bismarck's incapability of admitting
the existence of an equal. 'If I must choose,' he said, 'I will choose
Austria; a constitutionally governed, pacific State, which lies under
Germany's guns; whereas we can't get at Russia.'

The treaty of alliance was ratified in October 1879. It was to be
enlarged three years later into the Triple Alliance, to include Italy.
This did not prevent Bismarck from reviving the Three Emperors'
League (Hohenzollern, Habsburg and Romanov) in the summer of
1881, or from renewing it for a further three years in 1884. In 1887
this hoary institution died a natural death as a result of the Austro-
Russian quarrel over Bulgaria. Bismarck's response to that, while still
clinging to the Triple Alliance, was to arrange his famous Reinsurance
Treaty with Petersburg, under the terms of which Germany promised
neutrality towards Russia unless Russia attacked Austria-Hungary,
while Russia promised neutrality towards Germany unless Germany
attacked France. Thus an apparently watertight system of treaties
designed to secure peace in general and the immediate peace of the
Balkans in particular was woven by the man who in the past had
shown a horror of all systems. In this last phase, instead of riding the
waves, Bismarck sought to quell them. When one element in the
system failed the entire defensive apparatus was turned into a trap.
That happened when the old Emperor died and his son, Wilhelm II,
replaced Bismarck with Caprivi, whose first act was to denounce the
Reinsurance Treaty with Russia. That left Germany tied to Austria
and Italy in face of a resentful Russia, who was, as the old Emperor
had foreseen, indeed driven into the arms of France and her *bête noire*,
England. So that the net result of the treaty of 1879 was to place
Germany and Austria 'between two fires'. It was to force Germany to
support Austria's 'forward' policy in the Balkans (though Bismarck
would never have allowed this); it was to force Austria to support
Germany against France (which Andrassy never contemplated). It

was to be the pivot on which swung the jaws of the monstrous trap which was to crush the body of Europe just thirty-five years later, destroying the grandson of the German signatory, the nephew of the Austrian signatory, the grandson of the Russian Tsar. Designed by two men, one a man of genius, the other a statesman of very considerable parts, for the sole purpose of maintaining the peace and the integrity of Europe, signed by two monarchs, also desiring peace, but above all honour, it contributed more than any other single act to the greatest holocaust in history and, at a later stage, to the supersession of Europe as the centre of the universe by the two young giants, America and Russia, who, even before they could relish their remarkable translation, themselves discovered to their untold chagrin that each, separately, was unable to command a world which also contained Africa and Asia.

CHAPTER FOURTEEN

THE LULL BETWEEN STORMS

In many of his attitudes the man who was to dominate the politics of the Empire for the next fourteen years, Count Taaffe, was curiously English. Profoundly sceptical of all ideologies, moved by an invincible sense of humour, he was concerned to have round him men who could see a joke and take the problems of each day as they arose rather than men of large ideas who were inclined to treat the common stuff of humanity as guinea-pigs for their social, economic and constitutional theories. He was not English, of course. Although he invented the term 'muddling through' (*fortwürsteln*) to describe his own activities years before it became fashionable in England he was in fact very much an Irish Viennese. Descended from one of Wallenstein's men in the Thirty Years War, his family had settled in Bohemia, accumulating large estates there, while also keeping themselves on the list of Irish peers: they were not struck off until 1917. Taaffe himself had been a childhood playmate of Franz Josef: the two so very different men knew each other inside out and trusted each other absolutely. Unable to work any more with the German liberals, who had opposed the occupation of Bosnia, Franz Josef decided that the time was ripe for another attempt to make his inheritance work: he wanted a compromiser, a conciliator, an adroit negotiator uncommitted to any theory of government, undesirous of making his mark in the Great Game of nineteenth-century diplomacy, content to knock heads together in the gentlest manner and make Germans lie down with Slavs. He turned to Taaffe; and Taaffe, for his part, was content – was proud even – to regard himself not as a haughty statesman in his own right, but as what he called an 'Imperial Minister', a kind of fixer and contact-man for his master.

It was a remarkable partnership. Taaffe was the negation of all the great forces then at work. He was not interested in nationalism (how could he be with that background?), but he wanted fair play for those who were – Germans, Czechs, Poles, Slovenes, Italians and the rest. He was not interested in social theories, but he did more than any man to help the oppressed. He appeared to take nothing seriously, but for fifteen years he made things work as they had never worked before and were never to work again. Under his light-hearted, light-fingered regency, groupings took shape and forces emerged which were to change the face of the world; but, until his fall, he kept them all in check. The Austria he established (he could not legislate for Hungary) was the Austria of legend. And the legend survived his downfall.

The 1880s and the first half of the 1890s were remarkable all over Europe, and in America too, for the illusion of steady progress towards the light. While nasty and dangerous international incidents arose, products of diplomatic positions already taken up, there were two broad governmental movements. Grover Cleveland in America, Ferry in France, Gladstone (and also Salisbury) in England, Bismarck in Germany (Bismarck the anti-liberal social reformer), Taaffe in Austria, were all working in their very different ways towards an era of secular enlightenment and economic amelioration. On the other hand, in Africa and elsewhere, it was the period of cruel, predatory imperialism, which, nevertheless, was soon to be complicated by a dawning sense of responsibility on the part of the master-nations to their subject-peoples, later to be symbolized in the phrase 'the White Man's burden'. Only Russia remained unaffected by these tendencies. Just as Taaffe came too late in Austria, so Witte and Stolypin, thirty years later, were to come too late in Russia. For what was going on was not a gathering of strength for a new leap forward into concord, but a belated rearguard action, an attempt of the old order to conciliate the new forces, which were, however, to prove themselves unmerciful.

The impression which Taaffe so diligently sought to make, that he took nothing seriously, was, of course, a blind. He had been a public figure for a very long time. Much of an age with Franz Josef, he had entered the Imperial civil service at the height of the Bach régime in 1852 and shown himself an assiduous and gifted organizer as Governor first of Salzburg, then of Upper Austria. After the Hungarian Compromise he had moved into politics, serving as Minister of Defence under Auersperg and Minister of the Interior under Hohenwart, with a brief intermission of Prime Minister. With the coming of Andrassy he had gone back to the country to govern Tirol, briskly, efficiently, and with benefit to the workers and the peasants. Now, as 'Imperial Minister', he was determined to create and develop a State of which his master could be proud and which would prove strong enough internally to make its weight felt in the world. He was not given to public polemics or to philosophizing; but he was moved by much the same spirit which had already been expressed in England by the Disraeli of the 'Two Nations' (only in Austria there were more than two) and was later to inspire Lord Milner in his losing fight against *laissez-faire*. His most particular concern was with fostering equality of opportunity among the peoples of the Empire – or at least those in his care: about Hungary he could do nothing. When it came to protecting individuals from the excesses of *laissez-faire* he was not alone. There had always been strong voices to protest against the spirit of economic determinism as preached by the Manchester School. And the whole concept of government in Imperial Austria, as in Imperial Germany, was constantly working against the unbridled rule of *laissez-faire* (as represented, above all, by the German liberals) and for a degree of Statism which was to remain wholly distasteful to the English until after the Second World War: this was the other side of the absolutist medal. What Taaffe had to do was to apply this principle to the various peoples. This meant, above all, to the Czechs, who were the strongest, most selfconscious and most materially advanced of all the peoples of the Empire other than the Germans.

Everywhere, except in Bohemia, the central government had to do with essentially peasant peoples. But in Northern Bohemia the peasant pattern was being broken irreparably by the impact of the industrial revolution. To break the force of the German liberals Taaffe thus had to rely on three main elements: the clericals, who represented the Catholic peasants of the Empire; the German aristocrats; the Slavs, above all the Czechs and the Poles. By playing variations on Schmerling's electoral system he managed to forge these three minority elements into a majority coalition, which was known as Taaffe's 'Iron Ring', or 'Government above Party', which survived until 1894. The most remarkable feature of this coalition was the presence of the Czech deputies, who had boycotted the Vienna Parliament during all the time it had been dominated by the German liberals. The Czechs came, under protest: at the opening of each parliamentary session the leader of the Bohemian delegation made a formal statement about the historic rights of the lands of St Wenceslaus; but the dream of historic rights was in fact wearing a little thin. While the veteran leader, Rieger, remained faithful in his heart to the romantic dream which would restore to Bohemia the lands of St Wenceslaus, a younger generation was showing itself far more interested in participating actively and equally in the government and privileges of Empire than in the reassertion of past glories. What they needed, above all, was for Czech to be recognized as an official language in Bohemia, Moravia and Silesia. And this Taaffe achieved with his Language Ordinance of 1880. This made Czech co-equal with German throughout what was known as the 'outer service' – i.e. where communication between government and judicial officials with the outer world was concerned (the 'inner service', referring to correspondence between officials of State, still had to use German). But this language reform was quite enough to lay the bureaucracy wide open to penetration by Czechs: almost all Czechs knew German, very few Germans knew Czech. The younger generation had found a way of making their weight felt, of pushing their careers and their ideas, without tears. The same applied to other parts of the Empire – e.g. in Styria, where the Germans had long had things all their own way *vis-à-vis* the Slovenes. It was the beginning of the great mingling of races which was to make Vienna a city of all the talents: the new Slav officials did not all stay on their own ground; they also came to the capital and helped to run the Empire from the Centre. So, while in the Hungarian half, Budapest was developed into an exclusively Magyar preserve, and there were no jobs for members of the minority races unless they identified themselves completely with the master race, which many were only too pleased to do, in the Austrian half Vienna became the headquarters of a truly cosmopolitan government machine, with Poles, Czechs, Slovenes and Italians working side by side and intermarrying.

The Germans did not sit down under this. Just as there was a new generation of Czechs far removed from the romanticism of Rieger, so there was a new generation of Germans who were not bound closely to the ageing liberal centralists, whose interest had now dwindled to the maintenance of a free capitalist system and who looked down on the German masses no less than on the Slavs. These new Germans embodied many moods, many aims and many classes. They ranged from those who still dreamed of a centralized, Germanized Empire on the lines of Bach and Schmerling, to those who would have been happy to cast off considerable parts of the Empire which were entirely Slav in order that what remained might be more easily Germanized. Some believed in the virtues of unrestricted capitalism, some in the protection of the little man; some saw in Bismarck and the Hohenzollern Empire the true leader and home of all German Austrians; others sought revival through Catholicism. All were suspect to Franz Josef, who considered that the Germans presumed too much; all were hostile to Taaffe and his multi-national reforming Cabinet.

The new mood found its first expression in what was known as the Linz Programme, a pan-German manifesto drafted in 1882 by the oddest coalition of young men it is possible to imagine. The three leaders did not stay together long: it was only extraordinary that they ever coincided, an indication of the extreme desperation with which the Austrian Germans regarded Taaffe's cosmopolitanism, or refusal to regard the Germans as the 'people of State'. They were Georg von Schönerer, who was later to emerge as the forerunner of Nazism and to go to prison for sedition, a violent anti-Semite (the father, indeed, of Austrian anti-semitism), and the first political proponent of the Teutonic myth, later to be adopted by Himmler for his SS: he invented a new calendar from which the B.C. and A.D. were eliminated: Year One was the Battle of the Teutoburg Forest (A.D. 9). Co-signatories of the Linz manifesto were two Jews of the highest distinction: Heinrich Friedjung, who was to become one of the greatest Austrian historians and live out in his own life and writings the eternal contradiction between loyalty to the Emperor and loyalty to Germanism; and Viktor Adler, who was to be the father of Austrian socialism, founder of that Marxist Social Democratic Party which, when the Empire had gone, was to be shattered in street battles by the successors of Lueger under Dollfuss, who themselves were soon to be destroyed by the successors of Schönerer under Adolf Hitler.

Formative years . . . the years of the Taaffe era were nothing if not that. This tolerant, adroit and highly civilized politician, who expressed all that was best and most constructive in his Imperial master, thought he was muddling through, sidestepping one crisis after another, turning the Austrian Empire into a smiling land of common sense and order, where, shielded by the army's might, all kinds and conditions of men might develop their faculties, follow their bents in peace and concord – and, indeed, all this he did to a remarkable extent. But he was also doing something else: he was clearing an arena which was to be the scene of embittered and savage conflict. Taaffe's main driving force was expediency: he wanted to make the Empire work. Cynical he might be called, superficial he certainly was, but he made the same deep error as the idealist Adolf Fischhof.

Fischhof was still plugging away. At the time of the Compromise he had published a book called *Austria and the Guarantees of her Existence* in which he tried to revive the ideals he had so nobly expressed in his speech to the crowd on the first day of the 1848 revolution. A little later, at the height of Andrassy's fame, he wrote in a letter: 'In the long run it is not an alliance of princes nor an *entente cordiale* of diplomats that is going to help us, but unity at home and the friendly co-operation of all the nationalities that make up our State, for the chasm that divides our nationalities will one day be the grave of the monarchy.'[1]

Both Fischhof and Taaffe in their different ways were unable to see that the peoples may be brought to the waters of concord, but they cannot be made to drink.

And so in these years, the 1880s and the early 1890s, we see crystallizing out the pattern of internal forces which were to plunge the Empire to ruin just as in the previous decade there crystallized out the pattern of the external forces which were to push it irresistibly towards the brink.

The Linz Programme was remarkable in that it reflected a total lack of political sense on the part of highly intelligent Austrian Germans, even in the matter which affected them most closely. Its main object was to make the Empire manageable by Germans, and to this end it invoked the aid of the greatest German, Bismarck, against Franz Josef and Taaffe. There was to be no nonsense about those parts of the Empire which the Germans knew they could never dominate successfully. Thus the Poles were to be given a free hand to suppress their own subject-peoples in Galicia; Vienna's control of Dalmatia was to be delegated to the Italian minority, who would be allowed to lord it over the indigenous Croats; the Hungarian Compromise would be undone in favour of the old idea of Personal Union – possibly, even Dalmatia would be handed over to Hungary provided Budapest would guarantee support for the Germanization of Austria. All this was a direct challenge to the dynasty, and the man who was to force it on the dynasty was Bismarck. The underlying fallacy was that Bismarck would be only too pleased to back his co-nationals in face of the Slavonic hordes. The Austrian Germans were unable to grasp the fact that it had been Bismarck who had expelled Austria from Germany, not Austria which had contracted out. They could not understand that the Habsburg Empire, as constituted, was a vital necessity in Bismarck's scheme for a continental balance of power. Their plans and resolutions thus foundered ignominiously in a void. As time went on they went different ways. Adler came to see a way to greater German unity through the Socialist workers' movement, then abandoned nationalism for the Socialist International. Friedjung remained a German nationalist all his life; but he could not stomach anti-semitism and was too honest for the political game: his romantic Germanism, to which he clung, in spite of his intellectual awareness of the fatal contradictions in his position as a loyal Austrian and a believer in the German mission, served to infuse his great histories with their boding sense of tragedy. Only Schönerer persisted to the logical conclusion, and, in calling on his fellow-citizens to transfer their allegiance from the Habsburgs to the Hohenzollerns he marked out the course – the counter-colonization of Germany by the German Austrians – which was to be followed to the bitter end by Adolf Hitler. Born in 1889 when Schönerer was at the height of his notoriety, the young Schickelgruber, just seventeen years later, was to inherit the spirit of this bullying demagogue when he went to Vienna to seek his fortune.

All that remained of the Linz Programme while Taaffe held the ring was the constant and perpetual obstruction by the German nationalists of all efforts to conciliate the Slavs. All that remained of the great Bohemian programme was the determined efforts by the young Czechs to establish themselves and their people as indispensable components of the governing machine. Moderates both among the Czechs and the Germans were brought together on the defensive against the radicals on their own side.

2

The foreign policy of the period was uneventful. Andrassy had been succeeded as Foreign Minister for a very short time by an able but colourless bureaucrat called Haymerle, who soon died. Then Andrassy thought his chance had come round once more. But just as Franz Josef needed an empiricist at home, so he needed caution and neutrality abroad. He brought in Count Kalnocky, a Moravian aristocrat from an old Transylvanian family, who could be relied on not to start any adventures or to nurse far-ranging schemes. Kalnocky had two main tasks: to convert the Dual Alliance into the Triple Alliance, which he successfully achieved with the accession of Italy in 1882, and to keep the peace with Russia. This was not so easy. Austria's essay in prestige politics which had culminated in the humiliation of Russia at the Congress of Berlin and the occupation of Bosnia and Herzegovina in 1878, had sown dragon's teeth. It was all very well for Franz Josef now to decide that Austria must go carefully in the Balkans and avoid all possibility of a clash with Russia in south-eastern Europe. By virtue of the occupation, she had planted herself firmly in the very heart of the storm-centre. She had, in effect, made herself an accomplice with Russia in rocking that very leaky boat. And in 1887 it took all Kalnocky's caution and all Bismarck's weight to damp down the first consequences of that action. This was when Russia, predictably, started behaving as though Bulgaria belonged to her, arresting and deposing Prince Alexander and sending a Russian general to Sofia to assume command. Austria had to object to Russia's treating Bulgaria as her own sphere of influence. Bismarck, his aged Emperor now approaching death, apprehensive about the drawing together of Russia and France and the open talk in France about a war of revenge, had to act quickly. He had no intention of allowing himself to be dragged by Austria into a war over the Balkans against France allied with Russia. He was not at all prepared to jettison Austria. But, in his great peace speech to the Reichstag on 11 January 1887, he sailed as close to the wind as he dared. Taking the line that, as he saw it, the Treaty of Berlin had given Russia a perfect right to interfere in Bulgaria, he went on with a passage which was an uncanny pre-echo of Neville Chamberlain's remark about Czechoslovakia at the time of Munich – 'a far-away country, of which we know nothing'. 'What's Hecuba to us?' he demanded. 'It is a matter of perfect indifference to us who governs Bulgaria, or what becomes of that country. Not for Bulgaria's sake shall we suffer anyone to cast a lasso round our necks and drag us into a quarrel with Russia.'

Austria had to climb down: the word 'appeasement' had not then been invented. Bismarck then had to apologize to Franz Josef for being a little rough, while assuring him of Germany's unbreakable loyalty. But a few months later, with an eye to Germany's own security, he had concluded his highly secret Reinsurance Treaty with Petersburg, whereby Germany promised her neutrality in case of an attack by Austria-Hungary, in return for Russia's neutrality in case of an attack by France. At the same time Germany formally recognized Bulgaria and Eastern Rumania as falling within Russia's sphere of influence. It was the master-stroke. It was the apogee of the secret treaty as a guarantee of peace. The man who had coldly and collectedly provoked three wars to win for Prussia what he regarded as her due, had for seventeen years, ever since 1870, been Europe's great man of peace. It was he, now, through this brilliant and complex series of alliances and treaties, who was saving Austria from war with Russia. But in March 1888 the old Emperor William died. The Crown Prince, Frederick, desperately ill with cancer, reigned for exactly ninety-nine days. On 15 June 1888, the twenty-nine-year-old Wilhelm II became Emperor. Two years later Bismarck was dismissed 'like a dog', and with him went the understanding with Russia and the Reinsurance Treaty.

3

In twenty years, since 1867, the whole character of the Empire had slowly and imperceptibly changed. Franz Josef was now fifty-seven, and he presided over a State which had little in common with the Austria of his inheritance and which had developed under the parliamentary régime and with the increasing freedom of the Press a life of its own. Franz Josef did not read the newspapers, only the brief summaries which were served up to him every day; but, had he done so, he would have seen that the life of the people of the Austrian half of the Empire was no longer to any considerable degree regulated from the centre but was broken now into multitudinous fractions, interest groups and pressure groups, banging away at each other with great vehemence and some savagery, almost as though he himself no longer existed. He was, of course, in some manner aware of this, but, possessing intact his authority over foreign affairs and the army, he was unable to take the shrill ferment of ideas and conflicting interests with sufficient seriousness. He was very much Atlas now, more or less consciously supporting on his trim shoulders the whole weight of his universe. There was only one flaw in this graven image of patient, long-suffering, sacrificial wisdom: this was the need to prove to himself that he was something more than Atlas. The preservation of the *status quo*, the avoidance of war with Russia, were not enough. Deeply within him, invisible and unsuspected by those who brawled and bickered in his shadow, there burned a lasting shame at having been forced to surrender a part of his inheritance. This was his last infirmity. And so, against all reason, against the main current of his developed character, there still lingered a flicker of the burning fire which forty years before had sustained the young autocrat in the teeth of his mutinous subjects. What he had lost on the one hand, he must compensate on the other. Bosnia and Herzegovina were not to him far-flung provinces, a tangle of wild mountains inhabited by passionate Slavs reckless in their desire for freedom to the point of self-destruction: they were symbols of Imperial Majesty reborn. Fischhof – it is the last time we shall encounter this man who for so many decades was the unheeded conscience of the Monarchy – saw what was happening. He saw, that is, the advance of Austria into the Balkans by agreement with Russia as a trap which, in the end, whether Russia willed it or not, would embroil the Monarchy with Russia:

> A victorious war against Russia might delay, but could not prevent, the downfall of Austria, so long as our constitution, instead of being the wax which welds our territories into a whole, is the wedge to drive them apart. Thence and thence only can salvation come. As it is, what is happening at home? What are our monarch's popular assemblies doing at the moment when Russia presents the hemlock? They are engaged in a desperate feud against a halfpenny tax on their cup of coffee.[2]

4

While Taaffe manipulated the balance inside the Empire, while Hungary went her own way building up a legacy of woe, while Kalnocky and Bismarck skirted the very brink of war, Franz Josef, as a man, found troubles multiplying. Elizabeth was quite out of hand, though he still loved her to distraction. After the great reconciliation in 1867 there had been another child, and for a long time it had seemed that her devotion to this youngest daughter, Valerie, had been Elizabeth's only link with reality. It seemed that the growing girl was the only object that bound her to life itself. With or without Valerie, her restless travelling had moved from the compulsive to the obsessive. Now in her fifties, she was more magnificently beautiful than ever: her devoted, worshipping – but she worshipped without illusions – lady-in-waiting and confidante, Marie Festetics, even after twenty years of her incessant company, found that beauty heart-breaking. Elizabeth had only to smile, to gesture faintly with her hand, to melt the sceptic into adoration. But her smiles were rare now; they were kept for some of her Hungarians and for the English and Irish house-parties where she went for the riding and the hunting: there was nowhere on all the continent of Europe which could offer the sort of riding she wanted. Only the English shires would do; and soon, partly to escape scandalous publicity, partly to test herself further, she abandoned England for Ireland, her constant escort being Captain 'Bay' Middleton, the most intrepid of all English horsemen.

This was one side of her life. The other approached the melancholy mad. She was now in love with Greece and with Heine. Greek she learnt from a queer, ambiguous figure called Christomanos, half confidant, half factotum, whom she took around with her. She fell in love with Corfu and built herself there a dream palace hidden from all eyes. But between Corfu and the English shires she was everywhere, always solitary, always incognito. Franz Josef was still deeply in love with her, still living for the rare moments when they were together – usually at Gödöllö in Hungary or in the Hermes villa in the great natural park at Lainz, near Schönbrunn, built specially for her. Only at the Court was she scarcely ever seen, and the Viennese gossiped about her, and wondered whether, once Valerie was married off, she would abandon the world altogether, like the grandest of all the Habsburgs, Charles V, or retreat into total and insane isolation at Corfu, like her mad uncle Ludwig of Bavaria, who gave firework displays for himself in solitary places and built a theatre in Munich for the production of Wagner's operas for himself alone.

But she was never mad in this sense. She cared passionately for Valerie. She had lost touch with her son, Rudolf, now in his thirties and, as she knew very well, in his temperament owing all too much to her: she was touched beyond measure when Rudolf went to great trouble to procure for her as a surprise the original MSS. of some of Heine's poems. It was clear by now that it was herself she hated above all; and while in a sense her endless journeying meant an attempt to escape from herself, at the same time she had also an indistinct feeling that in some way her presence in the bosom of her family was a taint and that the least she could do was to hold herself at arm's length. She was plagued with sciatica and to cure it went to the oddest places, to Bournemouth, to Cromer. There are people alive who remember that sad figure. Sir Compton Mackenzie was four years old in the summer of 1887, and he remembers a tall, slender woman dressed in brown alpaca, who sat on the beach alone, with a small lace parasol, staring out to sea, then writing, writing, staring out to sea again.[3] This was the Empress of Austria, dreaming about Heine. Perhaps she was writing her own verses, perhaps she was writing to Franz Josef to say that she proposed to visit Queen Victoria at Osborne and then come home. For it was to her at Cromer that he wrote: 'My endlessly beloved Angel – Your dear letter gave me so much happiness, for it was one more proof to me that you love me and that you will be glad to come back to us. . . .'[4] Poor Franz Josef, then fifty-seven, and wrestling with Russia over Bulgaria – he was not beloved. A few months later Elizabeth was to write to her daughter the strangest and most oppressive of letters, which Count Corti has called a formal declaration of love:

> It is you alone that I love, and if you leave me, then my life is over. But one loves like this only once in a lifetime. Then one thinks only of the beloved creature, and it is all on one side – one demands nothing from the other and expects nothing. I can never understand how anyone can love several people at once. With my other children Sophie took the mother's place, but with you from the very first moment I said, this time it must be different. You had to be my own, most only child, my pledge, on whom nobody had any claims but me, and all the love in my heart, quite closed until then, I have poured out over you.[5]

Poor Valerie: but she married to escape and be happy. Poor Rudolf, who had eighteen months to live before he killed himself. Poor Elizabeth. . . . Here is another side. It is Marie Festetics writing to her friend, Ida Ferenczy, another devoted servant of Elizabeth:

> I am so oppressed, dear Ida, by what I hear and see here. To be sure Her Majesty is still dear and kind when we are alone, and talks as she used to do. But she is no longer what she was – there is a shadow over her soul. I can use no other word, for when somebody denies the very existence of fine and noble feelings what can one call it but bitterness and cynicism? I can tell you, my heart sometimes bleeds. Sometimes she does things that make not only the heart but the reason stand still. . . .[6]

And as though to emphasize that with all this desolating obsession with herself, she yet knew that she had failed, with the sane fibres of her mind she tried to give Franz Josef what he needed: in Katherina Schratt, an enchanting, quiet, happily extrovert young actress from the Burgtheater, she laid at his feet all that she was not, guarding her from the least breath of gossip, and providing with the utmost delicacy of discretion and tact the means to enable her husband to enjoy young, untroubled company, home-cooking and easy chatter. It was all the domestic life the Emperor ever had.

And yet several times in the life of Franz Josef and Elizabeth she showed a perfect consciousness of what was required of her and gave a glimpse of what might have been. She had done this after König-grätz; she was to do it again in the most terrible crisis of her husband's far from easy life.

5

On 30 January 1889 the report went round Vienna that Rudolf, the Crown Prince, had been found dead in his bedroom in his hunting-box at Mayerling among the wooded hills to the south-east of Vienna. Then came another report, that in the same room was the body of a young girl of considerable beauty and local fame, Baroness Marie Vetsera.

The world knew nothing of this attachment. Nor did it know that twice before the final act Rudolf had tried to persuade other girls, one of them a cheerful, common little dancer, called Mitzi Kaspar, to agree to die with him. His whole life was lived out behind a smoke-screen of gossip, which had plenty to feed on in his last two years, but the brooding morbidity was well-concealed. Towards the end his brilliance went wild: he drank compulsively, made love compulsively, took drugs; his hand writing went to pieces;[7] then feverishness turned to apathy and exhaustion and he looked much older than his thirty years. But everybody put this down to dissipation, as such: he could still turn on his old charm and delight all who met him. Franz Josef himself, when Rudolf's young wife, Stephanie of Belgium, greatly daring, sought a private interview to beg the Emperor to send her husband on a long voyage to recover his health and his balance, could see nothing wrong. 'What he needs', said the Emperor, 'is to spend more time with you.'

In fact the marriage was a disaster. Stephanie was a dull girl with a narrow outlook. She was the daughter of Leopold II of Belgium, who worked the Congo, the 'Heart of Darkness', as his own private estate and built up an immense fortune on the proceeds. Her mother was a Habsburg. Her marriage to Rudolf was arranged by Franz Josef himself, in spite of Elizabeth's protests, when Stephanie was fifteen: it had to be put off once when it was found that the poor girl had not even begun to menstruate. She was a cheerful child, though colourless and narrow, and Rudolf, at twenty-three, seems to have been quite taken with her: also, in spite of the deep rebelliousness of his nature, there was another side: he was fully conscious of the demands made by his station in life and his duties as heir to the throne. He never lost this consciousness, which was one of the motives for his suicide seven years later, when he had compromised himself in so many ways and was so steeped in deceit *vis-à-vis* his father that he could see no honourable way out. His ideas soon left Stephanie far behind.

He was an angry young man, but he also had a strong vested interest in the Establishment, which he came to detest in its working but still accepted in principle as a mystique: one day he would dominate it and breathe new life into it. He was a liberal. He detested Russia as a reactionary Power and was full of contempt for his father's and Kalnocky's attempt to appease the Tsar. He had warm feelings towards the Hungarians, but objected to the Compromise. Starting off with strong sympathies towards the Czechs, he came to dislike them because of his dislike and distrust of Taaffe and his feudal-clerical affiliations. He objected with passion also to Taaffe's policy of muddling through from day to day, from year to year, which appeared to him both unprincipled and flabby. But he quite lacked the intellectual power, or the political sense, to substitute for this a grand design of his own. He took his stand with the German liberals, who nourished his radical ideas; but he never understood their limitations: he was for free-thinking and against outdated conventions, for science and against the Church – so were many of the liberals; but the common ground was insufficient. On top of that he loathed the Hohenzollerns, above all Wilhelm II, then still Crown Prince, whom he could hardly trust himself to meet. He had no real home, except, paradoxically, the army: with all his eccentricities, his iconoclasm, his flirtation with revolutionary ideas, he could find no new direction for the Empire, and he echoed in his heart the famous words of Grill-parzer about Radetzky: 'Thy camp is Austria.' This fine-drawn and sensitive intellectual was also, paradoxically, the very type of Imperial officer. And although, from the age of fifteen, he was convinced that the days of monarchies, of ruling castes, of the exploitation of the masses by the few, were at an end, his father's dynasty, so long as it could last, was for him an object of veneration and of awe. It was because of this profound contradiction that he could never be captured by any group or any cause. He would go along far enough – with the German liberals, with the Magyars – to be compromised by them, perhaps fatally; but they could not capture his heart.

Yet he was more than a dilettante prince. It is true that his politics were as a rule half-baked and never thought through, bound up, too, with prejudices of every kind and liable to be influenced by moods. It is true that his impassioned interest in science, in geography, in economics – in the power of reason – could not turn him into a scientist or an economist. But he *felt*, and at first with little assistance from anybody, the new spirit of the times and tried to find expression for it in his intellectual life.

Thus, when he was fifteen, we find him writing down his thoughts about the mysteries of life in general and human society in particular. In one moment he is brooding about First Causes, about the point of differentiation between man and beast, about love as the universal solvent; in the next he is prophesying the doom of his father's dynasty: 'The kingdom still stands, a mighty ruin, continuing from one day to the next, but doomed finally to fall. For centuries it has endured, and so long as the people allowed themselves to be led blindly, it was good; but now its task is at an end, all men are free, and the next storm will sweep away this ruin.'[8] That was in December 1873. Two years later, now seventeen, he is still brooding:

> The spirit of the individual never dies, it continues into the next generation. . . . This is what differentiates us from the beasts, who repeat themselves for generation after generation. . . .
> The individual must strive towards spiritual development, always with the ultimate aim of establishing here on earth a spiritual kingdom, embracing the whole of mankind, whose laws shall approach the harmony of the immutable laws of the universe. . . .
> There will be wars until the peoples and the nations have completed their development, until they at last unite themselves and mankind has become one great family which will seek the highest spiritual life and the highest culture in striving forward all for all and identifying themselves through the laws of their life and action with the natural law. . . .[9]

These were some of the thoughts of a young prince in adolescence immured with his tutors, allowed no contact with the real intellectual life of his father's Empire, and denied by that father any insight into the affairs of government.

They did not remain the broodings of adolescence. As Rudolf reached technical maturity he was still excluded by his father from matters of State. He turned to journalists and lawyers for stimulus and in search of sounding-boards for his own ideas. Above all to Moritz Szeps, founder of the *Neue Wiener Tagblatt*. 'A great and powerful reaction must come,' he wrote to Szeps one day, 'social upheavals from which, as after a long period of sickness, a wholly new Europe will rise and bloom.'

The difference between Rudolf and other dreamers was that to him would fall the power to make these dreams come true. There was no escape from this. Others may dream and sigh for power, knowing they will never hold it; free, thus, to blame for every failure those who have the power. Rudolf's position was less comfortable: it was, indeed, intolerable. He was to be a monarch endowed with great power within his own realm and immense influence outside it. He could not retire from his dreams into passivity. He had been vouchsafed a vision, and one day he would be put to the test. How could he forget this? Others would not allow him to forget, even if he could forget himself:

> . . . To keep your right arm and your spirit strong for the day of action, that is the task, which you, Imperial Highness, have set yourself; and this task you fulfil day in day out with unceasing endurance and activity. You will not weary, as so many weary, giving in to the inevitable and because the Crown Prince does not weary, we pin our hopes to the future of a great, glorious, free and prosperous Austria. . . . We know that you desire great things, are equipped to achieve great things – and those who don't know, guess it. Because of this you are already being opposed in a variety of ways, your path obstructed by many foes. But you rely on yourself and on your character, on your genius, on your strength and steadfastness, and you are right to rely on these.[10]

Thus Moritz Szeps to Rudolf on New Year's Day 1889. Within a month Rudolf was dead.

Who can wonder?

In that schoolboy essay about the universe and the monarchy, the fifteen-year-old Rudolf had written:

> Thoughts of every kind race endlessly through my head, all is confusion, my brain seethes and works away all day; no sooner has one thought gone than another takes its place, each one compels me,

each one says something different, now gay and cheerful, now raven black with rage; I fight them and struggle with them, and out of it all the truth at last will come.[11]

It went on like that for another fifteen years – until the brain snapped. The ideas were too big for the brain. Rudolf was not a genius; he was a dynast who saw too much, who asked too much of himself, who knew that much too much was expected of him by others. He had one refuge, the army, and its extension, the hunting-field. The army was all that was left to him in practice of the dynastic mystique. In any land, under any system of government, in any foreseeable future, there had to be an army. And the Imperial and Royal Army of the Dual Monarchy in particular was a State within the State. It was in the army and the army alone (for not even the Church was all embracing) that the concept of the Empire with the Emperor at its head was translated into reality. All races served in it. Hungarians too. All who served in it, their families in civilian life divided from each other by religion, national hatreds, conflicts of political and economic interest, political ideas, found in their military duties a common tongue, a common ideal, a common loyalty. '*In deinem Lager ist Oesterreich.*' In the simple, hierarchical organization of this great closed society with its career officers, its unceasing flow of conscripts from half the lands of Europe, there was indeed something splendid and unearthly, a glimpse of the true supra-national society. In membership of this unique institution, which transcended all civilian bitterness and lifted them up and set them apart from the welter of nationalist and party strife, individuals of all kinds found fulfilment in service. For many short-term soldiers the brief time of army service was a return to a golden age when all problems were solved by simple obedience in a mood of universal brotherhood to a remote and ineffable father-figure, Franz Josef. It was an army in which the young Dr Sigmund Freud, who hated Vienna and everything to do with it, would perform his compulsory service as a surgeon-lieutenant quite ungrudgingly, marching many miles a day on manoeuvres, and turning doctor when the men were billeted for the night.[12] It was an army remembered with nostalgia by some of the most sophisticated characters of a highly sophisticated age. Thus the great Prime Minister, Max Vladimir Beck, perhaps the first Austrian statesman after Schwarzenberg, who, had he retained power, might very well have averted the First World War, looked back on his year with the Saxony Dragoons (they had as their regimental call the opening bars of the Blue Danube Waltz) with the utmost tenderness:

> The long marches on horseback, going on for days at a time, through the lovely landscape of Lower Austria under the autumn sunshine, the ever-changing staging points in picturesque villages, the nightly billets depending on accident and the Quartermaster's mood – all this came together to make a romantic harmony taking one back to simple rural existence and giving to life an enchantment never known before, and never to be known again.[13]

Rudolf escaped from the thoughts chasing through his brain more and more into these simplicities and certitudes. One of his young protégés was his cousin, Franz Ferdinand, over whom he took endless pains. This strange, awkward, glowering, morbidly sensitive youth cannot in the least have appealed to Rudolf with his universal interests, his quickness of perception and apprehension, his easy facility, his contempt for the slow and the ponderous, his perfect manners, his radiant charm. But, in his middle twenties, he went out of his way on many occasions to befriend Franz Ferdinand, to bring him out, to make him feel wanted and loved, to divert him from his devouring egocentricity to the delights of army life and the open air. Already at twenty-two he was writing to the seventeen-year-old cousin like an uncle, suggesting to him, as one asking a favour, that he should see the 1880 manoeuvres in Bohemia through to the end – everything he saw, he said, should fill him with interest and delight 'in our craft, which is the finest and grandest in the world'.[14] On at least one occasion, too, he was to save with perfect tact his young cousin from the Emperor's wrath. Franz Ferdinand, then twenty-one, had not been taking his duties seriously enough. He was bored with the garrison life at Enns where his regiment was stationed; he had been coming up to Vienna far too often, and his enemies, who were legion, had been painting him to the Emperor as an idle good-for-nothing. Franz Ferdinand, always on the edge of exploding in black fury, would have made a scene; but Rudolf restrained him: the only answer was to ignore the malicious gossip and put himself above criticism by his future conduct. 'One must, in life, above all be clever. . . . When the Emperor sees that you now come up less frequently – and he will certainly learn this, for he knows everything – he is bound to mention it to me, and I can then explain that you used to come up more often because you had time on your hands, but that now. . . .'[15]

There is something boding about Rudolf's almost tender solicitude for this most unpromising young cousin, the next but one in line to the throne. It was as though he already had foreknowledge that he himself would never wear the Crown and was determined to do his best to see that Franz Ferdinand should make the best possible showing, should base his career firmly on the Emperor's good graces, should avoid the mistakes he had made.

'The Emperor will learn of this, for he knows everything. . . .'

The Emperor certainly knew little or nothing of Rudolf's inner turmoil, but he knew enough to be deeply disturbed – though it never seems to have occurred to him that he might save his son and heir by taking him into his confidence in matters of government and life. He knew, for example, that Rudolf, at twenty-nine, had applied to the Pope to annul his marriage to Stephanie.

The Mayerling story was one of the great sensations of the late nineteenth century. It is understandable enough that people, and not only sensationalists, should look for hidden causes for this tragedy. Rumour piled on rumour and the behaviour of Franz Josef and the Court gave a free run to the wildest gossip. Only the obvious was ignored. Rudolf was the legendary prince, brilliant, accomplished, handsome, sophisticated to a degree, adored by women: how could a man to whom all things came so easily kill himself for love of a seventeen-year-old child just out of the convent? There had to be quite another reason, and the reasons suggested ranged from involvement in a conspiracy, discovered, to have himself crowned King of Hungary, to the American duel theory, an affair of honour arising from his alleged seduction of the Countess Auersperg. There are still letters which have never been brought to light, and one day these may add something to our knowledge of Rudolf's state of mind when he persuaded Marie Vetsera to die with him. He loved her, clearly, but he did not die for love of her; she died with him, evidently gladly, because her love for him was hopeless. By her voluntary death she proved to him something that had to be proved before he himself could die. 'Love', he had written in his adolescent testament, 'is certainly the most beautiful thing in the life of all organic beings, it is the one feeling which man still possesses in its animal purity; in this he comes into perfect accord with Nature itself.'[16]

There was a fatality about poor Marie. She was seventeen, the daughter of an undistinguished diplomat's wife, sister of one of the rich Baltazzi brothers, who were sons of a Levantine banker. The mother, aspiring to the highest society, had long before aroused the suspicions of Elizabeth and her entourage. Ten years earlier, when Rudolf was twenty, when Marie was only seven, Marie Festetics had laughed at herself for her alarm at the way in which the Baroness was running after the young Crown Prince; but she could not laugh her fears away:

> The temptations that surround a young man in his place! Among them that Madame Vetsera . . . it can't really be dangerous, because, God knows, she isn't in any way attractive, but she is so cunning and knows so well how to use people to get herself to Court and make herself and her family count for something. Meanwhile her daughter is coming up, slowly, to be sure, but one builds from the ground up![17]

The Emperor, too ('he knows everything'), saw what was going on. 'The way that woman goes on about Rudolf is incredible,' he said one day to Marie Festetics. 'She chases him everywhere. Today she even gave him a present.'[18]

In the end the Baroness paid. Rudolf, who could cope no longer, threw himself into dissipation at a last attempt at escape, but found no comfort there, rediscovered love, and died. It was clearly no sudden impulse. The police reports, now published, the affidavit of Count Josef Hoyos, written and sworn the next day, then hidden away, and various other documents, show that the suicide was planned in advance.[19] Rudolf went to meet Marie at Mayerling knowing that they would both die there, and arranging that the discovery should be made by a most trusted friend. He wrote farewell letters to Elizabeth and Stephanie, but not a word to the Emperor. If he left an explanation and a justification, it is still held secret. We do not know the immediate cause of the terrible decision; but this is unimportant. It was the tragedy of a man of vision who could not exist on visions alone because the powers he held demanded the translation of the ideal into practical politics, and this was beyond him. His father's character and policies, and Taaffe's, were leading the Empire to ruin, as he saw it. Had he had a lucid set of practical policies to put in their place he might have had the patience to wait (he was still only thirty and he could not foresee that Franz Josef would reign for another twenty-eight years), or at least to set to work tenaciously and 'cleverly' to counteract those attitudes and policies. But he had no clear practical goal, and he knew it. This meant that by his own high-flying standards he was a failure, and he knew it. He was not alone. Failure was in the air. Later that year his cousin, the Archduke Johann Salvator, another highly gifted, but far less sympathetic, character, who had collided head-on with Franz Josef, renounced his title, his position, and assumed the name of Johann Orth. Two years before he had written to his old tutor: 'Believe me, I know that I have failed; yet I have conducted an inquest on myself of a kind I would not wish on my worst enemy, which (I openly confess) has for the time being broken my spirit and clouded my soul.' And again: 'My life – it is no life – my existence is like nothing more than the fog-bound, gloomy, hopeless, void autumn day in the mountains. Why can't the human soul be tuned up like a piano at five gulden a time?' Johann ended up by driving his ship on the rocks off Cape Horn.

The Imperial family was breaking up, losing direction, losing the will to live. Tough old Uncle Albrecht could write to Franz Ferdinand as the new heir about the disgrace of Rudolf's suicide, followed by Johann's 'desertion' – 'two unheard-of ignominies in a single year on the hitherto immaculate honour of our House'.[20] But the very foundations of that House were shifting. They rested on the simple assumption that duty was duty, that one carried on regardless, that the soul was an affair between God and the individual and wholly in the former's charge. Franz Josef carried on because he could and because it was the only thing to do. He was furious with Johann, and he did not understand Rudolf; but he loved Rudolf in his way, and he was already deeply convinced that the dynasty was coming to an end: it must go down with colours flying. Elizabeth, after rising magnificently to the occasion when it came to breaking the news of Rudolf's suicide and sustaining Franz Josef in his grief, now, dressed for ever in black, virtually contracted out of life, until she was stabbed to death on the quayside at Geneva by the Italian Lucheni. And Franz Josef was near enough to Elizabeth to understand that what had gone on in Rudolf's heart was not a personal aberration but symptomatic of a profound sickness which had undermined the certitudes on which he based his own life and must still, since he had nothing else, continue to base it on. Less than a mile away from the Hofburg at this time there was living and working in considerable adversity, but with official support from the Government of which Franz Josef was the head, Sigmund Freud, who was to be the living answer to Johann's appeal, the great piano-tuner of the human soul, then gestating his ideas about dreams, about infantile sexuality, and preparing for the great voyage into the unknown which was to unearth in himself the Oedipus complex – a discovery which would have interested Rudolf deeply had he lived for ten more years.

The personal tragedy of Rudolf and Marie Vetsera is peripheral to this narrative; but the motives behind it and the reactions of Franz Josef and Taaffe are not. The motives have been touched on; the reactions, too, are revealing. The news came to the Hofburg out of a blue sky, shattering the daily routine. The Empress was having her daily lesson in modern Greek; Stephanie was in the middle of a singing lesson; Franz Josef himself was on the point of knocking off work for the morning to spend his usual hour with Katherina Schratt. In that splintered and arrested moment it took a little time for the truth to be grasped, then digested. Rudolf was dead; he had died side by side with a seventeen-year-old girl. She must have poisoned him, and then herself. No, it had been a shooting. Then she must have shot him, and then herself. No – and here the Court doctor was wonderfully firm, maintaining his professional integrity in the full blast of the Emperor's wrath and indignation (neither lasted long) – it was painfully clear that the Crown Prince had done the shooting; he could say nothing else in the official death certificate. Franz Josef bit on this bullet: he knew honesty when he saw it; after the first short outburst of Imperial rage, he knew how to respect professional duty. His only son and heir had murdered a seventeen-year-old débutante, then shot himself: so be it. This did not mean that he had to waste pity on the Vetsera. It did mean that Rudolf had to be buried in the Imperial vault, the Kaisergruft, among his ancestors, below the little church of the Capuchin Friars, and then mentioned no more. It meant a furious row with the Cardinal-Archbishop of Vienna and the Papal Secretary, who frowned on suicide. It meant clearing the remains of the Vetsera out of the way. It meant turning Rudolf's favourite hunting-box, hidden in one of the smiling uplands in the heart of the Wienerwald, into a shrine where nuns should pray for his soul for ever. It meant carrying on as though nothing at all had happened, so that nobody, nobody but Elizabeth and Katherina Schratt, and then the few who saw him break down at the dedication service at the Mayerling chapel, should have the least idea of the depth of his suffering, or its nature. All this was enough for one man. The removal of Marie Vetsera's body was the affair of Taaffe and Baron Krauss the head of the Vienna police.[21] Rudolf had asked that the unfortunate girl should be buried with him in the parish church at Alland, the village nearest to Mayerling. But

Taaffe in those first panic-stricken moments when it still, improbably, seemed that the truth might be hushed up, knew very well that this dying request could not even be considered. It was he who was responsible for the swift train of action which expressed itself in the macabre and cruel story of Marie Vetsera's transfer, in a coach, in torrential rain, at dead of night, held upright between her two Baltazzi uncles, to the swiftly dug grave at the ancient and lovely monastery of Heiligenkreuz. Taaffe was afraid, above all, of the Press. Already, before the full news was released, he knew that certain journalists had been putting two and two together, had been watching the house in the Salesianergasse close to the palaces of the Metternichs and the Schwarzenbergs, where Marie had lived, had been interrogating neighbouring tradesmen about her movements and about the movements of her mother, who, alarmed at her disappearance, plunged wildly and appeared before Elizabeth almost in the moment that the dreadful news reached the Hofburg.[22] The Press had to be kept away and misled at all costs. And the Vetseras and Baltazzis must pay for their fearful indiscretion. They did. The whole weight of the bureaucratic machine was summoned up in a moment to suppress the truth. For this Franz Josef has been blamed. By the time the truth was out it was too late to compose the affair more elegantly. The deed remained, exposed for all to see, undefended and unexplained. The deed was the deed of men harassed beyond endurance, striking out savagely in defence of a sacred principle, the principle of the Monarchy. It was not done in cold blood. And there was, thereafter, no cold-blooded attempt to twist the facts in mitigation.

Franz Josef had superbly the courage of his convictions. This meant, among other things, that he went on making, with an iron countenance, the same mistakes. The story of Marie Vetsera's last earthly journey was to be repeated, in another key, after the assassination at Sarajevo, when Franz Ferdinand, the new heir, was bundled off with his morganatic wife, again by night, again in tempestuous weather, to be buried out of sight and mind at Artstetten across the Danube from Pöchlarn in the Wachau. Franz Josef let it happen.

He also made the same mistake over Franz Ferdinand in life as he had made over Rudolf in life. He refused to take him into his confidence as heir to the throne. But Franz Ferdinand, very much less gifted than Rudolf, very much narrower, was also very much stronger. He made his own career.

CHAPTER FIFTEEN

GERMANS, SLAVS AND MAGYARS

With the suicide of the Crown Prince the Empire entered its last phase. Almost imperceptibly, the movement concealed by the continuity of Franz Josef and the Court, it had developed into a modern State. But it was a modern State ruled over by a monarch who had gone to school under Metternich. Franz Josef had stopped developing: he was rising sixty, still physically active, still springy in his step, but increasingly withdrawn from all effective contact with younger and inquiring minds. He had effectively lost his wife, he had lost his son and heir, he did not like the new heir apparent (the technical heir, Franz Ferdinand's father, Franz Josef's brother, was nearly as old as the Emperor himself). He was content in future to hold the ring. He could do nothing radical about the constitution of the Empire because nothing radical could be done without revoking Dualism: the Magyars blocked all useful reforms, and the Emperor could not turn against the Magyars because he had sworn on his apostolic oath to maintain the Compromise: the fact that the Hungarians offended against the spirit of the Compromise with every action, and against the letter of the Compromise with most, was neither here nor there: if they liked to prove themselves false that was their own affair. The Emperor was not false. So the drama of the next twenty-five years was played out under the aegis of a man bound hand and foot.

Taaffe had still four years to go, but by 1890 it was clear that he had failed in his attempt to reconcile the Germans and the Slavs. At the elections in that year two things happened which marked a climacteric. The old Czechs were overwhelmingly defeated by the young Czechs and the German liberals suffered heavily at the hands of the petty-bourgeois Christian Socialists and the proletarian Social Democrats. What Taaffe had failed to understand was that the conditions of life had changed: the Slavs and Germans who had to do the living together were different from those for whom he had been legislating. For all practical purposes the middle classes had long swamped the aristocracy, and now the middle classes themselves were threatened by the rise of the masses. The peoples had developed lives of their own. The men to whom they now looked owed nothing personally to the Emperor or to high connections; this meant that between the multitudes, growing ever more conscious of their strength, and the dynasty which held them together, the organic links had worn very thin. Unless they were to be left to tear each other to pieces, or to be swallowed up by predatory Powers, they still had to be held together, and their more responsible leaders knew this very well: the last thing they wanted to assist at was the dissolution of the Empire, and it was not, indeed, until 1914 that the greatest of all the Czech nationalist leaders, the man who created the Republic of Czecho-slovakia, Thomas Masaryk, finally and reluctantly reconciled himself to the idea of secession. Even the less intelligent felt a personal loyalty to the Emperor, which did not, however, prevent them from doing their utmost to make it impossible for him to rule. Taaffe and Franz Josef have been criticized, and rightly, for their failure to understand the true nature of the forces at work and to think their policies through. But it is also the responsibility of those seeking to change the *status quo* to provide alternative policies of a practicable kind. The national politicians of the component lands of the Empire, unharassed by the day-to-day conduct of high policy, had plenty of time to think; but there was amongst them an almost complete dearth of constructive political thought. Just as Franz Josef failed to appreciate the new forces, so the national politicians failed to appreciate their new responsibilities. Germans, Czechs, Poles, Magyars, all failed in their different ways (the smaller peoples could not be blamed for irresponsibility, since responsibility was out of their reach: they were either, like the Croats and the Slovaks, held down by Magyars or, like the Slovenes of Styria and Carinthia, swamped by Germans). They took the broad framework of the Empire for granted and instead of asking themselves how this extra-ordinary institution, on whose continued existence they severally depended, could be improved, strengthened, and made more equit-able, contented themselves with fighting amongst each other for their own immediate interests and advantages.

Thus the Czechs, instead of asking themselves how best they could make themselves felt in matters of State, were busy colonizing their own land at the expense of the Germans who had lived for so long in Bohemia and Moravia, bringing much material and cultural benefit (Karl Marx was largely right about this). At the same time they sought to penetrate as deeply as possible the Imperial civil service, not so much with the object of influencing policy as with the object of securing jobs for themselves. Thus in 1856 the population of Prague had been 133,000, of whom 60,000 had been Czechs and the rest German. By 1886 the population had grown to 180,000, of whom 150,000 were Czechs.[1] By that time the Germans had not a single seat on the City Council. It was the same with other towns. Under the impact of the industrial revolution the old aristocratic feudalism had largely broken down in the countryside, and the Germans in the towns, for so long the bourgeois standard-bearers of culture, were being swamped by displaced peasants and their progeny, driven into industry and trade by the development of industrial crops and mechanized farming. Thousands of poor Czechs emigrated; but many more flocked, for example, to the coal mines of Northern Bohemia, taking over jobs from Germans who moved west to find higher wages. In addition to the great coalfields there was a swiftly growing textile industry; while porcelain, glass, beads, buttons, all kinds of cheap consumer goods, were poured out in masses from factories and peasant homes. Two main trends were showing. The first was the paternalistic development of immense manufactures in which the worker was sustained by clubs, special shops, tied houses, kindergartens, technical schools and sickness benefits. The pioneer of this peculiarly Bohemian development, which was to reach its apotheosis during and after the 1914 war in the Bata shoe concern – a forerunner of Henry Ford at Dearborn and the Cadburys at Bournville – was Johann Liebig, a journeyman weaver who became a textile millionaire. The other was the development of a widespread cottage industry, depending for its viability on cheapness, and desperately vulnerable to changing fashions. The one produced a highly self-conscious type of worker, the other drove its liveliest spirits into the towns or to emigrate in despair. Both trends came together to assist in the foundation, thirty years later, of the Czechoslovak State, the *émigrés*, working as a pressure group in the United States of America, stimulating the political consciousness of workers of Skoda at Pilsen and other great steelworks and making President Wilson aware of the existence of a highly developed Bohemian economy, run by Czechs, and, as he erroneously supposed, exploited by Vienna. What nobody pointed out was that this remarkable economic transformation of a backward agrarian land had been carried out under the aegis of the man, the Emperor Franz Josef, whom everybody had written off as a reactionary anachronism.

At the International Socialist Congress in Paris in 1889, Victor Adler, then approaching forty, told the assembled delegates about his homeland.

> Austrian liberty [he said] is a hybrid creature, midway between Russian liberty and German liberty. In shape it is German, in execution Russian. Apart from France and England, Austria has perhaps the most liberal legislation in all Europe, it might almost be a republic, with a crowned head instead of a president at the summit. Unfortunately, in practice what counts are not the statutory provisions but the whim of the police official. The police official is empowered to suspend all statutory liberties, and, as you may imagine, he makes abundant use of this right. The Government of Austria is incapable of carrying out with thoroughness either an act of justice or an act of oppression. It sways from one side to the other. It is a system of despotism tempered by inefficiency [*Schlamperei*].[2]

Considering that Adler at that time was the leader of a powerful socialist movement working on Marxist principles, yet not proscribed, considering that he had been allowed to go from Vienna to Paris to attend the inaugural meeting of the Socialist International and would be allowed to return to Vienna, this is not quite a fair characterization of the age of Taaffe. Certainly Taaffe relied far too much on his police, who tended to be arbitrary and jumpy, and stupid too. But there was another side of the medal. When Adler was speaking, the Bach system had been dead for just thirty years. During those thirty years there had arisen among the parties hardly a politician who showed the least appreciation of the needs of the Empire as a whole. All desired the continuance of the Empire, but to none did it ever seem to have occurred that he might be required to make a contribution which transcended the interests of his own particular group or nationality. To be a party politician in Austria was, and so it remained until the end of the Monarchy, with the rarest exceptions, to be a fanatical and uncompromising defender of a sectional interest. Even the few who had a wider vision – like Adler himself, like Karl Lueger at the head of his Christian Socialists – were incapable of compromise and never hesitated to inflame base passions to win base men to their side. Besides Franz Josef, almost the only men who ever tried to see the Imperial problem as a whole were the high officials of the bureaucracy, and from these Franz Josef was only too happy to choose his Ministers: he did not like party politicians, and the party politicians did little to recommend themselves to him.

He had, moreover, constantly before his eyes a terrible example of what happened when, in central Europe, party politicians won control. He was King in Hungary, but in 1867 he had abdicated his authority, except in the matter of the army and foreign policy. Hungary under the premiership of Kolomon Tisza was not a model of enlightenment to show up the black reaction of the Hofburg. It was the other way round. Franz Josef's authoritarianism in the Cisleithnian lands was all sweetness and light compared with the rule of the Magyar Parliament. Tisza, as well as he could, held the Magyars to the bargain with the Emperor: Hungary, he knew, could not exist without that partnership. He had broken the power of the great magnates and based himself on Kossuth's 'gentry'; to keep their favour he had to show himself the most determined Magyarizer of them all; and it was under his régime that Magyar oppression of the minorities reached its zenith. There was a great deal of talk about the prison-house of nations governed from Vienna, and when it came to the showdown in 1918 this phrase stuck and had much influence on the decision of the Western Powers to dismember the Empire. But, in fact, since the end of the Bach system in 1859, the only part of the Monarchy which could reasonably be called a *Völkerkerker* was Hungary, ruled by chauvinist politicians in Vienna's despite. Even Galicia, where Franz Josef allowed far too free a hand to the Polish aristocrats in return for their loyalty to the Crown, by no means qualified as a prison in this sense.

Hungary, however, was a special case. Every individual of whatever nationality who was prepared to learn Magyar and embrace the Magyar cause was welcomed within the magic circle and absorbed by it. This was the secret of Hungarian strength; for in this way gifted individuals of comparatively backward nationalities could rise to the top. They often became more Magyar than the Magyars. Kossuth, a Slovak, was a case in point. The great poet Petöfi, also a Slovak, was another. What was forbidden was the cultivation of national consciousness, of national political life among the minority races of Hungary. A Croat could be a good Magyar; but if he wanted to be a good Croat he was proscribed. This invited that growing irredentism which made nonsense of Magyar pretensions and was to be one of the chief causes of the downfall of the Monarchy.

How exalted these pretensions had become may be seen in these words spoken in 1897 by the son of Andrassy, now a politician in his own right: 'The power balance of the Monarchy makes it inevitable, and its interests make it desirable, that in political matters we, the Magyars, play the leading role. We form a unified State of great antiquity. Austria is a mosaic of nationalities and provinces without an inner unity.'[3]

Andrassy junior did not add that the 'unified' State of Hungary was based on a rejection by Budapest of the national rights of many subject-peoples; that the lack of 'inner unity' in Cisleithnia was due to the refusal of Franz Josef to employ Hungarian methods. Nor did he add that the astonishingly swift transformation of Hungary's material existence was due to economic advantages gained from the Compromise; or that the relative strength of the Magyar population was partly due to the mass emigration of countless Slovaks, Croats, and Transylvanians. He did not add, again, that for Hungary to play the leading role within the whole Empire would have been a direct repudiation of the Compromise, from which she derived so much of her strength; that it would have meant the concentration in the hands of ten million Magyars of political power over forty-five million members of a dozen races, including more than twelve million Germans, more than six and a half million Czechs, nearly five million Poles, and many more besides.

For the Magyars to fight like wild cats for their independence, for their very national existence, driven by the fear of being swamped by a sea of Slavs and Germans, was one thing. They had won that battle, with their stubborn mixture of recklessness and calculating blackmail. They ruled over half the Empire, in which they occupied a position of extraordinary and indeed disastrous privilege, under a King to whom they professed romantic loyalty while doing their best to stab him in the back. They paid less than their share of everything; they had enjoyed more than their share of influence when it came to policy-making; they had striven with all their might to nullify the efforts of Franz Josef, Taaffe and others to achieve harmony and equity in the Austrian half, which they had also contrived to saddle with their own sins. They contributed nothing but some dashing regiments of cavalry, a large number of surpassingly beautiful women, and an infinity of woe. If this is parliamentary government, Franz Josef might justifiably have said, God save us from it!

But he went on trying in Vienna, manoeuvring now with now against the conflicting opinions of the nationalities and of the classes which had grown up beneath his 'tyranny'. From 1890 to 1897 he manoeuvred very wildly indeed before giving up and returning finally to bureaucratic rule. Faced with the elections of 1890, with a Parliament which Taaffe could no longer manage, he plunged for a solution recommended by Baron Steinbach, Taaffe's Minister of Finance. It was nothing less than a sudden move towards universal male suffrage: if the prosperous and powerful middle classes insisted on making Parliament unworkable he would call in the poor and the exploited and buy their support with votes; at the same time he would give Steinbach his head by introducing advanced social reforms – the limitation of working hours, social insurance, a whole far-reaching system of social security. Instead of smoothing his path, the new Bill, introduced in October 1893, was Taaffe's downfall. It was received with all but unanimous disapproval. Czechs, Poles and Germans rose in wrath and, in so doing, provided at last a parliamentary opposition capable of action. The Emperor was quite prepared to bow to Parliament if only Parliament would function. Taaffe went, and, first under a grandson of old Field-Marshal Windischgraetz, Austria prepared for her last fling at parliamentary government. The grand union of parties was unnatural and fleeting; opposed only by an equally unnatural alliance of young Czechs and Lueger's Christian Socialists, no progress was made with the Suffrage Bill or anything else. This coalition was wrecked not on strife between Czechs and Germans, but on the affair of the grammar school at Cilli, a small town in Styria surrounded by a largely Slovene countryside. The Germans bitterly resisted Slav demands for Slovene classes in the local grammar school. The same sort of dispute was going on between Germans and Slavs in many other towns; but it was the grammar school at Cilli that became the great symbolic issue which dominates Austrian politics through the whole of 1894, led to the withdrawal of the Germans from the Vienna Parliament, and thus effectively crippled parliamentary government in Austria. Within two years, after watching the interminable quarrelling between sectional interests and nationalities, Franz Josef had his revenge, or what he thought was his revenge: he appointed a man he had long had up his sleeve as a strong and resolute administrator who would knock the heads of the politicians together, Count Casimir Badeni, who had achieved fame, particularly with the soldiers, in a very specialized sphere as Governor of Galicia. The appointment of Badeni was a queer regressive action on the part of a harassed and frustrated ruler who was getting no help from anyone. After so many

years of dealing in one way and another with politicians, after dis-
covering that he had a remarkable talent for ruling through them, he
quite suddenly slipped back forty years, seized with an overwhelming
need for the harsh, incisive certitudes of his first mentor and Prime
Minister. In Badeni, the Polish Count, who was quite at home and
strong among the simplicities of Galician feudalism, he thought he
had found another Schwarzenberg. It was an error of great gravity.
Badeni could not do much for the Slavs, but he could, and did,
appearing himself as a presumptuous Slav from the backwoods,
alienate the Germans. He managed to push through a Bill which
enshrined the principles of universal suffrage, Steinbach's own Bill,
without really conceding it: only 72 out of 425 deputies could be
elected by popular vote. He then applied himself to achieving a new
decennial settlement with Hungary, the second since the 1867
Compromise. In face of Magyar demands, concessions had to be
made to which there was strong objection in Cisleithnia. Badeni then
decided to kill two birds with one stone: he would carry Taaffe's work
of conciliating the Czechs a stage further, and they in their gratitude
would support him in the matter of the Hungarian settlement. His
way of conciliating the Czechs was to introduce a new Language
Ordinance which in theory was to put the Czechs on an equal footing
with the Germans, but which in practice gave them an immense
advantage over the Germans in Bohemia: except in intercourse with
the Court and the Vienna Ministries, the Czech civil service was to
be bilingual. Since every Czech knew German and very few Germans
knew Czech, since the civil service in a Monarchy which favoured
Statism had innumerable jobs to offer, from stationmasters to
professorships, the way was clear for the Czechs to dominate their
own land. The whole German element within the Empire exploded
with fury at this high-handed attempt by a Polish aristocrat to break
their supremacy and worse. Parliament broke down in uproar. The
Czechs in their day had excelled at parliamentary obstruction, but
they had never used violence. The Germans used violence, even
towards the Speaker, and, in the end, the police had to be called in to
clear the Chamber. The rioting was then carried into the streets and
the military had to be called in to reinforce the police in their efforts
to put down first the rioting students, then the rioting workers,
brought out by the Socialist politicians. Franz Josef was not in the
least afraid of another revolution; but he dropped Badeni. That little
episode had made it finally clear that there was not the slightest chance

of reconciling Germans and Slavs by force, at least without the help
of the Hungarians. The only thing to be done was to tack and trim.
And this he did. He dropped Badeni, but he kept the Language
Ordinances for two more years. Parliament had broken Badeni, but it
was never to work again. The Germans had found that they could
paralyse parliamentary government and they continued to do so. Two
short Ministries were brought down on the Language Ordinances by
the Germans, then these were repealed, and the Czechs retaliated by
bringing down a third. By now Franz Josef hardly cared. He went
back to using men. Instead of opposing Karl Lueger and seeing the
whole unscrupulous force of this man's demagogic powers turned
against the administration, he confirmed, after three successive
refusals, his position as Mayor of Vienna, and watched him build up
the Vienna municipality into an example for all Europe. Once the
Language Ordinances were repealed he chose as his next Prime
Minister a man of outstanding gifts, Ernest von Koerber, who ruled,
as Taaffe had ruled (but more blatantly), as the Emperor's supreme
functionary or factotum for five years, from 1900 to 1904. Parliament
still existed, and politicians thundered away at one another, but the
business of administration went on over Parliament's head, a consummation made possible by falling back on a loophole in Schmerling's ingenious constitution, Article 14, which enabled the Emperor
to rule on occasion by emergency decree. It was like old times –
except that the course now set was in the direction of economic
expansion and social amelioration, and Koerber was, besides being a
manager of genius, a man of liberal and constructive ideas who set in
train vast new developments in the way of railways, canals, roads and
other public services.

The party politicians let it happen. Things were running fairly
smoothly, and, so long as they could not be held immediately responsible for any enactment affecting adversely the circumstances of the
sections they represented, they were content to let them run. Koerber
ruled, quite simply, but with immense skill, by balancing the claims
of the various pressure groups, playing one off against another,
striking bargains between them, making a concession here, demanding a service in return, favouring this one, sending that one away for
the moment with a flea in his ear. It was to this that Parliament had
reduced itself: the real battles between the parties were being
organized and conducted away from Parliament, a noisy sham, with
demagogy in the streets, the political clubs, the public halls of the

capital and the provinces. The real evil of this system was that the political leaders who represented the pressures, and stimulated them by their rabble-rousing, lacked all responsibility, and this lack of responsibility led to demagogy run riot. This has been blamed on Koerber; but the system was not his creation. The party politicians had never accepted responsibility, even when it was thrust on them. All that Koerber did was to regularize an existing situation, put through his social reforms and his economic measures, produce elaborate and excellent drafts for legislation on the nationalities problem, which he did not take in the least seriously, and stand up to the Hungarians who, in the first decade of the twentieth century grew more overbearing every day: their culminating demand, amounted virtually to a claim to a separate army.

Koerber also drastically curtailed the powers and the activities of the police, so that Victor Adler's massive 'but' was at last removed. By the time Koerber resigned in 1904 the Austrian half of the Empire enjoyed a very high level of freedom for the individual and a much higher level of social welfare than, for example, England. Politics and administration were open to all the talents. The Emperor found among members of the Senate, the Upper House, individuals of the old aristocracy whose views and opinions he trusted, and when it came to appointing Foreign Ministers he turned instinctively to members of the First or Second Society who were career diplomats. But government was very largely a middle-class affair. There was no effective Parliament, but this was not for want of opportunity: if the bourgeois party politicians had shown themselves capable of conducting a Parliament they could have had things all their own way. There was nothing to stop them from proving their capacity at any future time.

Professor Josef Redlich, himself an active parliamentarian, decided that the violence displayed by the German parliamentarians in the Badeni affair, had irrevocably shattered the constitutional principle. 'Looking back on those days', he wrote, 'their meaning is clear: no one saw it at the time. *From this moment the Habsburg realm was doomed.*'[4] It is impossible to agree. Redlich was writing in 1926, only eight years after the débâcle. He was writing as one who had once striven with might and main by his own excellent example to infuse a sense of responsibility into Austrian party politics; he had once believed, like an Englishman, in parliamentary government as the only way. Looking back across a slightly longer stretch of time, garishly floodlit by that arch-illuminator of the human spirit, Adolf Hitler, it seems certain that he was wrong: quite clearly the Monarchy did not founder because its bourgeois politicians failed to model their conduct on Westminster. It did not even founder because it was composed of a number of irreconcilable nationalities. Both these made it vulnerable; but it foundered because it lost a war to people who hated dynasties. Perhaps, also, because Franz Josef lived too long and, in 1914, at eighty-four, was tired to death.

As to the cause of the war, which Austria lost, most responsible historians are now agreed that this, in the words of Benedetto Croce, was 'at the same time simpler and a great deal more complex' than any of the *ex parte* analyses offered during and soon after that war: Europe (and also 'that part of Europe which became America') was suffering from a deep-seated moral sickness.[5] Or, as Sir Harold Nicolson has said: 'The war was caused by an unhealthy state of mind in Europe: that state of mind had been created by the amassed unintelligence of international thought from 1878 onwards: it displays a false sense of historical values to lay disproportionate stress upon the intricate diplomatic evolutions which took place during the last twelve days.'[6]

Austria shared in that sickness, but it was not peculiar to her, and it did not arise in any way from her special internal stresses – although these were aggravated by it. Austria was uninterruptedly at peace from 1866 to 1914, for just on half a century: the Emperor and most (but not all) of his Ministers and advisers were above all intent on keeping the peace, yet it was they who, in the end, precipitated the war when it came. The great mainstay of peace in Europe since 1870 had been Bismarck: it was his diplomatic genius which devised a system strong and flexible enough to control, almost miraculously, a tempest of forces all making for war on a continental scale. He did this because he had obtained for Germany all that he considered necessary or desirable; but by his methods in achieving this end, a combination of diplomatic chicanery and military hammer-blows, he had infected his people with the disease of violence and cynicism; in particular by a blunder of a kind almost incredible in a man so far-seeing, he had ensured the perpetuation of a divided Europe by taking, against his better instincts and under pressure of the victorious army, Alsace and Lorraine from France, alienating her irretrievably and filling her with thoughts of revenge.

The immediate cause of the 1914 war, the reckless pursuit of prestige politics, was itself only a symptom of a deeper sickness. Certain Austrian statesmen, above all the Foreign Minister, Baron Lexa von Aehrenthal, were heavily engaged in this insane activity, which was, however, the fashion of the day, and the reflection of an attitude that was not in the least peculiar to Austria. More will have to be said about this. For the moment it is sufficient to insist that grave as were the failings of the Dual Monarchy, some of them special to itself, there was no reason why, given peace, the Empire should not have lasted longer, transforming itself as time went on; further, that the forces, to be considered in more detail later, which brought about the 1914 war, did not arise from the internal conduct of the Empire.

Indeed, at the turn of the century, with the opening of the twentieth century – the century of dictators risen up from the masses and established by the masses, so aptly called the Century of the Common Man – there was nothing inherently unstable about the Habsburg Empire. There was a great deal wrong with it, but nothing that time could not have put right, if only, in the manner of time, by substituting new woes for old. The thing that was most wrong, and which obsessed serious thinkers and drove them almost to despair, was the abuse by the Magyars of their special position, which hamstrung all attempts at reform elsewhere. But, given a ruler who did not feel himself tied by his sacred oath to maintaining Dualism, cost what it might (and Franz Ferdinand, the heir, was determined, also cost what it might, to end it quickly and ruthlessly), there was no reason to suppose that sooner or later Budapest could not be put in its place.

Outside Hungary things were going very well. The quarrel about the grammar school at Cilli had effectively made an end of Parliament, but Cilli had its Slovene classes. The Emperor still held in his own hands the conduct of foreign policy and the army: when, in 1905, with surpassing demagogy, the Magyars tried to split the army, Franz Josef showed that he could still act, summoned to the Hofburg the Magyar leaders, now using Kossuth's ungifted son as a chauvinistic figurehead, and dictated terms to them. Shortly afterwards, and with considerable skill and a clever bit of timing, he bowled the magnates over with a master-stroke by proposing to impose universal suffrage on Hungary. He then had to do the same for Austria, appointing a new Prime Minister, Max Vladimir Beck, as the man most fitted to carry out a difficult task. Beck was on the face of it still another civil servant; but in fact he was much more than that: he was also a politician of great gifts, and he broke new ground by including politicians in his Cabinet and managing to control them. Thus, by the summer of 1906, Franz Josef had shown that the Magyars could, when it came to it, be defied. He had also, while still retaining the outward appearance of an autocrat, brought Austria into the industrial and capitalist age, where business men had to treat with organized workers, and where the needs of economic development were beginning to cut across nationalist prejudices. He was much closer now to a president than to an autocrat, and he knew it. Had he lived longer and been able to retain his vitality there is not the least doubt that sooner or later, as opportunity arose, he would have surrendered his last provinces, the army and foreign affairs, to his Ministers and become in the fullest sense a constitutional monarch. Opportunity only waited on the rise of suitable political leaders, and the appearance of Koerber and Beck was a clear indication that the Empire was at last beginning to produce responsible statesmen from families far removed from the old familiar Court circles. The war put an end to all that.

2

'The situation is serious but not desperate,' we sometimes say. The old chestnut makes the Austrians turn the phrase round: 'The situation is desperate but not serious.' This is supposed to illustrate the cynical flippancy of the Viennese – who in fact have suffered a good deal by being neither flippant nor cynical, though good at jokes and phrases. It illustrates much more exactly the real situation in the last two decades of the Monarchy: almost every issue, taken separately, was desperate, in the sense that there was no immediate solution, but all these issues taken together were not serious: they did not prevent the State from functioning, and they showed no signs of doing so. In the last decade of the Monarchy moderate Czechs and moderate Germans were beginning to come together. There were other movements of a highly promising kind. Politicians have to work for 'solutions', and it is understandable that many Austrian politicians and even Franz Josef himself at times despaired of a situation which held in suspense so many insoluble problems. Because of this there were frequent prophecies of doom; but the sense of doom sprang from deeper causes, scarcely apprehended, which in fact had little to do with the domestic political failures of the Monarchy. It was one thing for politicians and thinkers, striving to find a way out of a dark wood, to despair of the future; it was one thing, indeed, for Professor Redlich, who was a politician as well as a historian, and to whom many looked to find solutions, to see in short-term retrospect the seeds of doom in the failure of the Austrian Parliament to solve the question of the grammar school at Cilli. It is quite another thing when historians accept this view as their own, and propagate it. They, if anybody, should know that 'solutions' to political issues are, if not irrelevant to the continued existence of a State, at least secondary; that although every society may indeed bear within it the seeds of its own decay or disintegration, it takes violence from outside (though it may itself provoke that violence) to smash it. As for Austria and her quarrelling peoples, these disparate races, fragments, flotsam and jetsam almost, of the great migrations of an earlier age, stranded in and around the great arterial river basin, inextricably intermingled and with no clear-cut ethnic boundaries, banded together under pressure from the Turks, thereafter squeezed between new pressures from the east and west – certainly they quarrelled under the Habsburgs, but they were doomed to quarrel, Habsburgs or no Habsburgs, and their liberation from Vienna neither ended their quarrelling nor made an end of oppression; the sources of oppression simply multiplied.

A great deal was also written in those last decades about 'the Austrian mission'. This was in keeping with the age: societies, particularly predatory societies (and, in the last decade of all, the Habsburg Monarchy caught the universal infection and started to be predatory again), felt impelled to justify their existence and their greed by inventing missions for themselves. Russia had a mission – immediately to liberate the Christians from the Turk, then to revive and rejuvenate an ageing, effete and cynical civilization: backward as she was, in her very backwardness she had preserved herself from the mercenary taint of the West, to whom she was destined to bring a spiritual purging. Britain had a mission – it was to spread the two-party system of parliamentary government throughout the world; this was mixed up with freedom and the White Man's burden. France had a mission – to continue as the exemplar of light and reason and, as the focus of high civilization, to serve as a model to the world. Other lands had other missions: few reflected with much accuracy the activities in which most of their citizens were engaged. Only

Austria had no mission. She had had missions in the past. The first, and most famous, had been to stand as the bulwark of Christendom against the Turk; the second was to unite Germany and bring into being the Empire of Seventy Millions. The Turk was now broken, and it had been Prussia, not Austria, who united Germany. Good and honest men, as well as knaves, scratched their heads to find a new mission for the twentieth century: they scratched in vain. The best they could think of was a programme of economic and cultural amelioration for the lands that made up the Empire. This did not seem enough. It was a dynamic age, given over to Croce's disease of 'activism'. Germany, with Bismarck gone, was active in Africa and preparing to challenge the lead of Britain; Russia was energetically expanding towards India, towards the Far East, while extending her influence in Persia and, her eye always on the Straits, threatening Austria's position in the Balkans; Italy had aspirations in the direction of South Tirol, Istria, Dalmatia and Albania – as well as being engaged in Africa; France, the most active of all in Africa, to say nothing of south-east Asia and elsewhere, burned for her revenge on Germany. All these Powers, and America also in her way, were on the flood tide of imperialism. Only Austria was passive. It is easy to understand how the more active sons of Vienna, infected by the mood of the times, so deadly in its vulgarity, sighed for an outlet through which they too could prove their dynamism and demonstrate their mission. It is less easy to understand why a modern English historian should jeer at them for failing: Austria had outlived its mission; therefore Austria must die. In fact, why Austria died was because she thought she had found a new mission, to be carried out in the late-nineteenth-century manner. Until the annexation of Bosnia-Herzegovina by Aehrenthal in October 1908, she was doing very well without one and, indeed, in her international conduct setting an example to the world.

3

Politically, the disintegration of European civilization expressed itself in nationalism; morally, in Bismarckian diplomacy and the technique of using calculated aggression as an instrument of policy; spiritually in romanticism, the glorification of the individual impulse. All was fission. The process of disintegration revealed new and forgotten truths: philosophy and the arts were being forced apart, either by the simple process of pushing one element to extremes, or by direct analysis. In Vienna, quintessentially European, special conditions existed which accelerated all these processes. Freud, Mahler, von Hoffmanstal and Schönberg were all active in that first decade of the twentieth century.

That the last twenty years before the 1914 war was a period of accelerated decadence is one of our received ideas. It is worth asking whether it holds water. Another received idea, and one which seems to contradict the theory of decadence, is that the 'old order' was doomed to be swept away by the wrath of the downtrodden masses. Unless one holds the belief that everything that happens is inevitable, that because it happened it had to happen, that because it had to happen it was 'right', it is impossible to sustain these ideas. Who was decadent? The dynamic masses, who were more and more at the turn of the century making their weight felt and causing the administration to take their needs into account? The administration itself, which was producing new ideas much faster than at any time in history? The business men, who were turning the Empire into a modified capitalist society with confidence and verve? The middle classes who, besides making their contribution to administration and industry, were bursting out in all directions in the sciences, in medicine, in the arts? Certainly some of the old ruling families were decadent, but these had already been left far behind; and although, partly because of their inherited wealth, more largely because of the anachronistic composition of the First Society, they were still unduly prominent, they carried little weight and, except in Hungary, where the peculiar character of Magyardom enabled them to rule the countryside like feudal lords, and in Galicia where the Polish nobility could still treat their Ruthenian peasantry like helots, they were not in a position to impose their own decadence on the course of economic development. Groups of ancient families, whole classes, can give way to new forces without creating the sort of disturbance which ends in the destruction of the State they inhabit.

For many years now we have laughed at the men of the Victorian Age who believed in what they called progress. In some parts of the Western world people went on believing in progress even when faced with the cataclysm of the 1914 war: this was seen as an appalling aberration; it was to be, positively, the last, the war to end war, to clear away the last remnants of domestic tyranny and international injustice. When it was seen that the war to end war did none of these things and that very soon afterwards a large part of European society could revert, without turning a hair, to the barbarities of the sixteenth century aggravated beyond measure by the growth of populations and the inventions of the industrial revolution, we stopped believing in progress. It may be that the men of 1900, out of touch as they were with the realities of human nature, had grasped a corner of the truth that we have lost. They were even beginning to find out about human nature. It was Hitler, reacting against the Vienna of that fatal decade, who finally took the lid off and demonstrated the hideous forces so close to the easy surface, but this was an extravagantly expensive lesson and, in a sense, supererogatory: that other product of Vienna (who hated the place almost as much as Hitler hated it, though for very different reasons), Sigmund Freud, had fifty years earlier begun his long, slow, gentle course of instruction. All Europe was moving forward. Freud, and others, were telling us what we were made of. At the same time, in the world of practical politics, remarkable things were happening. In England the Boer War taught a lesson which the best citizens did not forget; Lord Lugard was perfecting his blueprints for the dismantling of the colonial system; the Lloyd George budget of 1906 was laying the foundations of the Welfare State. In Russia, in spite of the futility of the Duma, the reforms of Stolypin promised in a measurable time very great amelioration of the existence of the peasantry, while the belated but swift development of industry was promising a vast transformation of the whole fabric of society. France was doing well. Germany was the wonder of the world. The Habsburg Monarchy, as we have seen, was in the process of transformation, and a new prince was waiting in the wings, strong and masterful, the reverse of decadent, determined at all costs to break the deadlock produced by Magyar reaction.

Why, in 1914, when the current of civilization was moving with such majesty and speed, did the whole process suddenly have to break down? And if the answer is the deterministic answer, that the masses had been held back too long, that the improvement of their condition, while swift, was not swift enough – what then did this cataclysm achieve for them? Are they more advanced now than they would have been had Europe worried on in 1914 and not gone to war? Certainly now, all over the world, they are on the march. But they had already begun their march. The 1914 war and its consequences interrupted that march catastrophically and brought them forty years of suffering and misery unparalleled. It was, by common consent, the 1914 war and the suffering produced by it which drove the Russian peasants to achieve their great revolution and so create the chaos which made it possible for Lenin to stage his *Putsch*. Was this cataclysm really necessary before Russia could produce a tractor, a mannequin parade, a sputnik? The 1914 war and its consequences broke up Europe and gave rise to Hitler. In what conceivable sense can that war and its consequences be said to have advanced the condition, material or spiritual, of the German workers? How did it benefit the workers and peasants of France? How, to come closer to our subject, did it benefit the workers, the peasants, the masses, the nationalities, even of the Habsburg Empire?

It is only if one holds with conviction the Leninist view, that one can regard the 1914 cataclysm as either desirable or, from the standpoint of developing European society, inevitable. It set in train a process which enabled the Russian Bolsheviks first to establish a dictatorship over the Russian lands, then to extend that dictatorship over other countries, including the greater part of, precisely, the Dual Monarchy – Bohemia, Moravia, Gelicia, Transylvania and Hungary proper. This can be regarded as a good thing only by those who believe that the Soviet system is the highest form of government yet achieved on earth and wish to see it triumph everywhere. Those who do not believe this must ask themselves whether the catastrophe which led directly to the Sovietization of a large part of Europe by way of Hitler's 'new order' was in fact inevitable. It was Austrian action that precipitated that catastrophe. Was this action inherent in the Austrian situation? Or could the Monarchy have continued indefinitely as a unit of the European complex? If it is concluded that it could so have continued, who was to blame for the smash? Indeed, was the smash itself irredeemable? There is a good deal to be said for the argument, most recently put forward by Professor Kennan, that had Lord Lansdowne's appeal for peace been listened to in November 1917 the final break-up of Europe might well have been arrested. The Tsar would have gone all the same, but there would have been no Leninist apotheosis.

The peasants of Moravia and Bohemia are worse off than they were under the Empire. The peasants of Croatia and Slovenia under Marshal Tito are about the same. The Slovenes in their smiling, hilly countryside, still gather their grapes, collect them in great mounds by the roadside, press them down with their bare feet. Their homesteads in Tito's Yugoslavia are the same whitewashed cottages and farmsteads lived in by their grandfathers. They still use immemorial carts of wickerwork to bring in the apples from their fertile orchards; soon they will have television (but it did not need two world wars to bring them television); they have in Ljubliana their own university for the cleverer of their sons and daughters – but Franz Ferdinand would have compelled Budapest to give them a university. All over the wide Croatian plain, where the black and white storks stand hunched above the irrigation ditches, little girls still watch over great flocks of geese, old women still gossip under the trees in the wayside meadows watching the cow, or the two or three cows, brought out from the steading for the evening bite. They have a university in Zagreb, but the Austrians built it for them. A great high road now links Zagreb with Belgrade; but it did not need two world wars and bitter, religious civil war with their fellow-Slavs, the Serbs, to bring them a motor-road. It would have come. The 1914 war, seen as an episode in the development of peoples, was not inevitable, it was a disaster, and it was due not to human progress but to human failure. The peoples of central and south-eastern Europe lived together under the Habsburgs more harmoniously than they were to live together without the Habsburgs. There was oppression and injustice, harshness and cruelty, bitterness and strife, chicanery and exploitation, jealousy and bullying. But as the Monarchy approached its term there was progressively more light and less iniquity, and, compared with what happened next, the age of Franz Josef was an age of enlightenment.

Earlier, mention was made of the forces of fission and disintegration; and these indeed existed. Disintegration, or dissociation, is not another term for decadence. Certainly there were many in Vienna at the turn of the century who found the mental climate of Vienna enervating and insufferable. This was entirely reasonable in anyone possessing an original brain. The young man up from the provinces found a great deal of emptiness behind the splendid façade. In the midst of splendour the ageing Emperor lived like an anchorite. The courtiers swarmed, but there was no Court. Up on the hill in the Belvedere Palace Franz Ferdinand waited for his uncle's death: never, with his overbearing nature, an ingratiating figure, he alienated popular sympathy by his intimacy with the High Command, winning for himself a reputation as a militarist, which he was not. The behaviour of the young archdukes reflected badly on the Crown, and the great nobles, spending much of their time on their vast country estates, appeared to have little or no connection with either culture or administration. The thin rigidities of the bureaucracy embraced the whole of life. Politics appeared to consist either of pressure groups doing deals with the administration or else of brawling demagogy. The cultural life of the city was dominated by Jews to an extent which was clearly unhealthy: pouring in from Bohemia, Moravia, Galicia and Bukovina, they quite failed to realize their own strength and, by pushing too hard, made it all too easy for crude and unscrupulous men to play on the latent spirit of anti-semitism. The nationalities quarrelled incessantly and, over all, there hung a heavy pall of bourgeois philistinism of the kind which blanketed England, and indeed all industrial Europe, during the last years of Victoria and the reign of Edward VII. The vulgarity of new wealth was an offence. In the dark and stinking slums which were the workers' quarters, the unemployed, tattered and half-starved, filled doss-houses and goulasch kitchens: one of these was the young Adolf Hitler, shabby-genteel and down on his luck, brooding over the intolerable situation in which he, a racial German, counted for less than Slavs and Jews.

The surface of life for the well-to-do and those patronized by them was, of course, of a surpassing elegance. Vienna was still the cultural capital not only of the German-speaking world, but also of all central and south-eastern Europe. Throughout the nobility and the higher bureaucracy, amusement, usually highly cultivated, came before work. The opera was splendid, so were many of the theatres and concert halls. But there was no creative drive, only splendid opportunities for the display of talent. For over a hundred years Vienna had been the musical centre of the Western world. During all that time there was no other city east or south of Paris to compare with it: the Court provided the centre, the great magnates from Galicia, from Bohemia, from Hungary provided the patronage; the mingling of cultural streams provided the stimulus. Gluck, Beethoven, Wagner, Brahms all came from outside the Empire to gild its capital, often enough for little reward. But Haydn, Mozart and Schubert were Austrian, and so were countless lesser figures. Then came Bruckner and Mahler, the first living wholly to himself, the second stamping his image on an epoch. Brahms died in 1897, but Bruckner and Mahler were both active at the turn of the century, and so was Hugo Wolf. These three, indeed, expressed two aspects of what was thought of as the decadence of a remarkable civilization centred on the rich administrative capital of a disintegrating Empire. But what, in fact, was decaying? Surely no more than a specialized culture deriving from a limited ruling caste who lived, directly or indirectly, on the labours of exploited millions. This caste was assuredly in decay. It had had its day. It had built up, almost without knowing it, and largely for no other motive than personal gain, an economic machine, partly capitalist, partly State run, which was already beginning to serve as a base upon which the millions could raise themselves up. This caste, less adulterated under the Habsburgs than anywhere else in the world, still lent tone and colour and manners to the life of every day as Vienna swung into the twentieth century. It was still very rich. Its obvious decline affected very closely the mood of the middle classes, who for so long had identified the Court and the great families with the Empire itself; this alone would have been enough to induce in the thoughtful a mood of uncertainty and self-questioning. Uncertainty all too easily turned into defeatism in face of the apparently insoluble problems posed by the nationalities in their drive for self-expression, by the presumption of the Magyars, and, as the century grew, by the entirely new problem presented by the resurgence of Serbia who, with Russia in the background, appeared to threaten not only to upset the uneasy balance in the Balkans but also to set fire to the whole of the Danubian basin. These local difficulties were exacerbated by the continuing rise of an immensely strong and prosperous Germany. Although it was far from the truth, all over the world and in Vienna too it was felt that the Monarchy was now wholly subservient to Berlin. With defeatism in politics went desperation in the arts – in Vienna, above all, in music and literature. The great composers of the day, Mahler and Hugo Wolf, still used the old forms, perfected in a more positive age: the one in his symphonies, the other in his songs found himself caught up in an agonizing exploration of the furthest reaches, sometimes backwaters, of individual sensibility. Both *The Song of the Earth* and the *Mörike Lieder* may be seen, looking back over more than half a century, to have been the final inarticulate cries of the individual now struggling against, now submitting to, a destiny the workings of which he did not comprehend. Forms developed to please the ear had proved well suited to carry the meditations, the simple statements and the doubts, acceptances, and rejections of the late-eighteenth-century composers. They had proved strong enough to carry the asseverations and profound heart-searchings of Beethoven; they could contain with distortions the self-exploration of the

Weltschmerz and the later romantics. Brahms, dominated by nostalgia, Bruckner, sustained by religious faith, turned back to them with perfect naturalness. But, long before, in France, that extraordinary genius, Hector Berlioz, the first truly modern composer, with his passionate rejection of too easy synthesis – too easy, because too excluding – had discovered their limitations. Now Wolf transformed the *Lied* by pouring into it the discoveries of the new self-consciousness, and Mahler tried to make a new synthesis of good and evil, using a form which was well enough for conveying the consciousness of good and evil, seen in simple antithesis, but totally inadequate to convey the sense, scarcely apprehended, of good and evil inextricably intertwined in disturbing symbiosis.

This was the new sense: it disturbed writers as various as von Hoffmanstal and Kajka, both sustained by the scaffolding of the old society. It disturbed Rilke, supported in material ease by one of the princesses of the old Empire, Marie Thurn and Taxis, in Duino Castle looking across the Adriatic bay to Miramar from whence Maximilian had set off to conquer Mexico. It drove Mahler to a frenzy. And then it caused the young men struggling in Vienna to keep body and soul together, Arnold Schönberg and von Webern, to break the mould and, by taking apart the physical body of music, to fashion out of its bare and meaningless component tones a new vessel. All their energies were bent on this craft, which seemed to be an end in itself; but what in fact they were doing was extending the vocabulary of music to contain new thoughts. A corner of the new thought had already been seized by Freud. In despair at the magnitude of the task they, too, mistook their blindfold strivings for decadence. It was the very reverse of decadence. It was new life. Unless we are to regard the lusty, brute peasant as the summit of human achievement (in which case all else is decay), we must recognize that the highest intellectual life of the Habsburg Empire on the eve of the catastrophe marked one of those immense leaps forward: man was on the verge of understanding his own condition and being articulate about it, no longer relying on images and parables for his highest flights into the unknown. Exhausted by this effort, he fell back. But ground had been won, soon to be submerged, which, once seen, could never be forgotten: we know it is there. And not all the barbarities of Hitler (which, indeed, confirmed the validity of the new discoveries), nor all the inanities which the Russian communists have sought to impose on their own society to keep it in step with the medieval crudities of their own political ideas, can destroy the fertilizing memory of that vision. This was the crowning achievement, unrealized at the time, of a complex and difficult society held together by a monarch who knew next to nothing about culture and only one thing about civilization – that, to achieve it and sustain it, large societies had somehow to be held together. Franz Josef, seventy years old at the turn of the century, had long been Atlas. After he died he was made the scapegoat for all the ills of central and south-eastern Europe. Even today, few recognize across half a century that the social, political, scientific and aesthetic processes commonly regarded now as good were developing at speed in the Europe of 1914, unobstructed, and not least in the Hapsburg realm.

4

The hub of the great complex was Vienna, the *Kaiserstadt*. There were other fine cities in the Habsburg hereditary lands, provincial capitals enjoying a great deal of local autonomy, governed by men of the calibre of Taaffe, and enjoying strong and ancient cultures of their own: Innsbruck in Tirol, the Emperor Maximilian's medieval seat; Graz in Styria, which for long rivalled Vienna, the birthplace of many Habsburgs, including Franz Ferdinand of Este. There were national capitals: Zagreb (Agram) for the Croats; Ljubliana (Laibach) for the Slovenes; Bratislava (Pressburg) for the Slovaks; Brno (Brünn) for Moravia; Lvov (Lemberg) for Galicia. Cracow with its ancient university stood alone: then, as still today in Communist Poland, a proud enclave of independent tradition. Budapest, adding to its ancient foundation the nineteenth-century splendours which turned it into one of the most beautiful cities of Europe, was at last beginning to produce a strong cultural life of its own, a sudden flowering of poets, dramatists and musicians to take up the banner of Petöfi, the revolutionary poet. Above all there was Prague, which outshone them all, and, on the wings of the new national culture born in the music of Smetana and Dvořák, swept into the twentieth century, there to deposit two strange and remarkable offerings: the writer Kafka and the musician Janaček.

But Vienna was the centre. Every city in the Monarchy, even those whose histories went back far beyond the Habsburgs, even Cracow and Prague, owed much of their appearance and their culture (some owed almost all) to Habsburg rule. Vienna was Habsburg and nothing but Habsburg, as it had discovered painfully in 1848, when, with the Court removed, first to Innsbruck, then to Olmütz, it found that the very reason for its existence had vanished into thin air. It had been called into being, over the ages, as the administrative centre of an Empire, and its people were either the servants of the Monarchy or they were nothing.

On the surface this beautiful city had never seemed more vital than when it was dying. It drew vitality from its past, which lived in the streets, and also from its incomparable setting between tall hills, with beeches, vines and gemlike meadows, and the great arterial river curving out across the plain to Hungary and the far-off delta on the coast of the Black Sea. From the heart of the city those hills are in sight; and it is never possible, as it is all too easily possible in London, Paris, or Berlin, to lose touch with the movements of the earth and the sky and to fall into the delusion that what is going on from day to day, from minute to minute, in palaces, government buildings and newspaper offices, is the only important interest in the world. It may be the consciousness of life going on beyond the immediate horizon which gave the Viennese their markedly provincial quality, a quality which was never absent even in those moments when the Court and the Ballhausplatz were virtually the pivot of Europe, a quality which went with a strong and sometimes tiresome local patriotism. To this, no doubt, was added an instinctive effort on the part of the native Viennese to preserve their sense of identity in a city which for so long was the magnet attracting a constant stream of the most gifted men from all over Europe. There is also a relaxing wind called the *Föhn*, which is commonly said to be the enemy of resolution, of concentrated purpose: it might better be known as the inhibitor of blinkered absorption in self-glorifying business. Sometimes at night, even now, in spite of petrol fumes, the faint odour of pinewoods in the mountains beyond the hills of the Wienerwald may be caught inside the inner city.

Nineteenth-century Vienna suffered, like every other city, from the galloping blight of tenement housing, as the fields were put down to slums. But the compact centre of the city remained intact; and, at the height of the industrial expansion, this living heart, with its steep-roofed Gothic cathedral reared high above the Baroque palaces and churches of Fischer von Erlach and Hildebrandt, was encircled by the finest street in Europe. The Ringstrasse was built on the old open glacis left by the Emperor Josef when he pulled down the city walls late in the eighteenth century. Planted with multiple rows of limes and plane trees, it took in the palace of the Habsburgs and raised a new skyline composed of massive buildings which might have been put up to celebrate the founding of an empire rather than its end: the Opera, which had first call on the finest native singers from a dozen lands; the Burg Theatre, the shrine of a great tradition expressed in the brilliances of Sonnenthal and Kainz; the Parliament building, to replace Schmerling's wooden 'circus'; the monumental twin museums of art and science; the great new university; the City Hall; the Palace of Justice; the Ministry of War – all splendid among gardens, parks and trees. This feverish institutional building in the grandest manner must have filled the city with a sense of power and purpose, although it did not get into its stride until after the loss of Italy. It was designed as the crown of Empire; but it turned out to be a tomb.

It would be pleasant to dwell on the life of this great capital as it was at the turn of the century. But although in one way it was a microcosm of the polyglot Empire, in another way so rich in life and so vast was that Empire, it was no more than one city among others, all of which would call for individual chapters. Vienna was indeed the cross-roads. Hungarians, Bohemians, Italians, Poles, Croats, Slovenes, Serbs, Rumanians, Germans of all kinds – all who wanted to shine in the world came to Vienna: politicians, diplomats, lawyers, doctors, journalists, priests, painters, musicians, writers, artists of all kinds, to say nothing of men of business, came there not only from the great cities, but also from the smaller towns and the hamlets of the central European complex of mountains, plains and river valleys, to found their careers, and often to continue them. They came, even though many of them had been brought up to hate the name of Habsburg, to regard 'Austria' as the enemy – some to be absorbed into the governing machine, others to fight in workers' movements, others for the education they needed for the business of destroying their educators, others to enrich with their native talents the cultural life of the city, many more simply to earn a living and to live to themselves in an environment of unique quality – and to intermarry to the point at which the Viennese became almost a separate race.

The comic-opera legend of Imperial Vienna was far from being a reflection of reality; but it was no farther from the truth than the counter-legend of a city empty and heartless beneath a surface charm. Bureaucracies do not have hearts, and in so far as Vienna was the headquarters of the most extensive bureaucracy in the world, outside Russia, regulating the lives of tens of millions and trying to hold the balance between a dozen races, obviously it was heartless. But the bureaucracy was not all, and the surface charm was the reflection of a deeper spontaneity and warmth. This charm, deliberately cultivated, came in some degree to permeate the whole of life, changing it a little. It was something more than whistling in the dark: it was a refusal to recognize the night, a half-conscious agreement to pretend that artificial light was daylight. When all is said, this was no more than a local manifestation of the spirit which has sustained Western man throughout his history, through his fleeting triumphs and his long calamities. Perhaps by excluding too much it did not demand enough. But it gave warmth and some contentment, as well as cheerfulness, to untold millions on their sparrow-flights from darkness into darkness. Can more be asked? Can more be given? The Habsburgs never pretended that they were gods who could order the life of this planet on lines of universal equity and justice to make a paradise on earth.

More particularly, the usual criticism of the Viennese is that they were not what they pretended to be. They boasted of their culture; but most of them preferred Lanner and Strauss to Beethoven. They boasted of their good living; but there were slums and goulash kitchens as well as *Heurigen* and cafés. They danced and were gay; but their gaiety masked a lack of purpose. All these criticisms may be levelled against other cities. The simple fact remains that the Viennese on the whole took pleasure and found stimulus and relaxation in music of one kind or another, always a decent kind; they enjoyed their food in the open air and in entrancing surroundings, and worked to get it; they preferred young wine to gin; they danced and were gay – and as for purpose. . . . All these aspects existed and helped to make life tolerable and on the whole cheerful for millions who had no more, and no less, sense of purpose than the millions of brothers elsewhere who did not dance or drink in garden restaurants and were rarely gay.

We have been told often enough that the image symbolized by the Vienna opera was a consciously deceptive image to conceal a cynical, aggressive and militarist society. In that case the deception went very deep: in what other city in the world has a part of the auditorium been especially designed to accommodate army officers in uniform – and standing-room only at that? In what other army in the world have officers, in or out of uniform, been prepared to stand to listen to an opera? And those who now, in this day and age, are pleased with themselves because they can now understand the music of Webern may reflect that what they now hear with a sense of delighted discovery was composed half a century ago in a city ruled over by Franz Josef. It could be done. Very few Viennese paid any attention at the time. But they were not alone in this.

The 1914 war shattered a civilization which by no stretch of the imagination can be said to have reached a dead end. It is not enough to regard either the increasing self-consciousness of the nationalities, or the gathering strength of the masses, or the smashing of old moulds by new thinkers and artists as the signals for the inevitable collapse in flame and thunder of a political and social system. Vienna was not sutured off from the main stream of development. Schönberg, Webern, Wellesz, Berg, the Hungarian Bartok, the Czech Janaček, were matched in other Empires, if not by musicians (apart from the Russian, Stravinsky) then by painters and writers: Picasso and Braque, Ernst, Modigliani (Austria, not a painting country, had Kokoschka). Robert Musil might delicately analyse the universe in a mirror of Viennese society. But France had Proust, and the English-speaking world James Joyce. Tsarist Russian business men bought the works of Picasso and Matisse. Kafka's sleep-walking reflected a universal nightmare. The 1914 war and the disintegration of Europe did nothing to dispel this nightmare. The workers' movements were in full swing, with nothing to stop their development: no catastrophe was needed to assist the triumph all over Europe of organized labour – which was indeed most grievously checked by later catastrophes in the shape of Lenin and Hitler and their admirers. Most remarkable of all, now, fifty years later, as we laboriously try to patch together a new civilization which shall atone for the disgrace of the years between the wars, we turn for nourishment increasingly to the sustenance offered and ignored by the creative spirits of a society once considered moribund and useless.

PART FIVE

AUSTRIA MUST STILL BE GREAT

CHAPTER SIXTEEN

RUSSIA PRESENTS THE HEMLOCK

The remarkable quietism of the Ballhausplatz between the Russian crisis of 1887 and the annexation of Bosnia-Herzegovina in 1908 has often been attributed to the preoccupation of Franz Josef and the Vienna administration with domestic conflicts. Up to a point this was true, but the striving for peace and tranquillity also had deeper causes.

The European Powers during that epoch were largely occupied with extra-European affairs, above all with the partition of Africa, but also with the Middle East and with China. Austria sent a token force to help suppress the Boxer rising in 1900, but although there were voices demanding that she too should become a colonial Power these were not listened to. She even sent an expedition to the Antarctic. There was no money to build a large fleet, and the Hungarians, who did not have to look outside Europe for their markets, were flatly opposed to any sort of expansion. Italy's African adventure and Russia's preoccupation with the Far East, which in 1905 ended in war and revolution, suited Austria to perfection. Franz Josef was determined to keep the peace, and he clung to the German alliance as to a rock of ages, in spite of a growing feeling against Berlin in many parts of the Empire, and in spite of the fact that Wilhelm II, without Bismarck, had succeeded in achieving a position of quite unsplendid isolation.

The two main external worries were Italy and the new kingdom of Serbia. The fact that Italy was technically an ally (the Triple Alliance of 1882 was renewed, with modifications, several times before 1914) did not prevent either the development of an active and bitter irredentist movement seeking possession of the Trentino, and Istria (with Trieste), or the formulation of an official policy, involving the extension of Italian influence in Albania, designed to gain for Italy control of the Adriatic. No alliance was ever more uneasy or more flimsily based: long before the showdown came in 1914 and Italy declared herself neutral, her hostile attitudes had driven Conrad von Hötzendorf, the Austrian Chief-of-Staff, to preach a preventive war against her. By that time von Hötzendorf was also calling for a preventive war against Serbia, which he finally and with great difficulty (and much too late) achieved. It was the activities of this remarkable and immensely attractive man, a brilliant soldier who also thought he was a politician with a mission, which contrived to attach the label of militarism to the most unmilitaristic of all the continental Powers.

The existence of Serbia as a sovereign Power was in itself a complication and a nuisance. The new kingdom, however, was in no way a serious threat until she had Russia behind her. This did not happen until Russia turned away from the Far East and back to the Balkans after her catastrophic defeat by the Japanese in 1905.

The Serbs, like the Croats, their fellow Slavs, had a very ancient history. Unlike the Croats, they received Christianity not from Rome but from Constantinople, which meant that the two peoples grew apart. It also meant that, sooner or later, Russia, the great schismatic Power, was bound to take a special interest in her. The summit of Serbian glory was achieved under Stepan Dushan in the middle of the fourteenth century. Dushan was one of the greatest warrior-kings. He shattered the Bulgars and made the original Serb territories, the mountain areas of Novibazar and Montenegro, the nucleus of an imposing Empire. He took all Macedonia up to Salonika, all Albania, and a great part of Greece. By the time of his death in 1355 he had made Serbia the lord of the Balkans, and had he lived he might well have taken Constantinople, for which consummation he was actively preparing.

Instead, the Empire collapsed. The Turks had been making themselves felt in Europe even during his lifetime. In 1371 they had defeated the Serbs at Maritza, and in 1389 came the Battle of Kossovo, the Field of Blackbirds, where the Serbs were finally routed and their king, Lazar, killed. For five hundred years the memory of Kossovo, and nothing else, was what held the Serbs together as a people. Great national legends are usually based on a victory; the Serbs based theirs on a defeat. To complicate the mood still further, the great national hero of the Serbs, whose deeds have been told and retold through the centuries at every Serbian hearth, was not Stepan Dushan himself, but Marko Kralyevich, a vassal prince of the Turks, who had to fight against his countrymen in the Turkish army, but prayed that the Serbs might win, even if it meant his death. He died.

Turkish rule was not immediately oppressive. Many Serbs fled to Hungary (their descendants forming the population of the Voivodina), but there was no real rebellion for two hundred years. After the Austrians had occupied Serbia in 1690 many Serbs retreated with them when the Turks drove them out. But still there was no organized resistance: only the Serbs in the heights of Montenegro, the Black Mountain, managed to defend their independence intact. Their brothers in Serbia proper and in parts of Bosnia managed to accommodate themselves, and many became Moslems for the advantages offered by this expedient: the heavily carpeted mosques of Sarajevo and Mostar which lend their peculiar colour to Marshal Tito's Yugoslavia owe their existence to this development. The real trouble did not begin until towards the end of the eighteenth century with the misrule of the Janissaries, given to murder, robbery and rapine. After some decades of violent unrest, with the Serbs themselves sometimes encouraged by the Sultan to resist the Janissaries, a full-scale rebellion broke out under Kara George in 1804. Kara George, Czerny Dyorde (in English, Black George), was a peasant of gloomy but heroic nature whose real name was George Petrovich. He succeeded in rallying his people behind him to such effect that they beat back the Turks and, in 1808, elected him hereditary chieftain and lord, or Hospadar, the first native ruler since the death of King Lazar over four centuries before. For five more years he managed to keep his government going. Convinced that the very existence of an independent Serbia depended on Russian support, yet profoundly suspicious of Russian intentions, during these five years he was used now as a convenient instrument, now as a scapegoat, by the Russians in their manoeuvres *vis-à-vis* the Turks. In 1812 he received his reward: during the second part of the Seventh Russo-Turkish War of 1809–12 he threw his weight behind the Russians, although the Turks tried to bribe him with the promise of turning Serbia into a new Principality, on the lines of Moldavia and Wallachia: by the terms of the Treaty of Bucharest the Russians deserted him and left him to the mercy of the Sultan, having secured for themselves parts of Moldavia and Bessarabia in exchange for their recognition of Turkish sovereignty over Serbia. This betrayal of Kara George by the Russians on 28 May 1812 was the first of a series of actions which were to determine the ambivalence of Serbia's attitude towards their fellow-Slavs of Muscovy which has persisted to this day. It was apparent even in the behaviour of Kara George himself, who, when

Turkey pulled herself together and in 1813 utterly crushed the Serbs, fled to Russia by way of Austria. Two years later, in 1815, there was a fresh revolt, led this time by Milan Obrenović, Kara George's bitter rival, who defeated the Turks and, in 1829, managed to get himself declared as a virtually independent prince (Kara George, meanwhile, had made his own second bid, reappearing in Serbia in July 1817, only to be assassinated in his sleep, his head sent as a trophy to Constantinople, a month later).

For nearly forty years the Obrenović's ruled with Turkish consent. It was not until 1867 that the last Turkish garrisons were got rid of, and not until 1878, with the ill-fated Treaty of San Stefano, that Turkey formally recognized Serbia's independence – which she thus owed to a Russian victory. Independent Serbia, nevertheless, under Milan Obrenović, turned to Austria rather than to Russia for support, and for the first twenty-five years of her existence followed the Habsburg line. There was a reason for this. Taking their cue from memories of the greatness of Stepan Dushan, the Serbs were at first less interested in achieving union with, or domination over, their fellow-Slavs of the Habsburg Monarchy than in recovering Macedonia and Albania. Their most immediate enemy, furthermore, was the newly independent Bulgaria; it was impossible even for the most labyrinthine Muscovite to encourage the expansionist ambitions of the Bulgarians, whom they dominated, and at the same time win the confidence of the Serbs.

Serbia, moreover, was riven by the rivalry of the Obrenović and Karageorgević factions, which expressed itself in frequent assassinations. On top of all this, the Austro-Russian agreement of 1897 to preserve the *status quo* in the Balkans, to consult harmoniously together, not to take Balkan territory themselves (though Austria reserved the right to annex Bosnia-Herzegovina and the Sanjak of Novibazar in case of need), to prevent others doing so, and to combine in opposition to domination of the Balkan peninsula by any single Balkan nation, helped to stabilize the situation for another decade. This Austro-Russian rapprochement was highly popular throughout the Empire. There were dreams of a grand continental league, which, however, ignored a number of points. France, allied with Russia, could hardly be expected to join in an alliance which would embrace the Germany on which she sought revenge. Russia, though for the moment otherwise engaged, was bound to return to her old, old aim of achieving Constantinople. England would sooner or later realize that she could not exist for ever in her splendid isolation and would herself begin to seek for friends on the mainland, a consummation that was to be accelerated by the growing challenge of Germany, to whom Austria was bound.

2

The general European situation in the first decade of the twentieth century remained, nevertheless, remarkably fluid – to a degree, indeed, almost incredible when contemplated in retrospect over the gulf of fifty years. The Austro-Russian understanding survived the fearful troubles in Macedonia in 1903; the two countries refrained from taking sides when Serbs, Bulgarians and Greeks were all fighting for advantage in that barbarous ethnical no-man's-land. It survived the bloody and treacherous murder in his palace at Belgrade of King Alexander Obrenović and his wife Draga and the succession of Peter Karageorgević, the grandson of Kara George, with his Russophile, pan-Serb feelings. It was an understanding, however, which rested on no sure foundations and might be broken overnight. The Triple Alliance, which looked so fine on paper, was very much a mockery: feeling sure for the time being about Russia, Austria felt that she need not bother too much about Italy, and Italy, in any case, was actively plotting against her ally and allowing popular irredentist feeling full expression. Already in 1896 with the final fall of Crispi, the Italian architect of the alliance, after Italy's Abyssinian failure, the Italians had recovered from the Francophobia produced by the French occupation of Tunis. Their rapprochement with France made them bolder in their conduct towards Austria in the Balkans and elsewhere. By the time of the Moroccan crisis in 1905–6 the very existence of the Triple Alliance seemed threatened. At the Algeciras Conference Italy lined up unequivocally on the side of the French and the British, against her other ally, Germany, and, with Britain's belated but fateful move to put an end to her isolation with the Anglo-French Entente, found herself increasingly being pulled along in the slip-stream of Anglo-French and, indirectly, Franco-Russian policy. At Algeciras, indeed, even Austro-German solidarity was seriously impaired. Austria gave her ally only lukewarm support and the subsequent friction was serious. The whole pattern of twentieth-century Europe was in flux. Germany, under Bismarck the centre of the most elegant system of alliances and reinsurance policies, found herself virtually isolated. She was already deeply committed to von Tirpitz's naval building programme, which filled England with dismay and indignation; she had achieved her fatal breach with Russia by Caprivi's repudiation of Bismarck's Reinsurance Treaty, and Russia was now allied with France. Austria, treated in the past with considerable high-handedness, was now her only friend, and a friend whom von Bülow and Wilhelm II (as far as his tactlessness would allow) set out to cultivate with the utmost sedulousness. The outer world, looking not only at the facts of power, of military might and internal cohesion, but also at the mood displayed by Berlin and Vienna, the one sabre-rattling and overweening, the other mild and self-effacing, not unnaturally drew the conclusion that Germany could order Austria about as she chose. This was a persistent and a fateful miscalculation: in fact, as Wilhelm and von Bülow saw it, Germany, if she was to make an appropriate noise in the world, was very much dependent on Austrian support, and they set out to prove their loyalty by demonstrating their sympathy on numerous occasions. Austria, for her part, while building on the German alliance, was determined to assert her own interests and not to play second fiddle. This revived spirit of assertion was embodied, above all, in the person of Count Aehrenthal, appointed Foreign Minister in 1906. Forty years earlier, before Königgrätz, Bismarck had rather insolently informed Count Esterhazy that Austria's destiny lay in south-east Europe. Aehrenthal was sure of this. A major element in the tragedy which now began to unfold was the almost simultaneous appointment to the Foreign Ministry in St Petersburg of Alexander Izvolsky, who had similar plans for Russia.

3

No twentieth-century statesman has been more persistently underrated and treated with more unmerited contempt than Aehrenthal. He failed because he thought too much about Austria and not enough about Europe. If he cannot be designated a tragic figure in the classical sense it is only because he was too easily at home in a vulgar age: like almost all his contemporaries in the chancelleries of Europe he served the goddess of prestige.

He was a career diplomat. When he took over the Ballhausplatz he came direct from the Petersburg Embassy, where he had been a brilliant success. He was devoted to the idea of bringing about a lasting understanding with Russia and thought in terms of a revival of the Three Emperors' League. He was desperately afraid of pan-Slavism and of the disruptive effect an antagonistic Serbia might have on the Slavs of the Empire. He set out from the beginning to conciliate the Serbs. He was resolute and stubborn in his determination to resist war, any war, when war was being called for by the Chief-of-Staff. He was vividly aware of the damage the Magyars were doing to the Empire, but he advocated handling them patiently and gently at a time when all parties in Austria were calling on the Emperor, in the words of the Social Democrat, Renner, to 'mount his horse' and break them if necessary by force. And yet, by the time of his death at the end of 1911, he was to leave a situation, to be inherited by his much weaker successor, Count Berchtold, of precisely the kind he had most feared and striven to avoid.

A member of an old aristocratic family, crossed with Jewish blood, he was certainly a most gifted diplomat. But it is questionable whether he had the first elements of a statesman. It is the hardest thing in the world to get a clear picture of him. Sir Harold Nicolson, who knew him, saw him as 'an unwieldy man, with heavy, hapless jaws, a stubble head of hair, and sad turbot eyes'.[1] But to Mr A. J. P. Taylor (who never knew him but whose picture has stuck) he was 'self-confident and arrogant, with the cocky yapping of a terrier'.[2] Somebody is wrong. Mr Asquith, when Prime Minister, regarded him as the cleverest and perhaps the least scrupulous of Austrian statesmen.[3] Sir Arthur Nicolson, later Lord Carnock, recorded in his diary after their first meeting in Petersburg: 'An amiable and chatty man, but not brilliant.'[4] It would be possible to go on like this for page after page; but the more sympathetically this unfortunate man is studied the more it seems that the Nicolsons, father and son, came nearest to the truth. His cleverness was extreme, but not under control: it was likely to degenerate into being too clever by half; he had deep and far-ranging perceptions, but these were disconnected and fragmented, never adding up to a coherent view of Europe as a whole. He was vain, and a show-off. His arrogance, of which much has been made, was not natural but willed: he was always having to prove, to himself as well as to others, that he was a man of the world, and a ruthless one at that; but he was neither. He was a romantic at heart. He dreamed dreams and saw visions: his dreams and visions were of grandeur and prosperity for the peoples under his charge, but, in practice, because of the spirit of the age, he confused prestige with grandeur and brilliance with prosperity. His dream of a resurrected Three Emperors' League, which would attract France into its orbit and put England and Italy in their places, was a romantic dream: it had nothing to do with statesmanship; since a statesman would have recognized that England would rise against such a conception in fury – as indeed she did when the Russian envoy to Vienna helpfully leaked the whole affair to London. His one great *coup*, the annexation of Bosnia-Herzegovina (which, because of the way it was done, was wholly disastrous) was not a deeply considered act. It was not pondered and thought through. It was partly an instant response to a very real threat – that the Young Turks after their successful revolution against the Sultan would revoke the occupation agreement; it was partly a gesture to put Austria on the map and escape the charge of subservience to Berlin; it was partly a display of vanity, compulsive vanity, which made it seem the most desirable thing in the world to outsmart his Russian counterpart, Izvolsky. Time and time again he expected to be admired for his brilliance and diplomatic finesse; time and time again he woke up to find himself execrated for his trickery. This was romantic too: he thought he had to be like Metternich. While alertly and, indeed, creatively aware of half a dozen perils, he could be totally blind to the one that really mattered. Thus in 1908 he went to Bad Ischl with Franz Josef to meet Edward VII of England and Sir Charles Hardinge (later Lord Hardinge of Penshurst), then head of the Foreign Office. He took with him five sheets of foolscap, handwritten, headed: 'Briefing for the conversations with Sir Charles Hardinge.' Most of the points had to do with the state of Turkey and the Balkans. But the last paragraph dealt with the German alliance:

> To the German alliance we are indestructibly bound, because it serves our interests and the peace of Europe. The rivalries between Germany and England have nothing to do with us, particularly the competition in naval armaments, which we regard as not without danger. We are justified in expecting that these frictions between Berlin and London will not be allowed to affect the relations between Austria-Hungary and England.[5]

That was in August 1908. The conversations took place when England's suspicion and alarm at German maritime intentions were at their peak. For what conceivable reason could a great continental Power want a High Seas Fleet to match that of a great maritime Power if not to challenge her? Only two days before, at Kronberg, Sir Charles Hardinge (Edward VII holding tactfully aloof, puffing away at his post-luncheon cigar in a summerhouse) had boldly tackled Wilhelm II on this subject and got nowhere – afterwards telling Herr von Jenisch, acting German Minister of Foreign Affairs, that if Germany went on with this competition, forcing England to spend vast sums in keeping ahead of her, next year's proposed State visit of Edward VII and Queen Alexandra to Berlin might have to be cancelled in view of popular indignation.[6] And yet Aehrenthal, bound absolutely to the German alliance, aware of the bitterness of the quarrel, could calmly state to Sir Charles Hardinge that it had nothing to do with Vienna and ought in no way to affect relations between Vienna and London. This was not statesmanship; it was not even cleverness.

Three years later, when he was already a dying man, he showed a clearer awareness of the true state of affairs. At the close of a long memorandum to the Emperor, dated 12 December 1911, the initiation of which was one of his last acts, he concluded on a note of utter defeatism, transferring his own death-wish to the Monarchy itself:

> As has already been indicated in the course of this survey, it is the tension between England and Germany which gives the political situation its world-historic complexion. This tense relationship, which has its repercussions on all sides, compels us to adopt a sharply defensive but, at the same time, cautious and groping policy. Even if the Imperial and Royal Cabinet desired to find a solution to the most immediately pressing problems through action in Italy or the Balkans, it would not succeed in finally disposing of them, *for the great decision which will determine the future of Europe will be taken in the Vosges and on the oceans which wash the coasts of Germany and England.*[7]

Aehrenthal was a desperately sick man when he put his signature to those words, which expressed the effective abdication of Habsburg power, only three years after the great annexation. But the words of a man preparing to die may be taken as the reflection of an element in his character which may have been concealed or even inhibited in his days of vitality and health, but which nevertheless helped to determine his activity. And that astonishing paragraph, apparently accepted not only by Franz Josef, but also by Franz Ferdinand, to whom it was sent by Aehrenthal himself for information ten days later, throws a new light on a man whose diplomacy was commonly seen (in the words of one of his biographers) as being 'composed more of hard arrogance and dissolvent intrigue than of prudent reserve and ingratiating *souplesse* . . . a mixture of pretension and subtlety, of force and ruse, of realism and cynicism; his readiness to cheat, to circumvent, to outwit, hid a harsh and ruthless will'.[8]

There was no ruthless will. There was vanity, energy, and a desire to shine, competing with a profound pessimism which could be obscured by sudden action, by bursts of arrogance, a sort of auto-intoxication, by a disconcerting refusal to connect facts – and also by a queer trick of rationalization which enabled him to fortify himself with elaborate reasons for pursuing, between bursts, a policy of wait and see. The memorandum just cited contains an excellent example of this. Most of it is concerned with Aehrenthal's Russian policy, or what he thought was his Russian policy. After a swift recension of the history of Austro-Russian relations since the Congress of Berlin, he goes further back still, to prove that, ever since the days of Kaunitz, Maria Theresa's great man of State, Russia had always in times of serious trouble come closer to Austria. This, he says (and he was writing when England had lately come very close to Russia through the Triple Entente, when France was formally allied to Russia, when he himself was hated above all men by the Russian Foreign Minister, Izvolsky), will happen again: 'The Monarchy is Russia's reserve – and it waits for a favourable moment when Russia will once more approach her. This tactic, to allow Russia to make her own advances to us, was employed by Prince Kaunitz nearly a century and a half ago, and it has been used since then, always with success.' The moral is that although Russia is in a strong diplomatic position now, 'thanks to Anglo-German contradictions', the time will come when England and Russia will get at cross-purposes, and England will fall away. Then Germany herself can afford to cease paying court to Petersburg. Then Russia will turn to Vienna. . . .[9]

The supreme moment of this queer, mixed-up man, whose friends loved him very dearly, was the Bosnian crisis of 1908.

In October 1907, just a year after his accession to the Ballhausplatz in the footsteps of the prudent, cautious Pole, Goluchowski, he was still doing splendidly and had excellent ideas: the main idea was to treat Serbia in a conciliatory way in order not to drive her into the arms of Russia, and to maintain the spirit of the 1897 under-standing with Russia by refraining from unilateral action in the Balkans generally. Relations with Serbia in 1906 were poisonous to a degree. There was another 'pig war'* in being, this time caused by the demands of the Magyar farmers, who wanted protection against Serbian pigs, maize and plums (the little kingdom's only exports), and by the determination of Vienna to force Belgrade by economic sanctions to go back to buying their arms from Skoda instead of France, and, generally, to make the Serbs realize their economic dependence on the Monarchy and translate this into terms of politics. The Serbs fought back hard, found other markets for their agricultural products, installed their own meat-packing plants, and agitated more and more sharply for the railway to the Adriatic which would have made nonsense of Austria's position in Bosnia-Herze-govina. In Austria it was an unpopular war of nerves, because the cutting off of Serbian exports, and consequent reliance on substitutes from Hungary, so accomplished in blackmail, sent the price of meat in Vienna sky-high. Aehrenthal took immediate action to put an end to it. At the close of his first year he could say at a Cabinet meeting in Vienna:

> Our policy of making Serbia economically and politically dependent and treating her as a negligible quantity has foundered. Only a third party would profit by a conflict between Serbia and the Monarchy. Politically we must urgently beg for such a conduct of Croatian, Dalmatian and Bosnian affairs as would place the centre of gravity for the Serbo-Croat peoples within the Monarchy.[10]

This was a perfect echo of the line being taken by one of the most dis-tinguished, thoughtful and far-seeing Austrian politicians, J. Baern-reither, a man close to Franz Josef, and in direct opposition to the preventive-war policies of the Chief-of-Staff, Conrad von Hötzendorf. It said almost all that needed saying. But within a few months the mood had suddenly changed. Aehrenthal was not only the most hated man in Serbia, but had made himself a suspect figure who was feared (if only because unpredictable) by the Powers. He had also turned the new Foreign Minister of the Russia he was so intent on conciliating into an enemy whose fanaticism bordered on hysteria – the hysteria of the trickster who finds himself tricked.

* The name given to periodic attempts by the Monarchy to coerce the Serbs by refusing to accept their exports, chiefly pigs.

4

Aehrenthal's first essay in the higher diplomacy, or the statesmanship of the *fait accompli*, was his announcement in January 1908 that he had done a deal with Turkey about a projected railway-line across the Sanjak of Novibazar. The Ottoman Empire was divided into provinces called *vilayets*, and the *vilayets* were broken down into administrative divisions called *sanjaks*. The Sanjak of Novibazar was part of the Vilayet of Kossovo and thus stood at the heart of medieval Serbia. Lying between the modern kingdom of Serbia and Montenegro, it cut Serbia off from Dalmatia and the sea. Under the Treaty of Berlin of 1878 it, like Bosnia, was occupied by Austria, while still under nominal Turkish sovereignty. Before starting negotiations with the Turks, Aehrenthal had informed the other European Powers of his intentions, as he was required to do under the provisions of the Berlin Treaty. It was a project that had been discussed off and on for many years, designed to link the railway system of the Monarchy and the rest of Europe with Salonika. It had obvious strategic advantages for Austria, but it had strong economic advantages too. In 1908 nobody was thinking of Austria in terms of aggressive expansionism, and nobody objected to the idea of the railway. It was the manner of Aehrenthal's announcement of the concluded deal (which never came to anything in the end) which startled Europe. His speech was flamboyant to say the least, and although the governments of the Powers took it quietly at first, there was an immediate uproar in the Press, above all the Russian Press, part of which was controlled by pan-Slav enthusiasts: here was Austria again pushing forward into the Balkans and threatening the Slav idea. But this time there was a general conviction, perfectly unfounded, that Berlin was behind it: nobody believed that Austria would start a thing like this on her own initiative. Yet that was just what Aehrenthal had done, and he had done it, very largely, as part of a gesture to prove that Vienna was not dependent on Berlin. It was a situation which was to be repeated in a different part of the world on a larger scale nearly fifty years later with the Suez operation: no Russian would then believe that France and Britain could conceivably be acting without American support and consent, if not under direct instructions from Washington.

Izvolsky, in Petersburg, had, like the other Foreign Ministers, casually agreed to the Sanjak project. He was not in the least interested

334

in pan-Slavism as such, and did not believe that anybody else was: he reckoned without the Press, the voice of the people. A number of statesmen and kings were to make mistakes in these years because they forgot the voice of the people, which, interestingly, was almost invariably angry and belligerent. In fact, Izvolsky knew better than to believe that Germany was behind the affair. But he had his own position to think of and he bowed before the storm. He managed to quieten public opinion – which, had the Russian army been better equipped, might have forced drastic action – and sought to capitalize on Serbian fury by supporting the much-desired line from Belgrade to the Adriatic. But the damage had been done. Austria had put herself back on the map with a vengeance – though not quite as Aehrenthal wished: pretty well everybody outside the governments of Germany and Russia believed that this new show of energy had been made in Germany.

It is time to consider Izvolsky himself, the Russian member of that dire partnership in woe, which, seeking peace and harmony, produced disaster, arising directly from character defects in two men very different in many ways but like enough in others to appear at times unheavenly twins. Izvolsky was a far more integrated character than Aehrenthal. The Austrian could on occasion give the impression of a German university professor who had strayed into high politics:[11] his rash acts accorded ill with the general shape of his temperament and sprang from his spasmodic efforts to be somebody else. Izvolsky was all of a piece, his actions shaped predictably by extreme ambition combined with a timidity scarcely less extreme, which came out in an exaggerated sensitiveness to public opinion: he was one of those sad statesmen who are kept awake at night by a hostile leading article.[12] But, unlike Aehrenthal, he was a statesman through and through: not for him the death-wish and poetic dreams of his country being dragged into the abyss by obscure naval actions between blue-eyed sailormen peering through the mists of the Baltic and the North Sea. Little, dapper, bright-eyed, with a very determined chin above a high starched collar, he was the antithesis of the cumbrous, hesitant Aehrenthal, who nevertheless was the sharper of the two: remembering Aehrenthal's 'hapless jaws' we return to Sir Harold Nicolson:

> He was obviously a vain man and he strutted on little lacquered feet. His clothes, which came from Savile Row, were moulded tightly upon a plump but still gainly frame. He held himself rigidly with stiff shoulders. He wore a pearl pin, an eye-glass, white spats, a white

slip to his waistcoat. His face was well cared for, but pasty and fattening, with loose and surly lips. His hair and moustache were carefully parted; he had a way of turning his short Russian neck stiffly above his high white collar, glancing sideways, as so often with Russians, away from the person with whom he was shaking hands. His voice was at once cultured and rasping. He left behind him, as he passed onwards, a slight scent of *violette de parme*.[13]

He was a great Anglophile: more than any other Russian he was responsible for the Anglo-Russian Convention of 1907, which was above all the work of Sir Arthur Nicolson, who got to know him inside out and liked him. Sir Arthur was aware of his defects, which included a desire to shine in high society, but found him likeable and honest, loyal too, and with a quick and subtle intelligence.[14] He did not want to quarrel with Austria, with Aehrenthal, nor did Aehrenthal want to quarrel with him. Izvolsky was interested in the Dardanelles; Aehrenthal was interested in Bosnia. The old, old question of control of the Straits had very much come to life again after the Russo-Japanese war. Then Russia had fumed at the thought of her Black Sea fleet, which might, she thought, have made all the difference, locked up uselessly in the Levant. The newer question of Bosnia-Herzegovina was revived in Aehrenthal's mind by the necessity of constructing a South Slav bloc within the Empire to counter the attractions of Serbia, by the difficulty of doing this without first securing Bosnia-Herzegovina, and, finally, by the advent of Enver Pasha's Young Turkish revolution which to many seemed to solve at one sweep the problem of Turkey in Europe: if the Young Turks would carry out the reforms the Sultan had resisted for so long, then the whole Balkan problem would subside – and with it would be eliminated Vienna's justification for occupying Bosnia.

The two interests coincided. Izvolsky had had some very rough things to say about the Sanjak operation: he had called it a bomb thrown between his feet; he had said never again could there be true co-operation between Austria and Russia in the Balkans. But these objurgations did not go very deep. And on 2 July 1908 he made nonsense of them by inviting Aehrenthal to meet him to discuss 'in a friendly spirit of reciprocity' the two things that interested them most. It had occurred to him that Austrian backing for his new campaign to get the Straits opened to Russian warships might be secured in exchange for Russian backing for Austria's annexation plans. The meeting did not take place until 15 September: both men being unwilling to take the decisive initiative. It only came about because Berchtold, Aehrenthal's successor at Petersburg, was at Carlsbad where Izvolsky was taking a cure, and persuaded the Russian to meet Aehrenthal at Buchlau, his country seat, which lay conveniently to hand.

Exactly what happened at Buchlau has remained, and will remain, one of the major diplomatic mysteries. The two men were together for six hours, and neither kept a record of what was said. All that the world knew, a little later, was what both men said they had said – and not said.

The first thing the world knew was that on 6 October the Emperor Franz Josef, apparently out of the blue, formally announced the annexation of Bosnia-Herzegovina and the simultaneous evacuation of the Sanjak of Novibazar. This sudden act was a direct breach of the provisions of the Treaty of Berlin. For a moment it looked like war. England, France and Russia called for a European Conference. Then the explanations – and the recriminations – started up.

Aehrenthal took the line, and held to it, that Izvolsky at Buchlau, just three weeks earlier, had agreed to the Annexation in exchange for assurances of Austrian support in the matter of the Straits. Izvolsky denied that there had been any hard agreement: it had been one thing to agree to support Austria's claim to Bosnia in principle, but he had not the least idea that Aehrenthal was meditating immediate action; such action, therefore, was a deliberate breach of faith and Aehrenthal himself was a liar and a rogue.

In fact it is virtually certain that Izvolsky had to call Aehrenthal a liar to save his own face: it was bad enough for him to have to admit to being duped by a barefaced rogue; but for a man of his vanity it would have been insupportable to have to admit that he had, quite simply, been caught napping. Yet this was clearly what had happened. Furthermore, Izvolsky did not wake up until well after Franz Josef's proclamation.[15]

After the Buchlau meeting, he returned to Carlsbad to continue his cure. He then proceeded in a leisurely way to London, via Bavaria and Paris, in order to canvass his ideas about the Straits. At Berchtesgaden he met von Schön, the German Foreign Minister, and told him in confidence that he expected the annexation to be declared on 8 October: von Schön, who had no axe to grind and may be believed in this matter, formally reported this interesting item of news to Berlin. Izvolsky was in Paris when the proclamation was made, and at first he took it calmly. By the time he got to London Europe had exploded. Izvolsky then exploded too.

What seems to have happened is that Izvolsky made a whole series of mistakes, none of which he dared admit in face of the hurricane of wrath which arose in Russia. In the first place he committed himself too definitely to Aehrenthal in giving his general blessing to the annexation scheme; then, in discussing the Straits, he failed to realize that he and Aehrenthal were talking about two different things: by freedom of the Straits, he meant freedom for Russian warships to move out of the Black Sea, but not for Western warships to move into it, whereas Aehrenthal meant both; then, when he talked to von Schön about the date of the announcement of the Annexation it had not occurred to him that this would be announced by the Emperor as a *fait accompli*, but, initially, as an imminent project to the Austro-Hungarian Delegations in Vienna. Finally, and fatally, he repeated the very mistake he had made in the Sanjak affair. Then he had discovered too late that Russian opinion was not at that time in the least interested in the Straits (an academic matter when Russia had no navy left immediately after the Port Arthur disaster), but was highly inflammable in the matter of pan-Slavism in general and Serbia in particular. It is almost inconceivable that he should have made this mistake again so soon after the rude awakening nine months earlier; but make it he did. And he was in good company, for Aehrenthal too repeated, letter for letter, his own mistake. The outrage produced by the Sanjak railway deal taught him nothing: he was to be shocked once more and for just the same reasons.

There is no place in this narrative for an exhaustive study of the Buchlau affair and its repercussions. It is of interest here only for the light it throws on Great Power relations on the eve of the First World War and the sort of men who were conducting those relations. They were frivolous men. They were quite wantonly playing with fire. There was a difference in kind between a Buol and an Aehrenthal. Buol, in 1853, was trivial, vain and superficial, but he was a deeply harrassed man, too small for his job, but trying, nevertheless, to do that job according to his lights: to keep Austria afloat. This was a serious and desperate matter, and serious and desperate mistakes were made. In the first decade of the twentieth century the seriousness had departed. Aehrenthal, as we have seen, had room for good ideas; but he moved among his own good ideas like a shadow, play-acting. He had a number of courses open to him. The annexation of Bosnia-Herzegovina, the creation of a strong, independent Bulgaria to stand against Serbia, the creation of a strong, contented Serbia under Austrian patronage – all these were reasonable courses. He chose the course of annexation. There is no reason in the world why he should not have achieved that end by perfectly honourable means and with the full approval of the Powers. But he had also to prove that he was a great diplomat in what he took to be the Metternich-cum-Bismarck tradition. He had to turn what might have been reasonably presented as an act of forward statesmanship into a diplomatic victory, into a score off Izvolsky. And he was allowed to get away with it. He was allowed to get away with it because Britain and France rallied round to save Izvolsky's face, and because Germany came to his rescue by offering unconditional support. Wilhelm II was furious, and for more than one reason: he was genuinely alarmed at any disturbance of the peace and he was angry because Aehrenthal had nullified the hard work he had put in cultivating the goodwill of Turkey.[16] But von Bülow, the wretched heir to Bismarck, could think of nothing but the alliance. Regardless of the fact that Austria's new activity was clearly running her into a head-on collision with Russia, and that this could be the moment for Germany to secure herself by returning to her old understanding with Petersburg, he telegraphed frantically from his Baltic holiday resort (as in 1914, so in 1908, Austrian action caught the leadership of Germany, from the Emperor downwards, dispersed among beaches and mountains) that to save the Triple Alliance Germany must at all costs back Austria up to the hilt.[17] The Emperor, who had sacked Bismarck, gave in. Austria was having her revenge for 1866. She was now the active element, and she was dragging Germany in her train.[18]

CHAPTER SEVENTEEN

THE DOOMED INHERITOR

Franz Josef at the time of the Annexation was seventy-eight. He was still very much the Emperor and he could still take decisive action of that sudden and unexpected kind always characteristic of him. In 1905, as we have seen, he broke the Magyar government and in the following year appointed Max Vladimir Beck as Prime Minister of Cisleithnia to introduce universal suffrage. He did not initiate the Annexation, but he presided over it and derived, with at least a part of his mind, profound satisfaction from the thought that by adding two new provinces to the Monarchy he had in some way atoned for the loss of Italy and the failure to win Germany. With the rest of his mind he was intent on two things only: to keep the peace and to keep the Empire in being while he lived. What happened after his death he was past caring about. No doubt the Empire would break up: there was nobody, in his view, to hold it together. But he would have done his duty. He could be no more responsible for the future than he had been for the past. He had been called, at eighteen, to assume an overwhelming burden, not of his making. God and his ancestors were responsible for that: he had done what he had to do; he had carried the burden; he would continue to carry it until he dropped. What happened then was a matter for God.

He was now so used to being alone that solitariness had become his second nature. He could move in and out of it at will, emerging from his isolation to enjoy the long conversations with his immediate advisers, his Ministers, and still more with men of all parties, above all intelligent senators from the Upper House: men like the liberal-minded Baernreither, so full of excellent ideas. He liked meeting socialists, too. Indeed, in his old age he showed more curiosity about the workings of other men's minds than he had ever done in the past. It was as though the realization that he had no longer to strive forward, but only to hold, enabled him to relax and even to enjoy. He certainly took pleasure in being the elder statesman of Europe, of the world, and whatever he may have thought of the brash and devious self-confidence of his juniors – of Edward VII, of Nicholas II, of Theodore Roosevelt, of the unpredictable, showy, emotional, slightly mad yet desperately serious Wilhelm II – he liked having them visit him at Vienna, at Ischl, suing for his counsel or support, and offering him glimpses of strange and interesting new ways. He could afford now to look at new ways and new ideas: since there was no longer any question of his being caught up in them, he no longer had to repel them at sight. In 1906, at seventy-six, he allowed Edward VII to persuade him to go for a spin in a motor-car: the courtiers at Ischl were thunderstruck, but the old man took it well.

The Empress had died on 10 September 1898. For ten years, since the suicide of Rudolf, she had been out of this world, dressed always in black, and wandering incessantly. One day her wanderings took her to Caux, in the mountains above Montreux on Lake Geneva. She hoped that perhaps Franz Josef might be able to join her there for a few days after the summer manoeuvres, but this was out of the question. She was now so far removed from the everyday concerns of Court and Government that she had to be reminded that her husband was already plunged into the tiresome and exacting arrangements for the celebration of the jubilee of his accession.[1] So Elizabeth went on with her sightseeing alone. She went to Geneva by steamer in dreamy September weather, to visit the Rothschild garden and the aquarium, where she was enchanted by the tiny gemlike tropical fish. From the Hotel Beau Rivage, looking across the lake at the gleaming mass of Mont Blanc, she went off next morning with one of her ladies-in-waiting, Countess Sztaray, to a music-shop which had on show a brand new contrivance called the Orchestrion, which played tunes from *Carmen*, *Tannhäuser*, *Rigoletto* and *Lohengrin*. She liked the *Tannhäuser* extract best and asked for it to be repeated.[2] The afternoon came and it was time to catch the steamer for Caux. With Countess Sztaray she walked from the hotel, a short distance along the quayside, to board the steamer. A young man hurried towards them, barred their path, leapt at the Empress and stabbed her violently and swiftly in the breast. Countess Sztaray saw the blow, but not the weapon. Elizabeth fell to the ground as the young man rushed headlong away. But, with help, she got to her feet, was dusted down, refused to go back to the hotel, said it was nothing, and resumed the walk to the steamer. Countess Sztaray had to help her up the gangway, but she did not collapse until she had set foot on deck; then she sank down and died. The young man was Luigi Lucheni, an Italian builder's labourer, twenty-six years old. He was not one of the ragged, undernourished poor: he was bronzed and strong and healthy. He said he was an anarchist, an individual anarchist who belonged to no party or society and he was acting on his own. He wanted to die for his act, which had no political effect except to bring the peoples of the Empire closer to Franz Josef.[3] 'Nothing has been spared me in this world,' the Emperor exclaimed, as though to himself, as he tore open the final telegram from Geneva. And then again, though this time as though he wanted all the world to hear: 'Nobody knows how much we loved each other. . . .'[4]

Elizabeth's death brought him closer to his people, but not to what remained of his own family. Indeed, in his eyes, very little remained. Only to his daughter Valerie and to his very young grandnephew, Archduke Karl, did he seem in the least attached. Between Franz Ferdinand, the heir apparent, and himself there was no spark of human warmth. Indeed for some time he had made it abundantly clear that he found it impossible to think of Franz Ferdinand as his heir at all. It was a failure which had heavy consequences.

2

Franz Ferdinand, difficult and complex, had every reason to feel disgruntled. Quite soon after Rudolf's suicide he was saying that to judge by the way his uncle talked, the Mayerling 'idiocy' had been his fault.[5] Then he fell ill. The lungs in that heavy, plethoric body were in a very bad state indeed. He was sent away for treatment; he travelled down the Nile, he travelled round the world. It was common belief that he would die, and during his long enforced absences everybody from Franz Josef downwards treated his younger brother Otto as the future Emperor. Franz Ferdinand knew all about this. He should have died, but he was determined to recover and live and one day to have his revenge. He grew into a man suspicious, morose and violent, seeing enemies everywhere and, because of this, all too easily turning would-be friends into enemies. 'You always expect that every man will prove an angel,' he said one day to Conrad von Hötzendorf, more in sorrow than in anger. 'I always assume that everyone I meet is a rogue until the contrary is proved.'[6] He had been extrovert and cheerful as a youth, in the days when his cousin Rudolf had taken him by the hand. But the latent paranoia was always there: it may have come from his maternal grandfather, who was none other than King Bomba of Naples. The violence, too. But he did not inherit a trace of his grandfather's cowardice, and even in his most insane moments a certain grandeur of a very strong character, always slightly larger than life, came through. It came through especially when, realizing the deficiencies of his education, he put himself to school under Max Vladimir Beck, then a civil servant, later to become Prime Minister: of course he quarrelled with Beck in due course. It came through in his fight against illness. It came through in his obstinate refusal to conciliate the Emperor. It came through, above all, in the circumstances of his marriage.

He was thirty-seven, and supposed to be paying court to one of the daughters of Archduke Friedrich at Pressburg, when it suddenly came out that he was using her simply as a cover for his love for one of the ladies-in-waiting, Countess Sophie Chotek von Chotkowa und Wognin, who belonged to an old Bohemian family fallen on hard times. One day, after a tennis party at the Archduke's castle, Franz Ferdinand left his watch behind. It was found by a servant and taken to the Archduchess, who opened a locket attached to the watch and nearly fainted when she found it contained a miniature not of her daughter but of Sophie Chotek. The fat was in the fire. Sophie was dismissed immediately and bundled out of the house: Franz Josef was informed.[7]

This was the musical-comedy opening to the tragic history which ended at Sarajevo. The Choteks belonged to the nobility, but they were not in the list of families into which a Habsburg might marry. This list had nothing to do with the Imperial statute-book: it was a product of the Habsburg House Law, by which every Head of the House of Habsburg considered himself indissolubly bound. Franz Ferdinand said he was aware of the Law, naturally; but if he was to be any good for anything in life he had to marry Sophie. Franz Josef replied that he could have either the Chotek or the Crown, emphatically not both. But Franz Ferdinand was stubborn too. He would marry *and* be Emperor. Franz Josef could do nothing with him. Archdukes, archduchesses, the Cardinal-Archbishop of Vienna, were all turned loose on him – in vain. He wrote a long, reasonable, dignified, circumstantial letter to the Emperor setting out his determination and declaring categorically that with Sophie he could do his full duty to the Empire, without her he would be useless.[8] Franz Josef, very angrily, gave in. He rejected the easy solution that the Chotek family, entirely worthy, might be further ennobled to qualify them for intermarriage with the Habsburgs: that was a trick.

The marriage might take place, but it must be a morganatic one, provided the lawyers and the constitutionalists could find a case. The working out of this affair occupied the best brains of the Empire for most of 1899 and the first half of 1900.

Franz Ferdinand found his happiness. Sophie, ambitious as she was, put up with the humiliations heaped upon her. The Emperor relented enough to raise her from being Countess Chotek to be Duchess of Hohenberg – although even then, when attendance at Court functions was unavoidable, she, the wife of the heir to the throne, had to tag along behind the youngest Archduchess. But the Court, and especially the High Chamberlain, Count Montenuovo (himself the child of a morganatic marriage), never forgave her. She never allowed her bitterness to appear; a splendid wife and mother, she steadily played her part. Meanwhile, her hidden influence made itself felt only in the way in which her husband felt impelled to assert himself increasingly. The contrast between his behaviour as a husband and a father, which in many ways approached the ideal, and his rough and overbearing conduct as heir to the throne was in every way remarkable.[9]

3

Franz Josef had no luck. He himself, at twenty-one, had embarked eagerly, head over heels in love, with perfect confidence, on his own disastrous marriage. Now, while this unprepossessing nephew, with his gooseberry eyes, his hair *en brosse*, his Hohenzollern moustachioes, was mulishly informing him that love was the only thing that mattered, he was losing Katherina Schratt. Elizabeth, during her lifetime, had splendidly protected Katherina Schratt and her strange, dream-like relationship with Franz Josef from the least breath of scandal and from every intrigue. When Elizabeth was murdered, when the Emperor needed Frau Schratt more than ever before, she was suddenly vulnerable. Her enemies came at her in two ways. She was still an actress with a contract at the Burgtheater. She still liked to appear on the stage; but she had played fairly fast and loose with the terms of her contract. Now, approaching fifty, she wanted to play Ibsen, and the directorate had its revenge. She was not, they said, the type for Ibsen: Franz Josef, if he had ever heard of Nora or Rebecca West or Hedda Gabler, would have heartily concurred. She had also taken too much time off. The contract was not renewed. If it seems inconceivable that the Director of the Burgtheater, a Dr Paul Schlenter, could have dared behave in this way to the Emperor's favourite, it is because of a failure to understand the remarkable fullness of the autonomy of everyday life within the Empire. Dr Schlenter needed support, of course, and he obtained it from Count Montenuovo, Franz Ferdinand's dedicated enemy, who, as Court Chamberlain, had ultimate control over the two Court theatres – the Burg and the Opera. Katherina Schratt thought, not unreasonably, that Franz Josef should intervene; but the old Emperor refused to intervene: it would be bad for her reputation, he said, and it would lower the dignity of the Crown.[10] At almost the same time there was an issue of a new Order, the Elizabeth Order. This had been inaugurated just before Elizabeth's death: it had been intended by the Emperor as a present to Elizabeth; she was to nominate its recipients. But she was dead before the first list came to be compiled. When it was made out, Katherina Schratt was not on it. She was deeply hurt. Franz Josef said again that he could do nothing. Had Elizabeth been alive, Frau Schratt would have headed the list; but he himself could not put her down, for obvious reasons. Again, when she received a formal invitation to visit Valerie and her husband at Wallsee, Franz Josef advised her to refuse: she might find things unpleasant.[11] The whole family was turning against her, and the Emperor seemed to think that she should put up with it gladly. But it was too much. She felt a need to get away from the poisonous atmosphere and also to find younger company: she could not, at fifty, be shut off from the whole world, friendless except for an old man who would do nothing, could do nothing, he said, to make people respect her. In March 1899, while Franz Josef was wrestling with the Chotek problem, things came to a head. There was an open quarrel, exactly what about nobody knows. But Katherina Schratt went off. Franz Josef poured out his heart in an agonizing letter, less intimate, more inhibited than his letters to Sisi, but sufficiently abandoned:

> My dear, kind friend! I don't really know whether I may still use these words, or whether I should not write: *Gnädige Frau* – but I simply cannot abandon the hope that yesterday's black storm clouds will roll away and that the old, happy friendship will be restored. You rejected my suggestions, which were meant only for the good, in the interests of both of us, so stubbornly and passionately that I was carried away myself and spoke with a violence for which I am

sorry, and for which I beg for your forgiveness from the bottom of my heart. I too will forget the sudden, wounding, and, for me, most painful way in which you left me yesterday.

Poor Franz Josef – he should have left it at that, but he went on:

Listen to the voice of your own kind heart, think things over quietly, and you will find that we simply cannot part, that we simply have to find each other again. Think of the long years of our unclouded friendship, of the joy and the suffering we have shared, more suffering, alas, you helped me to bear, think of the Unforgettable One, whom we both loved so much and who hovered over us like a guardian angel – and then I believe you will find yourself agreeing. I am unspeakably wretched. The thought that I may lose the one who has sustained me through so much misery, the one with whom I can talk over all things, is too terrible. . . .[12]

But Katherina Schratt had made up her mind. She went away. Later there was a formal farewell. That was at Ischl on the Emperor's seventieth birthday, when Valerie, who herself had turned against Frau Schratt since her mother's death, was nevertheless horrified and deeply moved when he told her he was going to call on her to see her for the last time. He came home in tears, and the next day wrote:

It is just twenty-four hours since I set out to come to you for the last time, my so deeply beloved angel! When we had said goodbye I ran into a chimney-sweep outside the smithy. They say such a meeting is a sign of good luck, so perhaps that sweep will bring me luck, and luck for me means one thing: to see you again. I cannot describe my feelings; it is altogether beyond me, and would anyway be too sad, when what you need is to be comforted and cheered. Silent, dull misery – we can leave it at that. . . .[13]

They wrote sometimes. Several times Franz Josef begged her to give him the solace of at least another meeting. In the following year they did indeed meet and walk together at Ischl, but for the Emperor this brought more pain than joy. In 1902, at seventy-two, he was writing from Budapest: 'You will find me much aged and mentally enfeebled. I think a great deal about the past and a great deal about the sad, hopeless future, and about death. The last is useful, for one cannot prepare oneself enough for the final moment.'[14] He had still fourteen years to go.

This was the man who appeared to the princes and statesmen of the world in the crisis-ridden years which were even then preparing as the Grand Old Man, the embodiment of an elder statesman, courteous, grand, aloof and serene, alien to all human feeling. This was the man who was laughed at by his first biographers because he was supposed to be incapable of tenderness, of any emotion save anger, and because his sole correspondence with Elizabeth and Katherina Schratt was sincerely supposed to consist of a sparse handful of formal telegrams.[15]

4

He was not merely a Grand Old Man. He was still astonishingly active. His back was straight and he strode out briskly. He undertook long and tiring journeys to be with his troops on manoeuvres and to inspect depots and barracks. Increasingly he had periods of lassitude; increasingly he let things happen which, earlier, he would have sharply resisted. But he was still crisp and firm about the things that really mattered. He might write to Katherina Schratt in 1902, from the depths of self-pity and loneliness, telling her that his mind was going and that he thought a great deal about death. But in fact he did not give himself much time to brood or to think about anything but the affairs of the Empire and the dynasty. He still rose before it was light from his iron bedstead; he still worked steadily all day, consulting with his Ministers, receiving diplomats and petitioners, reading every document deep into the night. Even up to 1910, when he was eighty, he could gather himself to undertake the long hard journey to Bosnia in high summer, to take a parade in Sarajevo, to visit one of the mountain fortresses high above the city. The next time a Habsburg visited Sarajevo, just four years later, it was Franz Ferdinand, who went in the Emperor's place.

5

It was not until 1906 that the Heir Apparent began to make himself felt as a power. Until then he had concerned himself above all with military affairs, working through the small Military Chancellery which his uncle allowed him to establish in the Belvedere, and in trying to educate himself about the affairs of the Empire. He took up certain fixed positions. Russia, he thought, should be bound to Austria with hoops of iron. He believed that Goluchowski, as a Pole, was working deviously for war against Russia, regardless of the fact that it was to Goluchowski above all that the long accord between Russia and Austria, from 1897 to 1908, was due. He had no understanding of England, and, long before the Anglo-Russian Convention of 1907, regarded Goluchowski's attempts to reach an understanding with her as a betrayal:

> This fraternization with England which he has staged I consider exceedingly dangerous, or, to call it by its right name, nonsensical; because England is the most calculating, deceitful and unreliable ally on earth. I believe there is no longer a sensible, thinking man who does not know that the Armenian horrors and the affair at Crete were directly inspired by England. By this close association with English ideas he estranges us entirely from Germany which has just now spoken very plainly and created discord with Russia.[16]

That was in 1897 to the new Austrian Ambassador in St Petersburg. France he regarded as a land of anti-monarchist Freemasons. Poland irritated him. Italy he despised. The Magyars he pursued with a deep and choking hatred.

The Magyars had indeed, from 1897 on, insisted on behaving as though they owned the Empire. Instead of regarding the decenniel revision of the Compromise as an affair of amicable fiscal adjustment, they insisted that really it meant a complete renewal: in a word, that every ten years the Compromise came to an end and had to be negotiated again (or not) as between sovereign States: negotiation meant, invariably, more concessions from Vienna to Budapest, and, at the turn of the century, these concessions were extended from the sphere of finance to the sphere of the army; so that, in the end, Hungary was denying the very basis of the Compromise by demanding, in effect, an entirely separate army. Her mood had passed from arrogance into insolence. Thus, in 1903, Stepan Tisza could get up in the Budapest Parliament and refer to a mild criticism of the Magyar attitude towards the Compromise by the Austrian Prime Minister, Koerber, as 'the dilettante utterance of a distinguished foreigner'.[17] This kind of thing drove Franz Ferdinand to a frenzy; and when he was angry he lost control. In a letter to Max Vladimir Beck, he could write:

> Again and again I come back to the conviction, which I shall go on expressing as long as I live, that the so-called 'decent Hungarian' *simply does not exist*, and that *every* Hungarian, be he a minister, a prince, a cardinal, a tradesman, a peasant, a hussar, or a stable-

boy is a revolutionary and a — (I exempt the cardinal from being a
—, but he is a republican none the less). *Every one* of them thinks
precisely what the most rascally Deputy says.[18]

This attitude was fixed. Among his papers there has been preserved
the draft of a letter in his own hand (it may or may not have been
sent) to Wilhelm II, undated, but evidently written in the summer of
1909. In this he insists again that all the ills the Monarchy has to
face spring from Budapest, and that 'the so-called noble, chivalrous
Magyar is in fact the most vile, most perfidious, most unreliable
fellow'.

Normally he would write in more reasonable tones. Thus, during
the long battle for the introduction of Magyar as a language of army
command, he could point out, with perfect truth, that the Magyars
had freely conspired with the enemies of the House of Habsburg in
the past (e.g. with Bismarck in 1866 and with Cavour in 1859), and
were continuing to do so; that, nevertheless, they had been rewarded
for this at the expense of other nationalities, 'always staunchly loyal,
in difficult times, to the Imperial cause'.[19] He foresaw the day, as
certainly the extreme Magyars did, when Budapest would dominate
Vienna and when Magyar would become the official language of
command, which meant that 55 per cent of the troops raised in
Transleithina would have to learn Hungarian, 'a difficult and useless
language'.[20] He could write quite politely to Aehrenthal, who was
then advocating further concessions to Hungary to prove that the
dynasty was strong, that he was unable to see how the granting of
such concessions, 'which would mean dividing the army into two',
could conceivably be expected to impress foreign opinion as a sign
of strength.[21]

This violence, which came out again and again in face of the
Magyars, was his worst side. That and a queer manifestation of autocratic avatism. There were times when it seemed he could not fit
himself into the framework of his age. For example, as the heir to the
throne he had, to put it mildly, many privileges and great estates.
But one day he fell in love with a hunting-box called Blühnbach, in
the neighbourhood of Salzburg, the property of an Auersperg,
which was rented by an aristocratic syndicate. He desired to possess
Blühnbach above all things in this world and to keep the shooting for
himself; its owners might have sold; but the tenants refused to
surrender the lease. It had the best hunting in the world, he insisted;
it had the best air: to own it would be his happiness and his physical

salvation. He brought every conceivable and inconceivable kind of pressure to bear. He went after it with the monomaniac intensity with which, earlier, he had pursued his marriage. He engaged Prime Ministers in his cause, and he finally won. 'Believe me,' said the old Emperor to his Prime Minister, Beck, 'you had better fix him up with Blühnbach, then he'll be better at once!'[22] This was in 1908, the year of the Annexation – the year, too, in which Franz Ferdinand, for quite different reasons, was engaged in a complex and ruthless operation to discredit and unseat poor Beck, who was his oldest and most loyal friend.

This was the worst side: much has been written about it. He was intolerably rude to his servants; he was mean; he turned against his friends. All this was true. It was true, also, that his idea of shooting was the wholesale *battue* – but he was one of the finest shots in Europe, and it was the age of *battues*, as it was the age of Tranby Croft and Dreyfus: pheasants were massacred in their thousands at Elveden in Suffolk, no less than at Konospicht in Bohemia. It is true that he had a mania for collecting and filled his houses at Artstetten, Konospicht and elsewhere with objects of art of every kind. But if we are to discuss Franz Ferdinand on this level, there was another side of it. As head of the Central Commission for the Care of Monuments he took his duties very seriously. He had a genuine feeling for architecture rare in that age of reckless 'restoration'. He expended very much care and energy, often very much to the point, on the preservation of ancient monuments. He could be rough about the Hungarians, but he could also be rough about the insensitive restorers, who, but for him, would have ruined many of those cool, unassuming little churches, Baroque on a medieval foundation, which point the sunlit hills and broad valleys of Austria today. He was no more elegant in his bullying of village priests than he was in his political barnstorming; but he was on the side of the angels:

> His Imperial Highness observes with disapproval that, above all in Upper Austria, where there are so many splendid artistic monuments, the restoration mania has assumed the grossest forms. Every priest seems to have got it into his head that he is in duty bound to have his church redecorated from top to bottom, regardless of the ruin of the ancient and beautiful objects in his charge.[23]

He also had a passion for flowers and gardens. At Konospicht and Artstetten he lavished enough energy for the lifetime of an ordinary man on creating gardens of extreme beauty. In the long file of telegrams from Wilhelm II to Franz Ferdinand, almost the last document is a characteristic telegram about Franz Ferdinand as gardener:

> Again thank you from my heart for the precious hours I was able to spend with you in 'Klingsor's Magic Garden'. I admire the organizational mastery and the fine colour sense which show through in your landscaping. Glorious weather here. The roses in my rose-garden nearly all in bloom. Rhododendrons still flowering in spite of three weeks' rain. . . .[24]

That telegram was dated 14 June 1914, after Wilhelm's return to Potsdam from his last visit to Konospicht. A week later the Imperial gardener had set out for Sarajevo.

6

But there is no need to continue the discussion on this level. There was more to Franz Ferdinand than his *battues* and his rose gardens. He was a bitterly frustrated man, heir to a great Empire, who saw his inheritance crumbling away from mismanagement and neglect. The Magyars obsessed him as the chief internal danger – as well they might. Plans for the future seethed perpetually through his mind, plans informed partly by ignorance, partly by prejudice, but always by a sense of urgency. Unlike Rudolf, whose dreams had been vague and large, concerned more with the future of humanity as a whole than the Empire itself, he thought in terms of immediate dynastic aims. The first and imperative step was, by breaking the power of Budapest to restore authority to Vienna. He would have staked everything on this, and the Hungarians knew it: what would happen after that was anybody's guess. The idea of a Triune Monarchy, to supplant the Dual Monarchy, with Prague as a centre to offset Budapest, was popular with some, but not with Franz Ferdinand. There was a time when he elaborated far-reaching plans for the creation of a Trialism with Zagreb, as the capital of a Southern Slav Union, as the other pole. He was impressed with the dreams of the great Archbishop Strossmayer, who, at the close of the nineteenth century, did so much to enrich the national consciousness of the Croats, 'the stepchildren of the Monarchy', and worked for a sort of resurrected Illyria, to include Dalmatia, Istria, and Carniola. But

Franz Ferdinand turned his back on this dream when in 1905 the Croats, in despair of receiving any help from Vienna in face of the Magyar tyranny, decided, with the Fiume Resolution, that the best thing they could do was to join Hungary in its separatist agitation and then seek to come to terms with Budapest direct. After that, he fell in love successively with the federal ideas of the Rumanian Popovici, which demanded a division of the Empire along lines of race and topography not at all dissimilar to the scheme worked out by the ill-fated constitutionalists at Kremsier in 1849 before Schwarzenberg turned his guns on them, and the formula of Baron Eichhoff, a senior Foreign Office official, under the slogan: 'Mutual dependence in the economic sphere – independence in the political sphere'[25] – which meant turning the Empire into a sort of glorified Customs Union of quasi-autonomous peoples presided over by the Emperor.

Nobody knows what solution Franz Ferdinand would, in the end, have favoured. He was learning all the time. Nobody knows what sort of Emperor he would have made, or even how his character would have developed once the ultimate responsibility was his: so many of his words and actions were the words and actions of a man in a fury at his own powerlessness to act at all. He was impatient; he was self-willed. But he was essentially a torrent constantly overflowing its too constricted banks. Thus he frequently swung quite wildly from one course to another. He was not without sense. He could apologize gracefully when he had lost his temper. He needed more than anything else the discipline of responsibility to contain his impulses. He was highly intelligent, though in some disastrous ways ignorant. He had imagination. Koerber, who knew all about his bull-headed ways, once said of him: 'Who knows but that as Emperor he might not have become a downright liberal?' Schönaich, the Minister of War, whom Franz Ferdinand attacked with venom – and success – observed: 'The Heir Apparent will make more concessions in twenty-four hours than the Emperor Franz Josef has made in twenty-four years.'[26]

He had an eye for reality. Because of his association with Conrad von Hötzendorf he was popularly regarded as a militarist and the leader of a war party: in fact he quarrelled incessantly with Conrad, his own nominee, on the matter of peace and war. He was indeed ready to fight the Italians, but throughout all the crises of the first fourteen years of the century he was immovable on the need to maintain peace with Serbia. He disapproved even of the Annexation.

He, with Conrad, strove manfully to reform the armed services and to be prepared for war; but, for all his verbal violence, he detested war.[27] Above all he was determined to avoid any cause for conflict with Russia. This is one of the few things we know about him for certain; that and the fact that in his view the only task for Austrian statesmen was to keep the Empire intact in face of threats from without and within until he was in the saddle. It was this not unnatural obsession that led to so many contradictions.

The year 1906 was the beginning of those contradictions. In that year Aehrenthal went to the Ballhausplatz, Schönaich became Minister of War, and Beck was made Prime Minister of Cisleithnia. In the same year, on Franz Ferdinand's insistence, Conrad von Hötzendorf was appointed Chief-of-Staff. The Military Chancellery in the Belvedere was simultaneously strengthened immeasurably by the accession of Major von Brosch, a man of extreme brilliance, knowledge, penetration, charm and tact, who was also a most gifted intriguer. With Brosch at its head the office in the Belvedere became very quickly a sort of shadow government, extending its influence far beyond the armed services, which were its ostensible concern, and furnishing the Archduke with more detailed information about the state of the realm in its multitudinous parts than ever came to the Hofburg. Franz Josef had to rely on what his advisers cared to tell him, above all on reports from official circles, politicians in power, provincial governors and the rest. Franz Ferdinand, through Brosch, built up an elaborate network of unofficial informers; thus, for example, while he knew what the Polish landowners were saying, he also knew all about the state of Poland as seen by the leaders of the Ruthenian peasants, held in subjection by the landowners; again, he did not rely on Budapest for information about conditions among the Rumanian minority of Hungary; he went to selected spokesmen of that minority. This is not to say that his interest was wholly dispassionate: his contempt for the Italians prevented him from cultivating members of the Italian minority, and his predilection for the Bohemian magnates, among whom, at Konospicht, he numbered himself, made it impossible for him to view with detachment the aspirations of the Czech nationalists. But at least he tried: he was the first Habsburg since Josef II to be imbued with the sense that he, as Emperor, must find his fate bound up with the destinies of the minority peoples of his realm.

For nearly a decade the heir was thus better informed than the

Emperor himself about everything that went on inside the vast realm, and a good deal more far-seeing about the nature of the forces working for its destruction. But, except on the rarest occasions, the Emperor did not consult him; the two men worked in isolation, often against each other – so much so, indeed, that sometimes it was only necessary for Franz Josef to hear (as he always heard) what Franz Ferdinand wanted to do to make him decree the opposite. The aged Emperor, trim, dry, reserved, ironical, but still astonishingly active, still rosy-cheeked, regarded the large, noisy, often blustering figure of his nephew with contemptuous distaste. Franz Ferdinand should have his due; more, indeed, than his due, if that was what he wanted; but to expect him, Franz Josef, to take an active interest in the shaping of his mind, or to put up with his company more than was unavoidably necessary, was to expect too much.

It was the failure of a very old man. Franz Ferdinand was full of energy and he was full of ideas, some of them half-baked, none of them thought through, but many of them very much worth thinking through in the light of accumulated experience. Franz Josef had the experience, but he had no new ideas. He was well aware that new ideas were called for and would have to be developed and translated into action after his death. But he was incapable of the effort, or the desire, even to criticize Franz Ferdinand's ideas: he simply ignored them. He could have told the younger man, for example, something about the Magyars (hadn't he had to live with them for more than half a century?), their vulnerable points and their real strength. Instead he was content to let Franz Ferdinand collide with them head-on. It was the greatest pity in the world. Franz Ferdinand was, in his way, much more a chip of the old block than the Emperor ever gave him credit for being. He was a dynast too, and he had at heart the most profound respect for his uncle, whom he never abused. When, at the time of the conflict over Sophie, he burst out against the narrowness of the field into which a Habsburg could marry ('The result is that half the children are idiots or epileptics!')[28] he was not inveighing against his uncle so much as against an insane tradition and the courtiers who upheld it. When it was suggested that Franz Josef might be moved to celebrate his Diamond Jubilee by revoking the law excluding Franz Ferdinand's children from the succession, the Archduke replied grandly: 'The Habsburg Crown is a crown of thorns, and nobody who is not born to it shall aspire to it.'[29]

7

When Aehrenthal, whom he respected for his pro-Russian leanings, Schönaich, whom he respected because he thought he was strong, and Beck, whom he respected and admired as his first preceptor – when these three came to office all in one year, Franz Ferdinand wrote gleefully to Beck: 'With such a trifolium, Beck, Aehrenthal and Schönaich, we shall get on *famously*.'[30] But within three years he had turned against them all. Schönaich, he thought, was weak about the army; Aehrenthal (who was married to a Hungarian) made too many concessions to the Hungarians and, with the Annexation, had turned Russia against Austria; Beck had also, he thought, shown weakness towards the Hungarians, and, on top of that, by introducing the Universal Suffrage Bill and pushing it through, had irreparably damaged the fabric of his inheritance. It was in this period that the Belvedere grew into a centre of effective opposition. The opposition essentially, as far as Franz Ferdinand was concerned, was to any policy that in any way changed the *status quo*, pending the day when he would be in a position to change it himself.

Beck, who was probably the best Austrian statesman since Schwarzenberg, and certainly the most likeable, had two great missions, which were interlocking: to keep the Hungarian extremists in check and to make the Austrian Parliament work. In a realm where even the most reasonable liberals, like Josef Redlich, were turning against Parliament in disgust, where the last strong Prime Minister, Koerber, had been content to rule over its head, Beck, a career civil servant, with the trim figure and twirled white moustaches of a cavalry general, proved that Austria could throw up as accomplished and dedicated a parliamentarian as anyone could wish for – could throw up, but could not sustain. He had a clear eye for reality. The most loyal servant of his Emperor, he nevertheless saw that popular nationalism was an elemental force inseparable within the Habsburg realm from that other elemental force of revolutionary progress. To deny the existence of these forces or to regard them, as so many still did, as being purely conspiratorial in nature, was to invite an explosion: they had to be recognized and canalized. He could do nothing about Hungary. He knew all about the perils latent in Magyarization; but he knew that in Magyar eyes, as Prime Minister of Austria, he was only, as Koerber had been before him, 'a distinguished foreign dilettante'. There was only one way of dealing with Hung that was first to negotiate the new decenniel agreement in the teeth of the most violent exhibition of Magyar chauvinism that had been seen since 1848, then to set to work to make Cisleithnia strong and viable so that, at a later date, a more unified Austria could face future Hungarian demands and break them. He tried to get a twenty-year agreement, failed in this, but came back, after a heroic struggle, with a new ten-year agreement (it was to be the last) which made it possible for Vienna and Budapest to continue to co-exist under one head and with a common army. For this he had indeed to make concessions; but later it was agreed, even by some of his bitterest opponents, that he had done better than could possibly have been expected, short of an attempt to compel the Magyars by economic sanctions, which might well have failed disastrously.

Franz Ferdinand could not forgive him for these concessions. Nor could he forgive him for the Universal Suffrage Bill, which was especially detested, for obvious reasons, by his friends the Bohemian landowners. The Universal Suffrage Bill was, in fact, the Emperor's own belated bid to drown the warring factions and make Parliament work by getting the peoples on his side. It did not in fact work out like that, but it was a brave attempt. So, in a less spectacular manner, was the Bill to nationalize the railways. Beck's whole object was to weld the Austrian half of the realm together, economically as well as politically, so that it could stand up to any crisis: the nationalization of the railways was carried out not for doctrinaire reasons, not even for strategic ones, but simply so that the vast and complicated network could be regulated to serve the complex economy of Cisleithnia for the benefit of the whole and of the individual parts. The Beck formula is perhaps best summed up in the words of one of his right-hand men, Sieghart, until he became Governor of the Boden-Credit-Anstalt, the most influential of Austrian government officials, but for personal reasons detested by Franz Ferdinand and his entourage: 'To establish the whole economy as an international possession of all the nationalities of the State, and, within its framework, to develop mutual understanding between the peoples through nationally autonomous institutions.'[31]

This dream, as far as the Austrian half of the Empire was concerned, was interestingly close to the ideal of Popovici and Eichhoff for the whole Empire, which Franz Ferdinand was later to favour. But during Beck's premiership, the Archduke would not hear of it. He was at that time very much under the influence of certain magnates and also, as always, of the Church. All too easily Franz Ferdinand could see in Beck's efforts to hold Parliament together nothing but opportunism of the grossest kind – 'the celebrated Beck', he could write of his old friend, 'who looks for support only to the Social Democrats, the Jews, the Freemasons, and Hungary'.[32] He listened to men like Count Czernin:

> The duty laid upon the ruler by God is to *lead* his people, and if the peoples – as in our Monarchy – are not ripe to behave with reason, then they must be *compelled*. Dictatorship and force are justified, even if they mean a limitation of national right! . . . The Monarchy's way to health lies along the path of Caesarian absolutism! The peoples must first be put under tutelage – then with the passage of time the longing for parliamentarianism will once more awake in them, and then they will know how to cherish this priceless gift of the Crown and behave in a manner worthy of it.[33]

That was in the year of grace 1909, while a concerted attempt was in being to discredit not only Beck himself but, through him, the whole parliamentary system. Franz Ferdinand, not knowing quite what he was doing, presided over this operation, which succeeded all too well. Beck fell, and he was kept down. It was Brosch, no less, who pursued him even after he had fallen, working on Franz Ferdinand's behalf to keep him out of all public posts. He must be barred from all appointments that would keep him in the public eye. 'Let him be regarded as a spent eminence, a dead man, then nobody will talk about him any more. . . .'[34]

And so ended the last attempt to make Parliament work in Imperial Austria. Franz Josef let it happen. But there was an ironic postscript. When in 1918 the Monarchy was on the verge of disintegration and the new young Emperor Karl and his advisers were looking desperately for a strong man who might conceivably hold it together, that same Count Czernin who had worked so hard for Beck's downfall, now began to move heaven and earth to get Beck appointed as the saviour. In 1909 he had written that if at some time historians should have to explain the swift downfall of the Monarchy they would all, to a man, point to Beck as the cause.[35] Now, in 1918, he was 'the only possible man' to save the Monarchy. Almost everybody else agreed. Only the young Emperor resisted. He resisted, most stubbornly, because Franz Ferdinand, his uncle, had so often told him that Beck relied on Sieghart, and that Sieghart was Austria's evil genius.[36] And Franz Ferdinand, of course, had learnt to think this way from Count Czernin and his friends.

Beck was succeeded by Count Bienerth, the Archduke's choice, a man almost totally useless, and then by Count Stürgkh, whose destiny it was to take the country into war. Beck liked Stürgkh, found him amiable, steady and pleasantly cultivated. Like Koerber, he was not a believer in Parliament; unlike Koerber he did not know how to seem to rule through it. He fell back on Paragraph 14 of the constitution, that legacy of Schmerling, and governed by emergency regulations. Beck fought this to the end. In a speech just before the outbreak of the war he said he knew very well what a wonderful thing was Paragraph 14. In the sphere of internal affairs it could do so much, almost everything, indeed: 'Like the man in the fairy-tale it can stamp recruits out of the ground. As the dowser with his forked twig knows how to find water, so Paragraph 14 knows how to find gold. Yes, and this is the most interesting phenomenon of all, like the prophets of a new quackery it knows how to make converts.'[37] That was the last outcry of the man who could tell the Vienna Parliament 'One must will in terms of Parliament, then one will be able to act in terms of Parliament.'[38]

8

The gulf between Franz Ferdinand and Beck was absolute, the gulf between Beck and Aehrenthal scarcely less. Yet Franz Ferdinand quarrelled with Aehrenthal too; and both he and Beck were against the Annexation. It was a strange, tortured muddle which expressed in all its fatality the muted agony of the Empire in its last decade. This splendid parliamentarian had nowhere to turn. At odds with the Heir Apparent and the Imperial Foreign Minister, he should have received support from all those who thought in terms of Parliament. But no support was forthcoming: such was the mood of the times that many of the most articulate and progressive men were joined in desperation with the more outrageous of the exponents of Austria's 'forward' policy, and with Conrad and his demand for preventive wars. These, instead of supporting Beck in his desperate attempt to make sense of the Monarchy in parliamentary terms, turned their backs on Parliament in despair and clamoured for the cleansing fires of action, any action. That distinguished parliamentarian, Josef Redlich, as we have seen, dated the end of parliamentarianism in

Austria from the fall of Badeni. But the real end was when Redlich himself, and others like him, turned his back on the Beck Parliament in 1909 and started calling for war.

It was the convinced belief of Beck that Austria's first task was a domestic spring-cleaning. It was his failure that he was unable to convince either the Emperor or the Foreign Minister, Aehrenthal, that foreign policy must be subordinated to the Empire's internal problems. He could hardly not have failed. Technically neither the Prime Minister of Austria nor the Prime Minister of Hungary was responsible for foreign policy: that remained the Emperor's own province, and the Emperor worked through and with the Austro-Hungarian Minister for Foreign Affairs. Stepan Tisza, or any other Hungarian Prime Minister, could interfere extensively in the policy of the Hofburg and the Ballhausplatz; but this was only because they had the whole blackmailing weight of Magyardom behind them. Neither Beck nor any other Austrian Prime Minister had any such weight: one of Beck's long-seeing aims in trying to make Cisleithnia a unity with a strong and effective Parliament was, precisely, so that he or his successors, speaking for the peoples, should have a stronger voice in foreign affairs: none of his critics understood this in the least. He could only hope to have such a voice if he kept in step with the most forceful politicians of the realm, who, if they could not behave in Parliament, could at least make public opinion. Beck was out of step. He was against war in principle and he was against the Annexation, but his voice counted for nothing beside Aehrenthal's. He was against it for the same reason that he was against war. But there is nothing to show that even he had a clear insight into the terrifying diplomatic impasse into which Aehrenthal, glorying in his victory, and supported by so many who should have known better, was leading the Monarchy. It is clear enough that Franz Ferdinand, who also opposed the Annexation, also lacked that insight.

As previously observed, the European situation at the turn of the century was, for a time, of exceptional fluidity. The flux was due to a number of causes: the emergence of England from her 'splendid isolation'; the new preoccupation of the Powers with empire-building in distant continents and the conflicts arising therefrom; the swift expansion of German industry and the consequent threat directly to British trade, indirectly to Britain's naval supremacy; the abandonment of Bismarck's sedulously cultivated intimacy with St Petersburg; Russia's own efforts to thrust deep into south-east Asia;

the continued decline of Turkey and the new hazards and advantages offered to both Russia and Austria-Hungary by the rise of independent States – Rumania, Bulgaria, Serbia – where the Turks had lately been.

Or, to put it another way: England feared Russian expansion in the Far East, India, Asia Minor and the Balkans; at the same time she was apprehensive of a conflict with France arising from mutual rivalry in Africa; on top of this she could not happily contemplate the prospect of a continent dominated by Germany, especially a Germany challenging her with cheap exports and heavy naval construction.

Russia, deeply committed in Asia and desirous for the time being of an amicably disposed Austria-Hungary on her south-western flank, was nevertheless bound to return sooner or later to her interest in Constantinople. At the same time her relations with Germany, so swiftly developing and allied with Austria, were, after Caprivi's denunciation of Bismarck's Reinsurance Treaty, to say the least, uneasy.

France was active in Africa, jealous of England and at the same time revengeful and fearful towards Germany.

Italy, technically a member of the Triple Alliance, was drawn increasingly to France, was deeply stirred by irredentist longings at the expense of Austria, and was also intent on strengthening her position in the Adriatic – at Austria's expense.

Austria-Hungary itself was dependent on the maintenance of the *status quo*. She had to keep an eye on Italy; she had to keep on the best of terms with Serbia, or crush her while there was time, or, by domestic action, decisively neutralize the potential appeal of Belgrade to her own South Slavs; she had either to keep on the best of terms with Russia, or else ally herself firmly with Russia's natural enemies.

The key was England; but nobody saw it. This 'most calculating, deceitful and unreliable ally on earth' also happened to be the strongest maritime Power on earth, with the strongest interest in curtailing the pretensions of Russia and, therefore, of maintaining order in the Balkans and sustaining Turkey in her guardianship of the Straits. Here was a situation with which the heirs of Kaunitz, and Metternich – of Schwarzenberg, Andrassy and Kalnocky too – should have made hay. But far from exploiting it, they did not even perceive it.

Austrian Balkan policy had ignored peoples: it had been based on agreements, often secret, with princes, who were liable to fall or be corrupted. Its general aim had been to keep Russia at arm's length; hence, for example, the immense importance attached by Vienna to the secret defensive alliance with Rumania, an alliance that was rotted from within by the behaviour of Budapest towards its own Rumanian subjects. France achieved her *entente* with Russia in 1891, followed by the military convention a year later. Austria was then in control of Obrenović Serbia by virtue of a secret agreement (some years earlier King Milan had offered union with Austria-Hungary, but this had been refused by Kalnocky, partly because Russia would not have stood for it, partly because the Serbs themselves would have revolted). The pattern was fairly fixed when, in the last year of the nineteenth century, England suddenly came into the market and, in effect, offered herself to the highest bidder. The attitude of the Powers during the Boer War had shown not only that she was friendless, but, more than this, that the continent of Europe was united in glee to see her arrogance so humbled. She had to have a friend. In spite of the inept irresponsibility of the Kruger telegram, the natural friend appeared to be Germany, so closely bound by dynastic ties. Wilhelm appeared to think so too. Defying his own domestic public opinion, he embarked on a State visit to London in November 1899, and ten days later, at Leicester, Joseph Chamberlain publicly announced that 'it must have appeared evident to everybody that the natural alliance is between ourselves and the great German Empire'. An awesome prospect opened out before the world: Britain allied with Germany, and, through her, with Austria-Hungary certainly, with Italy perhaps, in face of the Franco-Russian array. Bismarck had been in his grave just eighteen months.

But it was not to be. Von Bülow, who before very long was to be screaming across the telegraph wires of Europe that Austria must be supported up to the hilt over Bosnia because she was Germany's only friend, was in a manic mood. Where Bismarck had prudently sought security and power through his delicate system of alliances, his irredeemably inept successor was determined at all costs to throw his weight about. Inheriting the dire figure of Baron Holstein as head of the political section of the Berlin Foreign Office, he fell, as Caprivi had briefly fallen before him, under the spell of this monument of German obtuseness – the sort of obtuseness which, oblivious of reality, not only expects people and nations to conduct themselves along preordained lines but, worse than this, is incapable of registering the fact when they do not. Baron Holstein's theory was that the Triple Alliance of Germany, Austria and Italy would look after itself (he, of course, would see to that), and form a durable and overwhelming coalition, whereas France, Russia and England existed in a state of such exacerbated rivalry that they could never in any circumstances come together. He was so sure of this that he thought Germany could play with fire, not only holding the balance between East and West, but also, as occasion arose, and, indeed, sometimes just for the fun of it, blackmailing the individual Powers. No man was more surprised than he when, belatedly, the incompatibles got together to resist these affronts: he was more than surprised; he was outraged. For, in doing so, they were defying Holstein's Law, which he took to be a law of nature. Indeed, it very nearly was a law of nature, for France, Russia and England would certainly never have come together if Holstein had not with every gesture, with every tortuous scheme and stratagem, insisted that they must.

Thus it was that Wilhelm's initiative and Joseph Chamberlain's response were nullified within three weeks by von Bülow, who, on 11 December proclaimed to an interested world: 'The times of our political anaemia and economic and political humility must not recur. In the coming century the German people will be either the hammer or the anvil.' Thus it was that the Germans went on supplying the Boers, giving rise to the seizure by British warships of a German ship carrying contraband cargo. This incident played straight into the hands of the German Navy League and enabled them to put through the German Navy Bill which, in 1900, doubled the existing building programme and started the naval race in earnest. But even then all was not lost. Wilhelm did the right thing when Queen Victoria died, and once more, in 1901, there was talk of an Anglo-German alliance. The thing went a long way. By the spring of 1901 negotiations came to a head, in spite of Holstein's and Bülow's indignation with the British for declaring openly that, since they had to ally themselves with somebody, they would have to turn to Russia and France if they could not get on with Germany. The negotiations finally broke down because Holstein required a guarantee that Britain would go to the aid of Germany should she, Germany, be required to support one of her own allies – a situation which, in fact, arose in July 1914. . . . Had the alliance been achieved, Britain would then have found herself going to war with Germany and Austria against Serbia, France and Russia. The whole affair was clearly a pipe-dream. In the climate of the times there could in fact have been no formal alliance. German public opinion was not in a mood to guarantee the British Empire; British public opinion was not in a mood to guarantee the Habsburg Empire. But with care and imagination on both sides some sort of arrangement short of a formal alliance might well have been made to stop the naval race and to prevent a situation arising in which Germany would feel that she had no option but to support the war party in Austria. What is interesting about this whole episode is that Chamberlain's and Lansdowne's strenuous efforts to conclude an alliance with Germany at the turn of the century made nonsense in advance of the position adopted by Grey during the 1914 crisis when he took the line that Britain could not conceivably, in any circumstances, commit herself to military action in advance of any impending conflict between her enemies and her friends.

9

Austria, astonishingly, stood outside all this. Without anybody noticing it, her horizon had narrowed. She was still a Great Power, although in that last decade she spent far less on her armed forces than any other Power, less, even, than Italy.[39] From 1897 until 1908 she had been content to keep the peace with Russia while maintaining an alliance with Germany which could not in any circumstances be questioned. Naturally she desired friendly relations with Britain and France, but neither Franz Josef nor his Ministers, first Goluchowski, then Aehrenthal, showed themselves capable of making a serious attempt to enter into the thoughts and apprehensions of the British or the French. They were content to see both through the eyes of Germany, which meant through the eyes of Holstein and Bülow, to minimize, as we have seen, the inherent perils of the naval competition, and to echo unthinkingly the charge of encirclement which, with the creation of the Entente, was to become an obsession with Berlin. It did not even occur to them that they and the Germans meant different things by encirclement and that they could not both be right. When in 1904 Britain achieved her Entente with France and, three years later, her Convention with Russia, Aehrenthal – and, indeed, almost all Austrians who thought about these things – took it as axiomatic that Russia was allying herself with England and

France in order to carry out far-reaching designs on the Monarchy; Wilhelm II and Bülow, on the other hand, took it as equally axiomatic that England was actively engaged in welding Russia and France into a vast coalition aimed at Germany. Few in Berlin or Vienna seem to have been aware of this confusion, much less made any effort to clear it up. Gone for ever were the days when the Monarchy had sought its alliances far and wide, when what happened in London and Paris was of no less intimate concern to her than what happened in Petersburg or Berlin. One of the Monarchy's most gifted and unfair critics, Louis Eisenmann, wrote apropos of the October Diploma: 'In a critical moment for the Monarchy, traditional Austrian politics were incapable of modifying themselves, of changing their nature, of correcting their faults. They worked always by little means in large issues; they considered always, above all, Europe, forgetting Austria.'[40] But now Austria had forgotten Europe. And it was in this new and blinkered attitude towards the European picture as a whole that the real abdication of Habsburg power was revealed. The whole vast diplomatic and military apparatus of one of the great pillars of the old European order was now concentrated obsessionally on events taking place, as it were, in its own backyard. Bulgaria and Rumania became more important than England and France, Serbia and Italy more important than the rest of Europe put together. The highest flight of diplomacy to which the Ballhausplatz would aspire was a secret treaty with Rumania, which was a simple expedient of military strategy. On Austro-Rumanian relations Franz Ferdinand, who held King Carol and his family in highest reverence, lavished all his care. But although on his world tour he had been deeply impressed by the British as Imperial administrators and had returned with a conviction that to maintain her greatness in a changing world the Monarchy too must begin to think in terms of sea-power;[41] and although he made two visits to England, it never occurred to him that he might do anything to bring that strange, perfidious, above all Protestant, Empire (but Berlin was Protestant too) into fruitful co-operation with his own. Instead he allowed his prejudices free play: the thing that struck him most when he came to London for King Edward's funeral was the extraordinary spectacle of the King's horse, led with an empty saddle, with the King's riding-boots in the stirrups turned the wrong way round, and followed by the King's rough-haired terrier on a lead.[42] This struck him as bizarre to the point of offensiveness.

Besides King Carol there was one other monarch whom he respected greatly (he began by disliking him intensely) and that was Wilhelm II of Germany. It was an unlikely friendship between the suspicious, misanthropic Habsburg and the upstart Hohenzollern, flamboyant, loquacious, bursting with wishful thinking, and carrying braggartry to the point of the inane. But it was a genuine friendship all the same. It was founded on Wilhelm's championship of Sophie Chotek and it throve on Wilhelm's flattery and his desire for peace. Franz Ferdinand needed flattery and he also wanted peace. The Kaiser offered both.

At the time of Franz Ferdinand's marriage in 1900 Wilhelm was forty-one to the Archduke's thirty-seven. He set out deliberately to charm and flatter and woo the heir to the Monarchy with all his remarkable dynamism. He was clearly working with an eye to the future, when Franz Ferdinand would be Emperor, and the main tasks he set himself were to strengthen the Austro-German alliance and at the same time to check further Balkan adventures into which Germany might be dragged, or which might upset her own plans for peaceful penetration in the direction of Asia Minor and the Middle East. To this end, he wrote not as a ruling Monarch to a Crown Prince, but as a friend to an equal and contemporary. He began to weave the spell by standing stoutly, demonstratively indeed, by Franz Ferdinand on the issue of his marriage. He alone, with the solitary exception of King Carol of Rumania, another Hohenzollern, pleaded Sophie Chotek's cause; and, once the marriage had taken place, he alone accorded to the bride the honour and respect due to the consort of the heir to the throne. This was at a time, before Sophie's elevation to be a Duchess, when she was not allowed to appear at the dinner-table of her own house, the Belvedere, if royalty (including Wilhelm II) was being entertained, or to sit with her husband in the royal box at the Opera.

There can be no doubt at all that the German Emperor was able to influence Franz Ferdinand very considerably. At first sight it is hard to believe that a dyed-in-the-wool sceptic, of the kind the Archduke appeared to be, could have swallowed the sort of flattery dispensed so lavishly by Wilhelm, or that a high and mighty dynast who knew his own domestic problems inside out could have put up with the superficial nonsense about the relationships between the component parts of the Empire of which Wilhelm delivered himself, often in insufferably patronizing terms, in letters which have only lately been made accessible.[43] Even the physical aspect of those letters, as of all Wilhelm's letters – the crabbed, crossed, almost hysterical handwriting, the unfinished sentences, the breathless incoherence, and, beneath all, the megalomania of the colossal and flamboyant signature – would have made most men raise their eyebrows. But Franz Ferdinand was pleased with them. There are few replies in existence to prove this; but there is plenty of internal evidence. It is also perfectly understandable. Wilhelm was a 'strong' ruler, a constitutional monarch who was not happy unless he could play the autocrat, and whose dramatic gestures concealed a vacillating spirit; Franz Ferdinand, also by nature vacillating, wished to be a strong ruler too. Wilhelm assiduously encouraged him in the belief that he could be strong, and he needed reassurance desperately: he was a very lonely man, carried into extreme positions more often than not by pride and obstinacy rather than by conviction. Wilhelm wanted peace, but on his own terms; Franz Ferdinand did not at all clearly comprehend the terms, but he found immense moral support when Wilhelm endorsed and strengthened his own beliefs – especially in the face of Conrad von Hötzendorf. At the time of the Balkan wars, when the war party was in full cry for violent action to clear the Serbs out of Albania, the war for 'a few miserable goat-pastures', to use Wilhelm's phrase, Franz Ferdinand stood out for peace against a positive uproar from those who believed that Austria-Hungary must fight now or go under. Wilhelm wrote to him twice: first about 'the intolerable tension which has been bearing so heavily on Europe for the past six months':

> To lift it would be a truly epoch-making act of peace, worthy of an *energetic* man who has the *moral* courage to speak the redeeming word, even though it might not be understood at once everywhere, and even though it might make him unpopular with single groups for the moment. Therefore I ask myself often whether the issues at stake here – for example the goat-pastures of Scutari and similar things – are really important enough to justify you and Russia facing each other still half mobilized. . . .[44]

And then, two days later, on 28 February 1913, when Franz Ferdinand had written (the letter does not exist) to say that all would be well: and that there would be no war:

> How immensely pleased I was with your kind letter! One may rightly say in this case *Les beaux esprits se rencontrent!* Bravo my

friend! You have fingered and executed this brilliantly! I am sure it was not easy and that the sacrifice called for effort, patience, and perseverance. But the final success compensates for all the injuries sustained. You have won undying merit for saving Europe from this oppressive spell. Millions of grateful hearts will remember you in prayer. I think the Emperor Nicholas will also be glad that he can send home his reserves![45]

It was a young Hohenzollern prince who, in 1282, had brought the news of his election to be Holy Roman Emperor to Rudolf of Habsburg, in the middle of the night as he lay before Bâle. It was a Hohenzollern king who had shattered at Königgrätz the pretensions of a Habsburg to the leadership of the Germans. Now a Hohenzollern Emperor was, with an insupportable mixture of condescension and inanity, congratulating the heir to the Habsburg Crown on following a course recommended by him which had already been firmly determined on not only by Franz Ferdinand but also, and more importantly, by Franz Josef. The waste-paper basket, one would have thought, was the proper place for these effusions; but not a bit of it; Franz Ferdinand was pleased enough to be moved to show certainly one, probably both, of these letters to Conrad as a partial justification of his own attitude towards peace and war.

This is important, because it brings us round to the fatal blindness of Franz Ferdinand, Aehrenthal, and the rest to the perilous situation produced by the growing hostility between Germany and England. By 1908, at the time of the Annexation crisis whereby Aehrenthal so wantonly and irretrievably set the Monarchy at loggerheads with Russia, so that Izvolsky and his successor Sazonov were henceforth dedicated to the task of laying Austria-Hungary low, England had cleared her own decks. By reaching agreement with St Petersburg about Persia and India she had not only brought into being the Triple Entente, but had also made it possible for Russia to concentrate her energies and her capacity for intrigue on the Balkans. There was a contradiction here, of course: sooner or later, if Russia proved too energetic, there was bound to be an Anglo-Russian clash over the Straits, and it was this contradiction, above all, which encouraged Aehrenthal to believe that no Anglo-Russian understanding could be permanent (why then, did he so fear the encirclement?); but permanency is a relative conception. The Russia Aehrenthal so sharply offended in 1908 was a Russia now bound up to some considerable degree with England and France. And the England Germany was challenging was an England bound up with Russia and France. They screamed about encirclement, but they behaved as though it did not exist. The general attitude of Wilhelm II is an old, familiar story; even so, his correspondence with Franz Ferdinand offers fascinating sidelights on his morbid inferiority complex towards England, with its love-hate overtones, and his hopelessly inaccurate estimates of the British national character. What is relevant to this narrative is the way in which the whole vertiginous peril was displayed again and again, year after year, to Vienna, and how the Ballhausplatz in general and Franz Ferdinand in particular failed to draw the most obvious conclusions.

Thus, in a letter dated 12 February 1909, Wilhelm uttered the most reassuring sounds about the naval arms race. Edward VII had just made a State visit to Berlin at a time when the whole rather desperate aim of Britain's German policy was to get the German naval construction programme revised; yet the German Emperor could write of the English King that 'he fully recognized the legitimacy of the German standpoint' and that the implementation of the Navy Bill 'does not disturb him in any way'.[46] This lunatic assertion appears to have aroused in Franz Ferdinand no misgivings whatsoever. Nearly three years later, on 6 December 1911, Wilhelm is taking a very different line: 'To judge by the attitude of the English during the past six months – Grey's twaddle makes no difference to this – we had to count on possible tricks from them and take measures against them in the form of increased construction. Only strong power and brute force impresses these people on the other side of the channel. Politeness is considered weakness.'[47] And only three days later he is back with another tirade, this time about Lord Haldane's warning to Lichnowsky, the German Ambassador in London. Haldane, says Wilhelm, bursting with righteous indignation (no doubt because England was not being impressed with brute force), had told Lichnowsky that (in the Emperor's words) 'if Germany through her siding with Austria should become involved in a war with France and Russia, England without further ado would join France. She *could not tolerate* that we defeat France and that the *continent* should be *united* under Germany's influence. . . .' Then, after an outburst about Haldane's peace mission of the previous February and England's 'venom, hatred and envy', he goes on: 'I was not taken by surprise. It is a welcome clarification which puts the soothing assurances of the British Press about peace and friendship into their true perspective. It clearly reveals their policy in Europe – balance of power – in its naked shamelessness, playing the Great Powers against each other to England's advantage.'[48]

That was five months after the Agadir crisis, engineered by Kiderlen-Wächter, whose idea of diplomacy was to stamp on his neighbour's foot and display aggrieved surprise if he received a kick in return. It is clear enough now that neither Wilhelm II nor anybody else who mattered in Germany wanted a European war, but it did not look like that at the time. And, as we have seen, already four months before that letter, and a month after Agadir, Aehrenthal, half dead with cancer, but still grimly holding on to office because he could not bring himself to lay his burden at the feet of his Emperor, so much older, who himself had suffered so much,[49] had come to the conclusion that the ultimately deciding factor, which would make any Austrian initiative vain, was Anglo-German rivalry. He saw it too late, and threw up his hands in despair.

Others never saw it. Franz Ferdinand should have seen it, should have been alarmed and driven to action by Wilhelm's attitude and words, and, having seen it, should have used his friendship to warn and persuade Berlin, or, if that failed, his influence to divide the Entente, even if it meant loosening the rigid bonds with Germany. All, all were obsessed by the idea of encirclement: they stared at it hypnotized. Indeed, it existed. The encirclement of the Central Powers by England, France and Russia, with Serbia and Italy operating on the fringe, was real enough: that was the pattern. Looking at the matter from the point of view of Berlin and Vienna it was important to discover as objectively as possible what was the key to this pattern: was it, as the Austrians were convinced for so long, until Aehrenthal's dying vision, Russia manipulating England and France to crush the Monarchy? Was it, as Wilhelm believed, England manipulating Russia and France to hamstring Germany? This confusion was never resolved. More elementary still, it was very much in the interests of Austria-Hungary to discover whether the encirclement, no matter who was its inspiration, was aggressive or defensive. If it was aggressive, then it was clearly dangerous, so dangerous that Vienna's whole diplomatic force, which was still considerable, should have been directed at breaking it; then, too, there would have been everything to be said for Conrad's policy of picking off Italy and Serbia while there was still time. If, on the other hand, it was defensive, quite a small effort of diplomatic imagination could have discovered this fact. The effort was never made. Aggressiveness was assumed and yet not countered. Germany in her manic state thought she could neutralize the encirclement by frightening now the English, now the French; in her depressive state she was content to wallow in self-pity. Franz Josef, exhausted and very old, could be forgiven for clinging to the German alliance and to Dualism as in honour bound. Franz Ferdinand, committed to saving the Monarchy by smashing Dualism, proved incapable of saving it by diplomacy on a European scale. In this he had failed as Emperor before ever he wore the crown, and this failure turned his death into the occasion for the ruin of the Empire.

CHAPTER EIGHTEEN

THE ROAD TO SARAJEVO

It was a strange paralysis: the Franco-Russian alliance; Germany's refusal of British overtures at the century's turn; Bülow holding forth about being the hammer or the anvil; Algeciras; the Anglo-French Entente; the Anglo-Russian convention; the naval building race; Agadir. . . . From 1891 to 1911 Vienna watched the great European crisis like a hypnotized hen, incapable of warning Germany, incapable of talking sensibly with Britain or France, incapable after the one convulsive moment of assertion in 1908 of talking sensibly with Russia. Of course, as everybody knew, her internal problems made her position one of excessive delicacy; of course Magyar blackmail made the solution of those problems one of excessive difficulty. But there was nothing in them to inhibit constructive diplomatic action of all kinds. Beck, very naturally, wanted stability at home to come first. But had he been allowed to go on working for it, there was nothing to prevent Aehrenthal as Foreign Minister and Franz Ferdinand as the friend of Wilhelm II and the venerator of the Russian Tsar from questioning the inevitability of the direful impasse into which the Monarchy had allowed itself to drift and then taking action to escape from it. It was a failure not only of imagination but of mind.

Aehrenthal was succeeded by Berchtold, and still the drift continued. The voices of those who, almost hysterically, wanted to end the drift by violent action grew more strident. But the action they wanted to take – war on Serbia – was essentially peripheral. Josef Redlich who, after he ceased behaving like a parliamentarian and before he became a philosopher looking back across the storm, was as violent as any in his demands for violent action – *any* action, action to escape 'the burden of the brain' – saw with his own eyes the real situation, and recorded it in his diary – and yet failed, as Aehrenthal had failed, to draw from it the necessary conclusions. That was in April 1913, after the Balkan wars, when the smashing victory over the Turks by the Balkan League of Serbia, Bulgaria and Greece, sponsored and inspired by Russia, and then the defeat of Bulgaria by

Serbia and Rumania, had at last made reality of Conrad's worst fears. Redlich visited London.

> I found among a section of the Liberals a genuine desire to reach an understanding with Germany. Even so, these people, too, misunderstand Germany so deeply that they see in the army increase and the supplementary estimates the possibility of a German aggression. The great masses are Germanophobe – far more than they were ever Francophobe, and will remain so for a very long time. Germany is too strong for the English and fills them with apprehension as a European Power. Thus it was that the treaty of 1908 [sic] was concluded with Russia, thus it was that they sacrificed Persia and China to Tsarism! Austria-Hungary on the other hand is seen as being very weak, but even so as highly awkward: again above all in connection with Germany, whose satellite she appears to be. In London they would gladly see the Monarchy shattered: for the ideal of English policy is the formation of small States in Europe which can be played against each other. That is why they are now enthusiasts for Serbia, Greece, Bulgaria, even Montenegro. . . . In England they now want peace at any price, because business is going splendidly and England still needs several years to build her auxiliary fleets in India, Australia and Canada. . . .[1]

And here is Ottakar Czernin's *cri de cœur*, uttered from Bucharest a year later and just six days before the assassination at Sarajevo:

> Before our eyes the encirclement of the Monarchy proceeds in the full light of day, openly and explicitly, crystal clear, with shameless explicitness, step by step; under Russian patronage a new Balkan League is being welded together – against the Monarchy! And we stand by with folded arms watching with interest the progress of this deployment.[2]

This was also true – though what had suddenly, since Bismarck's day, become 'shameless' about the construction of alliances (Wilhelm had also used that epithet in the same sort of context) it is hard to tell. For the final failure of Aehrenthal and Berchtold, of Franz Josef and Franz Ferdinand, was that between them they proved themselves incapable of arranging matters sensibly in their own backyard.

Thus there was a good deal to be said for Conrad's policy of striking at Serbia, even at Italy, while there was still time. He went on about it in and out of season, until in 1911, Franz Josef rounded on him: 'I tell you here and now that I forbid these perpetual attacks and pinpricks directed at Aehrenthal. . . . They are really directed against me; it is *I* who make policy, and this is *my* policy.' Even in face of that Conrad went on arguing, but Franz Josef cut him short: 'My policy is a policy of peace. With this policy everyone must comply. In this sense my Foreign Minister is carrying out my policy. It is possible that it will come to war, even probable. But there will be no war until Italy attacks us. . . . Until now we have never had a war party.'[3]

That was on 15 November 1911, when Italy was embroiled in her war with Turkey, and when Conrad was making his final effort to use the last opportunity for a preventive war against Italy, Serbia and Montenegro in order to establish the Monarchy's position once for all in the Balkans with one hand, while, with the other, achieving some sort of permanent agreement with Russia. A fortnight later Franz Josef was to send for Conrad again to tell him that he was no longer Chief-of-Staff.

The attitude of Franz Josef and Aehrenthal, and, in this matter of war and peace, of Franz Ferdinand too, would have made better sense if they had pursued with imagination and conviction the alternative path to war. They did not do this. Until the Annexation, Aehrenthal had been intent on coming to terms with Serbia, but the row that followed, ending with Serbia and Austria-Hungary, up in arms and standing on the brink of war, left so much bitterness that neither side could see the other clearly. Even when Pašić later on made conciliatory gestures, Aehrenthal, though he would not fight, was too proud and angry to respond. Out of this mood the whole South Slav movement grew, aggravated especially by the dynasty's negative attitude towards the Croats. While Hungary was favouring her own Serbs in the Voivodina and the no-man's-land Serbs in Bosnia-Herzegovina (for no reason at all but to spite the Croats), Vienna would not raise a finger to help those same Croats, for the most part loyal to the Monarchy, who were thus driven on the one hand to try to make their own deal with Budapest, and on the other to develop their own South Slav movement. This movement received impetus from two court actions which dragged on in Zagreb throughout 1909.

Although there was no love lost between Serbs and Croats, and although the Serbs of Belgrade had no desire for any sort of union with the Croats, there were, nevertheless, cross-currents at work, and certain Croat politicians entered into conspiracy with certain

Belgrade Serbs. The Austrians knew this was going on, and struck. Unfortunately their knowledge was inadequate in detail, and they struck so clumsily that when at the Zagreb high-treason trial they tried to nail the conspiracy down they failed completely. The accused were sentenced, but the trial was so clearly corrupt that they had to be pardoned by the Emperor.

A consequence of this was the famous libel action brought by Serbo-Croat leaders against the distinguished historian, Friedjung. This great writer, who was a patriot as well as a scholar, had written a series of articles to justify the war that did not come, and these were found to be based on forged evidence supplied by the Austrian Minister in Belgrade. Neither Aehrenthal nor Friedjung had questioned this evidence, which was soon shown up for what it was for all the world to see. But all the evidence suggests that the Austrian Minister in Belgrade was the dupe of a clever fraud. Much has been made of Aehrenthal's guilt in this matter. Far too much, and with disastrous consequences. Aehrenthal himself was deceived, no less than Friedjung. And he had reason to be deceived, since, although Friedjung's documents were forgeries, a conspiracy of sorts did in fact exist. The tragedy was that the scandal of the Friedjung trial coming on top of the scandal of the Zagreb treason trial, made it easy for the enemies of the Monarchy to discredit Aehrenthal, and, through him, Austria. The real guilt of Aehrenthal lay in the fact that once the forgeries had been exposed and admitted he did not seize immediately the opportunity to re-establish reasonable relations with Serbia. Instead, while denouncing the conception of preventive war in quite specific terms, he went on behaving like a man preparing for war. His attitude to Italy was similarly ambivalent. If he was not going to fight Italy he must make a serious attempt to come to terms with her; if this failed, then at least the pretence of Italian membership of the Triple Alliance could be given up and Vienna could think again. This was not done.

Behind the Rumanian alliance, based on a secret treaty of 1883, there was the same sort of muddle. Vienna set great store by this alliance and devoted much energy and ingenuity to trying to maintain it. There was, indeed, a good deal to be said for it from a purely strategic point of view: 'Rumania formed as it were the pivot upon which the two great rivals could make the minor Balkan Powers revolve', to quote Seton Watson, 'and her adhesion meant a very great strategic advantage to one side or the other. To the Austrians she meant an addition of five army corps on the right flank, within striking distance of Odessa: to the Russians she gave direct access to Bulgaria and Serbia and the possibility of invading Hungary through the unfortified Transylvanian passes.'[4] That was all very fine, and the enticement of Rumania into the Russian camp became a main object of Sazonov's policy, which in the end succeeded. The only thing was that as time went on the 'minor Balkan Powers' ceased to be minor, so that Rumania became progressively of less importance. Further, it was quite hopeless for Vienna to expect permanent friendship with Rumania so long as the irredentist movement in Transylvania persisted, fostered by Bucharest.

Thus, while in the large world of Europe the Monarchy allowed Germany led first by Bülow then by Bethmann-Hollweg to drag her into isolation, in its own sphere, the Balkans, things went from bad to worse. When, in 1913, Serbia had trounced Bulgaria in the Second Balkan War, Austria found herself faced with a tough and brash new Power, looking for new worlds to conquer, which she had done nothing to placate and everything to infuriate. The only fruit of the long-drawn-out London Conference designed to sort out the aftermath of this war was Austria's successful bid to make the Serbs evacuate the Adriatic coast by setting up an independent Albania – and even this had to be a joint affair with Italy, who thus obtained at last her foothold on the Eastern Adriatic. The idea was that at all costs Serbia must be kept away from independent Montenegro, then an enclave in Bosnia-Herzegovina: if Montenegro went, then Bosnia and Dalmatia would go too. But by now it was too late. Belgrade had not been in the least interested in the South Slav idea until after the Balkan wars, but only in Greater Serbia. The South Slav idea was nurtured in Croatia as a direct result of the Monarchy's shortcomings. But now that Greater Serbia had been achieved, the Belgrade politicians began to think increasingly in racial terms. These had in effect been laid down for them in advance by the Monarchy itself, which had conjured the South Slav problem out of nothing by its treatment of the Croats, who wanted only to be loyal, and which, at the same time, had exacerbated Serb nationalism by its refusal to come to terms with a neighbour it did not wish to fight – if only for the reason that it would not have known what to do with Serbia, or any part of it, after a victorious campaign.

The Serbian government did not want to fight either – at any rate not yet (the army was exhausted after the Balkan wars), and not without Russia. But the Serbian government was not strong enough to control the activities of its own extremists, who, more and more, were finding a happy hunting-ground among the young Bosnian Serbs who were sharpening their knives, driven partly by Serb nationalism as such, still more by hatred of their own landlords, feudal tyrants inherited by the Turks and maintained in power by the anachronistic extension of Schmerling's electoral geometry to the most backward and primitive country in the realm.

It was against this background that Franz Ferdinand went to meet his death at Sarajevo on 28 June 1914.

2

The conspirators in Sarajevo on that June day in 1914 were all very young. They were fanatical student revolutionaries, of the type found in every backward country in Europe in those days. Since they were Bosnian Serbs living under Austrian rule, their revolutionary ardour took the form of Serb nationalism. None of them had known anything but Austrian rule. To be nineteen and a Bosnian in 1914 meant having been born into a world in which Turkish violence, cruelty and corruption were nothing but a memory. Although the Bosnians had resisted the Austrian occupation in 1878 by force, it was soon clear to most of them that their new masters brought great blessings. The country was ruled in an orderly way, but with a perfect lack of imagination, in the best colonial tradition: the colonists built roads and fine public buildings. They provided schools, but not enough. They brought material prosperity on a quite remarkable scale. But they were the masters of an alien race, and their symbol was the barracks. Their administration was carried out under nominal Turkish sovereignty, and they did not interfere with the big landowners, whose existence in the past had maintained the national soul – even though many turned Moslem to survive – but now was a drag on the development of the poor peasantry.

At the time of the Annexation, in 1908, Gavrilo Princip, Nedjelko Čabrinović and Trifko Grabež were all thirteen. Princip, the son of a postman, and Grabež, the son of an Orthodox priest, did their schooling first in Bosnia and then in Belgrade, and, while they were at school, became coffee-house revolutionaries. Čabrinović had a rather different background: his father was an Austrian police spy, and he left school at fourteen to become a printer and a socialist. All three were soon caught up in the activities of a terrorist organization known as Union of Death, or the Black Hand. The Black Hand was founded in 1911 to achieve a Greater Serbia through violent and conspiratorial means. In fact it proved to be nothing but an embarrassment to the Serbian government under Nikola Pašić, and its only successful deed of any note was the assassination of Franz Ferdinand and his wife: this indeed achieved a greater Serbia, but not of the kind envisaged by the Black Hand leaders, and at a cost from which even their strong man, Colonel Dragutin Dimitrijević or 'Apis', would have shrunk. The Black Hand knew nothing about foreign politics or the balance of power. It knew only that Serbia must first win Macedonia from Turkey, then Bosnia-Herzegovina from Austria – and that the Russian agents in Belgrade would help them as much as they dared. Austria was afraid of Serbia, by which it meant the government of King Peter and Nikola Pašić. The profound irony was that the men who arranged the killing of the Heir Apparent and thus goaded Vienna into belated action had nothing to do with official Serbian policy, and their instruments, Princip and his friends, were characters out of a play by Chekhov, so remote from reality and the great political movement which Vienna feared that in the eyes of Austrian authority they did not exist.

3

The legend of 'gallant little Serbia' (or Servia, as they used to call it), which sprang to life as soon as England found herself at war with Germany and Austria-Hungary in August 1914, at once obscured the fact that for the previous decade Serbia had been regarded generally as a thorough-going nuisance, a nest of violent barbarians whose megalomania would sooner or later meet with the punishment it deserved. There had been several occasions when the rest of Europe fully expected to see Austria lash out and wipe Serbia off the map.

On the face of it there was good reason for this. The circumstances of Peter Karageorgević's accession in 1903 were of an atrocity unparalleled in Europe outside Russia and the Scottish Highlands for many centuries. The shock was so great that England and Holland were constrained to break off diplomatic relations with Belgrade. Many believed that Pašić himself had connived at this crime. In June 1914, eleven years later, there was hardly a soul in Europe who did not believe that the assassination of the Austrian Heir Apparent had been directly engineered by the Pašić government: it was taken for granted that Austria would react swiftly and sharply, and with every justification. In fact it took a month for Austria to react, and, when she did, it was to start a European war.

It is necessary to be clear about the Serbs. This nation of proud and often splendid individuals has become familiar to us now. Everything in us which is attracted by the primitive, the unbending and the brave, responds to the appeal of these mountain warriors from the medieval Serbian heartland and their magnificent and heroic women who for centuries have borne the yoke as though it were a crown. But it takes more than an aggregation of splendid individuals to make a civilized society; and the extremes of bravery and self-reliance go all too easily with the extremes of treachery and cruelty. Centuries of existence under oppression may bring out the best in a people, but it may also magnify the worst. The manners of the oppressed are all too likely to take their colour from the manners of the oppressors; when the oppressors are Turkish Janissaries the result is likely to be bad. Further, the habit of conspiratorial violence which may be just the thing in a resistance movement operating against a tyranny is apt to be continued, with undesirable consequences, when the tyranny has been overthrown. Serbia proper achieved its final independence from the Turks in 1878 and had certainly not freed its government of the Turkish taint by 1914.[5] Aspects of this were clearly visible in the conduct of both Pašić and Dimitrijević. Pašić, who was a genuine radical at home but an ardent pan-Serb abroad, was a master of dissimulation and deceit. His particular talent was for establishing alibis: when violent courses were imminent he contrived to be well away from Belgrade. He could not be found, for example, at the time of the palace revolution in 1903, which he certainly knew about in advance, and from which he profited. In 1914, a venerable elder statesman with a serene manner and a large and silky beard, he was far away on an election tour when the Sarajevo crime took place, about which he also knew in advance, though he had tried to stop it. He survived to become the first Prime Minister of independent Yugoslavia. Apis was a very different sort of man. Thirty-seven at the time of the Sarajevo crime, he believed in violence, and he dominated the central committee of the Black Hand, of which he was nominally only one among ten. He had a brilliant military career behind him and, at twenty-six, had taken a leading and active part in the killing of King Alexander and Queen Draga. Wounds received in that operation made him unfit to fight in the Balkan wars. Instead, he had risen to be Chief of Intelligence on the Serbian General Staff, a position that suited him very well. His first activities, directed at the recovery of Macedonia from the Turks, met with full official approval: the Crown Prince, Peter, was supposed to have subscribed heavily to the funds of the Black Hand.[6] But he had then been by-passed by history. Turkish power in Macedonia and Albania and Greece was, in the event, broken not by the Black Hand but by conventional military operations conducted by the Balkan League (Serbia, Bulgaria and Greece) in 1911 and 1912. Dimitrijević then became a nuisance to Pašić: there was a great quarrel which Dimitrijević lost as to whether the newly acquired territories should have civilian or military rule. But the Black Hand, though ineffective in action, was strong in influence. It operated under cover of the National Defence League (*Narodny Obranje*), which had become a fairly innocuous patriotic society enjoying official recognition. Pašić could not afford to take strong measures against the Black Hand, because these could have been represented as a pro-Austrian attack on the best patriotic elements in the country. He could not afford to expose the Black Hand for what it was, because he was too deeply compromised with guilty knowledge of its terroristic activities. He was the victim of his own deceit. Dimitrijević, bounding, limitlessly energetic, an impassioned patriot, a believer in terror and assassination, was heavily reinforced by the Russian military attaché, Captain Artamanov, who lavished on him subsidies and assurances of Russian support should Serb nationalist activities provoke Austria into making war on Serbia.[7] For a long time Austria had been obsessed with the image of Serbia as the Piedmont of the Balkans. Apis, in 1911, gave colour to that obsession by producing his own newspaper, called *Piemont*. The Austrians knew all about the innocuous *Narodny Obranje* and its official connections (if any Black Hand member was caught crossing the border into Bosnia he at once admitted membership of that body); but they knew nothing at all about the Black Hand itself beyond the bare fact of its existence. Considering that its main theatre of operations from 1912 onwards formed a part of a State which set so much store by its network of police informers this ignorance was surprising. Had the Austrian police done their duty, the blame for the assassination could have been fixed fairly and squarely where it belonged, the head of Dimitrijević demanded, and Pašić left to swim for his life:

no Power would have gone to war for Serbia if it could have been proved, as but for this failure it would have been proved, that the assassination had been ordered by the head of a secret society sitting in Belgrade.

4

It should not be thought that Bosnia-Herzegovina was a seething mass of discontent, living for the day of its union with Serbia. The population of these two provinces in 1914 was approaching two million. Of these rather less than half were Orthodox Serbs; 30 per cent were Moslems, Serbs and Turks; just on a quarter were Roman Catholic Croats. From 1910 they had had their own Parliament. The majority of the Serbs would have liked union with Serbia, but only a minority of these were at all fanatical about it. The Moslems, almost to a man, preferred Austrian rule. The Roman Catholic Croats were divided. Some would have gone along with the Serbs; some were content as they were; some dreamt of a union with their co-racials in Dalmatia and Croatia as a Southern Slav entity within the Empire. There was, indeed, a great deal of very bad blood between the Serbs and the Croats of Bosnia. And this was to survive the creation of the Yugoslav Federation. Hence the appalling mutual massacres between Orthodox Serbs and Catholic Croats in the Second World War. In Bosnia, where the two races are hopelessly mixed, there are terrible monuments among the wild and glorious hills and valleys: villages utterly deserted because, as though the Germans and Italians were not doing enough killing, Serbs and Croats had to kill each other – men, women and children – while they slept.

An immense amount of nonsense has been talked about the Bosnian manoeuvres of June 1914. They were a deliberate provocation; they were the prelude to an attack on Serbia; and so on. In fact they were perfectly ordinary summer manoeuvres, carried out far from the Serbian border, south-west of Sarajevo, by the local Military Governor, Potiorek. Potiorek, early in the year, sent an invitation to Franz Ferdinand to attend the manoeuvres as Inspector-General of the armed forces, and then to make a ceremonial visit to Sarajevo, capital of Bosnia-Herzegovina, as heir to the throne. The manoeuvres were to be carried out by some 22,000 men – not 250,000 as certain Serb sources insisted![7] The country in question was barren Karst, high, treeless, waterless, commanding great views of the most rugged kind, but pitilessly hot in summer. Franz Ferdinand accepted the invitation as a duty. An earlier journey to Bosnia had been put off because of fears for his safety; but it was high time that a Habsburg showed himself there again: four years had gone by since the Emperor's own visit. Franz Ferdinand did not look forward to it. He still had to take care of himself because of the state of his lungs, and he feared the great heat. Further, although he was physically brave and also fatalistic, he had forebodings. These would have been stronger than in fact they were had various warnings been passed on to him. *Emigré* Serbs in America were setting the pace, as usual. On 3 December 1913, their Chicago journal, *Srbobran*, made a characteristic contribution to light and liberty: 'The Austrian Heir Apparent has announced his intention of visiting Sarajevo early next year. Every Serb will take note of this. . . . Serbs, seize everything you can lay hands on – knives, rifles, bombs and dynamite. Take holy vengeance! Death to the Habsburg dynasty, eternal remembrance to the heroes who raise their hands against it.'[8]

The official warning, such as it was, came from Nikola Pašić via the Serbian Minister in Vienna, Jovan Jovanović. A great mystery has been made about this warning, but the facts are pretty straight forward. Pašić learnt in late May about the Apis plan to murder Franz Ferdinand. He was in no position to challenge the Black Hand openly, yet he could not risk a war with Austria before the Serbian forces had recovered from the ardours of the two Balkan wars. His first thought was to stop the conspirators at the frontier, but this effort failed – whether because the order came too late, or because frontier officers working for the Black Hand chose to ignore it, has never been settled. He then had to decide whether to warn Vienna or to wash his hands of the whole business. In fact, he decided on a compromise, telling Jovanović, himself an ardent pan-Serb, to put the Austrians on their guard without revealing the Serbian government's detailed knowledge of the plot.

Jovanović did the best he could. He was a highly unpopular figure in the Ballhausplatz because of his known pan-Serb activities. Berchtold saw him as little as possible and left him to be dealt with mainly by the Common Minister of Finance, Bilinski. This was not quite as odd as it sounds because Bilinski was also responsible for the administration of Bosnia-Herzegovina. Jovanović went to Bilinski and did what he thought was his duty. He ought, he said, to warn Austria that the Archduke's life might be in danger if, as he had heard, he conducted the forthcoming manoeuvres on the Serbian frontier:

> If this is true, I can assure your Excellency that this will cause much discontent among the Serbs, who will consider it a provocative gesture. Manoeuvres held in such circumstances can be dangerous. Some young Serb might slip a live cartridge into his rifle instead of a blank, and fire it. That bullet might hit the man who provoked him. Therefore it might be good and reasonable if Archduke Franz Ferdinand were not to go to Sarajevo, and if the manoeuvres were not to take place either on St Vitus's day or in Bosnia.[9]

Since there was no question either of Franz Ferdinand's being in charge of the manoeuvres, or of the manoeuvres themselves being held anywhere near the Serbian border, and since the whole idea of a Serbian regimental soldier getting anywhere near headquarters with a rifle, whether loaded with blank or with ball, was far-fetched in the extreme, Bilinski brushed the warning aside and omitted to pass it on either to Berchtold or to the Archduke. There was also a little pique at work. Bilinski did not get on well with the Belvedere party; further, although Bosnia-Herzegovina was his responsibility, he had not been consulted officially about the forthcoming trip, all the arrangements for which had been made by Potiorek as Commander-in-Chief.

But even knowing nothing of the warning, Franz Ferdinand nearly put off the journey. He told the Emperor he was worried about the heat, and Franz Josef said he must decide for himself. He was not, as has been suggested, all eagerness to go in order that Sophie might be received at his side with the honours she deserved, denied her on more formal occasions: it was, rather, that having made up his mind, he decided that from his wife's point of view it was an opportunity not to be missed.

So the journey took place and the manoeuvres began. Franz Ferdinand and Sophie were put up in style in the little mountain-spa of Ilidže, which was cleared for the occasion. Everything went smoothly. Not a shot was fired. Franz Ferdinand, a very particular soldier, was pleased and even surprised by the bearing of the troops and the skill of the commanders. He sent a telegram to the Emperor to say so, and had his words of commendation read aloud by every regimental commander in the language of the regiment. Potiorek was as pleased as Punch.

The manoeuvres were spread over 26 and 27 June. The three conspirators, Princip, Čabrinović and Grabež, had been in, or close to, Sarajevo, thirty miles away from Ilidže, for nearly a fortnight, waiting. These three nineteen-year-old boys were all, not unnaturally, in a great state of nerves. Picked up by Major Vova Tankosić, who ran the Black Hand's training centre for guerilla fighting and sabotage, they were all ready enough to die for the cause; but it was one thing to die with a swift, heroic gesture, quite another to undergo the strain of waiting, all the time fearful of betrayal and discovery. All through May they had practised shooting with pistols, but only Princip, who was also the most clear-eyed and understanding, was much good at this. On 27 May they were issued with their weapons and their poison. There were four Belgian automatics of the latest kind and six bombs manufactured in the Serbian State Arsenal and designed to slip into the jacket pocket. On 28 May they set off from Belgrade for the frontier and were passed across into Bosnia by the Black Hand's underground route two days later. On 3 June, with twenty-five days still to go, they arrived in Sarajevo and scattered.

It has never been made clear why Tankosić and Apis put them through this comedy. All three were native Bosnians holding Austrian passports. All three could have gone openly to Sarajevo, separately or together, and picked up their weapons there. Mr A. J. P. Taylor has asserted that the whole operation as conceived by Dimitrijević had nothing to do with the killing of Franz Ferdinand but was part of an attempt to discredit Pašić.[10] His argument runs that the last thing Dimitrijević expected was for the attempt to succeed: all he wanted was a failed attempt which would cause an uproar and lead to the arrest of the three conspirators. It would then be discovered that they had started from Belgrade and crossed the frontier secretly with the help of Serbian frontier officials, thus implicating the Serbian government, but not Dimitrijević, of whom none of the youngsters had ever heard. Pašić would be in a cleft stick. 'If he went against the conspirators and the Black Hand, he would be discredited in Serbia as an Austrian tool. If he defied the Austrians he would need the support of Dimitrijević and his secret society. Either way, Pašić would lose; and Apis would win. The plot at Sarajevo was a move in Serb domestic politics.'

This is an ingenious theory; but the facts remain that the conspirators were supplied with enough lethal weapons of a compact and up-to-date kind to kill, and that in the end one of them did kill. The cyanide some of them took after the assassination did not work, and thus they were captured alive; but there is no evidence that Dimitrijević knew it would not work. Further, in spite of the cloak-and-dagger aspects of their journey from Belgrade to Sarajevo, their trail was not uncovered until much later. When a man sends out suitably armed fanatics with instructions to kill, at a certain place and on a certain day, a certain individual, represented as their country's most deadly foe, he would have to be a bigger fool than Dimitrijević to take it for granted that the target would be missed by all three of them. An operation of this kind had been planned for some time. The original idea was to have General Potiorek killed. Nobody knows exactly what was intended, except to create the utmost confusion by the most economical means. Nobody ever knows what goes on in the minds of terrorists: more often than not they do not know themselves. It is one thing to suggest that Dimitrijević, seeking to stir up active hatred against Austria, saw also a means of embarrassing Pašić; quite another to assert that the whole operation was aimed at Pašić and Pašić alone.

Be that as it may, the thing happened. Princip had picked up four other acquaintances during the waiting time, all ready for a desperate deed. They were Danilo Ilić, a school-teacher turned journalist and a member of the Black Hand, who had known of the plot from Princip for some time. Ilić, who was twenty-four, himself recruited a Moslem, Muhamed Mehmedbašić (who had already panicked in an attempt to stab Potoriek), Vaso Čubrilović and Cvjetko Popović, both high-school students aged seventeen and eighteen respectiyely. On the morning of 28 June they took up their stations.

Sarajevo, which lies on the River Miljacka, a swift-flowing torrent carving its way between steep and high hills, was not the mere cluster of houses so frequently imagined. It was a sizable provincial capital with a population of 50,000 and a bustling life of its own. Besides a large city hall, a museum, and other public buildings it had a splendid mosque, dominating the skyline with its shallow dome and tall minarets, and an Orthodox cathedral. The route from Ilidže to the city hall lay along the river embankment, the Appel Quay, and the seven conspirators strung themselves out along this quay to await the Imperial procession.

Their task was made easier by the fact that security precautions were practically nil. The best part of two Austrian corps lay outside in the hills, but the city was out of bounds to them for the duration of the visit. The general idea seems to have been that there was no real danger and that a display of armed might, with troops lining the processional way, would create a bad impression. Potiorek was a very vain man, quite out of touch with political reality, and he seems to have been unwarrantably sure that, as Governor, he had the situation in hand. Franz Ferdinand himself was notoriously averse to guards and detectives following him round and coming between him and what he took to be the people. Already, on the eve of the manoeuvres, he and Sophie had made a surprise unscheduled visit to the town in order to shop for antiques in the ancient Oriental bazaar. There, quite unprotected, they had been mobbed by an enthusiastic crowd, but no harm had come of it. It never seems to have occurred to anyone that among the enthusiasts there might be individuals with hatred in their hearts. One of them, in fact, was Princip himself, who came almost face to face with Franz Ferdinand in the crowd. He had his pistol and could have shot him dead; but this was not part of the plan, which called for a public execution by one of a group, three days later. So, instead of shooting, he looked long at the man he was to murder to be sure of knowing him when the ritual moment came.[11]

It came at a quarter past ten, in full sunlight, on the morning of the 28th. Franz Ferdinand in his tunic and his general's head-dress, a tumble of green cock's feathers, made an easy target sitting high in the back of Count Harrach's open car. Sophie in a picture hat and a high-necked white dress sat beside him; Potiorek sat next to the chauffeur in front. Čabrinović had the first chance. Earlier that morning he had burst into tears, overwhelmed by the thought of the fate in store for him. But he had pulled himself together, dressed smartly, and, with the bomb in his pocket, went to a photographer's shop to have his picture taken. He was ready when the Archduke came by, pulled the pin out of his bomb, threw it carefully, and nearly succeeded: the chauffeur saw the bomb coming and had the sense to accelerate sharply. So the bomb passed just behind Sophie, who was on the side nearest to Čabrinović. Franz Ferdinand, too, saw it coming, managed to deflect it at the last moment, so that it fell on to the hood of the car, folded back, and bounced into the street – in time to wreck the following car and to wound Potiorek's adjutant severely and the other occupants and several onlookers more or less slightly. It was a powerful explosion and Franz Ferdinand

and Sophie were very close to death. While Čabrinović swallowed his cyanide and jumped into the river, was caught, nearly lynched, and then dragged away by the police, both Franz Ferdinand and Sophie displayed extreme courage. For all they knew, there were other would-be assassins in that crowd (indeed, there were six), but Franz Ferdinand took command, saw to the safety of the wounded, said 'Come on, the fellow is a lunatic; let us get on with our programme', got back into the car with Sophie, and proceeded along the quay – past Čubrilović, who funked his task, past where Popović should have been (but Popović had run away and hidden his bomb), past Princip, who got mixed up in the crowd running towards the scene of the explosion and found things moving much too quickly, past Grabež, who also was paralysed by fear.

It has been held against Franz Ferdinand that when he arrived at the city hall he was rude to the Mayor. There the poor man was, ready to read his speech of welcome, and before he could get a word out the Archduke exclaimed: 'Mr Mayor – one comes here for a visit and is received with bombs! It is outrageous!' What was he expected to do? Congratulate the Mayor on the efficiency of Bosnian explosives? . . . He recovered himself at once. 'All right, now you may speak.' The Mayor spoke: 'Your Royal and Imperial Highness! Your Highness! Our hearts are filled with happiness over the most gracious visit. . . .' And Franz Ferdinand replied, finishing his speech with a sentence in Serbo-Croat: 'May I ask you to give my cordial greetings to the inhabitants of this beautiful capital city, and assure you of my unchanged regard and favour.'

It was his last public speech. But he had a few more words to say before he died. First he sent a telegram to the Emperor telling him not to take too seriously any reports he might receive about the bomb incident.[12] Then he had a characteristic comment about Čabrinović when they told him he had been arrested: 'You wait and see!' he exclaimed. 'Instead of locking the fellow up they'll be proper Austrians and give him the Medal of Merit.'[13] Then there was the condition of Potiorek's aide to be inquired about. Then the new plans. Potiorek himself and Gerde, the Chief of Police, both of whom might have considered themselves in disgrace, seem to have been remarkably unmoved – evidently they were both shocked into something like insensibility. They thought there would be no more attempts. It might be a good thing to cancel the visit to the museum, but there would be no harm in driving on down the Appel Quay to lunch at the Governor's Residence. No (this was Potiorek) it would be a bad thing to rush a company of troops into the town to line the streets: they were improperly dressed. Anyway, the Archduke was determined to go first to the hospital to visit the wounded. Sophie, he thought, should go straight to the Governor's Residence, or back to Ilidže. But Sophie refused to leave him. Very well. At any rate, the route had been changed. Instead of the advertised route, turning away from the river into the narrow streets of the city, the cars would go straight on down the Appel Quay. This time Count Harrach insisted on standing on the running-board of his own car, with his back to the quay where Čabrinović had been. Their journey took them once more past Grabež, who did nothing. They should have been safe. But when the leading car, with the Mayor, reached the right-hand turning into Franz Josef Street, which was on the original route to the museum as originally planned, instead of carrying on down the Appel Quay it turned right, as originally planned, and the Archduke's chauffeur followed it: he had not been told of the change of plan. He drove straight past, of all people, Princip, who was standing outside Schiller's provision stores* trying to head off the importunate questions of a friend he had run into by chance. All might still have been well if the cars had simply gone on and kept moving. But Potiorek, whose day it undoubtedly was, again took a hand. 'Wrong way!' he cried, leaning forward to the chauffeur. 'Straight along the Appel Quay!' So the chauffeur stopped and started to back, the whole operation taking place immediately under Princip's incredulous eyes. All he had to do was to step out into the street and fire point-blank at Franz Ferdinand, which he did. He fired twice.

Even when the whole procession was halted, with the passengers in the other cars crowded round to see what had happened, even when Princip had been seized, beaten up, had tried to shoot himself, had taken his ineffective poison, and been hurried away, nobody knew what had been done. The Archduke and Sophie continued to sit upright; the car resumed its reversing operation to drive off and it was only then that the Archduke's mouth spurted blood. Sophie, seeing this, cried out in dismay, then collapsed, as though in a dead faint. Franz Ferdinand, who knew he was dying, with a bullet in his neck, was the only one to realize that his wife might also be hurt. He managed to turn: 'Sopherl! Sopherl! Don't die! Keep alive for

* This is now the site of the Princip Museum. Outside, in the pavement, two footprints impressed in concrete mark the place where Princip stood.

our children!' Then he, too, collapsed, muttering again and again: 'It is nothing!'

Sophie, who had been shot through the lower abdomen, was already dead of an internal haemorrhage; a moment or two after the cars reached the Residency, Franz Ferdinand died too. Their bodies were laid out on twin iron bedsteads, and covered with flowers from the luncheon table in the banqueting hall below, which was cleared to form a temporary office for Potiorek and his Staff.

5

The only man who might have kept Austria from war with Serbia was dead, killed by a Serb for the glory of his people. Nobody thought about him any more: he had to be cleared away and buried, and the nature of this mopping-up operation set the tone for the weeks that followed. While the Austrians were apathetic after the first shock, all those who had anything to do with events seem to have suffered from a sort of paralysis of the brain, which manifested itself in a total incapacity to think, in a wild and meaningless alternation of feeling. Only a leader could have called them to their senses and whipped them into using their heads: there was no leader; there was only Franz Josef, who was eighty-four and sunk in fatalism: if we must go down, let us at least go down like gentlemen.

The confusion of purpose ran very deep. Among the few reasonable men in high places was Professor Josef Redlich, a man of intelligence and liberal ideas and strong historical sense. But in the long entry in his diary for 28 June 1914, under the first impact of the news of the assassination, there are nothing but contradictions.[14] For example:

> I called on Professor Singer in his editorial office who saw in the end of Franz Ferdinand and his wife a happy dispensation for Austria. Many thousands will think like that: I think differently. For Franz Ferdinand would by hook or by crook have made an end of Franz Josef's régime, which has become untenable through weakness and planlessness, and carried out a real attempt to make Austria-Hungary viable, internally and externally.

And then, a few lines later:

> This day is the day of a world-historical event. Whether it will lead to a turn for the better or the worse for Austria nobody can yet say.

The hour of destiny for the Habsburgs is drawing near: for the first time a Habsburg has been killed by the son of one of those Balkan nations which are the deadly foes of Austria-Hungary, of Germany and Catholicism. The impossibility of a peaceful co-existence [*sic*] between this half-German Monarchy, so closely bound to Germany itself, and the nationalism of the Balkan peoples whipped up to murderous intensity, must now be clear to everyone. I doubt whether the eighty-four-year-old Emperor has the strength to draw the necessary conclusions from this happening: and equally whether the bombastic coward of a Hohenzollern, Wilhelm II, who was so clever at neutralizing Franz Ferdinand's finest quality, his courage, in 1912. . . . Over there [in Hungary] they will say the 'God of the Magyars' guided the hand and the bullet of the miserable Serbian wretch. Perhaps God is much more 'democratic' and much less 'clerical' than the creatures at Franz Ferdinand's Court imagine in their particular religion. Perhaps one will be able to say: 'God meant well by Austria in that he spared her from this Emperor' – a man made sickly by the consequences of tuberculosis, a man who one who knew him well characterized as having the callousness and cruelty of an Asiatic despot.

If one of Vienna's leading political intellectuals could get himself into such a muddle immediately after Sarajevo, what could be expected of the Berchtolds?

Two men knew what they wanted; Prince Montenuovo, who wanted only one thing, though the heavens might fall: to humiliate Franz Ferdinand in death; and Conrad von Hötzendorf, who, still convinced that Russia would not intervene, was determined to crush Serbia while, as he thought, there was still time. The Emperor let each have his way.

CHAPTER NINETEEN

THE POWERS GATHER ROUND

Hardly anyone in Vienna thought immediately of war, even though the heir to the throne had been murdered by a Serb who was at once assumed to have got his orders from Belgrade, and even though for so many years there had been so much talk of war. The news of the assassination came as a profound shock on one of those high summer afternoons when the Viennese were out in the parks and the neighbouring hills enjoying themselves in much the same way as they had been enjoying themselves while Königgrätz was being fought half a century before. But there was no sudden uprush of belligerence. Indeed, so far as can be seen, no single foreign observer thought in terms of war: many, indeed, who had quite erroneously seen in Franz Ferdinand the leader of the war party, thought that his death removed an obstacle to the maintenance of peace.

The reception of the news by the Court and the government circles of Vienna was matter-of-fact in the extreme. Franz Josef, on holiday at Ischl, did not grieve, nor does he seem to have experienced the least apprehension as to possible consequences. It is to be doubted whether he ever uttered the words attributed to him by Margutti, which afterwards became a kind of symbol of his general attitude. According to Margutti he exclaimed to Count Paar, his adjutant: 'A higher power has restored that order which I was unable to maintain.'[1] That is not a Franz Josef sentence: as we have seen abundantly, he did not speak in rounded Churchillian periods. It is to be doubted, too, whether it was strictly a Franz Josef sentiment. He was never a blasphemer. He might have said: 'God's will be done. It may be for the best!' Much as he disliked Franz Ferdinand and distrusted his policies, he would not have gone further than that. But this would have expressed his attitude fairly exactly. He was happy about the new heir, the young Archduke Karl; and his daughter Valerie, more reliable than Margutti, recorded in her diary:

> I found Papa amazingly fresh; certainly he was shocked, and when he spoke of the poor children he had tears in his eyes; but, as I had imagined in advance, he was not personally stricken. Indeed . . .

when I said that Karl would assuredly do well, he said very solemnly and emphatically: 'For me it is a great worry less.'[2]

It was now Prince Montenuovo's turn. While in Sarajevo itself there was an outbreak of violent anti-Serb rioting by the riff-raff of the town, who were joined by a great many normally sober citizens loyal for one reason or another to the Monarchy, the remains of Franz Ferdinand and Sophie were dispatched with a show of Imperial pomp and circumstance on their homeward journey, first by train to the coast, then by battleship to Trieste, then by train to Vienna. There the pomp and circumstance came to an abrupt halt. It was understood that Sophie could not be buried in the Imperial vault in the Capuchin church. Franz Ferdinand had stated in his will that he wished to be buried side by side with her in the vault he himself had prepared at Artstetten. But first there had to be a lying-in-state.

Franz Ferdinand was heir to the throne and Inspector-General of the armed forces; but Sophie, in the eyes of the Court Chamberlain, was nobody. This meant that there could be no elaborate ceremonial – unless the corpse of Franz Ferdinand could be detached from the corpse of his wife, as, a quarter of a century before, the corpse of Rudolf had been detached from the corpse of Marie Vetsera. This could not be. So, while the coffins were both taken to the Capuchin vault, Franz Ferdinand's was surmounted with his crown, his helmet, his sabre and all his Orders, but Sophie's stood on a lower level, and on it rested only a pair of white gloves and a fan, the marks of a lady-in-waiting. The lying-in-state lasted just two hours; then the doors were closed and the waiting crowds were turned away.

That afternoon there was a Requiem Mass. No foreign royalty were present, though many had got ready for the journey: all were put off, this time not by Montenuovo, but by the Ballhausplatz. In view of the Emperor's great age, it was said, he must be spared the exertions of elaborate ceremonial and formal meetings. It was as though both Berchtold and Franz Josef wished to keep the rulers of Europe at arm's length until they had made up their minds for themselves what to do next. But by now the behaviour of the Court had stirred up widespread anger and resentment, even among those who had had no use for Franz Ferdinand while he lived. That evening, when the coffins set out on their journey to Artstetten via the Danube ferry at Pöchlarn, there was a great and spontaneous demonstration. Montenuovo, who had flatly refused to permit the display of full military honours, had to give a little ground: there would be no formal parade, no lining of the streets; but it would be permissible, he said, for individual unit commanders to turn out their men in uniform if they so desired. The result was that they put on a formidable show. Further, in direct defiance of Montenuovo's orders, the aristocracy turned out in strength in full regalia, formed up in a column of their own, and turned the dim little funeral cortège into a major State occasion.

The Emperor knew all about this. He also knew that Montenuovo had contrived that the special train for Artstetten from the West Station should leave at 10 o'clock at night, which would mean that the hearses would cross the river by ferry in the neighbourhood of midnight. He could not know that, as things turned out, there was to be a tremendous thunderstorm and that the thunder and lightning in the sheeting rain panicked the horses, so that it was a miracle that the coffins were not tipped over into the river. Montenuovo was not responsible for the thunderstorm, but he was wholly responsible for the midnight river crossing.[3]

The outcry against these arrangements, which the *Reichpost* called 'so insulting to a grieving people'[4] was considerable. The Emperor knew about that too; but he went out of his way, in a manner unprecedented, to thank Montenuovo in a letter for publication.[5] He also did something else: at a time when people were calling for the head of General Potiorek, who, after Princip and Dimitrijević, had been more responsible for the assassination than any other single individual, the Emperor made no move whatsoever (nor did anybody else) to institute an inquiry into the security arrangements at Sarajevo, or to censure Potiorek and Gerda, the Head of Police. Instead, he told Bilinski personally on the very day after the assassination, to 'say a few words', as Bilinski wrote to Potiorek, 'highly appreciative of Your Excellency's person.'[6]

The only inquiry was the investigation of the attempt itself. The object was to uncover the assumed connection between the conspirators and the Belgrade government. It was as critical an inquiry as could possibly be imagined, but it was conducted throughout almost casually and on an absurdly low level against a background of mounting diplomatic excitement. Once the first shock of the assassination had been assimilated Vienna began to think of punishment, perhaps of war. If there was to be war, it was imperative to show that

Belgrade was behind the act. But at first the Ballhausplatz did nothing. An amiable Sarajevo judge called Pfeffer had been appointed within an hour of Čabrinović's capture to investigate the background of the attempt. He had started on this task even before Princip had turned an attempt into a murder. And he was allowed to go on with it, even though it was soon clear that he was not up to the job. He kept at it for twelve days. With Princip he was getting nowhere; and he did little better with Čabrinović. It was Ilić who broke their story. He was picked up in the police net for a routine check four days after the assassination and said he would confess everything if his life were spared. He confessed a great deal (in the event his life was not spared), but not enough to implicate Dimitrijević and, through him, the Belgrade government. And it was only on 9 July that somebody in Vienna decided that the issue was too big to be left in the hands of a provincial justice and sent off a Foreign Office official called Wiesner to Sarajevo to collect together what facts had been elicited and see what sense he could make of them. For two days, from 11 to 13 July, Wiesner worked all day and most of the night on the files and in conference with the officials on the spot. He established that the decision to kill Franz Ferdinand had been made in Belgrade, that the conspirators had been assisted by Milan Ciganović, an Austrian citizen, a native Bosnian now employed by the Serbian State Railways, and Major Tankosić of the Serbian army, that the bombs had come from the Serbian Army Arsenal and had been supplied, with the pistols, by Tankosić, that the conspirators had been helped over the border by various Serb frontier officials. It was not enough; and Wiesner did not even make the most of what he had. He concluded his report, conscientious, and painstakingly honest: 'There is nothing to indicate, or even to give rise to the suspicion, that the Serbian government knew about the plot, its preparation, or the procurement of arms. On the contrary, there are indications that this is impossible.'[7] Not the slightest speculation about the Black Hand, or any organization at all that might link together the Serbian army major, Tankosić, the railway official Ciganović, and the Bosnian revolutionaries, Princip and his friends; not the slightest reference to Jovanović's warning to Bilinski. . . . Berchtold, instead of sending out a really high-powered commission to Sarajevo, accepted the Wiesner report and that was that. To Pašić, waiting helpless in Belgrade for the Austrian reaction, the whole affair must have seemed incomprehensible and altogether too good to be true. But true it was.

Hofburg and Ballhausplatz were meanwhile deciding how best to cut Serbia down to size. As Conrad, once again Chief-of-Staff, had warned them, their best opportunities were long past. Czernin, who had been making a desperate effort to salvage the Rumanian alliance, had had to announce that it had gone beyond recall.[8] Conrad, a week before the Sarajevo crime, had written to Berchtold to inform him categorically that the Monarchy was surrounded from the north-east to the south-west by hostile Powers pursuing aggressive aims: Russia, Rumania, Serbia, Montenegro; that she had an unreliable ally to the south-west, Italy; that her only loyal support, Germany, in the north-west, was herself threatened on two sides, by France and Russia, perhaps by Great Britain too. The very existence of the Monarchy, he insisted, depended on a positive deed, no matter what this cost. To make this possible great sacrifices would have to be made.[9] It was the last appeal of the soldier to the politicians, who were soon to abdicate responsibility to him.

But it was Princip who had performed the 'positive deed'. And the first thought of the Ballhausplatz was still for the Monarchy's back-yard. Serbia was the foe, and had to be reduced. With Rumania on the edge of defecting, that left only Bulgaria to play with. But Bulgaria was exhausted after her defeat by Serbia. Nevertheless, the first move in the diplomatic game which was to lead directly to the fatal ultimatum was a personal letter from Franz Josef to Wilhelm II saying that the primary policy objective must be the isolation and reduction of Serbia and the corresponding strengthening of Bulgaria.[10] This was a fairly long-term operation. . . . It was on the same day that Franz Josef said to the German Ambassador, Tschir-schky: 'The future is black. . . . If only we could detach England altogether from her French and Russian friends!'[11] This was a little late in the day.

It was three days later, on 5 July, while Judge Pfeffer was still plodding away at Sarajevo, that the Austrian Ambassador to Germany was able to tell Wilhelm II that the origin of the conspiracy had been firmly traced to Belgrade, that the Austro-Hungarian government would be putting in very far-reaching demands, and that if these were not met her troops would march in.[12] Time and time again during the past years Wilhelm had urged restraint towards Serbia on Franz Ferdinand and on Franz Josef, neither of whom needed to be restrained. This time, whether because he felt that his advice in the past had been partly responsible for Franz Ferdinand's death, or because he was in one of his manic moods, he said at once, without reflection, that the Monarchy could count on Germany's support.[13] There was nobody to restrain him. Bülow had long been gone. Bülow had been responsible for the policies which led to the encirclement. He had seen this too late, and retracted in his last days of office, in 1909, warning Wilhelm II, as he should have warned him a decade before, that England could be a dangerous adversary. Wilhelm had replied that England would never dare attack the German navy.[14] And now there was not even Bülow, only Bethmann-Hollweg, a mixture of vanity, irresolution developed to a pathological degree, and passive fatalism, 'a doctrinaire bureaucrat dressed in wolf's clothing', as Bülow himself said of him. Bethmann-Hollweg, without at all a clear idea of what Vienna proposed to demand of the Serbs, said the Kaiser was quite right. Germany would support her up to the hilt.[15] This was the famous 'blank cheque'. The general view in Berlin was that Russia was not ready for war. Two days later, on 8 July, Wilhelm II sent word to Franz Josef himself that the Monarchy could count on the full support of Germany, even in the case of 'a European complication'.[16]

Meanwhile the rest of Europe was beginning to be stirred. Russia was uneasy. She was not at all thinking of war (Wilhelm was right about that). Although Serbia was a Slav State there were ambivalent feelings towards her in St Petersburg: it was possible that the Belgrade government was getting too big for its boots; it was certain that individual Russian agents, like Captain Artamanov, had been working too closely with Serb nationalist extremists, like Dimitrijević. The sensible thing for the time being might be for Russia and Austria-Hungary to work on Pašić and stiffen him to the point where he could do away with the secret societies. The man who stood for this line was Baron Hartwig, the Russian Ambassador to Belgrade, who, having once been hand in glove with the Black Hand, had turned against it. But Hartwig had a heart attack and died in the study of the Austrian Ambassador, Baron Giesl, at the very moment when he was about to take Giesl into his confidence. 'The tragedy of Hartwig's death', reported Giesl, 'was that he, the great Slav patriot and diplomat, should have had to die in the Legation of the State which he so much hated and despised.'[17] The tragedy was deeper than that. There was nobody else to take up Hartwig's idea.

Who, meanwhile, was guiding Austrian policy? Berchtold did not want war with Serbia; yet many were clamouring for war, the war that had been put off for so long, the positive action that never took place. These feelings were expressed very exactly in the Redlich diary. As the days wore on, as each day that passed removed a little more the justification of a swift blow struck in anger, Redlich's spirits mounted. On 15 July this liberal Austrian wrote exultantly:

> Had half an hour with Alek Hoyos today: he told me in strictest confidence that war is as good as decided on. But we must have patience, there are important reasons for dragging it out. Berchtold, Tisza, Stürkh, Burian, are all agreed. Bilinski too! The Emperor himself is perfectly ready for war. Hoyos said: 'If it leads to a world war, then so be it.' Again: 'If our army is no good, then the Monarchy is finished, for today it is the sole prop of the realm.' Later I heard from Fritz that Tisza had likewise told Ullmann, the director of the Budapesth Bank, that war was unavoidable, but it must not be talked about yet: we must wait until the end of the harvest before speaking out to the Serbs. The news that Conrad and Krobatin have gone on leave is simply to disguise our intentions.[18]

It was not quite as simple as that. Berchtold had realized from the beginning that he would have to do something drastic. But he was not a man to undertake great decisions on his own. He had never wanted to be Foreign Minister and was horrified when he found that Aehrenthal had recommended him as his successor. An aristocrat of pleasant manners and great charm, he was liked by everyone, but none of his colleagues saw him as a statesman and, indeed, he never tried to conceal his own limitations. Nor did he try very hard to transcend them. He regarded himself as a diplomatic figurehead, as a liaison officer between his Emperor and his permanent officials. These he trusted, and some of them were clearly very good. Certain memoranda signed by him, notably to Franz Ferdinand, who was kept more fully informed by him, by almost daily messages and telegrams, than he had ever been by Aehrenthal, were model appreciations of Austria's position.[19] The trouble was that Berchtold never bothered to understand the memoranda issued over his own name, preferring to sign them automatically, then dash off to the races, or to spend the afternoon with his horses, which he loved. No man could have been more out of his depth than this amiable relic, employed by Franz Josef to keep the peace, yet beset now on all sides by men pressing for war. He went with the floodtide. At first Stepan Tisza was stubbornly against a war: not for moral reasons, but because he saw trouble ahead for Hungary, as distinct from the

Monarchy as a whole. But soon he too came round. He would agree to war, he said at the Ministerial Council on 7 July only if the Monarchy would aim no further than the reduction of Serbia.[20] The annihilation of the country he would not agree to, first because Russia would never stand by and let it happen, second because, as Prime Minister of Hungary, he could not agree to the annexation of any part of Serbia. This had been the Hungarian line for the past decade: the last thing the Magyars wanted was the accession to the Monarchy of a host of rebellious Slavs. As for the Emperor, he appeared to have moved into a fatalistic mood. He had Germany at his side: what must be must be.

The fatality was that what must be had not already taken place.

In London, in Paris and elsewhere, the Foreign Offices simply could not understand what was going on. Here was Austria-Hungary, for years straining for an opportunity to put Serbia in its place; the perfect opportunity had now arrived and nothing happened. The unfortunate Archduke had been killed on 28 June. All the world expected an immediate and very sharp reaction. But time went on and nothing happened. There was not even any open discussion in Vienna: Berchtold was meeting the Cabinet in secret and nothing at all came out. On 6 July the German Ambassador to London, Prince Lichnowsky, warned Sir Edward Grey that Austria was going to put in fairly high demands and asked him to smooth things over with St Petersburg. Grey, who had not imagined that Austria would do anything else, nevertheless went out of his way to pass the message on to the Russian Ambassador in London, expressing the confident hope that Russia would do nothing to embarrass Austria-Hungary or her allies. This made good sense in St Petersburg, where the Russians were also expecting the Austrians to show their teeth. Berlin was relieved and delighted: it is a reflection of the extraordinary picture of reality enjoyed by the Germans at that time that there should have been any question in their minds. They were incapable of seeing that France might object to being bullied in Morocco, that England might regard with genuine suspicion and anger the activities of von Tirpitz, and yet they were filled with anxiety about what might happen if their ally struck out in justifiable anger in response to a wanton provocation.

The failure to strike has usually been attributed to Conrad von Hötzendorf. But this is not fair. This extraordinary little man, this terrier of an embodied *idée fixe*, with his stiff white hair, his bristling white moustache, his unquenchable blue eyes, is represented as having fretted and fumed for his chance, year in, year out, and then, when at last it came, to have muffed it. He did nothing of the kind. The failure was due in the first place to the hesitancies of the Emperor and Imperial Foreign Minister, to say nothing of Stepan Tisza; in the second place to the total lack of comprehension on the part of the civilian Ministers of the military facts of life. Thus, for example, it has been said that Berchtold, still dithering, was deeply relieved on the day, 25 July, when the mobilization order was signed, and Conrad told him that it would be two weeks before the army could move.[21] But Conrad had told him that long before.[22] Nor was there anything peculiar about this. Regele has tabulated the mobilization periods of the Powers as follows: Serbia 16 days; Russia 21–25; France 18; Germany 10–17; Austria-Hungary 17–21. If immediate mobilization had been ordered on the day after the assassination (as Conrad himself demanded) operations could not have been started until 20 July.[23]

It was not Conrad's fault that mobilization took so long; it was in the nature of the machine, and the Ballhausplatz should have known about the machine. The Ballhausplatz, however, was not alone. In England, Germany, France and Russia, the politicians were all under a similar delusion: namely that at the call of a bugle regiments, divisions, corps, armies and army groups could immediately rise from the ground, equipped and fully deployed, to start the advance. Not only politicians, but historians too. Thus, for example, there was a fearful misunderstanding about the notional capture of Belgrade. All the Powers, one after another, thought it would be an admirable thing if the Austrians, with a lightning advance, should seize Belgrade as a pledge, and then stand there while all the world talked about what to do next. Conrad has been terribly blamed for not doing this. But Austria did not begin to mobilize until 26 July, with Conrad getting more desperate all the time. Until then, in order to avoid any appearance of provocation, Conrad was not allowed to move any extra troops into Semlin, across the river from Belgrade.[24] When war was finally declared, with both armies mobilizing fast, the quick seizure of that highly fortified hill city, towering on high cliffs between the confluence of the Danube and the Save, was out of the question. Belgrade could not be taken except in a major operation. But many of the calculations of the Powers were based on the illusion that it could be and would be. Conrad had nothing to do with the long delay between the assassination and the ultimatum: that was an affair of the Emperor and his Ministers. And there was precious little he could do during that unhappy interval: until mobilization was ordered by the Emperor he could not begin to bring his units up to strength.

Conrad's only failure, indeed, was diplomatic rather than military. That is to say, he meddled in politics too much and too little. He saw the immediate danger from Serbia and Italy: but he was not enough of a statesman to see the wider danger. And by nagging incessantly about the immediate danger he helped to take the eye of the Emperor, of Franz Ferdinand, of Aehrenthal, of Berchtold, off the ball, and concentrate their thinking on their own backyard.

2

The ultimatum went out on 23 July. It was the last ultimatum to be drafted in diplomatic French. It said that the Belgrade government must issue an official condemnation of anti-Austrian propaganda, declare its regret for the consequences of such propaganda, and admit that Serbian officers and officials had been spreading this propaganda and thus injuring friendly relations with a neighbouring State. It said that the Belgrade government must proceed with extreme severity against those found guilty of such activity, and make these proceedings known to the army in a royal Order of the Day. It said that the Belgrade government must agree to the participation of Austro-Hungarian authorities in the suppression of irredentist movements: in particular there must be a judicial investigation of those involved in the conspiracy of 28 June, in which Austro-Hungarian officials would take part. It said that Major Tankosić and Milan Ciganović must be arrested immediately. It said that steps must be taken to stop arms and explosives being smuggled over the border into Bosnia, and that those border officials who had helped the Sarajevo conspirators must be dismissed and severely punished. It said finally that the Belgrade government must explain the anti-Austrian utterances of high Serbian officials after the assassination and make clear to all those concerned the measures demanded in the Note. Acceptance of the conditions was demanded by 25 July.

Copies of the ultimatum, together with summaries of the evidence elicited by Pfeffer's court of inquiry, were sent to all the Powers. In London it was thought that no self-respecting country could possibly accept the terms. In Petersburg Sazonov fulminated; but not in belligerent terms: he wanted an international conference. Both Russia and England urged that Austria should give Serbia more time. The uproar in Serbia was complete. Everybody talked about the immediate breakaway of all the South Slavs, of a revolution in Bosnia-Herzegovina, of the Slav regiments mutinying. The Prince Regent sent a desperate message to the Tsar, begging him to come to the aid of Serbia with all speed. But Pašić saw things more soberly. There was nothing for it, in his first view, but to submit. He had been through crises in his time, and this was another: the less he personally had to do with it the better. It was election time again, so having said what he thought, he went off to make some speeches in the country, then to Greece to have a little holiday. He had managed to disappear in 1903, when the murder of Milan Obrenević and Queen Draga had brought back the Karageorge dynasty – and him. He had managed to disappear at the time of the Annexation. But this time he could not get away with it. The Prince Regent made him come back.

Even so, on the morning of 25 July the Serbian reply had been drafted, as an unconditional acceptance. Then, later in the day, it was changed. It still accepted most of the points, but it rejected the demand that Austro-Hungarian agencies should take part in the investigations, since this went against the Serbian constitution and the Serbian criminal law. Major Tankosić, the reply went on, had indeed been arrested, but Ciganović could not be found.

It has been suggested, often enough, that this change of mind was due to a promise of Russian support. It may have been so (only the archivists in Russia and Yugoslavia know), or it may not have been. It may have been simply that, on second thoughts, Pašić decided that he could not possibly risk a confrontation between Austrian officials and the conspirators: somebody might have boasted. Dimitrijević may even have threatened that he would let the cat out of the bag if Pašič surrendered completely. Certainly Pašić could not afford to allow the extradition of Ciganović. We do not know. All we know is that in 1917 Dimitrijević was arrested and tried for treason by a Serbian military tribunal, with Ciganović as a prosecution witness, that he agreed to die for his country's good, that he died with perfect bravery before a firing squad, and that he left a testament which began: 'Although sentenced to death by two competent courts, and deprived of the mercy of the Crown, I die innocently, and in the conviction that my death is necessary to Serbia for higher reasons.'[2]

Be that as it may, it is known that on the morning of 25 July

Belgrade was about to send a reply which would have made it impossible for Austria to go to war, that during the day the draft was changed, that when it was handed over to the Austrian Ambassador at two minutes past six that evening it was at once seen to be unacceptable, that the Ambassador at once broke off relations and drove across the frontier, that Serbia proclaimed immediate mobilization and that Court and government slipped away from Belgrade into the interior.

All this news reached Ischl, where Franz Josef was staying, at a quarter past seven. The Emperor, Berchtold, Bilinski and Krobatin, had been waiting about all day, heedless of the natural beauty of that enchanting resort, in a state of almost intolerable suspense. As the evening approached the Emperor sent them away, telling them that he expected to see them at Mass in the morning if the reply had not come by half past seven.[26]

When they brought him the news he listened like a man turned into a statue. He could hardly speak. He said: 'Very well then!' and that was the end. But it was not quite the end. He went on looking at the telegram, then with a sudden gesture he exclaimed: 'But breaking off diplomatic relations still need not mean war.' Then he brooded again. Then sent for Berchtold and Krobatin. Then, after another long pause, signed the mobilization order for war with Serbia and Montenegro.[27]

The rest of the story belongs to the history of the First World War. On that hot July evening the Monarchy had shot its bolt. Berchtold, now filled with revulsion, realizing that he was not the man for drastic measures, still sought a way out. He found great comfort in the Emperor's phrase about the rupture of diplomatic relations not meaning war.[28] But events were now beyond his control. 'The tension is now at its peak', wrote Redlich in his diary on 22 July. 'We in the know are quite calm.'[29] He had meant that all was going well; that the ultimatum was ready; that Serbia would be unable to accept it; that war was therefore certain. He meant, without knowing it, that blessed release was at hand: in a very few days now neither he nor anybody else would ever have to think again: he, and everybody else, could throw off all responsibility, shed the burden of the brain, abandon the dusty thankless task of trying to make society work, and advance with glad cries into the great inane of violent action. This abdication of reason was not an affair only of the responsible statesmen: these, for years, even though heavily blinkered, had clung to reasonableness. They were swept aside now by the second echelon, not the hereditary rulers but the politicians and the publicists who had put themselves forward as the men best qualified to make society work and had now given up because they found the task too hard – having in the process of finding it too hard helped to ruin the rare spirits among them, Beck above all, who were prepared to go on trying.

'The energy of patience'[30] – that had been Beck's private slogan: it was, as he saw it, the only useful sort of energy in any statesman. It was also the rarest. He was, as we have already seen, a man who knew all about the delights of soldiering and who looked back on his days of national service as to a golden age. But he had put away toy soldiers. In June 1911, long after he had been driven out of office, and at the height of the Agadir crisis, he had written in a Viennese newspaper:

> We have achieved wonders: in a bare fraction of a second we can destroy foes by the thousand; but the enemy can also destroy us by the thousand. Surely it would mean the dawn of a truly golden age if only we could switch to the cultural advance of mankind the whole force of mental labour and material resources whose ultimate aim today is the destruction of men and their labour. In the very heart of the realm there are not enough hospitals, in many of its provinces there are not even doctors – but there are dreadnoughts, submarines, torpedoes, rifles and machine-guns, howitzers and bombs of every kind. . . .[31]

The thought was not original; it has been shared by many since. But at least it showed the other side of the medal. There were still men who could stand against the hysteria of the party politicians and the professional diplomats. And one of them, as close in spirit to Adolf Fischhof as makes no difference, could rise to become Prime Minister of Austria just fifty-eight years after Fischhof had spoken out in the streets of Vienna for tolerance and sweet reason.

On 23 July, the day of the ultimatum, the day after Redlich had triumphantly written in his diary that 'we in the know are quite calm', Beck, in despair, was writing to his supporters at home in Styria, to tell them that he had just come from calling on the Finance Ministry and the Ballhausplatz: 'In both places my original impression was confirmed that they want to push things to war with Serbia, even at the risk of a European conflagration.'[32]

On 25 July, the day of Serbia's reply to the ultimatum, the British

Foreign Minister, Sir Edward Grey, went away for the week-end to get some fishing at Itchen Abbas. By the time he came back he found that what everyone until then had hoped was an Austro-Serbian crisis was now a European one. In reply to a hint from St Petersburg that the whole issue should be threshed out by the Powers, Sir Arthur Nicolson had immediately proposed a conference of Germany, France and England, while Russia, Austria and Serbia should be asked to suspend all active military operations. There still seemed some hope; but at this stage Germany did not help. Bethmann-Hollweg did not immediately reject the idea of a conference, but he refused to try to influence Vienna: 'It is impossible for us', he telegraphed Lichnowsky, in London, 'to summon our ally in this quarrel with Serbia before a European court.'[33] Later in the day he told the Austro-Hungarian Ambassador to Berlin that the German government was disinclined to acquiesce in Grey's proposal for a conference. The blank cheque was to be honoured.

Next day, on 28 July, Austria-Hungary declared war on Serbia. Franz Josef, still at Ischl, had first been assured that Serbian resistance would be negligible and that the whole country could be overrun within two to three weeks.

On 29 July Sir Edward Grey made another belated attempt, this time in desperation, to get Germany to co-operate in preventing a European war. For the first time he warned Lichnowsky that if Germany attacked France England would be unable for long to stand aside. At last Whitehall had done what should have been done much earlier.

Poor Lichnowsky, beside himself, telegraphed to Berlin:

England now shows herself in her true colours . . . the lowdown shopkeeping rabble. . . . Grey knows very well that if he utters a single word of warning in Paris and Petersburg, recommending neutrality, both will stand still at once. But he refuses to say the word, and threatens us instead, lowdown, cowardly blackguard that he is. England alone bears responsibility for war and peace, not us any more![34]

Prince Lichnowsky, dragged from his retirement to be the representative in London of a government that paid no attention to him and regarded him, not incorrectly, as a pronounced Anglophile, was normally the image of a gentle and polished man of the world. This shrill and desperate outcry, so completely out of character, shocked

Bethmann-Hollweg to the heart. At last he woke up to the appalling danger, and suddenly panicked. Bethmann-Hollweg faced about: Austria must, he signalled to Vienna, accept outside mediation; Germany 'must decline to be irresponsibly dragged into a world war'.[35]

But it was too late to be shocked. On the very same day Franz Josef at last spoke: the eighty-four-year-old Emperor, who had kept the peace for forty-eight years, was mounting his horse:

> It was my most profound wish to devote the years which God in His mercy may still grant me to working for peace and to protecting my peoples from the heavy burdens and sacrifices of war.
>
> But the fates have seen otherwise. The machinations of a hostile Power, moved by hatred, compel me after many long years of peace to take up the sword to preserve the honour of my Monarchy, to defend its integrity and its power, and to stand guard over its possessions. . . .
>
> In these solemn hours I am fully conscious of the meaning of my decision and of my responsibility before the Almighty.
>
> I have examined and weighed all.
>
> It is with a clear conscience that I enter the path to which duty calls me.
>
> I put my faith in my peoples, who have always gathered round my Throne in unity and loyalty through every tempest, who have always been ready for the heaviest sacrifices for the honour, the majesty, the power of the Fatherland.
>
> I put my faith in the Austro-Hungarian army, in its bravery and its dedicated loyalty.
>
> I put my faith in the Almighty, that He may grant victory to my arms.   FRANZ JOSEF.[36]

The blank cheque had been cashed.

On that day, too, Russia began to mobilize: the military districts of Kiev, Odessa, Moscow and Kazan were put on a war footing. On the evening of Thursday 29 July this partial mobilization became general. Next day Germany declared war on Russia. On 2 August Berlin sent an ultimatum to Belgium, demanding free passage for its troops. On the 3rd, Germany declared war on France. On 4 August at 2 p.m. Sir Edward Grey telegraphed his ultimatum to Berlin, requesting a reply by midnight German time. No reply came, and all Europe was at war. The 'positive deed' had been done.

FINIS AUSTRIAE

The last hours of peace, the queer, unguided nature of the train of events which set the armies in motion, should have filled the rulers of Europe with fearful surmise. Here was something happening that none of them wanted, that some of them had made desperate eleventh-hour attempts to prevent. The Austro-Serbian War, originally conceived by Conrad as a limited punitive action, had become the First World War above all because neither the monarchs nor the statesmen understood the mechanics of mobilization as applied to huge conscript armies; and by the time they did understand it was too late to countermand mobilization orders without losing face and without dislocating the various national economies. In the past the order for mobilization had been one of the cards in the diplomatic pack, an ace by all means, but a recognized part of the series, the last and most effective means of bringing pressure to bear. In all the Chancelleries of Europe there was not a statesman who realized that this was no longer so, that the ace had become the joker. The great armies of 1914 could not be put in a state of immediate readiness by the stroke of a pen, and then, by another stroke, sent back home. Even now it is hard to determine the moment of time when this had become true. The only certain thing was that it had become true by 1914. General mobilization meant war: the mass armies were no longer the obedient pawns of statesmen; they had taken on a life of their own. And what had happened to the armies was only symptomatic: the nations themselves had also changed. They had become mass societies. The truth that mass societies may be all too easily manoeuvred into fighting but can only with the utmost difficulty be extracted from a war once it has begun, was hidden in those August days from rulers who should have been appalled by the terrifying evidence of their own impotence. Caught up by a new and sinister situation for which there were no precedents to act as guides, they should at least have seen that a war which had come without any of them wanting it was likely to be very hard to check. By the end of that first week of August they should already have been thinking in terms of how most swiftly to disarm the devouring and uncontrollable monster of their own creation. But they were blinded, as well as impotent: the gods were active as rarely before. Having been swept against their will into a catastrophe of monstrous proportions, the rulers of Europe made no attempt to regain control of events. At best they savoured nostalgic phrases about the lights going out; more usually, refraining from drawing general conclusions, they applied themselves to extracting national advantage from universal calamity. The Russians dreamt of Constantinople; the French of revenge; the Germans aspired to mastery of the fertile Eastern borderlands; the British saw a chance to smash the German economic challenge; Italians, Bulgarians, Rumanians calculated their chances, ready to throw pledged alliances to the winds in the name of expediency; only Austria had what she wanted, her war against Serbia – but from the beginning she was so beset by Russia that Conrad's elegant planning had to go by the board.

The monarchs and the statesmen abdicated and, in effect, handed over their destinies, and the destinies of the peoples they were supposed to rule, to the generals. It was not until late in 1916, when it had been finally proved that in the day of mass armies and intolerable fire-power generalship was at a discount, that any of them began to ask the question all should have asked more than two years before: where was all this leading, and how were they to resume control before it was too late, while there was anything left to control. Characteristically, the first men to ask this question were the monarchs, not the politicians. But by then a fresh portent had revealed itself. The new barbarism had been born: the concept of unconditional surrender (though not yet the phrase) had taken hold of men's minds. Gone were the days when the chief aim of diplomacy had been to strike a balance between conflicting claims and interests and when war had been seen simply as an unfortunate extension of diplomacy, to redress the balance, or to change it in the light of changed conditions, when the diplomats had failed. The war on the side of the Entente had become a war of the people for the people run by men of the people; and the good people had got it into their heads that it must be the war to end war, that if the Central Powers could be crushed and totally humiliated, everlasting peace and concord would ensue. They really believed this, and for the most excellent of reasons: incensed by the way in which the crowned heads and professional diplomats had muddled them into war, they struck out blindly against what Disraeli had once called the 'traditionary influences'. The very men who for so many difficult decades had managed to keep in check the forces of the human jungle, so that ordinary men and women could go about their affairs in peace and often in decent prosperity, were now saddled with all the blame for what had become in the minds of the sovereign peoples of France, Italy, the United Kingdom and the United States, a fight to the finish, cost what it might, a war of annihilation. It was all or nothing. This concept, first expressed in the furious and spontaneous rejection of the Lansdowne letter late in 1917 – the voice of an aristocrat of the old school calling for the exercise of reason – was to lead through anarchy into totalitarianism and back into anarchy.

2

Austria had started the war, and Austria was the first of the belligerents to see a glimmering of the light. She was also to be the first to pay the price for not seeing it a good deal earlier, with the dismemberment of her own body.

From the beginning, the Monarchy was in the worst possible position. Although it had been the first to break the peace it was the only one of the Powers which had nothing to gain by victory and everything to lose by defeat. It had no war aims of an inflammatory kind, either good or bad. There was no desire to annex any part of Serbia. Serbia had to be chastized and weakened, and as a result of this the Monarchy might expect to strengthen her economic penetration into the Balkans and towards Salonika; nothing else at all was to be hoped for. But because of the way things had fallen out, and because of Vienna's fixation on her own backyard and failure to comprehend the movement of European politics as a whole, the Monarchy found itself harnessed to a dynamic Power with very definite war aims of an imperialistic kind, and opposed by other Powers seeking clear-cut territorial gains. Instead of executing a swift campaign to win for itself more elbow-room in the Balkans, it found itself fighting a war for survival in a Europe engaged in the first stages of a seismological convulsion. Forty years later, the distinguished Austrian historian, Hugo Hantsch, was to write:

> Because of its connection with the German Empire, the Monarchy now found itself caught up in the arena of the great world-political contradictions, with which it had nothing at all to do. It had no

reason whatsoever to be at war with Great Britain or France, yet when these Great Powers nevertheless declared war on Austria-Hungary, it was done not only for reasons of solidarity, but also because in their eyes the Central Powers formed a common bloc.[1]

Here, echoing down the years, is surely the voice of Aehrenthal – not the dying visionary of 1911 who saw that 'the great decision which will determine the future of Europe will be made in the Vosges and in the seas which wash the coasts of Germany and England', but the confident, blind Aehrenthal of 1908: 'To the German alliance we are indestructibly bound. . . . The rivalry between Germany and England has nothing to do with us.'

Austria was a Great Power or she was nothing. How could first an Imperial Foreign Minister, then a gifted historian, imagine that any European Power could for a moment contract out of 'world-political contradictions'? Or, more particularly, how could the heirs of Kaunitz, of Metternich, of Schwarzenberg, delude themselves into believing that they could attach themselves to a great, powerful and dynamic ally without incurring a share of the hostility in which that ally was held by its great rivals?

3

If the Monarchy had no war aims, it also had no guide. The old Emperor had held it together for sixty-six years, conducting it in effect from the eighteenth to the twentieth century, and bringing it, more or less united, into Armageddon. Having done that, for all practical purposes he abdicated his authority: in a sense his signing of the mobilization order had been an abdication. He was eighty-four, and he had two years and four months to live. He persisted, heroically, in his routine; but he was no longer an effective ruler. His presence was more necessary than ever before as the living symbol of the reality of the Dual State; but he no longer acted as a guide. Guidance, such as it was, was left to the politicians and the generals. But Parliament did not exist. It had not been called since its proroguing in the spring of 1914, and it was not to meet again until after Franz Josef's death. The German Austrians were afraid of it. They were obsessed by the fear of parliamentary agitation on the part of disloyal elements among the nationalities, above all the Czechs. They could not believe that the men who were preaching sedition in Bohemia, in Galicia, in Croatia – the Czechs, Kramář and Klofáč; the Ruthenian, Markov;

the Croats, Supilo and Trumbić – were only isolated figures commanding very little popular support. They could not see that it would have been better by far to have disaffected politicians letting off steam in the *Reichsrat* under the eye of the Vienna government than building themselves up in the provinces as symbols of national resistance to Habsburg rule. So the *Reichsrat* did not exist, and the resistance grew, but at first very slowly. It grew, chiefly, because the back areas, which included the most vulnerable parts of the Monarchy, were placed by the civilian government of Stürgkh under military rule step by step, and the soldiers, with their harsh repressive policies, sowed resistance wherever they went.

In a word, the German politicians had taken over from the Emperor, and instead of coming to terms with the brother races, they themselves abdicated in favour of the military, who could be guaranteed to keep down Slavs, while the Vienna Germans made increasingly common purpose with the Germans of the Reich. It was against this background, a sort of mirror image of the state of affairs in 1848, the year of his accession, that the old Emperor faded slowly away and died.

He died on 21 November 1916, two years short of the seventieth anniversary of his accession. For some time he had been having trouble with his chest. Now, quite suddenly, he was worn out. On the evening of his last day they got him to bed two hours before his regular bedtime. He was too weak to kneel at his *prie-dieu*, so he said his prayers sitting. Everyone knew that he was dying, and an imposing uniformed assembly had gathered in the anterooms at Schönbrunn. But he himself gave instructions that he was to be wakened at half past three next morning; he had so much to do. Within an hour he was dead, and Katherina Schratt, led forward by the new Emperor, Karl, laid two white roses on his breast.[2]

By now Vienna was feeling with great severity the strain of war. The real hunger had not yet set in, but the people were weary, apathetic and dispirited. It was too late for the death of the wonderful old man to strike them as a cataclysm; it was not even the last straw. It was to be expected, and it made no difference: a movement was in train which no Habsburg, not even Franz Josef, could withstand. For three days the Viennese filed past the corpse of their Emperor, of their history, as it lay in state at Schönbrunn; but the impact of his death was muffled. And when the final moment came and the coffin was taken to rest in the Capuchin church in the Neuermarkt, its small, plain façade concealing the tomb of so many Emperors, the last theatrical gesture offered posthumously in the traditional Habsburg way seemed more than just a repetition of Habsburg arrogance formally humbling itself at the gates of heaven. When the Court Chamberlain (still Prince Montenuovo) knocked with his golden staff on the closed door with its heavy sable hangings, demanding admission for 'His Apostolic Majesty the Emperor Franz'; when the monk behind the door replied that he knew nothing about His Apostolic Majesty; when the performance was repeated, and, finally, the haughty Montenuovo craved admission for 'Your brother Franz, a miserable sinner' – when the solemn ritual, as so often before, had been played out and the coffin received at last into the impersonal care of Capuchin Friars, it seemed that at last the symbol had become the truth itself.

4

At this time, at the end of 1916, the Empire was holding together well and the military situation was good. Serbia and Montenegro had at last been overrun; the Russian front was more or less static, with the Central Powers occupying practically all Galicia and the Bukovina, as well as Warsaw and Brest-Litovsk. At Gallipoli the Turks had long before brought to nothing the threat to the Straits, and the Allies were bogged down at Salonika. Italy could make no impression on the long Alpine front. Almost the last news the old Emperor had received had been of the great victory over the Rumanians and the occupation of Bucharest. There was stalemate in the West. But the situation behind the lines was much less favourable.

Already in October, deeply apprehensive about the political and economic effects of a continuation of the war, Franz Josef and Wilhelm II had decided that it was time to halt the Gadarene stampede and call for a compromise peace. But the tone of Berlin was arrogant and overbearing. When the Entente Powers, incredulous of the sincerity of their intentions, rejected their overtures in December, the Monarchy, not Germany, was the harder hit. So much so that the new Emperor, Karl, Franz Josef's grandnephew, pledged himself to work for peace and, almost at once, through his brothers-in-law, the Princes Sixtus and Xavier of Bourbon-Parma, put himself in touch with Paris. Serious conversations were carried on for the first three months of 1917. Poincaré and Briand sent word to Karl that they had no intention of seeking the destruction of the Monarchy: all they demanded was the restoration of Alsace-Lorraine and unconditional guarantees of the independence of Belgium and Serbia.[3] The climax came when Karl, pressed heavily by Prince Sixtus, put his assent to these terms into writing: he assured the French President that he would urge upon his allies 'with all means and with all my personal influence the just demands of France for the restoration of Alsace-Lorraine'.[4] The idea of a separate peace was now on the table. It was shattered by Italy's insistence on obtaining Trieste and the Trentino, long promised by the Entente as the reward for her changing sides, and, more importantly, by the conduct of Count Czernin, that same Count Czernin who had once adjured Franz Ferdinand to be Caesar, who now, as Imperial Foreign Minister, was determined to bind the Monarchy more closely than ever to Berlin. It was now indeed, when Clemenceau published the Sixtus letter in 1918 as a retort to Czernin's blustering, that Austria found her last escape route closed. Wilhelm II was not unnaturally indignant when he discovered that Karl had pledged himself to back France's demand for Alsace-Lorraine. Karl was summoned to the German Emperor's headquarters at Spa, there to explain, to apologize, and suffer his inheritance to be tied indissolubly to the Hohenzollern destiny: thenceforth the great Empire, already subservient to Berlin in all matters concerning the higher conduct of the war, was in every way a German satellite.

5

It is commonly believed that the Monarchy found itself in a state of suspended dissolution from the very outbreak of the war and that the end from that moment was inevitable. In the light of what happened it is impossible to sustain this view. The worst has been presented in previous chapters. If the worst had been the whole truth the Empire could not have held together for a month under the impact of the violence now let loose upon it. In fact it held together for four years, surviving by nearly two years the death of Franz Josef and the end of the mystique attached uniquely to his person.

To begin with, the obvious contradictions were scarcely felt at all. Even in the most disaffected provinces there was no attempt at revolt. The army was at first wholly loyal, and the greater part of it was to remain loyal, in the teeth of fearful punishment, for the next four years, justifying all the claims that had been made for its supra-national quality. Even the Czechs, who were later to go over in large numbers to the Russians, were for a long time staunch. The famous demonstration of two Prague regiments in 1915 was not a signal for revolt. They marched off to the front with banners saying: 'We march against Russia, but we don't know why!' The military authorities and the Vienna government regarded this as an anti-Habsburg demonstra-tion, and treated it accordingly. But the civilian Governor of Bohemia, Count Thun, saw deeper. He insisted that this was no political demonstration but, rather, a failure of discipline within the army, for which the officers, not the troops, must be blamed. It was, in fact, an early manifestation of war-weariness, that same war-weariness that was soon to be made articulate by the English poet, Siegfried Sassoon, and, much later, celebrated in innumerable books about the war. It was to produce the French army mutiny in 1917, to trigger off the Russian Revolution, and, in the end, to infect the armies of the Central Powers, so that – but only at the end – they got out of control. It arose in the field from the bombardment of too many ordinary human beings dressed in uniform by too much metal and high explosive as they struggled for too long in too much mud; it arose at home from hunger and privation. It was a revolt against the politicians who had started the war without knowing what they were doing and to no obvious end, and against the generals for not know-ing how to win it quickly. Even so, until 1918 the only serious defections were among the Czechs; and the Czechs defected because they felt they had somewhere to go, being closer to their Slav brothers of Muscovy than to the Germans, who, as the war went on, gained more and more the upper hand.

Masaryk, the university professor of genius, once he had decided that the Monarchy must be broken, had a hard row to hoe; but, unlike the extremists, represented by Kramář and Klofáč, who had clamoured for the destruction of the Habsburgs while Masaryk still saw them as a shield, once he had made his decision he knew what to do. He had to get America on his side.

Already in the spring of 1915 the Croat, Trumbić, had been able to set up a Yugoslav Council in London, dedicated to the liberation of the Southern Slavs of the Empire and their unification with those outside it. The sculptor Mestrović, from Dalmatia, was one of his right-hand men. But in fact he did not get far: his fellow-countrymen in the Imperial and Royal Army were, as good Catholics, not at all interested in uniting with the Orthodox Serbs: indeed, they were using the Habsburg war as a heaven-sent opportunity for punishing the 'barbarians' in Belgrade: Stepan Tisza in Budapest gave them their heads. Masaryk went more slowly; but, in the end, it was he, the father of Czechoslovakia, who was also the real creator of the Yugoslav State, mobilizing the whole weight of Slav émigré opinion, above all in America, and gaining the ear of President Wilson.

It was not until May 1916 that the Czech National Council was set up in Paris, and even then Masaryk received little support from Prague and Bratislava. Apart from Kramář and his friends (who were sentenced to death in June 1916, but never executed), the Czechs went very carefully while the war hung in the balance. Until 1917 every anti-Habsburg gesture was regularly condemned by the local Czech authorities and countered by formal declarations of solidarity with the Monarchy and loyalty to the throne.[5] The conduct of the military gave every cause for resentment, but what finally swung the Czechs was, at home, fear of Budapest, and, abroad, the gradual emergence of Allied war aims, which involved the dismemberment of the Monarchy. As Vienna fell increasingly under the dominion of Berlin, so Czech disaffection grew: the Czechs knew very well that Berlin would be a tougher nut to crack than Vienna had ever been. And in this connection it is sometimes forgotten that the Germans of the Sudetenland, whose incorporation into Hitler's Germany of 1938 was to be the occasion of Munich, had never been citizens of the Reich: until 1918 they had been subjects of the Habsburgs.

The attitude of the Entente was for a long time ambiguous. Certainly in 1914 there was no thought at all in Paris, London or Petersburg of the destruction of the Habsburg Monarchy. As we have seen, as late as the early spring of 1917 the French, through Prince Sixtus, were assuring the new Emperor Karl that they had no desire for any such consummation. But already by then there were new influences at work. Taking advantage of the peace feelers of the Central Powers put out in the autumn of 1916, President Wilson had invited all the belligerents to make formal statements of their war aims. The reply of the Entente was delivered in Washington on 10 January 1917, at the very time when Poincaré and Briand were engaged in their tortuous discussions with Vienna. The reply started, as was to be expected, with demands for the restoration of Montenegro, Serbia and Belgium and the evacuation of all those parts of

France, Russia and Rumania occupied by the Central Powers. It then, however, proceeded, almost as an afterthought, to develop a new and fateful theme by insisting on 'the liberation of Italians, of Slavs, of Rumanians and Czecho-Slovaks from foreign domination'. This, if it meant anything at all, meant the dismemberment of the Empire, which would have been left with the Austrian hereditary lands, less parts of Styria and Carinthia, and the rump of Hungary. It made nonsense in advance of the French avowals to the Emperor Karl. It meant the end of the dynasty.

But it seems that these far-reaching demands were not very seriously intended at the time, or even understood by the men who put them forward. The Entente, having rejected the peace offer of the Central Powers, were now concerned with impressing the democratic Americans with the purity of their cause. With this in mind they sought to emphasize their interest in the sacred concept of self-determination, without properly understanding what lay behind that all too facile phrase: certainly the British Prime Minister of the day, David Lloyd George, whose defeat of Mr Asquith at the end of 1916 reflected the new spirit calling for total victory and unconditional surrender, knew nothing of most of the minority races of the Empire. No less certainly the Russian Tsar had no intention of applying the principle of self-determination to his own subject-peoples. The use of the term Czecho-Slovaks in that document is interesting in itself: Czechs and Slovaks were not natural collaborators, and the concept of a new State of Czechoslovakia was Masaryk's own.

The important thing however was that this set of war aims, compiled in a hurry and for an *ad hoc* purpose, from now on began to assume a life of its own. The political exiles from the Habsburg lands, who had lately been thrown into despair by the fear that the fighting might be brought to an end before the old order had been irretrievably shattered, were strengthened; and the idea of self-determination, as well as sentiments of an anti-dynastic kind, increasingly coloured the thinking of the Entente.

The more so when, in March 1917, the Russian Monarchy was overthrown. So long as the Entente included among them an absolutist autocracy, the Russia of Nicholas II, it was difficult for Lloyd George and Briand, though not impossible (such is the stuff that politicians are made of), to pretend that they were fighting a war for democracy against autocracy. But with the disappearance of Nicholas from the scene, all that was changed. The British and the

French did not at first perceive their great good fortune: they were perturbed by the vacuum in the East and the prospect of the collapse of Russia as a fighting Power. But the Americans were farther away and not fighting for their lives: they saw it at once. On 20 March the American Secretary of State, Robert Lansing, was able to inform the Cabinet in Washington that the Russian Revolution 'had removed the one objection to affirming that the European war was a war between Democracy and Absolutism'.[6] America could now join in with a clear conscience. And this, three weeks later, she did, her passage being greatly eased by Germany's announcement of her new policy of unrestricted submarine warfare.

Germany, now dragging Austria in her train, had made one gratuitous blunder in the overbearing tone of her peace overtures in the autumn of 1916; she made a second with the launching of her submarine campaign; she made a third by failing to perceive that the Russian Revolution, allowed to proceed unchecked, must strike a death-blow to the principle of legitimacy which was the main prop of the Hohenzollerns, no less than of the Habsburgs. Instead of recognizing the nature of the avalanche that had been started she proceeded to aggravate it by introducing Lenin, like a bacillus, into Petersburg – all in the short-term interests of a quick victory on the Eastern front (but a victory for what?) and the conquest of the granary of the Ukraine. The war continued. When Lenin and his Bolsheviks seized power in November 1917 his immediate appeal for an end to the fighting went unregarded. At the same time, and for very different reasons, Lord Lansdowne, whom nobody could accuse of being less than patriotic, was launching his own appeal in London for a compromise peace on rational lines. The Third Battle of Ypres had been in progress during all the late summer and autumn. The French army had mutinied. In the atrocious mud of Passchendaele 400,000 men had fallen, without, apparently, achieving anything. Russia, under Lenin, was about to get out of the war. It seemed a sensible moment to talk peace; but things had gone too far: the Germans were already planning their great offensive for the spring of 1918; the Entente, disembarrassed of Russia and reinforced by the great transatlantic democracy, were engaged in a struggle to the finish with the forces of evil. Only the Habsburg Monarchy was interested in peace without outright victory.

Austria was now hungry. She was dominated by Germany and blackmailed by Budapest. From the very beginning Stepan Tisza had made his own arrangements for the war, which involved sacrificing Cisleithnia for the greater glory of St Stephen. He had fought intelligently and stubbornly to keep the destinies of his own minorities in the hands of Budapest. Above all he had contrived to keep Croatia out of the hands of the military government. The lands of St Stephen were to be held intact, come what might, let the Monarchy be shattered and the King of Hungary thrown to the wolves. In so doing he assisted the doom of his own country as well as of the Empire as a whole. Now he was virtual master of the Empire, using the immense reserves of Hungarian grain to put pressure on a Vienna which had nowhere to turn. Germany could have fed Vienna from the newly acquired resources of the Ukraine, and, indeed, had promised to do so. But Germany was selfish too. The Peace of Brest-Litovsk, known as the 'Bread Peace', brought no relief. Germany ate the bread. This was Germany's fourth great blunder. For the time was close when, with the launching of Ludendorff's great March offensive, Germany would badly need a restored, unified and revitalized Austria-Hungary at her side. Instead, the Monarchy was riven by strikes and threats of revolution. The immediate danger now was less the defection of the nationalities – though the Czechs had gone over in large numbers to the Russians, and the Budapest politicians, with the splendid and courageous exception of Count Karolyi, were now actively working against Vienna – than a working-class revolt, stimulated by the Russian Revolution.

The remarkable thing was that the Habsburgs had held on for so long and that their army had proved so loyal. The deeds of that great army remain unsung. For four years it fought, always with amazing tenacity, sometimes with great skill, first against the Russians and the Serbs, then, as well, against the Italians and the Rumanians, on a front that ran from the Adriatic to Central Poland, and then along the terrible Alpine barrier. From the beginning Conrad's dream of a swift conquest of Serbia had had to be abandoned – and with it the only meaning of the war. Instead of crushing the Serbs according to plan with a massive deployment, he had to move against the Russians advancing into Galicia. He relied on swift German assistance; but the Germans were otherwise engaged. They also were fighting an action the failure of which deprived the war of its whole meaning for them too. To sweep France from the board before turning to smash Russia they threw their weight into the execution of the Schlieffen Plan, the great turning movement, via Belgium, which was to envelop Paris.

But the young Moltke lacked both the genius and the nerve of his uncle: he wrecked the plan and finished up in front of Paris on the Marne – so that the Germans were indeed faced with their familiar spectre of a war on two fronts – the endless war of attrition on the Western Front, and the war of immense slogging battles, finally turning also into one of attrition, on the Eastern Front. Further, by invading Belgium, they had brought England into the war against them: Aehrenthal's dying prophecy had come true.

It was not until 1915 that Germany could go to the help of the Austrians. Meanwhile vast numbers of the Habsburg army had been engaged in a losing campaign against superior Russian forces, which, with climax on climax, lasted without interruption for four months on end. Two million men were locked together in those battles, of which nobody has ever heard. On both sides there were tremendous strategic deployments and dramatic advances, stormings and retreats. By the time the Italians came in, the Imperial and Royal army had already fought the greatest, bloodiest and most exhausting battles in the history of the dynasty, and the war was only beginning. It managed, nevertheless, to keep the fighting on Italian soil.

We have heard a great deal about the mud of Flanders and the torturing heat of Gallipoli; but we have heard little or nothing about the mud of the great Polish plain and the Serbian river valleys; the bitter and terrible fighting in the Carpathians, the Bosnian hills, the Karst of Istria – where the totally barren limestone rock, splintering under shellfire, magnified a thousand times the effect of every burst; in the high Dolomites, where Austrians and Italians in sub-zero temperatures and eternal snow tunnelled and counter-tunnelled through ice and living rock to emerge facing each other at point-blank range thousands of feet above the valley floor: the relics of that mountain war still, half a century later, clutter the sheer precipices of Monte Marmolata, so that it is possible to be freshly amazed and incredulous that ordinary men, Italians and Austrians alike, managed to exist at all, let alone fight, in such conditions – and to marvel at historians and military critics who generalize comfortably about the poor fighting qualities of both armies.

As for the great Galician deployments: who remembers the battles of the San, of Lutsk, of Lemberg? Some of the great moments of human courage and endurance have fallen into oblivion for no other reason than that both the winners and the losers were in the end defeated. It was not for Lenin to glorify the epic of the San. As for the Austrians, they lost the war and their Empire: it was not for the victors to celebrate the four battles of the Karst, the storming of Belgrade, the twelve battles of the Isonzo. In the end the whole terrible story was reduced to the horizon of 'the good soldier Schweik'. That, perhaps, could have been endured if only the good soldier Schweik had been determined to defend his birthright, instead of surrendering it to the first plausible rabble-rouser.

In Cisleithnia it was not until the beginning of 1918 that affairs got quite out of hand. Parliament had been recalled at last in May 1917; but it was too late. While academic politicians who had helped to drive Berchtold to the brink in 1914 now wrestled with liberal solutions, the nationalities, at last, backed by Allied promises, now entered the game in earnest. There were demands in the new Parliament for a federation of free and equal national States, for a union of all the Slavs under the Habsburgs, for sovereign constitutional national assemblies for every individual people. Budapest watched aloofly. This state of affairs did not prevent the army from breaking the Italian front in October 1917 in the Twelfth Battle of the Isonzo, better known as Caporetto. But the check after Caporetto, when Italy's allies stopped the gap, was too much. And then, on 8 January 1918, came the Fourteen Points of President Wilson. Lloyd George could still declare that 'the dissolution of the Monarchy is not one of our war aims';[7] but the Fourteen Points spoke differently: autonomy for all the peoples of Austro-Hungary, the rectification of the frontier with Italy 'on clearly recognizable national lines', the creation of an independent Poland with access to the sea. . . . 'Our programme is justice for all peoples and nationalities, be they strong or weak. . . .'

Kramář, amnestied, proclaimed the foundation of the State of Czechoslovakia. The Poles went over to active opposition. The Czech legion in Russia, which had fought for the Tsar but held aloof from the Bolsheviks, made it their business to obstruct the return of Austrian and Hungarian prisoners of war to the Habsburg army. In June 1918 the Czech National Council in Paris was formally recognized as the provisional government of a Czechoslovak State. The South Slav rebels, still a minority of the Croats and Slovenes of the Monarchy, proclaimed in Lubliana a new nationalist organization conceived as 'part of the general South Slav National Council in Zagreb, which will shortly assemble to prepare for the assumption of all rights of State sovereignty'.

On the Western Front the great March offensive had shot its bolt.

On the new Eastern Front Franchet d'Esperey, based on Salonika, had broken the Bulgarians, who asked for an armistice. In Vienna harassed intellectuals clutched at straws in a starving, mutinous city incapable of facing another winter of war. At what they took to be the eleventh hour they persuaded the Monarchy to offer to transform itself into a federation of democratic States; but they had misread the time. It was long past the hour. The Hungarians, clinging to their dreams with characteristic single-mindedness, regarded these manoeuvres with contempt. As the army prepared itself for a last stand against the threat from Italy, and while the Allies mopped up the Germans in the West, Budapest demanded the immediate return of all Hungarian units: they were needed at home by Tisza to preserve the integrity of St Stephen and the estates of the great magnates.

This was the end. While Karl still wrestled with the politicians in Vienna, seeking through expedient after desperate expedient to hold the Habsburg inheritance together, somehow, anyhow, round the unifying symbol of the Crown, the army at last began to break and the break became a rout. On 24 October the Allies mounted a great offensive against what was left of the army in Italy. It was a superfluous operation. The Monarchy existed no longer. There was only a monarch. The troops who tried to stem the attack belonged now to half a dozen countries, some of them already bound to the Entente. But the troops did not know this: they thought they were still Austrians, and they tried to fight back. There was nobody to tell them when to stop. In the end they simply broke away, not knowing where to go, or indeed where they belonged. Karl waited a little at Schönbrunn, while the German liberals and socialists wrangled endlessly about the exact shape their new State was to take. It turned out to be a socialist republic. On 11 November 1918, poor Karl, who was a peace Emperor or nothing, at last got the peace for which he had striven so long; but he was no longer Emperor. His formal abdication (from what?) he proclaimed in a note which he signed with a pencil; quite soon, after some absurd adventures, he died in Madeira. The peoples had taken over; but they were not ready. The stage was set for the dictators.

APPENDIX A

Transcript of holograph letter from Lord Cowley, British Ambassador
to Paris, to Count Buol-Schauenstein, Austrian Foreign Minister, after
the conclusion of Lord Cowley's visit to Vienna on a special mission from
Queen Victoria. See Chapter IX, p. 146:

MON CHER AMI,   Paris le 19 mars/59

Je profite d'un courier que Hübner vous expédie, pour vous écrire
quelques lignes. Je suis arrivé ici mercredi soir, ayant passé un
couple de jours à Londres. J'ai eu l'honneur de remettre à la Reine la
lettre dont l'Empereur a daigné me charger pour sa Majesté. Elle s'en
est exprimée fort contente et m'a beaucoup questionné sur tout qui
s'était passé pendant mon court séjour a Vienne. Je ne vous dirai pas
à quel point elle s'est dite satisfaite, satisfaction qui a été partagé par
ses ministres, du récit que je lui en ai fait. Vous deviendriez trop
raidi pour l'avenir, et nous avons encore besoin de toute votre
modération et de toute votre conciliation pour sortir des difficultés
qui nous environnent encore – Ici je n'ai rien trouvé de change, si
ce n'est que le désir pour la paix est encore plus puissant et plus
prononcé, que ce ne l'était à mon départ. *Soyez en convaincu,*
l'Empereur Napoléon cherche une porte de retraite. C'est à nous
tous de la lui ouvrir.

La Russie propose un congrés des cinq puissances, *non pas* pour
les affaires d'Italie mais pour prendre en considération l'état critique
dans lequel se trouve l'Europe. L'Empereur y voit un moyen honor-
able de se soumettre a la volonté des Alliés, et de se délier de ses
engagements vis à vis de la Sardaigne, mais il lui coute beaucoup
d'accepter une proposition qui exclut cette dernière des délibérations.
Je ne sais pas encore ce que l'on en dira à Londres. On voudrait
d'abord savoir ce que vous en pensez. Quant à moi, je ne goute
guère l'idée d'un Congrès. Le mot est trop gros pour les résultats que
l'on pourrait en attendre – Mais je serai très disposé d'accepter des
conférences soit à Londres, soit à Berlin pour examiner ce qu'on
pourrait faire. C'est un fait assez curieux, que la première question
presque que Walewski m'a posée était de savoir, si je pensais qu'une
ligue entre les petits états d'Italie pour leur sureté intérieure trou-
verait la chance à être acceptée par vous. Vous voyez donc qu'on est

ici jusqu'à ce certain point sur le même terrain que vous. A Londres l'idée n'a pas plu, parce-que au fond on préférerait une occupation Autrichienne à une occupation Napolitaine de Rome, si on est obligé de choisir entre les deux – Mais nous nous opposerons pas à un arrangement de cette nature.

Maintenant, que faut-il répondre à la proposition Russe? Je serai très fâché de la voir declinée, parceque je ne vois pas d'autre sortie de nos difficultés, dès qu'elle a été acceptée par la France. Pour vous il me parait une immense chose d'avoir le consentement de la France à l'éloignement de la Sardaigne. Cavour a déjà protesté. Sa protestation n'a pas produit d'effet jusqu'à présent.

Mais la moindre hésitation de votre part pourrait tout compromettre de nouveau. Je dis donc – acceptez – faites les reserves que vous trouvez necessaires pour vos propres possessions en Italie – Mais montrez-vous disposé à examiner franchement le situation des autres Etats Italiens. Un examin ne vous engage à rien. Je devine d'avance vos scrupules. Mais songez que la paix est dans la balance et je ne doute pas de quel côté elle penchera – Le Congrès accepté, la France s'engage à demander avec nous de desarmement en Sardaigne. Croyez vous que Cavour puisse sourire à ce coup?

Ce que j'ai pu dire a l'Empereur Napoléon au sujet des sentiments anciens de l'Autriche et de son Souveraine pour lui, m'a paru faire une bonne impression, mais l'irritation contre l'Allemagne est bien grande et, il ne faut pas se la dissimuler, cette irritation gagne du terrain en France même. Il y a donc lieu de hâter le dénouement de cette crise, et à rassurer les esprits ici et ailleurs. ∴.

Veuillez, cher Ami, lorsqu'une occasion se présente, mettre aux pieds de l'Empereur l'expression de mes hommages les plus respectueux. Je n'oublirai jamais de ma vie l'accueil gracieux, que Sa Majesté a daigné m'accorder.

Ma femme et moi nous causons souvent des délices de notre courte visite dont le souvenir ne s'effacera jamais de nos cœurs.

Mille et mille amitiés.

COWLEY.

APPENDIX B

Distribution of the nationalities within the Habsburg Monarchy as at the 1910 census:

THE MONARCHY AS A WHOLE

Germans	12·011 million	Serbs	2·042 million
Magyars	10·068 million	Slovaks	1·968 million
Czechs	6·643 million	Slovenes	1·371 million
Poles	4·978 million	Italians	0·771 million
Ruthenians	3·999 million	Moslem Slavs	0·612 million
Rumanians	2·888 million	Others	0·368 million
Croats	3·225 million		

These figures may more revealingly be broken down into the Austrian and Hungarian halves of the Monarchy:

Austria

Germans	9·950 million (2·468 million of these
Czechs	6·436 million lived in Bohemia; 720,000
Poles	4·968 million in Moravia)
Ruthenians	3·519 million
Slovenes	1·253 million (409,684 of these lived in
Serbo-Croats	0·788 million Styria)
Italians	0·768 million
Rumanians	0·275 million

Hungary

Magyars	9·944 million
Rumanians	2·948 million
Slovaks	1·946 million
Germans	1·903 million
Ruthenians	0·464 million
Serbo-Croats	0·462 million
*Croats in Croatia-Slavonai	1·600 million
*Serbs in Croatia-Slavonai	0·650 million

* For the purposes of this census, and in order to avoid showing the strength of the Slav minority in Hungary, the Magyars excluded Croatia-Slavonia from their figures.

NOTE ON SOURCES

Books, pamphlets, speeches, letters, and unpublished papers cited in the text are indicated in the Notes which follow.

For the most part this volume is based on printed sources. Its purpose is not to offer new material but to take a new look at facts already established. Many of these facts, however, have so far been accessible only to those who read German. Since the last war Austrian scholars have been extremely active and I have plundered them to such effect that much of the material brought to light by them is here presented for the first time to the English-speaking reader.

Thus the printed sources fall into two divisions: those generally familiar to the English-speaking reader and those likely to be new to all but a few specialists.

The main source of unpublished material is the vast collection of papers preserved by the Archduke Franz Ferdinand, access to which was controlled and severely limited by his son, Duke Maximilian of Hohenberg, until his death (a death hastened by maltreatment in Dachau at the hands of the Nazis) in January 1962. But I have also made free use of the State Archives in Vienna, less in search of new material to quote from than to check documents already published, to compare published extracts from letters, memoranda, etc., with the tone of the whole, and, generally, to feel myself into the chief characters in this narrative. The letters of the Crown Prince Rudolf were particularly revealing in this connection; so were some of Aehrenthal's memoranda, two of which are here cited for the first time.

Perhaps it is worth adding that I have spent a considerable fraction of my life in Vienna and, at one time and another and under various régimes, have visited nearly all the main centres of the old Empire, as well as the great battlefields and Sarajevo itself.

Unpublished Crown Copyright material in the Public Record Office transcribed in this book appears by permission of the Controller of H.M. Stationery Office.

NOTES AND SOURCES

Prologue. The House of Austria PAGES 3–15

1. *p.* 7 BENEDIKT, HEINRICH: *Monarchie der Gegensätze* (Vienna, 1947), p. 43.

2. *p.* 14 ASHLEY, E.: *Life and Correspondence of the Hon. John Temple, Viscount Palmerston* (Revised edn. London, 1876), vol. I, p. 103.

3. *p.* 14 *Ibid.*, p. 104.

4. *p.* 14 TAYLOR, A. J. P.: *The Habsburg Monarchy, 1809–1918* (revised edn. London, 1948), p. 47.

5. *p.* 15 CORTI, COUNT EGON CESAR: *Vom Kind Zum Kaiser* (Graz, 1950), p. 332.

Chapter I. Pre-March PAGES 19–25

1. *p.* 22 NEWMAN, ERNEST: *The Life of Richard Wagner* (London, 1933), pp. 151–72.

2. *p.* 23 SCHUSELKA, FRANZ: *Deutsche Worte eines Oesterreichischers* (Hamburg, 1843), p. 24.

3. *p.* 23 KOCH, M.: *Genesis der Wiener Revolution* (Vienna, 1850), p. 10.

Chapter II. Peoples in Revolt PAGES 26–37

1. *p.* 26 RESCHAUER, HEINRICH, and SMETS, MORITZ: *Das Jahr 1848. Geschichte der Wiener Revolution* (Vienna, 1872), vol. I, p. 10.

2. *p.* 27 GRILLPARZER, FRANZ: *Errinerungen aus dem Jahre 1848.* (5th edn. of collected works, Stuttgart), vol. XX, p. 191.

3. *p.* 28 RESCHAUER U. SMETS, *op. cit.* vol. I, p. 183.

4. *p.* 29 SCHWARZENBERG, ADOLF: *Prince Felix zu Schwarzenberg* (New York, 1946), p. 28.

5. *p.* 32 CORTI, *op. cit.*, p. 241.

6. *p.* 33 SCHWARZENBERG, *op. cit.*, p. 3.

7. *p.* 33 HANSLICK, EDUARD: *Aus meinem Leben* (Berlin, 1894), vol. I, p. 241.

Note. The most complete recent account in English of the Vienna revolution is R. John Rath's *The Viennese Revolution of 1848* (Austin University of Texas Press, 1957). The well-known nineteenth-century histories may be supplemented by the memoirs of the dramatist Grillparzer and Hanslick, the celebrated music critic, cited above, both of which give valuable insight into the mood of the times.

Chapter III. *Counter-Attack* PAGES 38–45

1. *p.* 38 ASHLEY, *op. cit.*, vol. I, p. 93.

2. *p.* 39 *Ibid.*, pp. 104–5.

3. *p.* 39 CORTI, *op. cit.*, pp. 16 *et seq.*

4. *p.* 40 *Ibid.*, p. 19.

5. *p.* 41 *Tagebuch der Erzherzogin Sophie*, 10 Jan. 1848. State Archives, Vienna.

6. *p.* 41 WEST, REBECCA: *Black Lamb and Grey Falcon* (London, 1942), vol. I, p. 6.

Chapter IV. *The Course is Set* PAGES 49–64

1. *p.* 50 ASHLEY, *op. cit.*, p. 104.

2. *p.* 51 *Bismarcks Briefe an General Leopold von Gerlach* (Berlin, 1896), letter of 25 June 1852, p. 235.

3. *p.* 51 Nicholas I to the Tsaritsa, 23 May 1849. Quoted REDLICH JOSEF: *The Emperor Franz Josef* (London, 1929), p. 51.

4. *p.* 52 Schwarzenberg to Metternich, 29 July 1850. *Ibid.*, p. 49.

5. *p.* 53 SCHWARZENBERG, *op. cit.*, p. 11.

6. *p.* 53 *Ibid.*, p. 14.

7. *p.* 53 *Ibid.*

8. *p.* 56 ASHLEY, *op. cit.*, vol. I, p. 98.

9. *p.* 58 SCHWARZSCHILD, LEOPOLD: *The Red Prussian* (London, 1948), p. 220.

10. *p.* 59 MARX, KARL: *Germany: Revolution and Counter Revolution*, pp. 119–20.

This work consists of articles written mostly by Friedrich Engels, but under Marx's name, for the New York *Daily Tribune* in 1851–2. They are reprinted in *Karl Marx's Selected Works*, edited V. Adoratsky (Moscow, 1935).

11. *p.* 59 *Ibid.*, p. 91.

12. *p.* 59 *Ibid.*, p. 93.

13. *p.* 59 *Ibid.*, p. 71.

14. *p.* 60 BIBL, VIKTOR: *Der Zerfall Oesterreichs* (Vienna, 1922–4), vol. 1, p. 186.

15. *p.* 61 Minutes of the Ministerial Council, Olmütz, 3 April 1849. Quoted by General Hugo von Kerchenawe in *Feldmarschall Windisch-Graetz und die Russenhilfe 1848* (Innsbruck, 1930), p. 35.

Chapter V. Palmerston in a White Uniform PAGES 65–77

1. *p.* 66 Franz Josef to Windischgraetz, 12 April 1849. Quoted *ibid.*, p. 40.

2. *p.* 67 Welden to Schwarzenberg, 20 April 1849. *Ibid.*, p. 46.

3. *p.* 67 Minutes of Ministerial Council, Olmütz, 23 March 1849. *Ibid.*, p. 29.

4. *p.* 68 REDLICH, *op. cit.*, p. 60.

5. *p.* 69 FRIEDJUNG, HEINRICH: *Oesterreich von 1848 bis 1860* (3rd edn. Berlin, 1908), vol. 1, p. 430.

6. *p.* 69 Bismarck to his mother-in-law, 1849. Quoted LUDWIG, EMIL: *Bismarck*. Translated by Eden and Cedar Paul (London, 1927), p. 113.

7. *p.* 71 FRIEDJUNG, HEINRICH: *The Struggle for Supremacy in Germany* (London, 1935), p. 5. This is a splendid translation of Friedjung's classic, *Der Kampf um die Vorherrschaft in Deutschland*. Although the original has been slightly abridged by the translators, the long preface, bringing Friedjung up to date, is indispensable. Future page references are to this translation by A. J. P. Taylor and W. L. McElwee.

8. *p.* 74 SCHWARZENBERG, *op cit.*, p. 156

9. *p.* 74 VITZTHUM VON ECKSTÄDT, KARL FRIEDRICH: *Berlin und Wien in den Jahren 1845–1852* (Stuttgart, 1886), p. 304.

10. *p.* 74 *The Letters of Queen Victoria, 1837–61.* Edited by A. C. Benson and Viscount Esher (London, 1907), vol. II, p. 458.

11. *p.* 75 *Ibid.*, p. 330.

12. *p.* 75 *Life and Letters of Lord Beaconsfield*: W. F. Monypenny and G. E. Buckle (London, 1910–20), vol. III, p. 184.

13. *p.* 75 *Ibid.*, p. 185.

14. *p.* 76 DISRAELI, BENJAMIN: *Life of Lord George Bentinck* (new edn. London, 1905), pp. 360–1.

15. *p.* 76 HANSLICK, EDUARD, *op. cit.*, vol. I, p. 149.

Chapter VI. I Command to be Obeyed PAGES 78–98

1. *p.* 79 CORTI, *op. cit.*, p. 344.

2. *p.* 79 REDLICH, *op. cit.*, p. 102.

3. *p.* 80 *Ibid.*, pp. 222–3.

4. *p.* 81 *Ibid.*, p. 91.

5. *p.* 83 BATTAGLIA, OTTO FORST DE: *Johann Nestroy, Abschätzer der Menschen, Magier des Wortes* (Leipzig, 1932), p. 41.

6. *p.* 88 SCHWARZENBERG, *op. cit.*, p. 208.

7. *p.* 88 BERGER, A. F.: *Felix Fürst zu Schwarzenberg* (Leipzig, 1857), p. 490.

8. *p.* 92 BEER, ADOLF: *Die Finanzen Oesterreichs im XIX Jahrhundert* (Prague, 1877), p. 235.

9. *p.* 92 SCHWARZENBERG, *op. cit.*, p. 67.

10. *p.* 93 *Ibid.*, pp. 87–8.

11. *p.* 94 BAUERNFELD, EDUARD VON: *Errinerungen aus Alt-Wien* (Vienna, 1923). Bauernfeld's memoirs throw a great deal of light on the period. The one-act *Posse* referred to (on p. 96), *Alfred der Grosse*, is printed in the memoirs, pp. 331–8. Windischgraetz had written that he would watch over his regiment from heaven: Bauernfeld shows him trying to do so.

12. *p.* 97 *Ibid.*, pp. 311–13.

13. *p.* 97 MÜLLER, PAUL: *Feldmarschall Fürst Windish-Graetz* (Vienna, 1934), p. 264.

14. *p.* 98 MALMESBURY, THE EARL OF: *Memoirs of an Ex-Minister* (London, 1885). Letter to Lord Westmorland 8 March 1852, p. 235.

15. *p.* 98 *Ibid.*, Diary entry for 11 March 1852, p. 240.

Chapter VII. The Heavenly Empress PAGES 99–109

By far the greater part of the material for this chapter in particular, and the relations between Franz Josef and Elizabeth as outlined throughout this volume, comes from Count Corti's *Elisabeth* (Vienna, 1934) and from the second and third volumes of his monumental life of Franz Josef. The first volume of this trilogy, entitled *Vom Kind zum Kaiser* has already been cited. The next two volumes, *Mensch und Herrscher* (Graz, 1952) and *Der Alte Kaiser*, which was finished after Count Corti's death by Hans Sokol (Graz, 1955), carry on the day-to-day life of the Emperor until the end. It is to Count Corti that we owe the flood of illumination from Franz Josef's letters to Elizabeth; from the diary of Elizabeth's daughter, the Archduchess Valerie; from the journal of Countess Marie Festetics and the papers of Frau Ida von Ferenczy, both for very many years the confidantes of the Empress. These documents, from which I have quoted freely, make nonsense of the popular image of Franz Josef and also, I think, though in a lesser degree, of Elizabeth herself.

1. *p.* 100 CORTI, *Mensch und Herrscher*, pp. 101–3.

2. *p.* 101 CORTI, *Elisabeth*, p. 28.

3. *p.* 102 *Ibid.*, pp. 225 and 239.

4. *p.* 102 *Ibid.*, p. 45.

5. *p.* 102 *Ibid.*, p. 54.

6. *p.* 102 *Ibid.*, p. 51.

7. *p.* 104 CORTI, *Vom Kind zum Kaiser*, p. 25.

8. *p.* 104 *Ibid.*, p. 28.

9. *p.* 104 CORTI, *Elisabeth*, p. 58.

10. *p.* 105 Sophie to Franz Josef, 29 June 1854. *Ibid.*, p. 56.

11. *p.* 105 *Ibid.*, p. 57.

12. *p.* 106 King Leopold to Queen Victoria, 3 June 1853. *Letters of Queen Victoria, 1837–61*, vol. II, pp. 544–5.

13. *p.* 107 Franz Josef to Elizabeth, 7 June 1859. Corti, *Elisabeth*, p. 88.

14. *p.* 107 Franz Josef to Elizabeth, 2 June 1859. *Ibid.*, p. 88.

15. *p.* 107 Franz Josef to Elizabeth, 13 June 1859. *Ibid.*, p. 89.

16. *p.* 109 Sophie to her father, 7 Jan. 1850. Corti, *Mensch und Herrscher*, p. 52.

Chapter VIII. Distrusted and Alone PAGES 113–131

1. *p.* 117 The correspondence between Nicholas I and Franz Josef, conducted in French, is in the State Archives, Vienna. A considerable part of it is quoted in Redlich, *op. cit.*, Chapter V.

2. *p.* 120 REDLICH, *op. cit.*, p. 148.

3. *p.* 120 GRILLPARZER, FRANZ: *Ein Bruderzwift in Habsburg.*

4. *p.* 121 REDLICH, *op. cit.*, p. 148.

5. *p.* 124 Metternich to Buol, 18 June 1853. In Burckhardt, Karl J.: *Briefe des Staatskanzlers Fürsten Metternich-Winneburg an den oesterreichischen Minister des Äussern Grafen Buol-Schauenstein aus den Jahren 1852–1859* (Munich, 1934), p. 91.

6. *p.* 124 *Ibid.*, 12 July 1853.

7. *p.* 124 Metternich to Hübner, 16 June 1853. Corti, *Mensch und Herrscher*, p. 118.

8. *p.* 125 Seymour to Clarendon, 18 May 1857. Record Office, London.

9. *p.* 125 BURCKHARDT, *op. cit.*, p. 158.

10. *p.* 126 Metternich to Franz Josef, 26 Sept. 1854. State Archives, Vienna.

11. *p.* 126 Bismarck to Gerlach, 19 October 1854. *Op. cit.*, p. 197.

12. *p.* 127 BURCKHARDT, *op. cit.*, p. vi (Preface).

13. *p.* 127 Franz Josef to Sophie, 8 October 1854. In Schnürer, Franz: *Briefe Kaiser Franz Josefs an seine Mutter 1838–72* (Munich, 1930), p. 232.

14. *p.* 128 REDLICH, *op. cit.*, p. 159.

15. *p.* 128 Lord John Russell to Clarendon, 6 March 1855. Record Office, London.

16. *p.* 128 *Ibid.*, 22 April 1855. Record Office, London.

17. *p.* 129 Seymour to Clarendon, 25 March 1856. Record Office, London.

18. *p.* 129 *Tagebuch Hübner*, 16 Dec. 1855. Quoted Corti, *Mensch und Herrscher*, p. 16.

19. *p.* 130 Franz Josef to Albert of Saxony, 28 August 1855. *Ibid.*, p. 163.

20. *p.* 130 Franz Josef to Buol, 7 Oct. 1855. State Archives, Vienna. There is a facsimile of part of this letter in Hantsch, Hugo: *Geschichte Oesterreichs*, vol. II, facing p. 432 (2nd edn. Vienna, 1955).

21. *p.* 131 Seymour to Clarendon, 29 Nov. 1856. Record Office, London.

Chapter IX. The Loss of Italy PAGES 132–168

1. *p.* 132 TAYLOR, *op. cit.*, p. 92.

2. *p.* 132 *Ibid.*, p. 92.

3. *p.* 132 *Ibid.*, p. 90.

4. *p.* 134 Bismarck to Gerlach, *op. cit.*, p. 266.

5. *p.* 135 *Œuvres de Napoleon III* (Paris, 1869), vol. I, p. 243.

6. *p.* 137 THAYER, WILLIAM ROSCOE: *The Life and Times of Cavour* (London, 1911) vol. I, p. 370.

7. *p.* 137 *The Greville Memoirs*, entry for 11 Dec. 1855. (London, 1887), Third Part, vol. I, p. 303.

8. *p.* 137 MALMESBURY, THE EARL OF, *op. cit.* Diary entry for 29 Nov. 1855, p. 372.

9. *p.* 139 CORTI, *Elisabeth*, p. 72.

10. *p.* 141 THAYER, *op. cit.* Quoting Sir A. H. Layard in *The Quarterly Review*, July 1879, vol. I, pp. 545–6.

11. *p.* 142 Disraeli's memorandum on the origins of the 1859 war. Monypenny and Buckle, *op. cit.*, vol IV, pp. 226–8.

12. *p.* 142 Disraeli to Lord Derby, 7 Jan. 1859. *Ibid*, vol. IV, p. 222.

13. *p.* 143 Cavour to La Marmora, 14 July 1858. Thayer, *op. cit.*, vol. I, p. 528.

14. *p.* 144 MARTIN, THEODORE: *The Life of H.R.H. the Prince Consort* (London, 1880), vol. IV, p. 341. Queen Victoria to Lord Malmesbury, 9 Dec. 1858.

15. *p.* 144 HÜBNER, COUNT JOSEF ALEXANDER VON: *Neun Jahren der Errinerungen eines oesterreischichen Botschafters in Paris* (Berlin, 1902), vol. II, p. 150.

16. *p.* 145 BENEDIKT, HEINRICH: *Die wirtschaftliche Entwicklung in der Franz-Josef-Zeit* (Vienna, 1958), p. 50.

17. *p.* 145 *Ibid.*, p. 51.

18. *p.* 145 Cavour to the Piedmontese Minister at Berne. Thayer, *op. cit.*, vol. I, p. 554.

19. *p.* 146 HÜBNER, *op. cit.*, vol. II, p. 310.

20. *p.* 147 MALMESBURY, *op. cit.*, Letter of 11 April 1859, pp. 475–6.

21. *p.* 147 Ministerial Council of 19 April 1859. Minutes in State Archives, Vienna.

22. *p.* 149 CORTI, *Mensch und Herrscher*, pp. 208–22.

23. *p.* 150 *Ibid.*

24. *p.* 151 For comparative figures of the opposed armies throughout the campaign *see* REGELE, GENERAL OSKAR: *Feldzeugmarschall Benedek* (Vienna, 1960), pp. 129 *et seq.*

25. *p.* 152 CORTI, *Mensch und Herrscher*, pp. 223–6.

26. *p.* 152 There is a fine collection of uniforms of the old Austria, together with contemporary paintings and engravings, in the Heeresmuseum, Vienna.

27. *p.* 152 SCHNÜRER, *op. cit.*, p. 232.

28. *p.* 153 REGELE, *op. cit.*, pp. 290 *et seq.*

29. *p.* 153 *Ibid.*

30. *p.* 159 Count Crenneville to his wife, 8 and 14 June 1859. Quoted Corti, *Mensch und Herrscher*, pp. 230–1.

31. *p.* 164 Franz Josef to Elizabeth, 26 June 1889. *Ibid.*, p. 235.

32. *p.* 165 *Ibid.*

33. *p.* 166 Franz Josef to Elizabeth, 8 July 1859. *Ibid.*, p. 238.

34. *p.* 166 *Ibid.*, p. 241.

35. *p.* 166 *Ibid.*, p. 240.

36. *p.* 166 REDLICH, *op. cit.*, p. 278.

37. *p.* 166 *Ibid.*

Chapter X. Autocracy is not Enough PAGES 169–186

1. *p.* 170 FRIEDJUNG, *The Struggle for Supremacy in Germany* (*op. cit.*), p. 62.

2. *p.* 170 Rechberg's memorandum to Franz Josef, July 1859. State Archives, Vienna.

3. *p.* 171 FRIEDJUNG, *op. cit.*, p. 29.

4. *p.* 172 CORTI, *Mensch und Herrscher*, p. 247.

5. *p.* 173 *Ibid.*, p. 102.

6. *p.* 173 CHARMATZ, RICHARD: *Minister Freiherr von Bruck. Der Vorkämpfer Mitteleuropas* (Leipzig, 1916), pp. 141–3.

7. *p.* 175 EISENMANN, LOUIS: *Le Compromis austro-hongrois de 1867* (Paris, 1904).

8. *p.* 177 Lord Loftus to Lord John Russell, 20 Oct. 1859. Record Office, London.

9. *p.* 178 Franz Josef to Napoleon III, 14 Sept. 1859. State Archives, Vienna.

10. *p.* 179 FRIEDJUNG, *op. cit.*, p. 76.

11. *p.* 181 CORTI, *Mensch und Herrscher*, p. 259.

12. *p.* 181 Franz Josef to Sophie, 21 Oct. 1860. Schnürer, *op. cit.*, p. 301.

13. *p.* 181 Minutes of Ministerial Conference, 28 Feb. 1861. State Archives, Vienna.

14. *p.* 181 Benedek to Crenneville, 18 Jan. 1861. Corti, *op. cit.*, p. 267.

15. *p.* 182 Franz Josef to Sophie, Schnürer, *op. cit.*, p. 299.

16. *p.* 182 Elizabeth to Franz Josef, June 1859. Corti, *Elisabeth*, p. 91.

17. *p.* 182 Franz Josef to Elizabeth, 1 July 1859. *Ibid.*, p. 91.

18. *p.* 184 CORTI, *Mensch und Herrscher*, p. 269.

19. *p.* 185 Franz Josef to Elizabeth, October 1867. Corti, *Elisabeth*, pp. 190–1.

Chapter XI. *Prussia Takes All* PAGES 187–230

1. *p.* 187 For the inferiority of the Austrian armament *see* Regele, *op. cit.*, especially pp. 272–84.

2. *p.* 188 Bismarck in the Prussian *Landtag*, 30 Sept. 1862. *Bismarcks Reden* (Stuttgart, 1892), vol. II, p. 30.

3. *p.* 188 Bismarck to Motley, 17 April 1863: *The Correspondence of John Lothrop Motley* (London, 1889), vol. II, pp. 126–7.

4. *p.* 189 Bismarck to Zedlitz. Quoted Friedjung, *op. cit.*, p. 55.

5. *p.* 190 Disraeli to Queen Victoria, Monypenny and Buckle, *op. cit.*, vol. VI, p. 332.

6. *p.* 191 Bismarck to the Prussian Foreign Minister, Schleinitz, 12 May 1859. Quoted Friedjung, *op. cit.*, p. 17.

7. *p.* 191 FRIEDJUNG, *op. cit.*, p. 33.

8. *p.* 191 Bismarck to Benedetti, 12 March 1866. Friedjung, *op. cit.*, p. 102.

9. *p.* 191 *Ibid.*, p. 120.

10. *p.* 192 Bismarck to General Turr, 10 June 1863. *Ibid.*, p. 190.

11. *p.* 192 Disraeli in the House of Commons. 1853. Monypenny and Buckle, *op. cit.*, vol. IV, p. 337.

12. *p.* 193 Bismarck to Disraeli, 1862. *Ibid.*, vol. IV, p. 341.

13. *p.* 195 CORTI, *Mensch und Herrscher*, p. 291.

14. *p.* 195 Franz Josef to Sophie, Schnürer *op. cit.*, p. 320.

15. *p.* 197 Franz Josef to Sophie, 2 Sept. 1863. *Ibid.*, p. 323.

16. *p.* 197 *Queen Victoria's Letters, 1862–78* (London, 1926), vol. I, p. 108.

17. *p.* 199 REDLICH, *op. cit.*, p. 300.

18. *p.* 206 Ironically, it was planned by von Moltke.

19. *p.* 206 FRIEDJUNG, *op. cit.*, p. 54.

20. *p.* 207 Franz Josef to Albert of Saxony, 16 Feb. 1864. State Archives, Vienna.

21. *p.* 207 FRIEDJUNG, *op. cit.*, has an abbreviated version of this explanation, as received from Bismarck's own lips; p. 314.

22. *p.* 211 FRIEDJUNG, *op cit.*, p. 318.

23. *p.* 211 *Ibid.*, p. 67.

24. *p.* 212 For the fateful disarmament of Austria under pressure of the German liberals in the years before the Austro-Prussian war *see* Regele, *op. cit. Neunte Abschnitt.*

25. *p.* 213 For details of the mobilizations *see* Regele, *op. cit.*, p. 406 and Friedjung, *op. cit.*, pp. 125–6.

26. *p.* 213 FRIEDJUNG, *op. cit.*, p. 94.

27. *p.* 219 The best account of the Benedek tragedy is contained in Regele, *op. cit.* This effectively challenges the conventional view nurtured by historians (notably Redlich, *op. cit.*) who tend to apply civilian standards when assessing the conduct of soldiers reared in the Imperial tradition.

28. *p.* 219 REGELE, *op. cit.*, pp. 398–400.

29. *p.* 221 FRIEDJUNG, *op. cit.*, p. 189.

30. *p.* 224 *Ibid.*, p. 228.

31. *p.* 224 CORTI, *Mensch und Herrscher*, p. 357. But for the whole question of Lt.-Col. Beck's interventions, *see* Regele, *op. cit.*, pp. 443–47.

32. *p.* 224 FRIEDJUNG, *op. cit.*, p. 228.

33. *p.* 225 *Ibid.*, p. 233.

34. *p.* 227 REGELE, *op. cit.*, p. 436.

Chapter XII. Two Crowns, One Head PAGES 233–248

1. *p.* 235 Franz Josef to Sophie, 17 Feb. 1866. Schnürer, *op. cit.*, p. 351.

2. *p.* 236 Elizabeth to Franz Josef, 15 July 1866. Corti, *Elisabeth*, p. 156.

3. *p.* 236 Franz Josef to Elizabeth, 17 July 1866. *Ibid.*, p. 157.

4. *p.* 237 *Ibid.*, 7 Aug. 1866, p. 164.

5. *p.* 237 *Ibid.*, 8 Aug. 1866, pp. 165–6.

6. *p.* 237 *Ibid.*, 10 Aug. 1866, p. 166.

7. *p.* 237 *Ibid.*, 25 Aug. 1866, p. 167.

8. *p.* 238 WERTHEIMER, EDUARD VON: *Julius Andrassy. Sein Leben und seine Zeit* (Stuttgart, 1910–13), vol. I, p. 243.

9. *p.* 244 '*Leges abominabiles, vehementer reprobandae et damnandae . . . irriter et nullius momenti.*' Pius XI in Consistorial Oration, 22 June 1868. *See* Engel-Janosi, Friedrich: *Oesterreich und der Vatikan* (Graz, 1958), vol. I, pp. 147 *et seq.*

10. *p.* 244 Bishop Riegler of Linz.

11. *p.* 247 CORTI, *Mensch und Herrscher*, p. 313.

12. *p.* 248 BAGGER, E.: *Franz Josef* (New York, 1927), p. 363.

Chapter XIII. The Iron Ring of Fate PAGES 249–270

1. *p.* 251 FELDMARSCHALL VON KUHN, Memorandum to the Emperor, 20 July 1870. State Archives, Vienna. But Napoleon III had the same thought in 1869. See *Œuvres de Napoleon III*, vol. III, pp. 24–5.

2. *p.* 252 WILLIAMS, W. A.: *American-Russian Relations 1781–1947* (New York, 1952), p. 21.

3. *p.* 252 New York *Herald*, 29 April 1867. *Ibid.*, p. 22.

4. *p.* 253 REGELE, *op. cit.*, p. 328.

5. *p.* 255 SCHÄFFLE, A. E. F.: *Aus meinem Leben* (Berlin, 1904), vol. I, pp. 201–6.

6. *p.* 256 14 Sept. 1871.

7. *p.* 260 TSCHUPPIK, KARL: *The Reign of the Emperor Franz Josef* (London, 1930), pp. 231–2.

8. *p.* 260 Encyclical of 7 March 1874. Engel-Janosi, *op. cit.*, p. 191. In general this work shows up vividly the extreme bitterness, verging on violence, of the conflict between the Pope and Franz Josef, with Beust at his side. At the heart of the storm was poor Hübner, who, after years of devoted service as Schwarzenberg's secretary, as Ambassador to Paris during critical days, and, briefly, as Chief of Police in Vienna, had been sent to the Vatican for a rest.

9. *p.* 262 Correspondence between Alexander II and Franz Josef in the State Archives, Vienna.

10. *p.* 265 Count Montgelas to Beust, 18 July 1877. Quoted Corti, *Mensch und Herrscher*, pp. 501–2.

11. *p.* 266 *Tagebuch Hübner*, 8 June 1878. Quoted Corti, *Mensch und Herrscher*, p. 511.

12. *p.* 267 Ludwig, *op. cit.*, p. 513

13. *p.* 268 A very readable account of the crucial struggle between Bismarck and his eighty-two-year-old master, who, at the end of it, exclaimed 'My whole moral strength is broken', may be found in LUDWIG, *op. cit.*, pp. 524–35. William's sense of outrage and despair was most intimately exposed in his marginal comments on Bismarck's letters from Gastein. But his own letters to Bismarck are in *Kaiser Wilhelms des Grossen Briefe, Reden und Schriften* (Berlin, 1906), vol. II, pp. 350 *et seq*. See also A. J. P. TAYLOR in his superb biography, *Bismarck the Man and Statesman* (London, 1955), pp. 184–93; and, for sidelights, LUCIUS VON BALLHAUSEN, *Bismarck Errinerungen* (Berlin, 1921), pp. 170 *et. seq*.

14. *p.* 269 Karl Marx to Friedrich Engels. Quoted Ludwig, *op. cit.*

Chapter XIV. The Lull Between Storms PAGES 271–293

1. *p.* 276 REDLICH, *op. cit.*, p. 396.

2. *p.* 280 *Ibid.*, p. 397.

3. *p.* 282 Sir Compton Mackenzie in conversation with the author.

4. *p.* 282 Franz Josef to Elizabeth, July 1887. Corti, *Elisabeth*, p. 387.

5. *p.* 282 Diary of the Archduchess Valerie, 9 December 1887. *Ibid.*, p. 405.

6. *p.* 282 Marie Festetics to Ida von Ferenczy, 1888. *Ibid.*, p. 405.

7. *p.* 283 The appalling deterioration of Rudolf's handwriting may be studied in holograph letters in the State Archives, Vienna. It makes it hard to understand how anybody – e.g. Hanslick in *op. cit.*, vol. II – who had contact with him in his last days could have been unaware of the impending breakdown.

8. *p.* 285 From an essay dated 26 Dec. 1873, dedicated to his tutor, Latour. Quoted MITIS, OSKAR VON *Das Leben des Kronprinzen Rudolf* (Leipzig, 1928), p. 24. This work remains the most useful biography of Rudolf.

9. *p.* 285 Extracts from further essays composed in 1875 and 1876. *Ibid.*, pp. 27–8.

10. *p.* 286 MITIS, *op. cit.*, pp. 383–4.

11. *p.* 287 Essay of 26 Dec. 1873. *Ibid.*

12. *p.* 287 JONES, ERNEST: *Sigmund Freud, His Life and Work* (London, 1953), vol. I, p. 211.

13. *p.* 288 ALLMAYER-BECK, JOHANN CHRISTOPH: *Ministerpräsident Baron Beck* (Vienna, 1956), p. 20.

14. *p.* 288 *Nachlass des Erzherzogs Franz Ferdinand*. State Archives, Vienna. Referred to subsequently as *FF Nachlass*, this vast collection of Franz Ferdinand's papers, preserved by his son, the late Duke Maximilian of Hohenberg, has been deposited in the State Archives, Vienna, arranged and catalogued by Count Georg Nostitz-Rieneck. During the past few years a number of historians have worked on these papers, by permission of the Duke of Hohenberg, notably Dr Allmayer-Beck (who himself disposes of Franz Ferdinand's correspondence with his grandfather, Max Vladimir Beck), Dr Rudolf Kiszling, whose *Erzherzog Franz Ferdinand von Oesterreich-Este* (see below) is the latest and most complete biography of the Archduke, and Professor Robert A. Kann, author of *The Multi-National Empire* (New York, 1950).

15. *p.* 288 Rudolf to Franz Ferdinand, 26 Nov. 1884. *FF Nachlass.*

16. *p.* 289 Essay of 26 Dec. 1873. Mitis, *op. cit.*, p. 24.

17. *p.* 290 Diary of Marie Festetics, 5 Nov. 1879. Corti, *Elisabeth*, p. 311.

18. *p.* 290 *Ibid.* (3 Dec. 1879), p. 312.

19. *p.* 290 For the police dossier on the Mayerling case, see *Das Mayerling Original – Offizieller Akt des K. K. Polizeipresidiums Facsimilia der Dokumente der authentische Bericht* (Vienna, 1955). The memorandum of Count Josef Hoyos, dated 30 Jan. 1889, is reproduced in Mitis, *op cit.*, pp. 385–99.

20. *p.* 291 Archduke Albrecht to Franz Ferdinand, 18 Oct. 1889. *FF Nachlass.*

21. *p.* 292 *Das Mayerling Original. See* Note 19 above.

22. *p.* 293 CORTI-SOKOL: *Der Alte Kaiser*, pp. 122–3.

Chapter XV. *Germans, Slavs and Magyars*, PAGES 294–320

1. *p.* 296 MAY, ARTHUR J.: *The Habsburg Monarchy 1867–1914* (Harvard, 1960), p. 204. This work, the latest general survey of the state of the Monarchy from the Hungarian Compromise to the outbreak of the 1914 war, is also in many ways the most complete account in English of its make-up and its domestic politics. Although rather shapeless, it is easy to read and is a mine of information for the student of the period. It contains an excellent bibliography.

2. *p.* 297 ADLER, VIKTOR: *Aufsätze, Reden und Briefe* (Vienna, 1922–5).

3. *p.* 299 CORTI-SOKOL, *op. cit.*, p. 214.

4. *p.* 303 REDLICH, *op. cit.*, p. 448.

5. *p.* 304 CROCE, BENEDETTO: *History of Europe in the Nineteenth Century* (London, 1934), pp. 341 *et seq.*

6. *p.* 304 NICOLSON, HAROLD: *Sir Arthur Nicolson, Bart., First Lord Carnock* (London, 1930), p. 412.

Chapter XVI. *Russia Presents the Hemlock* PAGES 323–339

1. *p.* 329 NICOLSON, *op. cit.*, p. 265.

2. *p.* 329 TAYLOR, *Bismarck the Man and Statesman*, p. 214.

3. *p.* 329 ASQUITH, H. H.: *The Genesis of the War* (London, 1923), p. 40.

4. *p.* 329 NICOLSON, *op. cit.*, p. 211.

5. *p.* 330 *Schlagworte für die Unterreden mit Sir Charles Hardinge*, August 1908. State Archives, Vienna.

6. *p.* 331 LORD HARDINGE OF PENSHURST: *Old Diplomacy* (London, 1947), p. 161.

7. *p.* 331 Aehrenthal to Franz Josef, 12 Dec. 1911. State Archives, Vienna. (It was Aehrenthal's custom to send copies of important documents (e.g. Note 5 *supra*) for Franz Ferdinand in the Belvedere to see and keep. But he did this to a far less extent than his successor, Berchtold, who bombarded the Belvedere with a constant hail of paper and reported to Franz Ferdinand, by letter or by telegram, on everything that happened in the Ballhausplatz.)

8. *p.* 332 HOIJER, A.: *Le Comte d'Aehrenthal et la Politique de Violence* (Paris, 1922), p. 14.

9. *p.* 332 Aehrenthal's memorandum of 12 Dec. 1911. See Note 7 *supra.*

10. *p.* 333 BAERNREITHER, JOSEF MARIA: *Fragments of a Political Diary* (London, 1930), p. 56.

11. *p.* 335 ALBERTINI, LUIGI: *The Origins of the 1914 War*, vol. I, p. 240.

12. *p.* 335 *Ibid.*, quoting the Russian Ambassador to Rome, vol. I, p. 188.

13. *p.* 336 NICOLSON, *op. cit.*, p. 216.

14. *p.* 336 ALBERTINI, *op. cit.*, vol. I, p. 217.

15. *p.* 337 *Ibid.*, pp. 206–10.

16. *p.* 339 *Ibid.*, p. 228.

17. *p.* 339 *Ibid.*, pp. 229–30.

18. *p.* 339 The most complete account of the Annexation is in SCHMITT, BERNADOTTE E.: *The Annexation of Bosnia 1908–1909* (Cambridge, 1937).

Chapter XVII. The Doomed Inheritor PAGES 340–370

1. *p.* 341 CORTI-SOKOL, *op. cit.*, p. 228.

2. *p.* 341 *Ibid.*, p. 230.

3. *p.* 342 *Ibid.*, p. 233.

4. *p.* 342 MARGUTTI, ALBERT VON: *Kaiser Franz Josef* (Vienna, 1921), p. 86.

5. *p.* 342 (MÜLLER-GUTTENBRUNN, A.) *Franz Ferdinands Lebensroman* (Stuttgart, 1919), p. 17.

6. *p.* 342 CONRAD VON HÖTZENDORF, FRANZ: *Aus meiner Dienstzeit 1906–1918* (Vienna, 1921–5), vol. I, p. 338.

7. *p.* 343 NIKITSCH-BOULLES, PAUL: *Vor dem Sturm. Errinerungen an Erzherzog Thronfolger Franz Ferdinand* (Berlin, 1925), pp. 21 *et seq.*

8. *p.* 343 The best accounts of the manoeuvres over Franz Ferdinand's marriage are in Kiszling, *op. cit.* and Allmayer-Beck, *op. cit.* For the life of Franz Ferdinand in general, besides Kiszling, *op. cit.*, *see also* Nikitsch-Boulles, *op. cit.* (he was the Archduke's secretary), SOSNOSKY, THEODOR VON: *Franz Ferdinand, der Thronfolger. Ein Lebensbild* (Munich, 1929), CHLUMECKY, L. VON: *Erzherzog Franz Ferdinands Wirken und Wollen* (Berlin, 1929).

9. *p.* 344 From verbal accounts to the author from many of those who knew the Archduke and the Duchess, particularly Franz Ferdinand's elder son, the late Duke Maximilian of Hohenberg.

10. *p.* 345 BOURGOING, JEAN DE: *Briefe Kaiser Franz Josefs an Frau Katharina Schratt* (Vienna, 1949), pp. 372 *et seq.*

11. *p.* 345 *Ibid.*, p. 273.

12. *p.* 346 *Ibid.*, pp. 291–2.

13. *p.* 346 *Ibid.*, p. 401.

14. *p.* 346 *Ibid.*, p. 438.

15. *p.* 347 *See*, for example, Bagger, *op. cit.*, p. 502.

16. *p.* 348 EISENMENGER, VICTOR: *Archduke Franz Ferdinand* (London, 1931), p. 172. Eisenmenger was Franz Ferdinand's personal physician, who accompanied him on his travels.

17. *p.* 348 18 Nov. 1903. Kiszling, *op. cit.*, p. 82.

18. *p.* 349 Franz Ferdinand to Max Vladimir Beck, 28 Aug. 1905. Kiszling, *op. cit.*, p. 83.

19. *p.* 349 Franz Ferdinand to Franz Josef, 24 Nov. 1908. *FF Nachlass.*

20. *p.* 349 *Ibid.*, 5 Feb. 1909. *FF Nachlass.*

21. *p.* 349 *Ibid.*

22. *p.* 350 ALLMAYER-BECK, *op. cit.*, p. 56.

23. *p.* 350 Written instructions to Major Brosch to be conveyed 'in a friendly manner' to the relevant authority. Dated from St Moritz, 20 Jan. 1909. *FF Nachlass.*

24. *p.* 351 Telegram from Wilhelm II to Franz Ferdinand, 14 June 1914. *FF Nachlass.*

25. *p.* 352 KISZLING, *op. cit.*, p. 255.

26. *p.* 352 Quoted *Ibid.*, p. 315.

27. *p.* 353 Franz Ferdinand's views on war are best studied in Kiszling, *op. cit.*, Conrad von Hötzendorf, *op. cit.*, and BARDOLFF, CARL VON: *Soldat im alten Oesterreich* (Jena, 1938). Bardolff was Brosch's successor as head of the Military Chancellery in the Belvedere.

28. *p.* 354 EISENMENGER, *op. cit.*, p. 31.

29. *p.* 354 FUNDER, FRIEDRICH: *Vom Gestern ins Heute. Aus dem Kaiserreich in die Republik* (Vienna, 1952), p. 496. This immense volume of memoirs by the veteran Christian Socialist journalist and thinker (he edited the *Reichspost* before the 1914 war and *Die Fürche* after the 1939 war), contains invaluable first-hand records and insights into the period.

30. *p.* 355 Franz Ferdinand to Beck, 26 Oct. 1906. Kiszling, *op. cit.*, p. 94.

31. *p.* 356 SIEGHART, RUDOLF: *Die Letzten Jahrzehnten einer Grossmarcht* (Berlin, 1932), p. 144.

32. *p.* 357 Franz Ferdinand to R. von Biegeleben, 28 June 1907. Allmayer-Beck, *op. cit.*, p. 216.

33. *p.* 357 Count Ottokar Czernin to Franz Ferdinand, 10 Feb. 1909. *FF Nachlass.*

34. *p.* 357 Brosch to Franz Ferdinand, 10 Feb. 1909. *FF Nachlass.*

35. *p.* 357 CZERNIN, OTTOKAR: *Politische Betrachtungen* (Vienna, 1908), p. 18.

36. *p.* 358 ALLMAYER-BECK, *op. cit.*, p. 269.

37. *p.* 358 *Ibid.*, p. 260.

38. *p.* 358 *Ibid.*

39. *p.* 363 REGELE, OSKAR: *Feldmarschall Conrad* (Vienna, 1955), pp. 160–3.

40. *p.* 364 EISENMANN, *op. cit.*, p. 241.

41. *p.* 364 *See* Franz Ferdinand's *Tagebuch meiner Reise um die Erde* (Vienna, 1895–6).

42. *p.* 364 Franz Ferdinand's personal report on his visit to London, May 1910. *FF Nachlass.*

43. *p.* 366 This fascinating correspondence is one-sided. Wilhelm's letters are preserved in *FF Nachlass*; but Franz Ferdinand's letters to Wilhelm, apart from the drafts for two of them, appear to have been destroyed in Berlin. The letters were first brought to light by Professor Robert A. Kann, who published English translations of the most important of them in *The American Historical Review*, vol. CVII, No. 2, 1952.

44. *p.* 366 Wilhelm II to Franz Ferdinand, 26 Feb. 1913. *FF Nachlass.*

45. *p.* 367 *Ibid.*, 28 Feb. 1913. *FF Nachlass.*

46. *p.* 368 *Ibid.*, 12 Feb. 1909. *FF Nachlass.*

47. *p.* 368 *Ibid.*, 6 Dec. 1911. *FF Nachlass.*

48. *p.* 369 *Ibid.*, 9 Dec. 1911. *FF Nachlass.*

49. *p.* 369 MOLDEN, BERTHOLD: *Alois Graf Aehrenthal. Sechs Jahre äussere Politik Oesterreich-Ungarns* (Stuttgart, 1917), p. 231.

Chapter XVIII. The Road to Sarajevo PAGES 371–389

1. *p.* 372 REDLICH, JOSEF: *Schicksalsjahre Oesterreichs 1908–1919. Das politische Tagebuch Josef Redlichs* (Graz, 1953–4). Entry for 15 April 1913, vol. I, p. 196. Redlich's political diary, published posthumously, is indispensable for the period from the Annexation to the end.

2. *p.* 372 Count Czernin, as Austro-Hungarian Ambassador to Bucharest, reporting 14 May 1914. State Archives, Vienna.

3. *p.* 373 CONRAD VON HÖTZENDORF, *op. cit.*, vol. II, p. 282 (15 Nov. 1911).

4. *p.* 375 SETON-WATSON, R. W.: *A History of the Rumanians* (Cambridge, 1934), pp. 468–9.

5. *p.* 378 For a picture of the survival of Turkish influence in Serbia and Bosnia by a decidedly pro-Serb writer, see Vladimir Dedijer's account of his own family background in his moving and beautiful autobiography, *The Beloved Land* (London, 1961).

6. *p.* 379 REMAG, JOACHIM: *Sarajevo* (London, 1959), p. 49. Source material for the Sarajevo affair is copious, tortuous, and largely unreliable. There can be no definitive account of the conspiracy until the Yugoslavs open the Belgrade archives. Until then the best guides through the labyrinth are the most recent. Albertini (*op. cit.*) has put down everything that is known in vol. II of his tremendous study of the origins of the 1914 war, cited above. He patiently interviewed, or caused to be interviewed, all available first-hand witnesses. More accessibly and readably, Joachim Remag in *Sarajevo*, cited above, has supplied a vivid, blow-by-blow account of the events leading up to the assassination and the assassination itself and its aftermath, using all the most recent material. He provides a valuable bibliography. There is no point in duplicating it, because Remag is the first author to be read by anyone freshly tackling this subject. But it is worth adding that the best record of the trial itself yet available to those who, like myself, do not read Serbo-Croat, is the one edited by Albert Mousset: *Un Drame historique, l'Attentat de Sarajevo, documents inédite et texte intégral des sténogrammes du procès* (Paris, 1930). The Greater Serbian movement may be studied best in S. WAYNE VUCHINICH'S *Serbia between East and West, the Events of 1903–08* (Stanford, 1954). Sosnosky, *op. cit.*, and Nikitsch-Boulles, *op. cit.*, contain good accounts of the crime and the funeral arrangements. A superb and incandescent account of what it would feel like to be a Serb patriot if one were Miss Rebecca West is contained in West, Rebecca: *Black Lamb and Grey Falcon* (London, 1942). The great British champion of the Slavs of the Monarchy was R. W. Seton-Watson, whose *Sarajevo*

(London, 1926), *The Southern Slav Question and the Habsburg Monarchy* (London, 1911), *Masaryk in England* (London, 1943), and other works, have long had a formative influence on the English view of the Monarchy.

7. *p.* 380 ALBERTINI, *op. cit.*, vol. II, pp. 82–7.

8. *p.* 381 Quoted Corti-Sokol, *op. cit.*, p. 408.

9. *p.* 382 This is the account of Ljuba (not Jovan) Jovanović, who had been Serbian Minister of Education in 1914, published in 1924. It was violently attacked in the Yugoslav Press and the story was formally denied by Pašić in 1926. *See* Remag, *op. cit.*, pp. 277–8, and Albertini, *op. cit.*, vol. II, p. 174.

10. *p.* 383 TAYLOR, A. J. P.: 'Murder at Sarajevo' (*The Observer*, London, 16 Nov. 1958).

11. *p.* 385 JEVTIĆ, BORIVOYE: 'Weiterer Ausschnitte zum Attentat von Sarajevo' in the journal *Die Kriegsschuldfrage*, vol. III, pp. 657 *et seq. See also* Remag, *op. cit.*, p. 103.

12. *p.* 386 REMAG, *op. cit.*, p. 132.

13. *p.* 386 SOSNOSKY, *op. cit.*, p. 207.

14. *p.* 388 REDLICH, *Schicksalsjahre Oesterreichs*, vol. I, pp. 234–5.

Chapter XIX. The Powers Gather Round PAGES 390–404

1. *p.* 390 MARGUTTI, *op. cit.*, p. 148.

2. *p.* 391 Diary of Archduchess Valerie, 29 June 1914. Corti-Sokol, *op. cit.*, pp. 412–13.

3. *p.* 392 *See* Nikitsch-Boulles, *op. cit.*, pp. 220–25.

4. *p.* 392 REMAG, *op. cit.*, p. 175.

5. *p.* 392 *Ibid.*, pp. 175–6, 7 July 1914.

6. *p.* 392 REMAG, *op. cit.*, p. 164.

7. *p.* 393 ALBERTINI, *op. cit.*, vol. II, p. 174.

8. *p.* 394 *See* Czernin's despatches, May and June 1914. State Archives, Vienna.

9. *p.* 394 Conrad to Berchtold, 22 June 1914. State Archives, Vienna.

10. *p.* 394 Franz Josef to Wilhelm II, 2 July 1914, quoted Corti-Sokol, *op. cit.*, pp. 414–15.

11. *p.* 394 Franz Josef to Tschirschky, 2 July 1914, *ibid.*

12. *p.* 394 Franz Josef to Wilhelm II, 5 July 1914. Albertini, *op. cit.*, vol. II, p. 134.

13. *p.* 395 ALBERTINI, *op. cit.*, vol. II, p. 139.

14. *p.* 395 For von Bülow's own comments on the naval building programme, see *Prince von Bülow's Memoirs 1903–09*, translated by F. A. Voight (London and New York, 1935), especially pp. 311–12.

15. *p.* 395 For a domestic view of Bethmann-Hollweg's capacity for worry and indecision, see *Prince von Bülow's Memoirs 1909–19*, translated by Geoffrey Dunlop (London and New York, 1932), p. 119.

16. *p.* 395 Wilhelm II to Franz Josef, 8 July 1914.

17. *p.* 395 CORTI-SOKOL, *op. cit.*, p. 416.

18. *p.* 396 REDLICH, *Schicksalsjahre*, 15 July 1914, vol. I, p. 237.

19. *p.* 396 *See especially* memorandum of 3 Oct 1912. *FF Nachlass.*

20. *p.* 397 Ministerial Council of 7 July 1914. Albertini, *op. cit.*, vol. II, pp. 166–7.

21. *p.* 398 TAYLOR, A. J. P.: 'Dead Man's Battle Orders' (*The Observer*, London, 27 Nov. 1958).

22. *p.* 398 For details of the mobilization of the Imperial army see Regele, *Feldmarschall Conrad*, pp. 227–54. For Berchtold's attitude to mobilization and the war *see* Albertini, *op. cit.*, vol. II, pp. 453–60; Regele, *op. cit.*, pp. 240–1; Conrad von Hötzendorf, *op. cit.*, vol. III, pp. 443–4 and 474, and vol. IV, p. 40.

23. *p.* 398 REGELE, *op. cit.*, p. 239.

24. *p.* 398 *Ibid.*, pp. 242–3.

25. *p.* 400 BOGIČEVIĆ, MILOS: *Le Procès de Salonique* (Paris, 1927), pp. 39–40.

26. *p.* 401 MARGUTTI, *op. cit.*, p. 403.

27. *p.* 401 CORTI-SOKOL, *op. cit.*, p. 420.

28. *p.* 401 ALBERTINI, *op. cit.*, vol. II, pp. 457–8.

29. *p.* 401 REDLICH, *Schicksalsjahre*, 23 July 1914, vol. I, p. 238.

30. *p.* 402 ALLMAYER-BECK, *op. cit.*, p. 96.

31. *p.* 402 *Ibid.*, pp. 18–19.

32. *p.* 402 *Ibid.*, p. 262.

33. *p.* 403 Bethmann-Hollweg to Lichnowsky. Albertini, *op. cit.*, vol. II, p. 394.

34. *p.* 403 29 July 1914. Corti-Sokol, *op. cit.*, p. 422.

35. *p.* 404 ALBERTINI, *op. cit.*, vol. III, p. 1.

36. *p.* 404 *Wiener Zeitung*, 29 July 1914.

EPILOGUE: Finis Austriae PAGES 405–419

1. *p.* 408 HANTSCH, HUGO: *Geschichte Oesterreichs* (Vienna, 1947–53), vol. II, p. 550.

2. *p.* 409 CORTI-SOKOL, *op. cit.*, p. 470.

3. *p.* 411 HANTSCH, *op. cit.*, vol. II, p. 560.

4. *p.* 411 *Ibid.*, pp. 560–1.

5. *p.* 413 ZEMAN, Z. A. B.: *The Break-up of the Habsburg Empire 1914–1918*. (London, 1961), especially pp. 43–5 and 114–16. This is the first detailed and documented study of the physical dissolution of the Monarchy with any pretence at objectivity. It came out after I had written this 'Epilogue' but in time to allow revision. It is indispensable for clearing the ground of the rank growth cultivated by nationalist writers and politicians, pan-German apologists, and Marxist historians.

6. *p.* 415 KENNAN, GEORGE: *Russia Leaves the War* (London, 1956), pp. 14–15.

7. *p.* 418 Lloyd George to the Trades Union Conference, 5 Jan. 1918. Quoted Zeman, *op. cit.*, p. 178.

INDEX

FOR THE BEST IN PAPERBACKS, LOOK FOR THE

In every corner of the world, on every subject under the sun, Penguin represents quality and variety—the very best in publishing today.

For complete information about books available from Penguin—including Pelicans, Puffins, Peregrines, and Penguin Classics—and how to order them, write to us at the appropriate address below. Please note that for copyright reasons the selection of books varies from country to country.

In the United Kingdom: For a complete list of books available from Penguin in the U.K., please write to *Dept E.P., Penguin Books Ltd, Harmondsworth, Middlesex, UB7 0DA.*

In the United States: For a complete list of books available from Penguin in the U.S., please write to *Dept BA, Penguin*, Box 120, Bergenfield, New Jersey 07621-0120.

In Canada: For a complete list of books available from Penguin in Canada, please write to *Penguin Books Ltd, 2801 John Street, Markham, Ontario L3R 1B4.*

In Australia: For a complete list of books available from Penguin in Australia, please write to the *Marketing Department, Penguin Books Ltd, P.O. Box 257, Ringwood, Victoria 3134.*

In New Zealand: For a complete list of books available from Penguin in New Zealand, please write to the *Marketing Department, Penguin Books (NZ) Ltd, Private Bag, Takapuna, Auckland 9.*

In India: For a complete list of books available from Penguin, please write to *Penguin Overseas Ltd, 706 Eros Apartments, 56 Nehru Place, New Delhi, 110019.*

In Holland: For a complete list of books available from Penguin in Holland, please write to *Penguin Books Nederland B.V., Postbus 195, NL-1380AD Weesp, Netherlands.*

In Germany: For a complete list of books available from Penguin, please write to *Penguin Books Ltd, Friedrichstrasse 10-12, D-6000 Frankfurt Main I, Federal Republic of Germany.*

In Spain: For a complete list of books available from Penguin in Spain, please write to *Longman, Penguin España, Calle San Nicolas 15, E-28013 Madrid, Spain.*

In Japan: For a complete list of books available from Penguin in Japan, please write to *Longman Penguin Japan Co Ltd, Yamaguchi Building, 2-12-9 Kanda Jimbocho, Chiyoda-Ku, Tokyo 101, Japan.*

FOR THE BEST IN HISTORY, LOOK FOR THE